MAJOR JOHN RICHARDSON.

RICHARDSON'S WAR ⚐ OF ⚐ 1812

✿✿WITH NOTES AND✿✿
A LIFE OF THE AUTHOR

By

Alexander Clark Casselman

COLES PUBLISHING COMPANY LIMITED
TORONTO, CANADA.

COLES CANADIANA COLLECTION

Originally published in 1902
by Historical Publishing Company,
Toronto.

Facsimile edition published
by COLES PUBLISHING COMPANY, Toronto
© Copyright 1974.

PREFATORY NOTE.

The preparation of the biography of Major John Richardson entailed a large amount of independent research. Before I had gone far in the study of his career I found that all existing biographies were meagre, fragmentary or wrong in many important details. Several of his relatives have been personally interviewed, other relatives have been communicated with; and for the first time the date and the place, both of his birth and of his death, are correctly given. The bibliography will be found to be more nearly complete and, as far as it goes, more accurate than any previous attempt to give a list of his works and of the editions published. Every positive statement in the biography or the bibliography is made on the authority of documentary evidence in my possession. Failing such evidence, I have been cautious in statement; and I shall gladly welcome any additional information on the subject.

The genealogy of the Richardson and the Askin families is not intended to be complete; but it is hoped that it will be found of some historical interest and value.

The letters of Colonel John Askin, Major John Richardson and Colonel Elijah Brush have never been published before; and it must be conceded that they throw absolutely new sidelights on that period of our history.

One promise made in the announcement of this book has not been fulfilled. No picture of Major-General Henry Procter could be obtained. Under a mistaken impression, which is by no means uncommon, arrangements had been made to publish the portrait of Lieut.-General Henry Adolphus Proctor, C.B., when I found that it was not his military achievements that occupy so large a share of Richardson's narrative. The careers of these two officers are briefly given in the Appendix.

No change has been made in Richardson's narrative

except to correct the manifest typographical errors, to which he refers in the advertisement at the end of his volume. But the official despatches of the British and American officers, as given in the original edition of 1842, were found on comparison with the Archives and other sources to be in many cases incorrect or abbreviated. Rather than impair the historical value of the volume by leaving the despatches imperfect, I have in each instance substituted without comment the full official account.

To the numerous friends and relatives of Major Richardson, I tender my sincere thanks for the aid they have given, which has enabled me to prepare the biography. I am particularly indebted also to Mr. C. C. James, M.A., Deputy Minister of Agriculture for Ontario, for valuable advice and many historical notes; and to my lifelong friend, Mr. John Stewart Carstairs, B.A., of Harbord St. Collegiate Institute, Toronto, for help in the revision of the proofs and in the preparation of the biography.

A. C. C.

Toronto, February, 1902.

CONTENTS.

INTRODUCTION.

On the Canadian side of the Niagara river, just where its foaming and turbulent waters issue from the narrow, rocky gorge, stands the straggling village of Queenston. The place at the present time is of very little importance except as a terminal port for a magnificent fleet of pleasure vessels that carry tourists and excursion parties to visit the Falls, five or six miles farther up the river. But as the scene of one of the proudest victories of Canadian and British arms during the War of 1812 Queenston has won a fame that is world-wide.

The settlement proper of the country dates from the close of the Revolutionary war, when the disbanded soldiers of Butler's Rangers and other United Empire Loyalists took up grants of land on the banks of the river. At the mouth of the river there soon grew up the town of Niagara (Newark), opposite Fort Niagara, at that time and until 1796 in the hands of the British. The great highway of the trade with Detroit and other western settlements was the Niagara, and as this trade increased the laden vessels from the lakes were taken as far up the river as possible, to shorten the portage around the Falls. This head of navigation was called at first the New Landing, and later Queenstown. Thus favorably situated for trade, the new town prospered and soon became the home of several pioneer merchants, who never dreamed that the stream of commerce could possibly find any other course.

Queenston derived an additional importance, at this early period, from its proximity to the seat of government of the new Province of Upper Canada. The first Lieutenant-Governor of the Province, Colonel John Graves Simcoe, selected Niagara as the capital; and to enforce his authority and protect his person a British Regiment was sent to Canada. This Regiment was recruited in England, Scotland, Nova Scotia and New Brunswick, and was called the Queen's Rangers, from a corps, commanded by Colonel Simcoe, during the war of the Revolution. Among the officers of the new corps who had not held commands in the old one was a young Scotchman named Robert Richardson, the Assistant Surgeon, a scion of the younger branch of the Annandale family, which had clung to the fortunes of the Pretender. The detachment of the Queen's Rangers, with which Dr. Richardson served, was quartered at Queenston. The young military surgeon became acquainted with the leading merchant of the place, Honorable Robert Hamilton, member of the Legislative Council, who had married Catherine Askin, daughter of Colonel John Askin, a wealthy merchant of Detroit. At his home Dr. Richardson met Miss Madeleine, another daughter of Colonel Askin, then on a visit to her sister. The visits of the handsome young Scotchman were as frequent as his military duties would permit, and the beautiful and accomplished Madeleine encouraged him in his wooing; for we see in the records of St. Mark's church, Niagara, that " Doctor Robert Richardson, bachelor, and Madeleine Askin, spinster," were married by Reverend Robert Addison on January 24th, 1793. In July of this year a part at least of the Queen's Rangers left Queenston for Toronto, and Dr. Richardson accompanied them, leaving his wife with her sister. We learn from a letter written in French by Mrs. Richardson to her stepmother, Mrs. Askin at Detroit, that she is passing a very sad time awaiting news from Toronto, as no boat has arrived from there lately ; and that, if she could only know that Mr. Richardson was well, she would be satisfied.

While Mrs. Richardson resided at Queenston their three eldest children were born : Jane, born May 19th, 1794, baptized at Niagara, August 17th ; John, born October 4th, 1796, baptized January 5th, 1797 ; Robert, born September 10th, 1798, baptized December 30th of the same year.

In the fall of 1801 a detachment of the Queen's Rangers was ordered to Fort St. Joseph, a post on the island of the same name, near the head of Lake Huron. Dr. Richardson accompanied this force to the western post, but the prospects of providing suitable accommodation for his wife and young family in this fort were not very promising, so it was arranged that Mrs. Richardson and family should live with her father at Detroit.

In the summer of 1802 the Rangers were disbanded, and the officers and men with their wives and children, were provided with transport if they wished to return to Great Britain.   Dr. Richardson remained in Canada, and was appointed surgeon to the Governor and garrison of Fort Amherstburg ; and on June 7th, 1807, he was appointed Judge of the District Court of the Western District, an office he held until his death in 1832.   Here all his children were reared and educated.   His eldest son John was particularly brilliant, and although he hated school he seems to have made considerable progress in Latin, French and Euclid, as well as in the ordinary branches of an English education.   Unfortunately this course of instruction was abruptly cut short by the United States declaring war and by the preparations for the invasion of his native province.   Much as he may have lost by his lack of schooling, no trace of such loss is perceptible in his writings.   And in estimating the formative influences that produced our first novelist of romance, our first delineator of manners and customs, we must look elsewhere.

In that generation such a home and such a family as those of the Richardsons must have been peculiarly stimulating.   The father, combining the strictness of the soldier, the kindness of the physician and the sternness of the judge, commanded the love and the respect, not only of his own family, but of the community.   Even the redoubtable Simon Girty, the Sampson Gattrie of '' The Canadian Brothers,'' was awed into decorum at the sight of the judge.   The gentler virtues and the gentler graces found their exponent in his mother.   Educated at the Convent of Congregation de Notre Dame at Montreal, the foremost institution for young ladies in Canada, Madeleine Richardson, with the national pride of her race, taught her children from their earliest years to speak and write the French language.   It has been said that he who knows only one language does not know any. In the learning of two languages young Richardson's mind was broadened, his observation quickened, and a nice perception cultivated—perhaps as only years of training in the class-room could have perfected.   His quick eye for natural beauty, his power in vivid description and his marvellous ability in handling the sentence, are an inheritance or an acquisition from his vivacious mother.

Nor was the influence of his grandfather's home less

marked.   Although a British subject, Colonel Askin had
been unable, owing to large mercantile interests, to remove from Detroit to Canada till April, 1802.   On the
banks of the river Detroit opposite the lower end of
Belle Isle, then called Hog Island, there soon rose the
modest dwelling named Strabane, after the family seat
in Ireland.   How greatly this removal influenced young
Richardson may be read in his after life.   Who can
doubt that this devoted British officer would impress on
his youthful grandson that to live under that flag which
he had served so long was worth the sacrifice of a home
and a vast estate?   Here it was that Mrs. Askin used to
tell the boy those thrilling stories of romance, of Detroit,
of Michilimackinac, that enchained his young imagination.   None made so deep an impression as the crafty
and well-conceived plans of Pontiac, the great chief of
the Ottawas, and his persistent efforts to capture Fort
Detroit.   The events of that historic siege were the most
exciting episodes in a life not lacking in exciting incidents.   She had been an inmate of the fort, and the
lapse of time had not bedimmed one of the startling experiences of those eighteen months.   Proofs of the
power of this accomplished lady as a story-teller still
exist.   Her youthful listener even at that early age was
enkindled with a desire, not to be realized till he had
passed through thirty years of vicissitudes in two conti-
tinents, when in 1832 he gave to the world his masterly
"Wacousta."

If the home life was thus wholesome in formative influences, the community also in which he dwelt was rich in a
novel and diversified life that presented itself to his daily
observation at an age when the sharpest and most lasting
impressions are made.   No other place on the continent
could boast of a floating population so varied in character and race, so rich in well-defined types of civilized and
barbarous human nature.   At Amherstburg there were
the officers and soldiers of the garrison, dressed in brilliant uniforms, moving about with apparently few duties
to perform, attracting the boyish fancy and exciting his
admiration and his envy.   Nor was the British officer
wholly unworthy of this adoration.   A scion of one of
Britain's best families, he obtained promotion oftener by
purchase than by proficiency gained from actual service ;
fully cognizant of his own importance, here he lived in a
community that fully acknowledged his superiority.

Next to the soldiers in attractiveness were the Indians that periodically repaired to the town to receive at the hands of the Superintendent of Indian Affairs their customary presents. Many a time young Richardson would wander to the shores of the Detroit to watch the large fleets of canoes in military array, heading for the camping ground of Bois Blanc island; or as the Indians marched to the storekeeper's with a pride and haughty mien that contrasted strangely with the object of their visit, or as they engaged in various games of leaping, wrestling, ball-playing, he would follow and delight in receiving recognition from some chieftain whose acquaintance he had made before. Often, on a visit to the island camp, he would be an interested spectator of their daily habits; it was thus that he acquired that close and accurate knowledge of Indian character and life that he afterwards so successfully used in his literary productions. His delineation of Indian character in "Wacousta" has never been equalled, even by James Fenimore Cooper himself. In "The Canadian Brothers" he gives us a description of the principal Indian chiefs who were allies of the British in the War of 1812, to be found nowhere else.

Besides the soldiers and the Indians, there were those engaged in the fur trade, now fast declining here owing to the march of civilization westward. The French-Canadian and half-breed voyageur had not wholly forsaken the Detroit; and at times was to be seen the trader, just returned from trafficking with the Indians at their homes in the wilds of the interior, and in dress or complexion scarcely distinguishable from the Indians themselves—in some cases not degenerate successors of the *coureurs de bois* of the French period.

It was among such varied surroundings, then, that Richardson must have accumulated almost all the material that he used so effectively in history, poem or novel. The scenes of his boyhood are the favorite setting for his characters; and never after his boyhood had he the opportunity for a lengthened stay in those beloved haunts.

The news of the declaration of war against Great Britain reached Amherstburg, and awoke this frontier garrison from its monotonous routine of regular work. The militia were called out. The marine department became active in fitting out trading schooners and small gunboats for the purpose of defending from invasion the western district. The academic life of John Richardson was brought suddenly to a close. Hull's army had appeared on its march to Detroit, whence as a base it was to invade the land of a contented and happy people, guiltless of wrong to the United States. All the martial spirit of his ancestors was roused in John Richardson, and at the tender age of fifteen he resolved to fight in defence of his native land.

Through the influence of his father, and his grandfather Askin, he was appointed a gentleman volunteer on the strength of the 41st Regiment, a detachment of which was in garrison at Fort Amherstburg. From a District General Order we learn that "The undermentioned gentlemen are appointed as volunteers in His Majesty's regular forces, from the periods specified opposite their respective names. They will continue to do duty with the 41st Regiment until further orders.

Henry Procter, Gent., 1st July, 1812.
Alex. Wilkinson, "   1   "   1812.
John Richardson, "   9   "   1812.

By Order.   Thomas Evans,
                        Brigade Major."

Richardson fought in every engagement in which the detachment of the 41st took part, until its disastrous defeat at Moraviantown on October 5th, 1813. On this occasion he was taken prisoner, and suffered close imprisonment until released in 1814. The story of these engagements and his experiences during his captivity are fully set forth in his history of the Right Division. With the exception of the official reports of the officers commanding, his account of these engagements, and of the captivity of the prisoners, is the only one that has been written by any of the participators. In his first novel, "Ecarté," Dormer, one of the characters, and Clifford Delmaine, the hero, meet after years of separation in Paris. Dormer describes his experiences since they were schoolmates. The adventures of Dormer in the army in Canada and his imprisonment coincide closely with the actual events in this part of Richardson's career. In "The Canadian Brothers" one can gather likewise the story of the events in which the Right Division took part, and the story of the imprisonment.

After his return from captivity he was given a lieutenantcy in the 2nd Battalion of the 8th (King's) Regiment.
In June, 1815, both battalions embarked at Quebec for
Ostend, to join the Duke of Wellington's army in
Flanders. But Waterloo had been fought and won
before they were half way across the Atlantic. As a
permanent peace with France seemed to have been made,
and as Britain had no need for so large a standing army,
several regiments were reduced. Transferring its men
fit for duty to the first battalion, the second battalion of
the Eighth disbanded on the 24th of December, 1815,
and its officers were placed upon half-pay. Within six
months Sir Henry Torrens, then Military Secretary, procured Richardson's appointment to his own, the Second
or Queen's Regiment ; and on the 24th of April, 1816,
the regiment embarked at Portsmouth for the West
Indies, and landed at Barbadoes on June 5th. How long
he remained with the Queen's is not known, but it is
probable that he was invalided home after a short term
of service in that exceedingly unhealthy climate. He
was subsequently transferred to the 92nd Highlanders,
and was again placed on half-pay on October 1st, 1818.

For the next ten years Richardson lived the life of a
literary man in London with occasional visits to Paris.
He wrote sketches of West Indian and Canadian life
that appeared in the periodicals of the time, and produced two of his longer works, the poem "Tecumseh"
published in 1828, and the novel "Ecarte, or the Salons
of Paris," published in 1829.

"Tecumseh," Richardson's only effort in poetry consists of four cantos of 188 stanzas of *ottava rima;* in the
first canto there are 45 stanzas, in the second 50, in the
third 48 and in the fourth 45. No evidence is at hand
from which we can judge how this poem was received
in literary circles in England. The generation born
during the Napoleonic wars would not be enraptured with
martial poems: they had experienced too many of the hardships of war. At that time the heroic deeds and states-
manlike achievements of our greatest Indian ally were
unknown in Britain, and could appeal to but a limited
number of readers. The poem itself is marked by a strict
adherence to the conventional stanza form, with which
Byron took such liberties in his Don Juan. With a few
exceptions, there is marked care in the choice of words

and in the workmanship. The epic theme follows closely the historical facts and presents many opportunities for effective dramatic treatment. But perhaps the measure chosen was ill-adapted to so stirring a subject. That Richardson was not quite satisfied with his poetic effort is proved by his confining himself to prose in future.

" Ecarte," said Captain R. H. Barclay, in a letter to the author, "is assuredly an able and dreadful essay against the most insidious and ruinous of all sorts of dissipation and idleness, gaming, bad enough anywhere, but perhaps in Paris it holds its throne." Paris was then a favorite resort for many young British officers absent on leave ; and Richardson, in his visits, appears to have entered fully into the gay life of that metropolis. He had an affair of honor with a French officer of Cuirassiers and probably indulged in play, but it is hardly possible that he lost heavily, got in debt and was given time to contemplate the fickleness of fortune, and form good resolutions for the future in a room in the prison he so accurately describes in "Ecarte."

This novel was published by Colburn, of London, and was well received in some quarters ; but, by a strange circumstance, was doomed in so far as it might possibly bring immediate fame to the author and wealth to the publisher. Jerdan, a leading influential writer on the staff of the Literary Gazette, had some disagreement with Colburn, and to be revenged wrote him that he would " cut up " his next book in his review. The next book published by Colburn was " Ecarte," and Jerdan was as good as his word. This unwarranted criticism, Richardson acknowledges in " Eight Years in Canada," prevented him from writing many more works.

However, he appears to have been busy with his pen as " Wacousta " appeared in 1832. This story was published in three volumes by T. Cadell, Strand, London, and from the first met with great success. A second edition was published in the same style in 1840. It is considered his best work.

The London Literary Gazette, the London Athenæum, the London Satirist, the Morning Post, the London Atlas and Miss Sheridan's Magazine spoke in very flattering terms of the novel and the author. He was at once recognized as a powerful rival of Cooper, then at the height of his popularity in England and America.

The story is founded upon the designs of Pontiac to possess himself of the fort at Detroit. The principal characters are drawn from the actors in that historic event, and are portrayed with a marked fidelity to historical accuracy. Even Wacousta himself may have been suggested by the career of some real personage. The only feature of the story that it is possible to consider weak may be found in the incident of the capture in the St. Clair river of the schooner, having on board the survivors of the massacre at Fort Michilimackinac. Here, to cause the capture to take place in the river, the author, departing from geographical truth, makes the St. Clair a narrow stream, with the branches of the tall trees meeting in an arch overhead. But even for this he may well plead the licence that is always granted to writers of fiction.

The interview between Pontiac and Governor De Haldimar in the great council hall of the fort is the masterstroke of all Richardson's literary work. For dramatic power and graphic description it has not often been surpassed or even equalled in the language. As a character-sketch, unfolding on the one hand the adroit craft and subtle deceit of Pontiac with all the varied play of motives, and on the other the defiant confidence and intrepid fidelity to principle of the governor, it will compare favorably with those searching analyses of human passions to be found in the works of George Eliot.

Richardson has been accused of imitating Cooper in this novel. How closely one author may follow the style and character of another's productions and still rank as a great writer, will never be very clearly determined. The only ground for such an accusation is that both wrote stories with Indians figuring prominently in the foreground. And it is doubtful that Richardson owes more to Cooper's works than the bare suggestion that a romance dealing with the Canadian Indian would prove both popular and successful. For such a work he possessed peculiar qualifications, in power, in material and in desire. His power had already been revealed in " Ecarte " ; his material had been gathered from the experiences of his boyhood and the stirring stories he heard from his grandmother ; the desire had been enkindled thirty years before when he heard those stories by the open fireplace at Strabane.

Richardson's characters are never impossible. His Indians have all the virtues and all the vices of the greatest prototypes of the race. He was personally acquainted with Tecumseh. His grandmother had been in the fort when besieged by Pontiac. The original of Captain Erskine is no doubt his grandfather, Colonel John Askin; Lieutenant Johnstone is probably his father's relative. Dr. Richardson belonged to the Annandale family, so did Lieutenant Johnstone; and further to prove the identity, one of Major Richardson's half-brothers was named Johnstone Richardson, plainly showing that Johnstone was a family name. The name of Bombardier Kitson for one of the minor characters is a reminiscence of an officer of that name in the Royal Artillery who fought with the Right Division in the War of 1812. No doubt a careful comparison of the incidents of the novel with the actual events would reveal many other similarities. This is an instance in which we must go to fiction for reliable history.

In 1834 the Spanish Ambassador to Great Britain recruited an army in that country to assist the regent, Christina, to preserve the throne of Spain for her daughter Isabella, against the forces of Don Carlos, who claimed the crown. This force, which consisted of ten regiments of 1,000 men each, was known as the "British Auxiliary Legion," and was under the command of Lieut.-General De Lacy Evans, a veteran officer who had seen active service in India and the Peninsula, at Washington and New Orleans, and as Quartermaster-General at Waterloo. Richardson was assigned a captaincy in the 2nd Regiment, which sailed from Portsmouth on board the transport Royal Tar, on July 23rd, 1835, and arrived at San Sebastian on the 27th. After a short stay here the Legion marched to Vitoria, where typhus fever carried off about 700 men and 40 officers. The soldierly qualities and executive ability of Richardson were recognized by his being appointed commandant of Vitoria; but on January 30th, 1836, he was stricken down with the prevailing malady. His splendid physique, however, enabled him to combat the disease, and he rose from his bed on the 17th of March. During his illness intrigue and jealousy were at work, and he was displaced on the staff by a relative of the Lieut.-General; and to add to his troubles his regiment and the 5th were broken up, but he was appointed senior captain in the 6th (Scotch Grenadiers). To recuperate, Richardson applied for and received two months' leave of absence to visit England. He left Vitoria in April and proceeded to the coast, but before he had an opportunity to embark for England the Legion marched to the attack of San Sebastian, now occupied by the Carlists. Although on sick leave, Richardson, in his anxiety to be of assistance, volunteered his services on the staff. His offer was refused, and, enfeebled as he was, he led his own company of the 6th Regiment in the battle of the 5th of May.

An account of this battle appears in his memoirs. On the 11th he left Spain for London by way of Paris. While in Spain he kept a journal which he was anxious to publish, as it would in a measure be an answer to the attacks and aspersions made against the character and actions of the Legion by the persons and the press that opposed interference with the internal affairs of a foreign nation.

While in London a Gazette appeared which contained a list of the names of officers decorated for their conduct in the action of May 5th. Richardson's name did not appear, and, to add to his disappointment, he was mortified to find in the announcement that a junior officer had been promoted to a majority over his head. In his anger he wrote an addition to the preface of his book, "Movements of the British Legion," in which he set forth his claims, and in doing so reflected somewhat on the conduct of the other officers. When his wrath had subsided he recalled the irritating paragraphs and substituted others less incisive ; but he had already sent a copy of the preface to the Lieut.-General, and had written a private letter to the military secretary in which was conveyed a mild threat that some officers had honors to which they were not entitled. Meanwhile Richardson started for Spain and at once carried out his plans against the Lieut.-General and other officers, which resulted in the appointment of a court of inquiry to investigate and report on the whole affair.

On the 29th of June, just one day before the assembling of the court, his year of service having expired, he tendered his resignation and signified his retirement from the service. He therefore appeared before the commission, not as an officer of the Legion, but as a private citizen, and at the investigation his superior talents, aided by the justice of his cause, enabled him to wring from a hostile court a verdict that exonerated him in every particular. After the announcement of the verdict the Lieut.-General intimated to Richardson that he would like to make reparation for the injury that had been done him. Consequently it was arranged that his resignation should be withdrawn. On this being done Richardson appeared in general orders as promoted to a vacant majority which was dated May 13th, and at the same time was transferred from the 6th Scotch to the 4th Queen's Own Fusiliers. With this regiment Major Richardson served till the 19th of August, being in command of it at an engagement at the " Heights of Passages " on July 30th, 1836. Soon after, he returned to England.

To Major Richardson's experiences in Spain we owe the existence of three of his works. " Movements of the British Legion," referred to before, recounts in the form of a journal the operations from their arrival at San Sebastian, July 27th, 1835, till the attack on the same stronghold, May 5th, 1836. The second edition, published in 1837, contains also the narrative to the close of March, 1837. The book in its first edition is a faithful account of the events of the campaign, and is a worthy tribute to the military capacity of Lieutenant-General De Lacy Evans, the commander-in-chief. But the failure of that officer to promote Richardson to a majority to which he was entitled by seniority, led to a bitter personal quarrel with the Lieutenant-General, who does not seem to have been averse to showing a desire for revenge on the Major, who had worsted him before the Court of Inquiry. As De Lacy Evans had estranged his officers, had infringed the rules of service and had secured a reputation for delay and indecision, he was not invulnerable, and Richardson was always a merciless assailant. Accordingly, in the second part of the second edition, the author seldom loses an opportunity of attributing every failure or disaster to the incapacity of the commander. As a fact, only ten of the fifty experienced officers who had originally embarked in the cause chose to remain. It was easy for the officers to withdraw from the service, but with the rank and file it was very different. They had to stay till their term of service expired, and when this time came their pay was in arrears and no passage to England was to be got. Some re-enlisted, others in their desperation joined the Carlists. Their plight was a melancholy one. Neglected by their native country and cast off without pay by the nation they served, the survivors managed to reach Great Britain in a penniless condition, deplorable examples of the neglect usually shown to the private soldier when the nation no longer requires his services.

The affairs of Spain were made the subject of a debate in the British House of Commons on the motion of Sir Henry Hardinge. In this debate the opportunity was seized by O'Connell and some other members to attack Richardson, but his character and conduct were clearly vindicated. His cause was championed by Captain Boldero and Sir Henry Hardinge, the proposer of the motion. It would be exceedingly unfair even to hint that anything but justice could influence a man of the integrity and noble character of Sir Henry Hardinge, but his interest in Richardson in this connection may have arisen from his kindly remembrance of Richardson's father when they served in the same regiment. Sir Henry Hardinge began that military career which shone so brilliantly at Albuera and at Ferozshuhr, as an ensign in the Queen's Rangers in 1798 in Upper Canada, when Dr. Richardson was assistant surgeon of the same corps.

No better example of the appreciation of the subtleties of language can be found than in the volume, "Movements of the British Legion." At p. 162, in discussing the unhealthy and uncomfortable condition of the hospitals at Vitoria, Richardson had said :

"Things are said to have been better managed in Portugal under Mr. Alcock, who is *second* in rank of the Medical Department here." Mr. Alcock, considering that he had been complimented at the expense of his chief, wrote to the author, asking that the statement be amended or omitted in any future edition. Richardson replied, begging him " to consider it, however, as one of the typographical errors, and that 'said' should be in italics, not 'second.' You cannot fail to observe that this alteration will give a totally distinct reading to the passage." This *amende honorable* has something so genuinely clever about it that it deserves this special notice. It is scarcely paralleled even by Lord Robert Cecil's famous apology to Mr. Gladstone as related by Justin McCarthy.

Richardson's second work on the affairs in Spain entitled "Personal Memoirs of Major Richardson," was published in Montreal in 1838.   Events, that will be referred to presently, caused him to come to Canada in that year; hence its appearance in this country.   In this volume the injustice that he had suffered is submitted to the public. The documentary evidence adduced clearly shows that he pursued the only course consistent with honor and dignity.   As he himself says, p. 144 :

"By the cold and the calculating—by the selfish and the prudent—I shall no doubt be considered as having adopted a course more chivalrous than wise in the uniform opposition I have shown to the various measures of oppression—so unworthily—so ignobly arrayed against me.   By those, however, of high honour—of proud and independent feeling—by those who are incapable of sacrificing the approval of the inward man to mere considerations of personal interests and expediency, I shall be judged in a nobler. spirit.   *They*, at least, will admit, that in adopting the line of conduct unfolded in the pages of this brief and local memoir, I have studied that which was most befitting an honourable mind.   As I have had elsewhere reason to observe, never did a more cruel system of injustice seek to work its slow and sinuous course beneath the mantle of liberalism.   Every engine of his power had been put in motion by General Evans, to accomplish the ruin of an officer, who had in no other way offended than by refusing tamely to submit—firstly, to his injustice—secondly, to his oppression, and that the utter overthrow of such officer has not been accomplished, is attributable, not to any forbearance on the part of his persecutor, but to his own innate integrity and right."

His third work was a satire, not issued, however, in book form, but as a serial in THE NEW ERA OR CANADIAN CHRONICLE, a paper published by Richardson in Brockville in 1841 and 1842.   Theodore Hook in his last volume had transferred his hero, Jack Brag, to the staff of De Lacy Evans in Spain as Acting Assistant Deputy-Deputy Assistant Commissary General.   Richardson saw his opportunity and took Hook's hero successfully in hand.   Hook was pleased with the continuation of his satire and made an effort to secure a publisher for it.

He went to Colburn and to Bentley, but they declined to accept it as they considered the delineation of the characters too faithful a reflection of the originals, and the strictures on the Radicals at Westminster too severe.

In 1837 the political affairs of the Canadas caused no little alarm to the British Government of the day. Richardson, eager again to see active service, more particularly in defence of his native land, against those who would have robbed Britain of her fairest colony, embarked at London on the 18th of February, 1838, for Canada, by way of New York. He was accompanied by his wife, a member of a family in Essex, whom he had married about the year 1830. Her family name is not recorded that I have seen, and a diligent inquiry among Richardson's relatives, who knew her, has proved fruitless in the matter. All, however, agree in saying that she was accomplished, talented, and possessed of some literary ability, and that they were devotedly attached to each other.

While waiting in New York for four days Richardson met the Earl of Gosford and Sir Francis Bond Head, who had lately arrived from the Canadas on their way to England. He had a letter of introduction from Lord Glenelg, Colonial Secretary, to Sir Francis, in which was expressed the desire that some official position should be given him in his native province. Sir Francis was so concerned and agitated, probably through fear that violence might be done him by some sympathizers with the rebels in Canada, that after reading the letter he returned it to the Major unsealed, with a request to present it with his compliments to his successor, Sir George Arthur.

On the 29th of March he went by boat to Albany, thence by railroad to Utica, then by coach through Auburn, Geneva, Rochester and Lockport to Lewiston, where he arrived on Wednesday, the 3rd of April. The mingled feelings with which he viewed his native village of Queenston, a spot hallowed with so many recollections, are well described at the close of the second chapter of his "Eight Years in Canada."

"We reached Lewiston a few miles below the Falls of Niagara about 6 o'clock; and from that point beheld, for the first time since my return to the country and in its most interesting aspect, the Canadian shore. Opposite to Lewiston is the small village of Queenston, and overhanging the latter, the heights on which my early friend and military patron—the warrior beneath whose bright example my young heart had been trained to a love of heroism, and who had procured me my first commission in the service—had perished in the noble but unequal conflict with a foe invading almost from the spot on which I stood. More than five-and-twenty years had gone by, but the memory of the departed Brock lived as vividly in the hearts of a grateful people as it had in the early days of his fall; and in the monument which crowned the height, and which no ruffian hand had yet attempted to desecrate, was evidenced the strong and praiseworthy desire to perpetuate a memory as honored as it was loved. This moment was to me particularly exciting, for it brought with it the stirring reminiscences of the camp, and caused me to revert to many a trying scene in which my younger days had been passed. Since that period I had numbered a good many years, and had experienced in other climes a more than ordinary portion of the vicissitudes of human life; but not one of these had the freshness aud warmth of recollection of my earlier services in America, in which (independently of the fact of my having been present at the capture of Detroit, under the gallant soldier whose bones reposed beneath the monument on which my gaze was rivetted, as if through the influence of an irresistible fascination) I had been present in five general engagements, and twelve months a prisoner of war with the enemy before attaining my seventeenth year. These were certainly not ' piping times of peace,' and I must be pardoned the egotism of incidentally alluding to them.''

Before leaving London, Richardson had been entrusted with the important duty of furnishing political information to the London *Times*. In availing itself of the services of a writer so singularly competent and eligible as Richardson, the foremost of English dailies showed both enterprise and sagacity. In those times it was well to have sources of information on what was taking place in the Canadas, other than the official despatches of the governors and the news letters appearing in the United States press. Richardson began at once to study the political situation in Upper Canada. His opportunities for obtaining information were excellent. His brother Charles, with whom he lived at Niagara, represented that town in the Legislative

Assembly of Upper Canada, and through him Richardson could learn without reserve the state of affairs in the country, and get a description of the events that led up to armed resistance to the Government. He soon began his journey to Quebec to meet Lord Durham on his arrival. While in Toronto he called on and was entertained by Sir George Arthur, and by his own old comrades in arms when Detroit was taken, the Honorable John Beverley Robinson, then Chief Justice, and Colonel S. P. Jarvis, then Superintendent of Indian Affairs. In Montreal he found out the feeling in the province of Lower Canada. His observations in Canada up to this time are embodied in two letters published in the *Times*, one written from Niagara and the other from Montreal, and signed Inquisitor. On his arrival at Quebec he called upon the governor, and was received by him with every mark of respect. He was invited to dine at the Castle of St. Lewis with a brilliant assemblage. Lord Durham made him the special object of his attention, and during the course of a long conversation he unfolded in their entirety all his plans and projects for the government of the colony. Richardson was convinced that these plans were not only the best for the country, but perhaps the only ones that would harmonize the various conflicting interests arrayed in arms against each other. If Richardson was impressed by the honesty and integrity of Lord Durham, and his thorough grasp of the political situation, on the other hand it is merely just to record that he possessed the confidence of that nobleman to the fullest extent.

By birth and training Richardson was personally opposed to the general policy represented by the Melbourne administration. He was the trusted correspondent of a paper that had assailed that administration with a bitterness rarely exhibited by any journal. His salary of £300 and travelling expenses along with his half-pay would have enabled him to live in affluence. Moreover, his work was congenial, and no favor that Lord Durham or any succeeding governor might grant could offer more attractions to a man of Richardson's temperament than his present employment. Accordingly every motive and every prejudice of worldly wisdom would have led an ordinary man into opposition to the governor, but it is very gratifying to know that Richardson viewed the affairs of Canada with notable impartiality, which leaves no doubt of his patriotism and of a marked disregard of any selfish interests. Richardson was convinced that Lord Durham would do for the colony what no other governor had ever attempted in respect to its permanent interests. He realized the wisdom of his policy and grasped the spirit of his plans for the future. Time has already vindicated the action of the governor, and it must in all fairness grant to Richardson credit and honor for the personal sacrifices he made in advocating the cause that has proved so beneficial to British North America. Unfortunately for him the " mighty engine" he was in Canada to represent did not approve his course. The editor did not see fit to publish all his letters, and informed him that his connection with that journal would cease at the termination of his year's engagement. It would seem that a paper that delegates to itself the high position of directing the policy of a great nation should place accuracy of information before every other consideration ; that it should have placed more confidence in the opinions of its correspondent than upon its party traditions. The awakening was too sudden for most Englishmen to see clearly. The many reforms that had been gained in England within a half-dozen years were alarming to one party, and the other party were not prepared to support their official in his advanced ideas of granting self-government to the colonies. It is therefore too much to expect that a paper like the *Times* could change its colonial policy so quickly. The disavowal of Richardson by the *Times* enlisted the sympathy of Lord Durham, himself suffering from a more cruel desertion. In a letter to Richardson he says :

" It is indeed most disgusting to see such proofs of malignity in those who ought to value truth and fair dealing as the best means of informing the public of which they profess to be the ' best possible instructors.' Your course has been that of a man of honor and integrity, and you can hardly regret the dissolution of a connection which it appears could only have been preserved by the sacrifice on your part of truth and justice —by the *suppressio veri*, if not the *assertio falsi*."

If subsequent events had not clearly proved that the course adopted by Richardson was the proper one, this letter is sufficient exoneration. Lord Durham's policy and his acts while in Canada are fully set forth in chapters III., IV. and V. of Richardson's "Eight Years in Canada."

On November 2nd, 1838, the day after Lord Durham embarked for England, Richardson left Quebec to join his friends at Niagara. At Kingston he was much impressed by a visit to Von Schoultz, the "patriot" leader recently captured at the Windmill at Prescott. While he was in Toronto the news of the defeat of the brigand invaders at Windsor by Col. Prince was received, and Sir George Arthur employed Richardson to carry the despatches of that event to Sir John Colborne at Montreal, but was anticipated by half an hour by an express from Colonel Dundas at Kingston, to whom also he had carried a despatch of the affair. This duty being performed he joined his wife at Niagara.

On his way to Quebec during the spring of this year (1838), Richardson took the earliest occasion to settle an affair with Colonel Chichester, for which no opportunity offered while at San Sebastian in Spain. It appears that Colonel Chichester seconded a motion to expel Richardson from the San Sebastian club. On learning the truth of the matter Colonel Kirby, the proposer of the motion, apologized to Richardson in England. Richardson now required a similar apology from Colonel Chichester, who granted it. All the documents that were necessary were now in his possession, consequently his "Personal Memoirs" were published this year.

During the winter he made preparations to take up his residence at Amherstburg. On his arrival there he is disappointed in the place. The charms that it possessed in his youth have all departed. No fleet of government vessels now make the little harbor their home. No Indian watchfires add a picturesqueness to the beautiful island opposite the town. No bands of Indians now come there to sit in solemn council or to receive their annual presents. And where in other days a half regiment of regulars and a battery of artillery enlivened the town, now, but a single company remains, to garrison a fort,—but a mere shadow of its former greatness.

Although the town appeared to have every mark of decay, yet Richardson could not hire a vacant house. The quartering of the regulars and militia there in consequence of the rebellion, had increased the population so quickly that all the houses were occupied. He then went to Sandwich, where he made his home in a small brick house "gable end to the street." The house still stands about 100 yards south of St. John's Church, and but for a covering of bright red paint and the addition of a verandah in front, presents the same appearance as 60 years ago. It was pointed out to me last summer by Mr. Thomas McKee, the genial County Clerk of Essex, who remembered Richardson well and had many interesting stories to relate of him. It was in this house that the finishing touches were put upon "The Canadian Brothers," a sequel to "Wacousta." Some chapters of this novel had appeared in "The Literary Garland," a magazine that had been started in December, 1838, in Montreal. One of these contributions was entitled "Jeremiah Desborough," and the other "The Settler or the Prophecy Fulfilled."

Having received the encouragement of 250 subscriptions among the military and the people of Canada, Richardson resolved to publish the sequel to "Wacousta" and went to Montreal to see the work through the press. The registration notice of this novel bears the date, January 2nd, 1840. It was published in two volumes in the original edition, and was dedicated to Sir John Harvey, Lieutenant-Governor of New Brunswick. The tale is an historic one and deals with the War of 1812 on the Detroit frontier. In a measure the work is autobiographical and covers the same period as that of his history of the war. General Brock, Colonel Procter, Captain Barclay, Tecumseh, Walk-in-the-Water, Split-Log and Round-head appear in the work under their proper names. Gerald and Henry Grantham, the Canadian Brothers, are Major Richardson and his favorite brother Robert. Simon Girty appears as Sampson Gattrie and the description of this personage in the book is the best ever written. St. Julian is Colonel St. George, Cranstoun is Brevet-Lieutenant-Colonel Short, and Middlemore, Lieutenant Gordon. The other officers all have places in the narrative, but to avoid a multiplicity of characters one personage in the story often represents two or more in the real events. For instance, Gerald Grantham is made to act the parts of Lieutenant Rolette, Lieutenant Irvine and Midshipman Robert Richardson. Some anachronisms occur for which the author prepares us in the preface. Captain Barclay and General Brock meet at Amherstburg

before the fall of Detroit and the battle of Queenston
Heights is not fought until October, 1813. The story in
many respects is not the equal of "Wacousta." The
purely fictitious characters are not so well drawn in " The
Canadian Brothers," while the historical ones are perhaps more faithfully pictured. The weakest part is the
attempt to make it a sequel. Jeremiah Desborough, the
villain of the novel, is a character without a purpose.
He is but an intruder in the insignificant place he has in
the tale. When Richardson knows the type of man he
is describing, we get a picture that delights us by the
boldness and clearness of the delineation of every phase
of his character ; but when he does not know him the
portrayal is a palpable failure. He found out, too late
to correct it in the first edition, that the Scotch dialect
he makes Cranstoun use is very imperfect. In the
second edition, published in New York in 1851, in one
volume, under the author's supervision, this imperfection
just pointed out does not occur.

After the publication of "The Canadian Brothers,"
Richardson made preparations to start for his home
in Sandwich. He decided to travel by means of his own
equipage, a method affording greater freedom and more
ease and convenience. He therefore purchased a sleigh,
a team of spirited French-Canadian ponies, and suitable
harness and robes, and engaged a servant to care for the
ponies at all stopping places. He set out from Montreal
during the last days of February. In Cornwall he
stayed some days, rehearsing old times with Judge G. S.
Jarvis, an old fellow-officer of 8th (King's). His fondness
for being entertained by his old friends on the way, and
an accident in the early part of the journey, delayed
him, and by the time Brockville was reached it was impossible to go farther by sleigh.

While waiting here some days to make the necessary
changes to travel by waggon, he was induced to purchase
a piece of land, beautifully situated on the high banks
of the St. Lawrence, on which were a good house, a barn
and other outbuildings. The journey, which occupied
about two months, the greater part of which time was
spent in visiting at Kingston, Toronto and London,
ended about the last of April.

Preparations were made for the return trip to his
"farm" in Brockville. Before the time for starting

came round, a grand demonstration was announced, which was to be held at Fort Meigs by the Whigs of Ohio in honor of their candidate for the Presidency of the United States. The place was appropriately chosen, as it was on the Miami that General Harrison won the military renown associated with his name, which contributed not a little to his success at the coming election. Richardson accepted an invitation from his friends at Detroit to be present, and to visit the place where he also had seen some hard fighting against the general whose exploits his party were now commemorating.

The trip to Brockville was begun in the last week in June. The ponies and waggon were again used, and by this picturesque and delightful method he and his wife reached Brockville in the first week in July. For some weeks his time was occupied in superintending the renovation of the house and the improvement of the grounds. But after this work was completed he became somewhat melancholy, a feeling that quite naturally follows when a person who has led a wandering life becomes a fixture in a place.

At this time he appears to have had no settled plans for the future. No event appears to have suggested itself as suitable for weaving into a romantic story. One alluring prospect seems to have taken possession of his very being. He hoped to be appointed to some office, in the gift of the Governor and his Council, which would enable him to live comfortably the rest of his days and to devote his leisure to literary work. He had strong and reasonable claims for such a position upon the government of Canada. His qualifications for many positions in the gift of the government were of the highest order. He was dignified in bearing and a thorough gentleman. He spoke English and French with equal fluency. His military training had specially fitted him to perform the routine duties of a public officer with promptness and attention to detail, necessary acquirements in a public official. He had done not a little for Canada. He fought in her defence at a time when she was most in need of assistance. He was for a year a prisoner of war, and for a part of that period suffered close imprisonment while two governments deliberated whether a certain number of their prisoners should or should not suffer death. When internal dissensions threatened again to make his native country the easy prey of a foreign power, he hastened to her shores to fight once more for British connection, if it were necessary. When he came to Canada in 1838 he represented the most powerful newspaper in the Empire.   Through the medium of that paper he endeavored to teach the public of Great Britain that the unity of the Empire depended upon the granting of Responsible Government to the Canadian people. For daring to express these views he was relieved of his position on the paper.   As he had not a sufficient income to support himself and his wife it became necessary for him to seek some employment.   In this extremity it was quite natural for him to turn, for the aid he required, to those he had served so conscientiously and so faithfully.   Lord Durham, cognizant of his devotion to the cause of Responsible Government and of the effort Richardson had made to shield him from the storm about to break about his devoted head, promised to exert himself in his behalf.   The early death of that nobleman left him without any hope of reward from that source.

The social conditions of Brockville in 1840 were in marked contrast to the refinement and culture of the large cities of Europe ; and it is not difficult for one to believe that Richardson felt himself imprisoned.   Of this he says : "There were moments when the idea of being buried alive, as it were, in this spot, without a possibility, perhaps, of again seeing the beautiful fields and magnificent cities, and mixing in the polished circles of Europe, and of matchless England in particular, came like a blighting cloud upon my thoughts, and filled me with a despondency no effort of my own could shake off."

He, however, felt the necessity of self-exertion. Some of his friends were confident that if a newspaper were started in Brockville, it would prove a profitable investment.   He resolved to adopt their advice.   His talents and tastes were literary and a periodical seemed to offer the best means of supporting the cause he had so much taken to heart.   His judgment in the matter was the more easily influenced in favor of the suggestion because he thought the dawn of a new order of things would quicken the literary activity of the colony.

Type, presses and compositors were necessary for the venture, and to obtain these Richardson went to New

York.   While transacting the business that brought him
to that city he received marked attention from several
persons who had been charmed and delighted by reading
his works.   In him they found a person who could accept
their homage with that ease and grace which marked the
man whose gentility and decorum had been fashioned in
the refined company of Europe.

His business having been completed, he started for
home, and arrived there on the last day of the year 1840.
In the early part of June of the following year the necessary machinery for printing arrived in Brockville, and
the first issue of the paper was published.   It was named
THE NEW ERA or CANADIAN CHRONICLE, a title sug-
gestive of the political change that Lord Sydenham came
to Canada to introduce, and which Lord Durham had
advised as a solution of the political problem.   The paper
was a weekly, and the subscription price was four dollars
for a year.   The leading articles and the other matter
were all from the pen of the editor.   No paying adver-
tisements or local topics found a place in its columns.
His " Jack Brag in Spain " and " Recollections of the
West Indies " were serials that ran through several
issues.   While the paper was interesting and enter-
taining, it had not that variety and freshness which
would secure and retain a long list of paying sub-
scribers at four dollars a year.   Consequently, the editor
became involved financially, and the paper was on
the verge of suspension.   Another brave effort, however, was made to reanimate it by appealing to the
patriotism of the Canadian people.   Richardson entertained the suggestion of his military comrades in the last
war, now in high positions in the country, to write a history of the War of 1812.   Although the immediate object
was to make money, there was a higher motive that
made Richardson eager to undertake the task.   The
various accounts of that war which had as yet found general circulation in Upper Canada were those contained in
United States text-books, which were used almost exclusively in the schools of the province.   The whole object
of the historians of the United States during the first
half of the 19th century seemed to be to create in the
minds of their readers a hatred of everything British.
A devotion to truth in historical writing, so pretty generally in evidence at the present day among her historians,

had not as yet been found acceptable to American readers or profitable to American historians.

Richardson was qualified in a special manner for such an undertaking. He had been an active participator in all the engagements in which the Right Division of the Canadian army had taken part. He had promises of assistance from several of his countrymen who had seen active service in the several campaigns. Sir John Harvey, then Governor of Newfoundland, promised to put at his disposal his personal narrative of the campaigns of 1813 and 1814. His experience in the several capacities of the service from gentleman volunteer to Major in command of a battalion in action, would enable him to comment intelligently on the skirmishes, battles and strategical evolutions of the combatants. The honesty and fairness he had shown in his letters on Lord Durham's administration was a guarantee that his prejudices would not lead him to give any but an impartial treatment of the incidents of the struggle.

The History of the War was to be written in Three Series. The first was to contain " A Narrative of the Operations of the Right Division," and was to be published serially in THE NEW ERA. The first instalment appeared in the first number of the second volume, which was issued on March 2nd, 1842. The paper appeared at intervals that varied from a week to two weeks ; and in fourteen numbers, the last of which appeared on July 15th, 1842, the Narrative was completed. Four more numbers were published in which was reprinted his poem " Tecumseh"; the paper ceasing with the 18th number on August 19th, 1842.

The Narrative was set up in wide columns in THE NEW ERA and by simply dividing the matter into pages, the work could be printed in book form. The history was dedicated to the United Legislature of Canada, to which Richardson applied for financial aid to reimburse him for his expenditure on the First Series and to enable him to complete the work. His petition was introduced and read by Sir Allan MacNab, and approved by the House, only one member dissenting. In consequence £250 was voted by the Assembly and paid to Richardson.

The appeal to the people of Canada to subscribe for THE NEW ERA, because the history of the War of 1812 was to appear in its columns, was not responded to by any large increase in the circulation. To bring the history generally before the people the author made an effort to get the district councils to recommend it for use in the schools within their boundaries. Johnstown district voted £50 to purchase copies to be used in their schools, but this vote was afterwards rescinded because the council had no power to vote money for that purpose. No other council took any action in the matter. The booksellers of the province with whom it had been placed on sale had disposed of about thirty copies, and in Kingston, the capital of the Province, all that a copy would fetch at auction was seven and one-half pence currency. The poor reception accorded the First Series of the History of the War caused the author to postpone the preparation of the other parts ; and as the prospect never became more promising during his lifetime the history was not completed. It is of some interest to know that this publication was the third for which a copyright was granted by the old Province of Canada.

THE NEW ERA supported in a general way the principle of Responsible Government and the " cabinet" that was administering the government ; but Richardson, like many others, became displeased because Sir Charles Bagot, a Conservative, had selected as his advisers persons belonging to both parties and had shown a similar impartiality in his appointments to office. Richardson may have had personal as well as public reasons for his action. However, he resolved to oppose the Ministry and to do so started at Kingston a paper called the CANADIAN LOYALIST AND SPIRIT OF 1812. The political articles that appeared were very severe upon the members of the Lafontaine-Baldwin Ministry ; Mr. Francis Hincks getting more than his share. The appointment to office of " men of more than questionable loyalty—of unmasked traitors and rebels—over the honest and self-sacrificing defender of the rights of the British Crown" was the " prominent ground on which the political principles of the CANADIAN LOYALIST were based." The paper fulfilled its mission. Sir Charles Metcalfe as Governor, maintained that he might appoint officials without consulting his Council ; disagreement followed, and all his executive except Mr. Daly resigned. The CANADIAN LOYALIST which was started at the beginning of 1843 was discontinued about the middle of the year 1844.

Parliament met next in Montreal on July 1st and during the session Richardson was as active as ever in his support of Sir Charles Metcalfe; and when the House was dissolved both parties made preparations for the coming struggle. In the elections that followed, the Conservatives had a majority. Richardson now expected some reward for the support he had given the party in power. The canals of Canada were being built and a system of police was instituted by the government to prevent disturbances of the peace. The office of Superintendent of Police on the Welland Canal, which was being enlarged, became vacant, and Richardson was appointed to the office by Lord Metcalfe on May 20th, 1845. The pay was only ten shillings a day, but he hoped for something better and entered on his duties with alacrity. To add to the smartness of the force he induced the men to purchase uniforms to be paid for in six equal instalments, he in the meantime advancing the pay for them. The force was disbanded on January 31st, 1846, on seven days' notice, and at that time there was due the Superintendent from the men for equipment £51. At the coming session of Parliament Richardson petitioned the House, complaining of the sudden dismissal of himself and the force, and praying compensation for losses sustained and for clothing for the force. The petition was referred by the House to a select Committee which reported that: An allowance for clothing had been made to the force at Lachine and Beauharnois; that they saw no reason why it should be withheld from the petitioner; that injustice had been done him by the abrupt dismissal; that he and the men be allowed a gratuity; and that he had discharged his responsible duties in a satisfactory and creditable manner. When the question upon the motion, to concur in the report of Committee, was put in the House the motion was negatived. It is very difficult for one at this distance of time to understand how the Legislature could make a distinction between the officials on the Welland Canal and those on the Lachine Canal. One thing is certain, the verdict of the House was not based upon the evidence as it appears in its Journals.

While Superintendent of Police, Richardson suffered the loss of his wife, who died at St. Catharines on the 16th of August, 1845. Her remains were interred in the Butler burial ground, near Niagara, where his eldest sister Jane and other relatives were buried. The inscription on the headstone that he erected to mark her grave is unique. Without indicating the lines or forms of letters the following is the order of the words :—" Here Reposes, Maria Caroline, the Generous-Hearted, High-Souled, Talented and Deeply-Lamented Wife of Major Richardson, Knight of the Military Order of Saint Ferdinand, First Class, and Superintendent of Police on the Welland Canal during the Administration of Lord Metcalfe. This Matchless Wife and This (illegible) Exceeding Grief of Her Faithfully Attached Husband after a few days' illness at St. Catharines on the 16th August, 1845, at the age of 37 years."

After being relieved of the duties of Superintendent of Police, Richardson prepared for publication " Eight Years in Canada," an exceedingly well-written description of his career in Canada from 1838 till March, 1847. The administrations of Lord Durham, Lord Sydenham, Sir Charles Bagot and Lord Metcalfe are very fully treated ; it is the only contemporary history we have of this transitional period, and in subsequent histories of this epoch he is very freely quoted. Although written after the position he filled had been abolished, and after he had abandoned all hope of receiving any office from the government, it exhibits a fairness one would scarcely expect from a person so unjustly used. Sir Charles Bagot and the Lafontaine-Baldwin ministry are severely handled, while the administration of Lord Metcalfe is eloquently praised. In defending the course of the latter he takes a position beside perhaps the greatest controversial writer of Canada, Reverend Egerton Ryerson.

In 1847 (the book bears the date 1848) Richardson entered for copyright a sequel to his " Eight Years in Canada," called " The Guards in Canada or the Point of Honor." In it the story is told of how differences were settled by duels if an apology was not forthcoming. Richardson never allowed an insult tendered him to pass unnoticed. The person offending would apologize if the insult was offered through some misunderstanding, or would meet him. His first duel was in Paris. I have no record of any being fought in England. In Canada he had several affairs: there is living yet in Ontario a person holding an honored and exalted position who, when a mere boy, acted, much against his will, as a second for Major

Richardson in a matter, which happily was settled through the seconds by asking mutual apologies from the principals.

"The Guards in Canada" was the last of Richardson's works published in Canada under his direction. The book was written to vindicate his character for courage in an affair with a resident of Montreal, and incidentally it was a setting in order of his Canadian affairs before taking up his residence in New York, a step he had contemplated for some time.

He did not leave his native province without just cause. He had tried by every honorable means to gain a livelihood among the people he loved best. He squandered his accumulations and all that he had derived from the sale of his best works in the hope that his countrymen would appreciate his efforts. His historical works, thoroughly patriotic in tone and written in a bright vivacious style, were not bought in Canada. In all probability they were as generally read here as any novels or histories of the time. The lack of interest in literature in Canada was general. Education was at a low-water mark, among the great mass of the population, who even as late as the middle of the century felt too keenly the struggle for existence. The intellectual energies of the few, who were educated, were directed into political channels; and the unsettled conditions of our government absorbed all their time, leaving no leisure for those avocations that exercise their benign influence in refining the politics of the Motherland. Even the clergy were drawn into the political whirlpool. The great founder of the educational system of Ontario, Rev. Egerton Ryerson, had been appointed to office only in 1844, and the fruits of his labors were not to be seen for some years. He also was engaged before 1844 in the most remarkable political controversy in the history of Canada.

Richardson's case was not an isolated one by any means. Other writers had started periodicals and magazines, Canadian in sentiment, of an undoubtedly high literary character, and were as hopeful of receiving support as Richardson ever was, but these all were compelled to stop after a few numbers were published. Writers in those days did missionary work and if they did not receive the reward they hoped for, they sow seed that in some cases fell on good ground. We are beginning to reap the benefit of their self-sacrificing labors and if we are in the morning of a brighter and a more appreciative day, a large share of credit for these hopeful conditions must be attributed to the earlier workers in this unprofitable and unfruitful field.

In New York Richardson was engaged in preparing new editions of his published novels and in writing others. "Hardscrabble or the Fall of Chicago" was published in New York in 1850 or before that year, since it is named on the title page of "Wacousta" published in 1851; but as I have not seen a copy except the one in my library, published in 1888, I cannot give any further information regarding the first edition. The story is much shorter than the author's previous ones and may be considered weak when compared with "Wacousta." The scene is laid at Fort Dearborn on the Chicago river in the year 1812. In all probability Richardson got the facts for the story from a pamphlet published in 1844, which described the events as seen by an actor in them. Two or three surprises and an affair of love are introduced by means of a slight change in the order of events. The names of the officers at the fort are but transparently disguised in the romance. Captain Heald, Lieut. Helm, Ensign Ronan and Surgeon Von Voorhees, appear as Captain Headley, Lieut. Elmsley, Ensign Ronayne and Surgeon Von Vottenberg in the story. In 1852 a work by Major Richardson entitled "Waunangee or the Massacre of Chicago" was published. I have not been able to see a copy of this work but in all probability it is either the same as "Hardscrabble," or a sequel to it. The leading Indian character of the historical narrative is Naunongee, who is called Waunangee in the novel; accordingly, the name seems to point to some connection with this romance. As a title "Waunangee" would certainly be both more appropriate and more attractive than "Hardscrabble." "Wacousta" and "Écarté" were revised by the author and published in cheap octavo form, the former by Robert M. De Witt and the latter by Dewitt and Davenport in 1851. In the same year a revised edition of "The Canadian Brothers" appeared under the name "Matilda Montgomerie," the heroine of the story. It will be readily seen that it would not be politic for the author to issue a story in New York entitled "The Canadian Brothers," even if the publishers gave their assent. "Matilda Montgomerie" is much improved in the revision. The Scotch dialect, which Richardson himself acknowledges to be so imperfect, he omits in this edition. Sampson Gattrie now appears under his proper name, Simon Girty. But the most marked change from the first edition is the suppression of the several passages in which the author had used all his eloquence to sound the praises of the British in the numerically unequal struggle they had been called upon to maintain. Notable instances are the omission of all reference to Col. Harvey's night attack at Stoney Creek and to the details of the victory at Queenston Heights. It is very interesting to compare the two editions and to notice the passages that are suppressed or modified, evidently to suit the tastes of his new audience.

His other works were "Westbrook, or the Outlaw," and "The Monk Knight of St. John." As I have not seen either of these books I cannot give any facts relating to them, except what are gleaned from other bibliographies. "Westbrook" is mentioned by Morgan, but the date of publication is not given. Dr. L. E. Horning, of Victoria University, Toronto, suspects "that this 'Westbrook' is only 'Wacousta' with another name." I think this scarcely possible. "Wacousta" was the most popular of Richardson's works, and the name had gained a vogue that had a definite cash value to both author and publisher. The names of successful books are not usually changed. If I were to offer any opinion, I should say that the scene is laid in the western peninsula of Upper Canada, and that the tale introduces the exploits of a renegade Canadian named Westbrook, an actual elusive personage who, at the head of some Americans and a few Canadian rebels, went about the district from Long Point to the Talbot Settlement robbing the people and burning homes during the year 1814. It is quite possible Richardson knew of this marauder's acts, but whether more than the name was suggested by this knowledge, can be settled only by a study of the book itself.

In the Dictionary of National Biography, 1850 is given as the date of publication of "The Monk Knight of St.

John," but as I have not a copy of the book I cannot confirm this date. It is a tale of the Crusaders, and those who have read it say that it is a unique story probably suggested by reading Byron and Moore.

These books were all published in cheap form, and consequently the revenue that the author derived must have been comparatively small. It was the day of the cheap novel. About 1840 two New York papers began to reprint in their columns the most popular English novels, which, when finished, were issued in parts at a very low price. No international copyright law protected the British author in the United States. "Wacousta" had been pirated and issued in Philadelphia in 1833. The regular publishers had to issue books in cheap form and at lower prices or go out of business. Richardson arrived in New York when this competition was perhaps the keenest. "Écartè," "Wacousta," "Matilda Montgomerie" and "Hardscrabble" appeared in paper-covered 8vo form at 50 cents a volume.

Major Richardson died suddenly on the 12th of May, 1852, at his lodgings No. 113 West Twenty-ninth street, New York. The obituary notice as it appeared in the New York Journal of Commerce of May 14th, 1852, is as follows :

"Died—On the 12th inst. Major John Richardson, late of H.B.M. Gordon Highlanders aged 53 (55) years. His friends are invited to attend his funeral, without further invitation, from the Church of the Holy Communion, corner 6th Avenue and 20th Street, this day, at two o'clock, P.M."

His remains were taken outside the city for burial, but diligent inquiry has failed to find his last resting place.

The immediate cause of death was erysipelas ; at first the symptoms were not considered alarming, but when medical aid was summoned it came too late. To his many friends the news, besides the shock of suddenness, brought qualms of self-reproach when they learned that Richardson had been living in more straitened circumstances than his appearance or his conversation indicated.

To die in poverty and neglect is no disgrace. Finding no means of livelihood in his native land, he sought a foreign city after his prime of life was past ; and if he was unsuccessful in gaining a competence, perhaps the causes arose from the training of his early manhood rather than from circumstances within his control. The camp does not train a man for the mart. He who has entered the army a youth of sixteen, to retire at thirty-nine, seldom, unless in official routine, can adapt himself successfully to the new environment of civilian life. The task of gaining a livelihood by literature in Canada was the harder because he had been accustomed to the cultured circles of London society. It is no reproach to the people of Canada, individually, amid the many difficulties they contended with, that they failed to appreciate and purchase the works of their first novelist. It is a reproach to them collectively, to their government, that Richardson was not given an opportunity of earning enough to enable him to live in simple comfort in his native land. He had no vanity of authorship. On this he says :—"I look upon the art of ingenious writing, not as a merit, but a mere incidental gift, for which one is more indebted to nature than to judicious application." As a man of letters he was publicly honored but once. Yet, because he was not honored more he felt inclined to pity rather than to censure his countrymen. In a careful study of his career, no mean, no dishonorable act will be found. Faithful to his friends, true to his convictions, loyal to his country, he unselfishly served friends and country better than he served himself.

One wish he asked to be respected by future generations of his countrymen, which has not been regarded. He says " I cannot deny to myself the gratification of the expression of a hope that should a more refined and cultivated taste ever be introduced into this matter-of-fact country in which I have derived my being, its people will decline to do me the honor of placing my name in the list of their ' Authors.' I certainly have no particular ambition to rank among their future ' men of genius,' or to share any posthumous honor they may be disposed to confer upon them."

Richardson's whole career was a noble and manly struggle. Pugnacious and exclusive in temperament, with but a slight sense of humor, he pursued undeviatingly a course of the strictest integrity. He knew neither tact nor compromise. He fought harder for the political principles he cherished, for the social code he respected, than he did for life itself.

Like the earliest English novelist, Richardson has suffered neglect in his own land. All that Scotland had for her greatest poet was an office worth £70 a year, but her succeeding generations remembered his exquisite productions. Canada could find not even such an office for her first novelist. His own generation refused him a living in his native land; subsequent generations of Canadians know him not. And his works, if obtainable, can be bought only at almost prohibitive prices. Yet three years before Scott died; when Thackeray was a stripling of eighteen; when Dickens had not yet become a reporter, Richardson was winning, by his first work of the imagination, applause from the English press and a large audience of English readers. In the very year of Scott's death, his masterpiece, "Wacousta" appeared; and the six editions through which it has run bear testimony to its popularity.

Whatever Richardson did he tried to do well. Unlike Cooper, he never trusted to chance to develop the circumstances of his plot; unlike Cooper he tells his story well, and tells it in faultless English. The interest is sustained to the end. There are no carelessnesses, no crudities, no notable mannerisms. Cooper often loses himself in the pathless mazes of his long sentences. Richardson, incisive and logical, builds clause on clause, phrase on phrase, here adding a limiting detail and there a defining circumstance, until you marvel at the accumulated result and you would not have a single word changed. Yet there is no straining after rhetorical effect, no attempt at fine writing. The lucidity of style recalls Macaulay, who at this period was writing his early essays.

A born literary artist, Richardson has drawn with a firm and skilled hand not only the children of his imagination, but the people of his own day. His autobiographical sketches, his historical works, as well as his novels, show us their foibles, their weaknesses, and their merits. His great interest is in men and their achievements; but there are delightful bits of painting from nature. Though a lover of nature, he seldom gives himself up to that revel in the life of nature which is so great a merit of Cooper's work. It is men and women in action that interest him. Only less perhaps did the brute creation claim his attention. His ponies are still a memory among the older people of Windsor and Sandwich. He delights in describing the capture of a young wild deer in the river opposite his grounds in Brockville, which eventually became a great pet. Its antics and actions are not too insignificant to be recorded in one of his most valuable literary productions. But though he took delight in the possession of the ponies and the pet deer, his intimate companions were his dogs. In Sandwich, in Brockville, in Montreal, he was always accompanied by a beautiful specimen of the Newfoundland species named Hector. His grief at the loss of this dog by poison in Brockville was great, and another named after the Trojan hero was his companion in New York till almost the last. At the end of a long and favorable notice of Major Richardson's career in "The New York Journal of Commerce" a few days after his death this pathetic anecdote is told : "A week or two since, he was heard by someone who met him in a bookstore, accompanied as usual by his faithful canine friend, to say, ' Ah, poor Hector, we must part or starve.' " And it is further related that the dog was sold a few days before his master's death to provide him with food.

His notions of life were by no means puritanical. He believed that solace and comfort were to be derived from an after-dinner cigar. In complete accord with the customs of the times among the circle in which he moved in his palmy days, he took his glass of wine, but none abhorred excesses more than he.

If we judge Richardson by the literary success that cheered him even amid his many days of adversity, we can merely wonder that a writer so wholesome in atmosphere, so buoyant in spirit, so notable in our literary development, is now almost completely forgotten. His works, whether we consider their subject-matter, their literary merits, or their position in the growth of the novel, place their gifted author high on that roll we choose to designate as our list of Canadian authors.

These productions of his genius are his sole monument. The bright young Canadian lad who left school to fight his country's battles had to seek in the land he fought against an unknown grave in the teeming solitude of America's greatest city. No votive garland can be laid on that tomb ; no admiring young Canadian may visit that shrine.

THE RICHARDSON GENEALOGY

Robert Richardson was born in Scotland, and came to
Upper Canada with the Queen's Rangers as assistant
surgeon in 1792. He was stationed with his regiment at
Queenston, Toronto, and St. Joseph's Island. When
the regiment was disbanded in 1802 he took up his residence at Amherstburg, where he acted as surgeon to the
garrison, and as such was with the Right Division in
every engagement until the battle of Lake Erie, where
he was taken prisoner but released through the intercession of his brother-in-law, Col. Elijah Brush. On June
12th, 1807, he was appointed judge of the Western District, an office he held till his death. On the 27th of
April, 1824, he was appointed one of the Commissioners
of Customs, an office he held till 11th January, 1826.
After the war of 1812 Dr. Richardson was appointed surgeon to all the tribes of Indians in the Western District.
His death took place at Amherstburg in 1832, and his remains were interred in the burial ground adjoining
Christ Church in that town.

Robert Richardson married (I) Jan. 24th, 1793,
Madeleine Askin, 2nd daughter of Colonel John Askin,
of Detroit, who died at Amherstburg Jan. 10th, 1811,
and was buried in Christ Church burial ground; (II.)
Aug. 8th, 1811, Ann McGregor, born at Detroit, April
1st, 1781, third child of Gregor McGregor, the first
Sheriff of the District of Hesse, appointed by Lord
Dorchester on July 24th, 1788, who lived in Detroit
till 1796 when he removed to Canada taking up his
residence at Petite Côte, on the banks of the Detroit
river.

Of the first marriage.

1.—JANE, born May 19th, 1794, married Captain
Robert Rist, of the 37th Regiment, Jan. 15th,
1816; died Oct. 31st, 1831, buried in the Butler
burial ground, Niagara.

2.—JOHN, born Oct. 4th, 1796, died in New York city
May 12th, 1852. This was Major John Richardson, the author.

3.—ROBERT, born Sept. 10th, 1798, joined the marine
department as midshipman, wounded severely at
the battle of Frenchtown Jan. 22nd, 1813. Received a pension from the Legislature which

amounted to £78 17s. from Jan. 22nd, 1813, till Dec. 31st, 1816. He died at Amherstburg June 7th, 1819, and was buried in Christ Church burial ground.

4. — WILLIAM, born Jan. 7th, 1801, married Jane Cameron Grant, youngest daughter of Honorable Alexander Grant and Thérésé Barthe, on Feb. 11th, 1834. Was postmaster at Brantford, where he died. His son James lived at London some years ago.

5.—JAMES A., born Jan. 19th, 1803, died Aug. 18th, 1828. He was Registrar of Kent from 1825 until his death.

6.—CHARLES, born March 26th, 1805, died 1847, married (I) April 2nd, 1827, Elizabeth Euretta Clench (born 1808, died Sept. 28th, 1833), youngest daughter of Ralph Clench, of Butler's Rangers, afterwards Colonel of Militia and Judge ; (II) Jane Clarke, daughter of William Clarke, Niagara.

He began the study of law in York (Toronto), was appointed cornet of the "Queen's Light Dragoons" (now represented by "The Governor-General's Body Guard for Ontario") at the organization in 1822 ; removed to Niagara, where he practised law ; was Clerk of the Peace for Niagara District ; elected by the town of Niagara a member of the Legislative Assembly of Upper Canada in 1835; re-elected in 1836.

Of the first marriage.

(1) Eliza Magdalene, born May 31st, 1828, died June 3rd, 1828.   (2) John Beverley Robinson, baptized Jan. 5th 1830. (Sponsors : Chief Justice John Beverley Robinson ; Captain Hanson, 71st Regt. ; and Miss Clench.) Was an attorney at Versailles, Missouri, U.S.A., where he died March, 1899, his wife dying the next year.   (3) Eliza Euretta, baptized June 14th, 1832. Married in 1853 Hugo M. Grout, born at Grimsby, Ontario, 1831 ; sometime civil engineer on the Great Western Railway, the staff of which he joined in 1850 ; went to the United States in 1863 ; returned to Canada in 1895 ; living at present in retirement at St. Catharines, Ontario. Two children survive ; George H. Grout, civil engineer in

southern United States ; and Mrs. F. O. Hall, of
Akron, Ohio.

Of the second marriage.

(1) Jeanie died, aged 6 years, (2) Kate died,
aged 18 years.

7.—ALEXANDER, born Feb. 15th, 1808. It is said
that he and his brother James were drowned in
Lake Erie, and if at the same time, his death occurred on Aug. 18th, 1828.

8.—GEORGE J., born Aug. 25th, 1810, died Feb. 3rd,
1811.

Of the second marriage.

1.—GEORGE MCGREGOR, born July 4th, 1812, married
March 2nd, 1836, Mary, daughter of Colonel
Robert Nelles, and had issue (1) Robert married
Minerva Hendershott and had issue Frank, Duf-
ferin, Minnie and Emily ; (2) William-Lock ;
(3) Abram married Emma Horne and had issue
George and one daughter ; (4) Emily-Fanning
married Francis Dougall of Windsor, Ontario, and
had issue, Frank ; Arthur ; Susan married Wil-
liam Davies, of Detroit ; Emily married Frank
Marcon, of Windsor, son of the late Frank E.
Marcon, of Windsor, Deputy Clerk of the Crown ;
Marion ; Delia.

For the Nelles genealogy, see '' Ontarian Families,'' by E. M. Chadwick, Vol. II., p. 154.

2.—HENRY WELLINGTON, born Aug. 12th, 1814, a
barrister, died unmarried at Amherstburg, Dec.
21st, 1841.

3.—DAVID JOHNSTONE, born Aug. 12th, 1816, for
many years Collector of Customs at Windsor,
Ontario ; died there 1885. Married (I.) Jan.
22nd, 1844, Margaret Watson, of Windsor ; (II.)
in 1856, Sarah Mercer, of Sandwich. Of the first
marriage : (1) Robert Watson, born Nov. 26th,
1844, married Aug. 10th, 1870, Katherine Donnelly, daughter of the late Dr. E. B. Donnelly.
Lives at Windsor. (2) Theresa Ann Grace, born
Oct. 10th, 1846, married Jan. 20th, 1876, William
H. Rowley, of Ottawa, Secretary and Treasurer
of The E. B. Eddy Co., Hull, Que. Of the second
marriage : (1) Mary Mercer, born May 27th,
1858, now living in Louisville, Ky. (2) Neville

Peto, born Sept. 12th, 1860, married Carrie Wilcox, May, 1878; lives in Windsor. (3) George Eccles, born 1862, married Bessie Baby, Nov. 17th, 1883; lives in Detroit. (4) Harvey McGregor, born Nov. 9th, 1864; lives at Port Townsend, Wash. (5) Joseph Mercer, twin brother of (4), married Harriet Payne, June 5th, 1895; lives in Detroit. (6) Mabel Treacher, born Feb. 17th, 1869; lives in Ottawa.

4.—ANN, born June 2nd, 1818, died March 23rd, 1869, married June 4th, 1842, William G. Duff, Jr., son of William Duff, Sr., of the Barrack and Ordnance Department of Amherstburg, who married Susannah McGregor, fifth child of Gregor McGregor, born at Detroit Oct. 4th, 1785. William Duff, Sr., who died July 12th, 1861, aged 82, was the son of a minister of the same name at Faveran, Aberdeenshire, Scotland. Had issue one daughter, Ann Susan, born March 19th, 1843, married Aug. 13th, 1866, Raymond A. LaCroix; lives in Detroit.

5.—CATHERINE GRACE, born Aug. 31st, 1820, died at Amherstburg Dec. 3rd, 1841, unmarried.

6.—THÉRESÉ LOUISA, born Oct. 6th, 1822, died in Ottawa, June 8th, 1878, married July 4th, 1848, Captain John Neville Peto, of the Royal Canadian Rifles, son of Rev. James Peto, Vicar of Preston near Faversham, Kent, England. Capt. Peto died at Amherstburg Sept. 6th, 1862, without issue.

7.—ROBERT HARVEY, born March 3rd, 1825; unmarried, died at Grasshopper river, Missouri, about 1851.

THE ASKIN GENEALOGY

The first of this name in Upper Canada was Colonel John Askin. He was of Scottish descent and was a kinsman of John Erskine, Earl of Mar, who headed the revolt of 1715 in favor of the Old Pretender. The failure of the rising led those concerned in it to leave Scotland. The father of Col. John Askin removed to Strabane, in the County of Tyrone, Ireland, and, there to conceal his identity, he took the name Askin. Some time previous to the commencement of the Seven Years' War, his son John emigrated to America, and at the time the British conquered Canada he was a merchant at Albany. There is a tradition in the family that he accompanied Major Robert Rogers to Detroit when that officer received its surrender to the British in 1760. However it is known that when old Fort Pontchartrain at Detroit was invested by Pontiac, John Askin was entrusted with the important duty of taking supplies from Albany to Lake Erie and thence to Detroit to relieve the garrison. This difficult undertaking having been successfully performed, John Askin was rewarded by the British with grants of land near Detroit. In 1764 he went as King's Commissary to Michilimackinac, and in 1780 he returned to Detroit to engage in trade. Here he amassed a large fortune which he was compelled to abandon, in part, when he removed to Canada and took up his residence on the bank of the Detroit just opposite the lower end of Isle aux Cochons or Hog Island, now Belle Isle, the beautiful island park of Detroit. This home he called Strabane, after his paternal home in Ireland, a name by which it is known at the present day.

In 1787 Mr. Askin received a commission as Captain of Militia from Lord Dorchester for the town of Detroit, and in 1796 was commissioned Lieutenant-Colonel of Militia for the Western District, and in 1801 was promoted to the position of Colonel in the same corps. At the formation of the Land Boards he was appointed a member for Detroit, the other members being Colonel England and Montigny. He was also one of the Magistrates of the District. On the evacuation of Detroit by the British in 1796 he did not immediately leave that city but he made his election as continuing a British subject, for which he was brought to trial before the magistrates of the United States Government, and then he came to Canada.

Colonel John Askin married (I.) a French lady whose name could not be ascertained, and (II.) Marie Archange Barthe, of Detroit.

Of the first marriage :

1.—JOHN, JR., many years Collector of Customs at Amherstburg and later storekeeper and interpreter at St. Joseph Island. He married an Indian woman of prominence among her people, who possessed a fair English education. Their son, John B. Askin, lived for many years at "Woodview," near London, Ontario. He was Colonel of

Militia and saw some active service in 1837-38. His death occurred Nov. 15th, 1869. The capture of Mackinac, July 17th, 1812, and its retention till the end of the war, was due largely to the influence John B. Askin and his father had over the Western tribes of Indians, a large body of whom they induced to make the trip to Amherstburg, to assist the Right Division. In the note on page 25 the inference is that John Askin, Jr., died in 1869. This error arose from confusing the father and son. John Askin, Jr., died about 1818.

2.—CATHERINE, died Dec., 1796, married (I.) John Robertson, (II.) Hon. Robert Hamilton, of Queenston, died March 8th, 1811, and had six children. For the Hamilton genealogy, see " Ontarian Families," by Edward Marion Chadwick, Toronto, Vol. I., p. 143.

3.—MADELEINE, died Jan. 10th, 1811, married Dr. Robert Richardson Jan. 24th, 1793, of whom see Richardson genealogy following.

Of the second marriage :

1.—CHARLES, born 1780, married Monique Jacobs, Captain of Militia, present at taking of Detroit (medal and clasp), was at Queenston Heights and several other engagements, appointed Clerk of the Peace and Clerk of the District Court in 1824 ; was Commissioner of Customs from April 27th, 1824, till 1836; inherited the homestead of Strabane which descended to his son, the present occupant, Alexander-Henry Askin, named after Alexander Henry the fur trader, a friend of Col. John Askin when he was King's Commissary at Michilimackinac.

2.—ADELAIDE, born May 30th, 1783, married in 1802, Col. Elijah Brush, of the Michigan Militia and Attorney-General of the Northwest Territory.

3.—THÉRÉSE, married Col. Thomas McKee, son of Col. Alexander McKee, Deputy Superintendent General of Indian Affairs. Col. Thomas McKee was elected M.L.A. for Kent in 1796 and for Essex in 1801. They had issue : Alexander married Phyllis Jacob, whose son Thomas is at present County Clerk of Essex, resides at Sandwich. William J. McKee, son of the latter, the present

M.L.A. for North Essex, married the eldest
daughter of Charles Baby.

4.—ELEANOR, born 1788, married Richard Pattinson,
of Sandwich, Captain of Militia, and had issue:
Richard, who served 16 years in India, rose to rank
of Major of 16th Lancers, was Adjutant-General of
Cavalry, was present at battles of Aliwal and
Sobraon (the Sutlej medal, two clasps), present at
battle of Maharajpore (star); exchanged to a
Highland Infantry Regiment and while stationed
at Halifax in 1848 visited his native town of
Sandwich; served throughout the Crimean War
(medal with clasps); appointed Governor of Heli-
goland, 1857.

5.—ARCHANGE married Lieut.-Col. Meredith of the
Royal Artillery.

6.—ALEXANDER, died unmarried.

7.—JAMES, married Françoise-Navarre-Godé Maran-
tette, Colonel of Militia, served as Lieut. at taking
of Detroit (medal with clasp), Captain in 2nd Essex
Militia at Frenchtown and the battle of the Miami;
appointed Registrar of Essex in 1831. They had
issue: (1) John, who succeeded his father as
Registrar in 1846, and who was in turn succeeded
by his son, J. Wallace Askin, in 1872. (2) Archange married Henry Ronalds, their only child,
Mary-Elizabeth-Lucy died 1901, married 1868,
George-Becher Harris, grandson of Lieut.-Col.
Samuel Ryerson (1752-1812), and had issue,
George-Henry-Ronald, born 1873; Edward Montgomery, born 1880; Amelia-Archange. (3) James
went to New Zealand in 1848 and afterwards to
Australia. (4) Charles, Lieut. of Militia, killed
accidentally by a sentry at Amherstburg in 1838.
(5) Jane married (I.) Daniel Murray, of Toronto,
(II.) Edward Skae. (6) Thérésé. (7) Alice.
(8) Ellen.

BIBLIOGRAPHY.

I. TECUMSEH, a poem of four cantos, and 188 stanzas of *ottava rima*. 1828 (?)

This poem was published *before* February 18th, 1828, but I do not know in what form. Captain R. H. Barclay, in a letter of this date, thanks Richardson for the flattering notice he gets in the poem. It was re-published in THE NEW ERA or CANADIAN CHRONICLE, in its last four issues bearing the dates, July 22nd, July 29th, August 12th and August 19th, 1842.

II. 1. ÉCARTÉ ; or the Salons of Paris, London, 1829. It is stated in Allibone's Dictionary of Authors that it was published in 3 Vols. Post 8vo.

I have not seen this edition.

2. ÉCARTÉ : | or, | the Salons of Paris. | by Major Richardson, | Knight of the Order of St. Ferdinand, | Author of " Wacousta," " Hardscrabble, &c., &c. | Author's revised edition. | New York : | Dewitt & Davenport, Publishers, | Tribune Buildings.

206 pp. Illustrated paper cover. Price fifty cents. Size 9x5¾.
Entered according to Act of Congress, 1851.

3. ÉCARTÉ ; or the Salons of Paris. New York, 1888. Pollard & Moss. 12mo.

Issued as No. 83 in the P. & M. 12mos., cloth at fifty cents, and as No. 31 of the Echo series, paper, at twenty-five cents.
" Ecarté," " Wacousta," "Matilda Montgomerie " and " Hardscrabble " were printed in 1888 by Pollard & Moss, New York, from the same plates as were used by Dewitt, & Davenport for printing their editions. The plates were cut down to fit a shorter page.

III. 1. WACOUSTA ; | or, | The Prophecy : | A Tale of the Canadas. |

" Vengeance is still alive ; from her dark covert,
　　With all her snakes erect upon her crest,
　She stalks in view and fires me with her charms."
　　　　　　　　　　　　　　　　The Revenge.

By · the author of '' Écarté.'' | in three volumes. | Vol.
I. | London : | T. Cadell, Strand ; and W. Blackwood, |
Edinburgh. | 1832. |

Vol. I. 4+280 pp. Vol. II. 4+332 pp. Vol. III. 4+
372 pp. Size, 7x4½. Dedicated to the 41st Regiment.

2. WACOUSTA : | or | The Prophecy. | A Tale of the
Canadas. |

"Vengeance is still alive ; from her dark covert,
With all her snakes erect upon her crest,
She stalks in view and fires me with her charms."

The Revenge.

| By the author of '' Écarté.'' | in two volumes. | Vol.I. |
Philadelphia : | Key and Biddle, 23 Minor Street. | 1833. |

Vol. I. 264 pp. Vol. II. 274 pp. Size 6½x4¾.
This edition was not issued with the author's sanction.

3. WACOUSTA ; | or | The Prophecy : | A Tale of the
Canadas, | by Major Richardson, | Knight of the Mil.
Order of St. Ferdinand. | Author of ''Ecarte,'' '' The
Canadian Brothers,'' &c. |

"Vengeance is still alive ; from her dark covert,
With all her snakes erect upon her crest,
She stalks in view and fires me with her charms."

The Revenge.

| Second edition. | In three volumes. | Vol.I. | London; |
1840. |

Vol. I. 4+280 pp. Vol. II. 2+332 pp. Vol. III. 2+
372 pp. Size 7½x4.

From a careful comparison of this edition with the
first, I have come to the conclusion that the author
brought several copies of the first edition, in sheets, from
London and had them bound in Canada, uniformly with
''The Canadian Brothers,'' with a new title page as
above, printed *here*, but bearing the imprint London. The
typography, paper, pagination and name of printer agree.
Dedicated to the 8th (or King's) Regiment.

4. WACOUSTA ; | or, | The Prophecy | An Indian
Tale. |

"Vengeance is still alive ; from her dark covert,
With all her snakes erect upon her crest,
She stalks in view, and fires me with her charms."

THE REVENGE.

| By Major Richardson, | Author of "Hardscrabble,"
"Ecarté," &c. | Revised edition. | New York : | Robert
M. De Witt, Publisher, | 33 Rose Street. |
224 pp.   Paper ; price, fifty cents.   Size, 9x5¾.
Introduction by author dated January 1st, 1851.

Some copies bear the imprint 160 & 162 Nassau St.

5. WACOUSTA ; | or | The Prophecy : | An Indian
Tale. |

_____

" Vengeance is still alive ; from her dark covert,
    With all her snakes erect upon her crest,
    She stalks in view, and fires me with her charms."
                              THE REVENGE.

_____

By Major Richardson, | Author of "Hardscrabble,"
"Ecarte," etc. | First Canadian edition. | Montreal : |
John Lovell, St. Nicholas Street. | 1868. | 168 pp.
Size, 9½x6¼.
6. WACOUSTA ; | or, | The Prophecy | An Indian
Tale. |

_____

" Vengeance is still alive ; from her dark covert,
    With all her snakes erect upon her crest,
    She stalks in view, and fires me with her charms."
                              THE REVENGE.

_____

By Major Richardson, | author of "Hardscrabble,"
"Écarté," &c. | New York : | Pollard & Moss, | 47
John Street. | ―― | 1888.
262 pp.   Cloth.   Size, 7¼x5.
No. 80 of the P. & M.   12mos.   Price, 50 cents.
No. 27 of the Echo Series.   Paper.   Price, 25 cents.
"Wacousta" was published as a serial in " The
Transcript" newspaper of Montreal.

IV. 1. MOVEMENTS of the British Legion.   First edition, London, 1836.   I have not seen this edition.
2. MOVEMENTS | of the | British Legion, | with | stric-
tures on the course of conduct pursued | by Lieutenant-
General Evans. | ―― | By Major Richardson, K.S.F. |
author of "Ecarté," "Wacousta," &c., &c. | ―― |
Second edition. | To which is added, with new views. |
A Continuation of the Operations from the 5th of May,
1836, to the close of | March, 1837. | ―― | London :

Published by Simpkin, Marshall and Co. Stationer's Hall |
Court ; J. Macrone, St. James's Square ; and E. Wilson,
| Royal Exchange, Cornhill. | —— | 1837. |
  XVI.+330 pp.   Size, 8½x5¼.
Contains seven lithographed plates.

V. PERSONAL Memoirs | of | Major Richardson, |
[Author of " Movements of the British Legion," &c.
&c. &c.] | as connected with | the singular oppression of
that officer while in Spain by | Lieutenant General Sir
De Lacy Evans. | —— | A man who is too proud to
acknowledge a fault when he is conscious of having com-
mitted | one, and thereby wounded the feelings of an-
other, shows himself to be, instead of elevated | rank,
very low indeed in the scale of intellectual worth.   His
pride is of the meanest kind, and | to him even more dis-
graceful than his fault.—*Anonymous*. | —— | Montreal :
Armour & Ramsay : | W. Neilson, Quebec ; R. Stanton,
Toronto ; and J. Macfarlane, | Kingston. | —— | 1838. |
  146+IV. pp.   Size, 9x5¾.

VI. 1. THE | Canadian Brothers ; | or, | The Prophecy
Fulfilled. | A tale of the late American War. | —— | By
| Major Richardson, | Knight of the Military Order of
Saint Ferdinand, | Author of " Ecarté," " Wacousta,"
&c. &c. | —— | In two volumes. | Vol. I. | —— | Mon-
treal : | A. H. Armour and H. Ramsay. | —— | 1840. |
  Vol. I., XIV.+220 pp.   Vol. II., 228+ IV. pp.
  Size, 7½x4¼.
This book, revised and slightly abridged by the author,
was published in the United States under the title of
" Matilda Montgomerie." The following are the editions
of this work under this title :

  2. MATILDA Montgomerie : | or, | The Prophecy Ful-
filled. | A tale of the late American War. | Being the sequel
to " Wacousta." | By Major Richardson, | Knight of the
Order of St. Ferdinand. | Author of "Wacousta," "Hard-
scrabble," " Ecarte," etc., etc. | No place.   No date.
No publisher's name.   192 pp., octavo, paper cover.

  Entered in 1851 by Dewitt & Davenport, New York.

  3. MATILDA Montgomerie : | or, | The Prophecy Ful-
filled. | A tale of the late American War. | Being the
sequel to Wacousta. | By Major Richardson, | author of

"Wacousta," "Hardscrabble," "Ecarte," etc., etc. |
New York : | Pollard & Moss, | 47 John Street. | 1888. |
226 pp., size 7½x5.
No. 28 of the Echo series, paper cover, price 25 cents.
No. 81 of the P. & M., 12mos., cloth, price 50 cents.

VII. War of | 1812. | —— | First Series. | Containing
a full and detailed narrative | of the | operations of the |
Right Division, | of the | Canadian Army, | by | Major
Richardson, K.S.F. | —— | 1842. | (Brockville.)
6+2+184 pp. Size 8¼x5¼.
Published originally in Vol. II. of The New Era or
Canadian Chronicle, a paper published by Richardson,
at Brockville. The first number of Vol. II. was published
on March 2nd, 1842.
This book was the third article for which a copyright
was granted in the Province of Canada.

VIII. Eight Years in | Canada ; | embracing | A Re-
view of the Administrations | of | Lords Durham and
Sydenham, Sir Chas. Bagot, | and Lord Metcalfe ; | and
including | numerous interesting letters | from Lord Dur-
ham, Mr. Chas. Buller, and other | well-known public
characters. | —— | By Major Richardson, | Knight of the
Military Order of St. Ferdinand, | Author of "Ecarte,"
"Wacousta," "The Canadian Brothers," &c. &c.
&c. | ~~~~~ | De Omnibus Rebus et Quibusdam Aliis.
| ~~~ | Montreal, Canada : | Published by H. H. Cun-
ningham, 50, Notre Dame Street. | —— | 1847. |
232 pp. Size 8½x5.
Some copies contain a lithographed portrait of the
author.

IX. The | Guards in Canada ; | or, the | Point of
Honor : | being a sequel to | Major Richardson's |
"Eight Years in Canada." | —— | Montreal: | Published
for the Author, | By H. H. Cunningham. | —— | 1848. |
56 pp. Size 8½x5½.
Yellow-coated paper covers. Title nearly as above in
two colors, with border, verso, arms of Great Britain.
Although this book bears the date 1848 on the title
page the registration notice is as follows : "Entered
according to the Act of the Provincial Legislature, in
the year one thousand eight hundred and forty-seven, by

Major Richardson, in the office of the Registrar of the Province of Canada.''

X. 1. HARDSCRABBLE ; | or, the | Fall of Chicago. | A Tale of Indian Warfare. | By Major Richardson, | Author of ''Wacousta,'' ''Ecarte,'' ''Matilda Montgomerie,'' etc., etc., | New York : | Robert M. De Witt, Publisher | 160 & 162 Nassau St. | no date, 100 pp. 8vo., paper cover. Published probably in 1850.

2. HARDSCRABBLE ; | or, the | Fall of Chicago. | A Tale of Indian Warfare. | By Major Richardson, | Author of | '' Wacousta ; or, The Prophecy,'' '' Matilda Montgomerie; or, The Prophecy | Fulfilled,'' '' Écarté; or, The Salons of Paris,'' etc., etc. | New York : | Pollard & Moss, | 42 Park Place and 37 Barclay Street. | 1888. |
114 pp. Size 7½ x 5.
No. 87 of the P. and M., 12mos., cloth, price 50 cents.
No. 42 of the Echo Series, paper, price 25 cents.
In Allibone's Dictionary of Authors it is stated that an edition was published in octavo form in 1856.

XI. WAUNANGEE ; or The Massacre of Chicago. A Romance. Octavo, paper, twenty-five cents. Long & Bro. New York and London. 1852.
I have not been able to see a copy of this work. It may be '' Hardscrabble '' under another name, or it may be a sequel to it. '' Hardscrabble '' describes the events that took place until the 4th of July, 1812. The massacre of the garrison at Fort Dearborn took place in August, hence this book may be a sequel.

XII. THE Monk Knight of St. John ; a tale of the Crusaders. New York. The Dictionary of National Biography gives the date of this work as 1850, while Morgan gives 1854.

XIII. WESTBROOK ; or, the Outlaw. 8vo.
I have not seen a copy of either XII. or XIII.

Amherstbury 4th February 1813

My Dear Uncle

You have doubtless heard ere this, of
of the engagement at the River Raisin on Friday the
2nd inst however you may probably not have heard
the particulars of the business, which are simply thes
On Monday the 18th we received information that the
Americans under the Command of General Winchester
after an obstinate resistance, had driven from the
River Raisin a detacht of Militia under Major Rey-
olds, (also a party of Indians) which had been statio
at there some time — That they had sustained
great loss from the fire of our Indians, and from
a 3 pounder, which was most ably served by Bombardier
Kitson (since dead) of the R.A. —

On Tuesday part of our men moved over the river
to Brownstown, consisting of a Detacht R Artill.y
with 3–3 pounders and 3–small howitzers – Captain
Mallor's Company (41 Regt) a few Militia, and the
Sailors attached to the Guns — An alarm was given
that the enemy were at hand — The Guns were
relimbered, & every thing prepared for action, when
the alarm was found to be false

On Wednesday the remainder of the army joined us
at Brownstown, where (including Regulars, Militia
Artillery, Sailors, and Indians) we mustered near
1000 men — We lay the night at Brownstown.
Next day The army commenced its march towards the River Raisin and encamped this night
at Rocky River which (you know) is about 12 miles

beyond Brownstown, and 6 on this side the Rio
Raisin. About two hours before day we resum
our march On Friday at day break we pe
ceived the enemy's fires very distinctly. All silent in
their Camp — The army drew up and formed the line
battle in 2 adjoining fields, and moved down t
towards th enemy; the guns advanced 20 or 30 pa
in front, & the Indians on our flanks — We had got
tolerably near their camp when we heard their Reva
drum beat /so completely lulled into security were the
that they had not the most distant idea of an enemy
being near/ and soon after we heard a shot or two
from the Centinels, who had by this time discovered
us— Their Camp was immediately in motion The
Guns began to play away upon them at a fine
rate, keeping up a constant fire The American
drew up and formed behind a thick picketting from
whence they kept up a most galling fire upon
our men, who, from the darkness of the morning
supposed the Pickets to be the Americans; however as
it grew lighter they discovered their mistake, and
advanced within 70 or 80 paces of the pickets, but fin
ing that scarcely one of their shot took effect, as they al
most all lodged in the fences Being thus protected
from the fire of our men, they took a cool and deliberate
aim at our Troops, who fell very fast, and them
of their men at the Guns being either killed or
wounded it was thought expedient to retire towards
the enemy's left under cover of some houses
I was a witness of a most Barbarous act of inhuman

the part of the Americans who, fired upon
poor wounded, helpless Soldiers who were endeavour
g to crawl away on their hands & feet from the
ene of action, and were they ~~tumbled~~ over like
many hogs — However the deaths of those brave
en were avenged, by the slaughter of 300 of the
wer of Winchester's army, which had been ordered
turn our flanks,—but who, having divided into
o parties, were met, driven back, pursued, tomahawk
& and scalped by our Indians (very few escaping)
carry the news of their defeat. — The General
imself was taken prisoner by the Indians, with his
n, aid, and several other officers — He immediately
ispatched a messenger to Colonel Procter, desiring him
acquaint him with the circumstance of his being a
risoner, and to intimate that if the Colonel would
nd an officer to his camp, to summons the remain
r of his army to surrender, he would send ~~an~~
der by him to his Officer then Commanding
surrender the Troops — Colonel Procter objected to
nding one of his own officers but permitted the
neral to send his aid, (with a flag) The firing instantl
ceased on both sides, and about 2 hours afterwards
he enemy (460 in number) laid down their arms
d surrendered themselves prisoners of war
good many of our Officers were wounded in the
gagement but none of them Killed — The
lowing is a List of them. R.A. Lt. Troughton, Solicitly
tached to the Guns. Cap. Rolette. Lt. Irvine Ensign Richards.

severely/ 45th ff. Capt. Tatton. Lt. Clemow /severely
Militia Thosd. A 6 ff. Lt. Col. St. George, Capt. Mills
Lt. a McCormick/ Paymaster Gordon /severely/ Ens.
Gowan /slightly/ R. N. F. Rt. Ensign Kerr /dangerously/
Indian Depart t Capt. Caldwell, Mr. Wilson /severely/
This is an accurate an account as I can give you of
the Engagement — I will now give you an account of
my feelings on the occasion — When we first drew
up in the field, I was ready to fall down, with
fatigue from marching and carrying a heavy mus
quet — Even when the balls were flying about my
ears as thick as hail I felt quite drowsy and sleepy.
And indeed I was altogether in a very disagreeable
dilemma, the night before at Rocky River. some
one, or other of the men took my firelock, and
left his own in the place — It being quite dark
when we sat out from that place, I could not distin
guish one from another — Enquiry was vain so I was oblig.
to take the other /without thinking that any thing
was the matter with it — When we come to the
firing part of the business — I could not get my
gun off, it flashed in the pan. I procured a
wire and worked away at it with that — Tried
it again; and again it flashed — I never was
so vexed to think that I was exposed to the tor
=rent of fire from the enemy without having the
power to return a single shot, quite disconcerted
the economy of my pericranium; though I
had fired fifty rounds, not one of them would

have had any effect, except un the pickets, which I was not at all ambitious of assailing like another Don Quixotte — Our men had fired a 5 rounds when I was called to assist my Brother Robert who was wounded, and who fell immediately, and which led me to suppose that he was mortally wounded — However when he was carried to the Doctors, I found the poor fellow had escaped with a broken leg, which torments him very much, and it will be some time before he gets over it — I think it is highly probable we shall have a brush with the valiant Harrison, who is said to be at the Rapids of the Miami River or near them — If so I think we shall have tight work, as we have lost, in Killed & wounded, in the action of the 22nd 180 men /exclusive of Indians/ Pray remember us to all my Cousins and,

Believe me
My Dear Uncle
Yours affectionately
John Richardson

Chal. Askin
Queenston

SKETCH MAP OF OPERATIONS OF THE
RIGHT DIVISION OF CANADIAN ARMY
AND THE
LEFT DIVISION OF AMERICAN ARMY
1812-'13

Scale of Miles

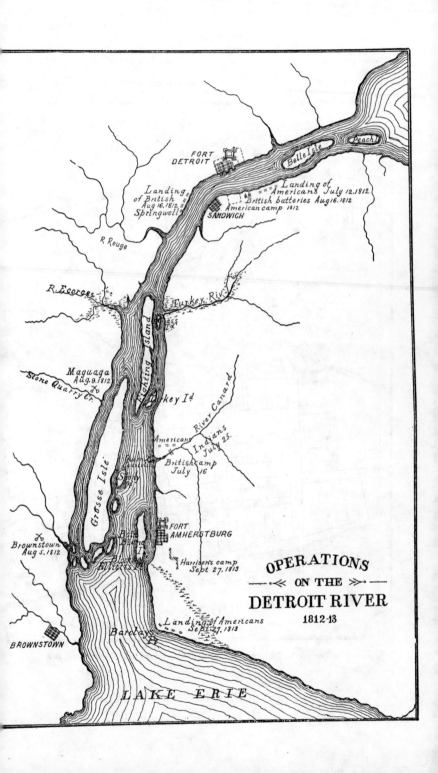

FORT DETROIT

Belle Isle

Peach I.

Landing of British Aug 16. 1812
Springwell

Landing of Americans July 12. 1812
British batteries Aug 16. 1812

SANDWICH

American camp 1812

R. Rouge

R. Ecorces

Turkey Riv.

255

Fighting Island

Maguaga Aug. 9. 1812

Stone Quarry Cr.

Turkey Id.

River Canard

Americans July 25

Indians

British camp July 16

Grosse Isle

Queen Charlotte
Sunk

Brownstown Aug 5. 1812

FORT AMHERSTBURG

Batte
Elliotts

Harrison's camp Sept 27. 1813

BROWNSTOWN

Barclay

Landing of Americans Sep. 27. 1813

OPERATIONS
—«— ON THE —»—
DETROIT RIVER
1812-13

LAKE ERIE

PLAN OF DETROIT 1812

Artillery Garden

Fort Lernoult

Magazine

Esplanade

River Savoyard

Wood Yard

Burying Ground

Bastion

Barracks

Officers quarters

Lerneau Street

St. James Street

St. Honore Street

St. Joseph Street

Catholic Church

Ann Street

Gate

St. Louis St.

McDougall Alley

Champaign

Alley

Bastion

A

Road

Bastion

Public Wharf

Merchants Wharf

Navy Yard

DETROIT RIVER

The site of Fort Ponchartrain is shown by the dotted enclosure, at A

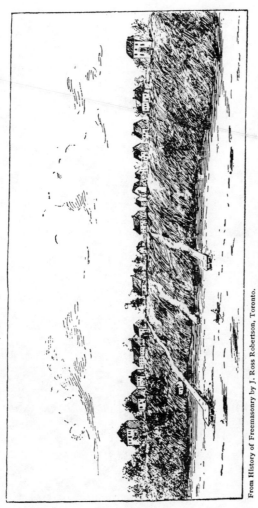

From History of Freemasonry by J. Ross Robertson, Toronto.

DETROIT, 1811.

WAR OF

1812.

FIRST SERIES.

CONTAINING A FULL AND DETAILED NARRATIVE

OF THE

OPERATIONS OF THE

RIGHT DIVISION,

OF THE

CANADIAN ARMY,

BY

MAJOR RICHARDSON, K. S. F.

1842

Facsimile of the title page of the original edition.

DEDICATION

To the present United Legislature of Canada, in whom has originated, and by whom has been carried into partial operation, one of the most beneficent measures which can be conferred upon a young country—that of a salutary provision for Education—this Historical Narrative, the first of an important series, (the completion of which must depend upon the countenance and support extended to the commencement) and compiled with a view to the furtherance of their object,   Is Dedicated,

By Their Very Obedient,

And Humble Servant,

The AUTHOR.

July 16th, 1842.

PREFACE

In preparing this first of a series of Historical Narratives for the use of Schools in Canada, the Author has been influenced by considerations, which he conceives will, more or less, govern the minds of those to whom the Education of the youth of the country is entrusted.

It is a humiliating, yet undeniable fact, that there are few young men of the present generation who are at all aware, except by vague and inaccurate report, of the brilliant feats of arms, and sterling loyalty displayed by their immediate progenitors, during the stern but brief struggle with the neighboring Republic, wherein numbers were fearfully against them, but in which, supported by true courage, and the consciousness of a good cause, they rode triumphant over every obstacle, and came forth unconquered from the strife. Or, if they have read of these matters, their information has been derived through the corrupt channel of American party publications bearing on the subject, all which have a tendency to pervert facts, and to instil into the youthful mind that diffidence and mistrust which operate as a check upon the generous aspirings, and weaken the energies of the national character.

Recovering as this country is, at this moment, from the severe shock which, although but of temporary duration, has deeply tested its general attachment and fealty to the British throne, and lapsing into that state of tranquillity from which it never should have departed, it will without difficulty be conceded that no compilation could, with greater propriety or consistency, be placed in the hands of Canadian students, than that which records the gallant deeds performed by their Fathers, fighting side by side, with the troops of England in defence of their invaded firesides : when, actuated by a devoted spirit of loyalty, and a generosity of emulation never exceeded, they won golden opinions from their Sovereign, and stood boldly forth in the hour of the country's greatest need—nor, although the youth of Western Canada have the greatest reason to feel pride in this fact, should it fail to be a source of satisfaction to the French Canadian pupil, whose Sire was, at the epoch treated of in the following narrative, ever forward in the demonstration of his attachment to British Institutions, and unwavering in his resolution to defend them with his life.　These were, indeed, happy and well-remembered days, when but one sentiment actuated the French and English races, who were knit together in one common bond of good fellowship, and knew rivalry only in their desire to tender to the parent, who had cherished and nursed them, the grateful evidence of their love.　This is no over-charged picture of the feeling which *then* existed in the Canadas, and on the direction given to the minds of its youth of the present day, French and English, must depend its utter extinction or revival.

In adopting the familiar style of the narrative, the Author has had two distinct inducements in view—firstly, because that species of composition relieves history of the dryness which is so great a barrier to interest with the student ; and secondly, because, in identifying himself with his subject, the reader is necessarily led to do the same. There are few Canadian youths who will fail to be inspired by a generous spirit of emulation, as they bear vividly before them the fact that the Author whom they are perusing, and who has written for their instruction and infor-

mation, was even himself a student [1] when summoned by
the trumpet of War, from a perusal of the military exploits
of the most renowned warriors of by-gone days, to range
himself in the next hour under the victorious banner of a
modern Chief not less daring, and scarcely less celebrated
than any of those and to defend, with his feeble yet willing
arm, the soil which gave him birth, and the Standard to
which he owed allegiance.

That the lot which was the Author's may be that of
the Reader, is a reflection which can never be lost sight
of by the generous of character whose rallying cry, whenever domestic rebellion or foreign invasion stalk throughout the land their Sires have consecrated to England with
their blood, will assuredly ever be "Aut vincere aut
mori." The past has pledged, the future will redeem
the bond.

---

[1] I had first breathed the breath of life near the *then* almost isolated Falls of Niagara—the loud roaring of whose cataract had, perhaps, been the earnest of the storms—and they have been many—
which were to assail my after life. My subsequent boyhood, up
to the moment, when at fifteen years of age, I became a soldier,
had been passed in a small town (Amherstburg), one of the most
remote, while, at the same time, one of the most beautifully situated in Canada. I had always detested school, and the days that
were passed in it were to me days of suffering, such as the boy
alone can understand. With the reputation for some little capacity, I had been oftener flogged than the greatest dunce in it, perhaps as much from the caprice of my tutor as from any actual
wrong in myself—and this had so seared my heart—given me such
a disgust for Virgil, Horace, and Euclid, that I often meditated
running away, and certainly should have gratified the very laud-
able inclination, had I not apprehended a severity from my father
—a stern, unbending man, that would have left me no room for
exultation at my escape from my tutor. It was, therefore, a day
of rejoicing to me when the commencement of hostilities on the
part of the United States, and the unexpected appearance of a large
body of their troops, proved the signal of the "break up" of the
school, or college, (for by the latter classical name was known the
long, low, narrow, stone building, with two apologies for wings
springing at right angles from the body), and my exchange of
Cæsar's Commentaries for the King's Regulations and Dundas.
The transition was indeed glorious, and in my joy at the change
which had been wrought in my position, I felt disposed to bless
the Americans for the bold step they had taken.
Eight Years in Canada, by Major Richardson, p. 87.

OPERATIONS.

OF THE
RIGHT DIVISION
OF THE
ARMY OF UPPER CANADA
DURING THE
AMERICAN WAR
OF 1812

&c., &c., &c.

I

INDIANS IN BRITISH WARS—RIOTS OF THE "WAR-HAWKS"[1]

Much has been said and written in respect to the Redmen of the forest; but I do not recollect having ever met with a detail sufficiently accurate to convey a just idea of the character of these people. As they will occupy a tolerable portion of my attention, and frequently appear under circumstances which may incline the reader to incredulity, I will merely observe, that no one incident will be found committed to these pages, which may not be attested by every officer who served with the Right Division of the Canadian army. In fact, to that division alone were the more savage of the Indian race attached; and when it is considered, that among the warriors of at

---

[1] " War-hawks " was a name given to a portion of the Republican party that clamored for war against Great Britain. Madison secured his second nomination for the Presidency by agreeing to their demands. The principal leaders of the war party were Henry Clay of Kentucky, Felix Grundy of Tennessee, Langdon Cheves, William Lowndes and John C. Calhoun of South Carolina, and Peter B. Porter of New York, having seats in the House of Representatives and William H. Crawford, in the Senate.

See The United States, an Outline of Political History by Goldwin Smith, D.C.L., p. 170.

least twenty different tribes, there were those who had
scarcely ever any previous intercourse with whites, and
had seldom approached a fortified place but in open hostility, the indomitableness of their natures will cease to
excite surprise.   As it is my intention to give a faithful
account of the various cruelties committed during our
struggle in Canada—cruelties we had not power to prevent, since perpetrated by an ally over whom we had no
control—it may not be improper to advert to the motives
for their employment. The Americans have invariably
been loud in their condemnation of a measure which
alone secured to us the possession of Upper Canada : with
how little reason, however, will appear from the well-
known fact, that every possible exertion was used, by the
agents of their Government, to detach the Indians from
our cause.   Embracing the system adopted and followed
by England for years, presents of all descriptions were
issued to the warriors ; while, in the council, the most
flattering promises were made, the most seducing offers
held forth, to induce them to make common cause with
the invader. The wary chieftains, however, were not to
be tempted by professions of friendship from those whose
perfidy had long been proverbial with the Indian race.
The bounties of England had been heaped on them with
no sparing hand—the faith of the Government had never
been violated—no spirit of interest or domination had
chased them from the homes of their forefathers—the
calumet of peace had never once been dashed from the
lips of those they were called on to abandon ; and they
remained true to the faith they had pledged, staunch to
the cause in which they had embarked. The natives
must have been our friends or our foes : had we not
employed them the Americans would ; and although
humanity may deplore the necessity imposed by the very
invader himself, of counting them among our allies, and
combating at their side,—the law of self-preservation was
our guide, and scrupulous indeed must be the power that

would have hesitated at such a moment in its choice. The act of aggression was not ours—we declared no war against America—we levied no armies to invade her soil, and carry desolation wherever they came:—but we availed ourselves of that right, common to every weak power—the right of repelling acts of aggression by every means within our reach. Yet though it is admitted that the Indians, while our allies, were in some instances guilty of those atrocities peculiar to every savage people ; let it not be supposed that these atrocities were sanctioned either by the Government or by individuals. On the contrary, every possible means were tried by the officer commanding at Amherstburg, and Colonel Elliott, [1] superintendent of Indian affairs for that post, to soften down the warlike habits of the natives. The most likely method of preventing the unnecessary effusion of blood

---

[1] Col. Matthew Elliott, Deputy Superintendent of Indian Affairs, whose name is inseparably associated with the events on the Detroit frontier from 1775 till his death on the 7th May 1814, entered the Indian Department as a captain. The influence that Britain exercised over the Indians was in a great measure due to his prudence, tact and firmness. Many of the hardships incident to a border warfare were much ameliorated by the power this officer possessed over the wildest and most savage tribes. The treacherous murder of his eldest son, a promising young lawyer, by some American Indians, his prisoners, was a sad blow to the Colonel. His humanity was well-known and Gen. Harrison bears testimony to his efforts to prevent the slaughter of American prisoners.

When he removed to Upper Canada he built a large house, still standing in part, on the Detroit river opposite the southern end of Bois Blanc island. This point is still called Elliott's Point.

Col. Elliott was exceedingly active during the first years of the war. On the evacuation of Amherstburg, he retreated with Procter to Moraviantown, and it is said he saved Procter's life there by throwing up the rifle of Tecumseh, who was going to shoot Procter for his contemplated retreat before the battle was decided. In this engagement, had he been less intent on his public duties, he might have saved both his personal baggage and his valuable plate which were captured by the Americans. The hardships of the trying campaign of 1813 told heavily upon him at his advanced age and hastened his death. He was M.P.P. for Essex from 1801 to 1812.

Frederick E. Elliott, the present representative of the family, lives on part of the land grant given to his grandfather for his services.

was that of offering rewards for prisoners. This, however, except in a very few instances, was found to be
ineffectual ; for the character and disposition of the
savage were not to be tamed by rewards, nor the impression of ages to be removed by such temptations. To
have employed force, would have been to have turned
their weapons against ourselves ; and a body of five hundred troops, composing the utmost strength of the garrison, could have effected little against three thousand
fiery warriors, unused to restraint, and acknowledging
no power but their own will. The Americans themselves
had Indians employed in their service—a few only it is
true—but if they had not more, it was not owing to any
want of exertion on their parts ; and if it is admitted on
the one hand, that they conducted themselves with more
humanity, it cannot at the same time be denied on the
other, that the feebleness of their numbers rendered them
more immediately subject to the authority of the American commanders, neither can it be disputed, that compulsion alone bound them to the adverse cause, their
families having been often detained as hostages to answer
for their fidelity.

On the 18th of June, 1812, a formal declaration of war
against Great Britain and her dependencies was passed
by both Houses of Congress, [1] and approved by Mr. Madison, the President—on the 20th it was officially notified
by General Bloomfield to the American army, and in what
spirit received by the war-party may be inferred from the
following account which appeared in the American papers
of that period.

Gazette Office, Boston, August 2nd, 1812.
This morning's mail gives us a few particulars of a most
barbarous riot in Baltimore, instigated by the friends of

---

[1] The majority for war was 30 in the House of Representatives
and but 6 in the Senate. The country divided almost geograph-
ically on the question. The vote on the Act declaring war with

the Administration, and completed by French Democracy.

Our blood stagnates with cold horror at the enormity of the scenes ; while our indignation is roused at the passive, and therefore encouraging deportment of the Police ; and our grief is deep and most painful from the loss of the eminent, the patriotic and the worthy characters who have fallen a sacrifice to the fury of the friends of War, and upholders of the Administration.

Baltimore, July 29th, 1812.

" The peace of our city has been again disturbed by the mob, the effects of which have been dreadful. On Monday morning, the ' Federal Republican ' was again issued from the press in this city. Mr. Hanson, one of the Editors, expecting an attack, had collected his friends in the New office (which is a brick house in Charles Street) to the number of from 50 to 75, completely armed with muskets, pistols, daggers, etc., determined to defend the house at all hazards. The mob collected and commenced the attack between 9 and 10 o'clock in the evening, by breaking all the windows with brick-bats ; and attempting to

Great Britain was as follows :—

	In House of Representatives		In Senate	
	Yeas.	Nays.	Yeas.	Nays.
New Hampshire	3	2	1	1
Massachusetts	6	8	1	1
Rhode Island	0	2	0	2
Connecticut	0	7	0	2
Vermont	3	1	1	0
New York	3	11	1	1
New Jersey	2	4	1	1
Pennsylvania	16	2	2	0
Delaware	0	1	0	2
Maryland	6	3	1	1
Virginia	14	5	2	0
North Carolina	6	3	2	0
South Carolina	8	0	2	0
Georgia	3	0	2	0
Kentucky	5	0	1	1
Tennessee	3	0	2	0
Ohio	1	0	0	1
	79	49	19	13
Majority for war	30		6	

force the door. The Garrison, after warning them of the consequences, fired a few rounds of blank cartridges, which had no other effect than to exasperate them. They then commenced firing with ball and slugs. Two or three were killed, and numbers were desperately wounded. The mob then retreated, and marched to Fell's Point and procured a cannon, with which they returned about 2 o'clock in the morning. The piece was loaded, and placed before the house ; but through some defect in the management of the gun they could not get her to go off. Partial attacks were in this way kept up until morning when the garrison, seeing no practicability of being rescued by the civil authority, found means to escape privately : all except about 25 who were determined to hold out. About 7 in the morning the Mayor of the City, and General Stricker, having collected a force of horse and infantry, amounting in all to about one hundred men, marched them to the scene of action, and paraded them in front of the house, but took no pains to disperse the mob by which they were surrounded. The small band of heroes who still garrisoned the house, now offered to give themselves up to the Mayor and General Stricker, if they would promise to protect them from the mob. This was acceded to by the Mayor and the General, who gave them their word of honor that they should have ample protection from all harm. They were accordingly taken from the house, surrounded by the military, who formed a hollow square, and in this manner marched to the City prison, where they were lodged and left without any guard, the troops being immediately dispersed, notwithstanding they were followed by the mob (often pelting them with brick-bats and paving-stones) and swearing that the prison should not protect the damned Tories, but that they should all be killed in 24 hours. At noon verbal orders were issued for the 5th Regiment of Infantry to turn out at 3 o'clock, P.M., and after the utmost exertions of some spirited officers, at 4 o'clock but about 30 or 40 men were collected ; they continued under arms about an hour, when orders came from the Mayor, as the mob had dispersed, to dismiss them. About 8 o'clock in the evening the mob again collected, attacked the prison, and forced the outer door, when the Sheriff it is said delivered them the keys of the inner apartments, which they opened, and brought the unfortunate men out two at a time, and beat them with clubs until they thought them dead—one they carried away, tarred and feathered him, beat him until he was almost dead; pricked him with sharp irons, and carded him with a wool-card. At 10 o'clock I saw five lying in front of the prison apparently lifeless, while these horrid savages were prowling over them, and exulting in their worse than savage barbarity; it was indeed a horrid sight, and it makes my blood boil when I think of it.

"I am informed this morning, that there is but one actually dead, that some can live but a few hours, and the lives of the greatest part are despaired of. They were secured, I am told, by meritorious exertions of the doctor who persuaded the butchers that they were dead, and had them conveyed away in carriages, as fast as they could get them out of their hands. The one who is ascertained to have been killed was General Lingau, an old Revolutionary Officer. General S. Lee of Virginia was also among them; the rest were chiefly young men whose connections were the most respectable in the City. The inhabitants are in the utmost consternation : all business is suspended : people collect in small groups in the streets, with a settled gloom upon their countenances, and every man looks with suspicion on his neighbor, for no man thinks himself safe whose *political* creed does not agree with that of the mob; lest that an unguarded expression may subject him to their fury. The number stated to have been massacred in the gaol exceeds twenty, and among these are Captains Murray and Lingau of the United States army."

Such is the picture drawn of American feeling on the occasion, by an American himself. Let me place in relief to it kindlier relations which existed at that period along the border, as exhibited in a letter dated

Niagara, (American side) June 28th.

"The news of war reached the British at (Niagara) Fort George the 24th by express, two days before it was received at our military station. General Brock, the British Governor, arrived at Fort George the 25th. Several American Gentlemen were there on a visit, who were treated very politely by the Governor, and sent under the protection of Captain Glegg, his aid, to Fort Niagara with a flag. The news of war was very unwelcome on both sides of the river. They have been for six

years in habits of friendly intercourse, connected by mar-
riages and various relationships.   Both sides were in consternation ; the women and children were out on the
banks of the river, while their Fathers, husbands, sons,
etc., were busily employed in arming.   It was said
Captain Glegg also bore a summons for the surrender of
Fort Niagara, but this was contradicted by Captain
Leonard commanding that post, who said the message
was merely to inquire if he had any official notice of the
war ; and that he answered in the negative.''

A more remarkable illustration of this feeling is the following
Answer of the Men of New York Inhabiting the Western District,
to the proclamation of Gen. Smyth addressed to them :

GENERAL.—We have seen your Proclamation. We have seen
this Country, not many years ago, the sole habitation of the beasts
of the forest and their prowling Enemy. We see it the habitation
of many thousand souls, rich in all the necessaries and in many
of the comforts of life. Till the day that the sound of war burst
on our ears from the Capitol at Washington, we scarcely experienced one moment of anxiety for the safety of our persons and
property.

The clamor of avaricious traders, and of factious office-seekers
trouble not our quiet. It reached us, but at the period of the elections, and it was then but like a blast of wind on our lakes, varie-
gating but for a moment the placid uniformity of the surface.

Why should our Swords be drawn in redress of injuries which
we have never felt, or which, if they exist, are beyond our reach ?
Why appeal to our valor for the destruction of our own happiness
or of that of others?

We are the descendants of the men that fought at Bennington
and at Saratoga. The labors of the field are proof, alike, against
degeneracy, and the rage of contending factions. You, General,
have been more exposed to their influence. The men who fought
at Bennington and Saratoga fought for the liberties of their Country. Foreign Mercenaries had set foot upon the soil which their
hands had redeemed from the desert and rendered fertile ; they
had entered the sanctuaries of their wives and children. Our
Fathers fought and conquered. You, General, who are taking the
place of these mercenaries, you cannot appeal to us.

The renown which you seek is not our renown. It is the renown
of Europe, not of America. The wrath of God precedes it, and
desolation follows in its footsteps. It delights in blood, and in
fields strewn with carnage, in the tears of the widow, and the
plainings of the orphan perishing of want and disease. This is
your glory. Ours has upon it the primeval blessing of the Almighty ; our Victories are Victories over the unproductive face of
nature ; our renown is in fertile fields, in peaceful homes and
numerous and happy families.

Go, General, if you will. Should you ever reach the Walls of
Quebec, the shade of Montgomery will reproach you for not hav-
ing profited by his example ; and when you fall, the men of New
York will lament that folly has found new victims.

II

HULL'S INVASION—CAPTURE OF MICHILIMACKINAC

The garrison of Amherstburg, at the commencement of the war, consisted of about 200 men of the first battalion of the 41st Regiment, a very weak detachment of the Royal Newfoundland Fencibles, and a subaltern's command of artillery. Situated at the head of Lake Erie, and forming the key to our relations with the Western Indians, this post became an object of additional interest to the enemy. With every opportunity of ascertaining the weakness of its defences, and the almost utter impossibility of its obtaining supplies, the fall of Amherstburg was looked forward to by the Americans, as an event which admitted not of doubt. With this view, the division under General Hull, consisting of two thousand three hundred men, had been urged forward with all possible despatch to Detroit, at a distance of eighteen miles beyond Amherstburg, an attack on which latter place was immediately contemplated. Having collected his boats, and made every other necessary preparation, the American General, on the 7th of July, [1] landed three miles above Sandwich, a small town nearly opposite to Detroit, and within view of a corps of observation, which, in conformity with its instructions, retired on his approach. Colonel St. George, Inspecting Field officer, and then commanding at Amherstburg, with that spirit and activity by which he was distinguished throughout

---

[1] This date should be 12th of July. Every authority that I have seen places it on this date. Anthony S. Baker in a despatch to Lord Castlereagh dated Washington, August 1st, 1812, says :

"General Hull entered Canada on the night of the 11th ult."

It is probable that the landing was on the night of 11th and morning of the 12th.

the war, made every judicious disposition for his reception. The militia were called out, and, through the exertions of the various agents of their department, a body of 600 Indians was soon collected. At a distance of eight miles from Amherstburg, and traversing the high road, is the Canard River, which empties itself into that of the Detroit, and is impassable even by cavalry. Over this, and near its mouth, a bridge composed entirely of timber had been constructed. Seizing at once the advantage of this position, and determining to profit by the delay the enemy must consequently experience, Colonel St. George instantly caused the bridge to be destroyed and a body of marksmen to be posted among the long grass and weeds with which the banks of the river are covered, for the purpose of annoying such of the enemy as appeared for its reconstruction. The Queen Charlotte, a vessel of twenty guns, was at the same time anchored at the mouth of the river, for the purpose of keeping them more effectually in check.

Meanwhile, General Hull amused himself and his enemy by the following piece of rhodomontade, in the shape of a

PROCLAMATION.

Inhabitants of Canada !

After thirty years of peace and prosperity, the United States have been driven to arms. The injuries and aggressions, the insults and indignities of Great Britain, have once more left them no alternative but manly resistance or unconditional submission. The army under my command has *invaded your country*, and the standard of Union now waves over the territory of Canada. To the peaceable, unoffending inhabitant, it brings neither danger nor difficulty. I come to find enemies, not to make them. I come to protect, not to injure you.

Separated by an immense ocean, and an extensive wilderness from Great Britain, you have no participation in her councils, no interest in her conduct—you have felt her tyranny, you have seen her injustice; but I do not ask you to avenge the one, or redress the other. The United States are sufficiently powerful to afford you every security consistent with their rights and your expectations. I tender you the invaluable blessings of civil, political and religious liberty, and their necessary result, individual and general prosperity—that liberty which gave decision to our councils and energy to our conduct, in a struggle for independence, and which conducted us safely and triumphantly through the stormy period of the revolution—that liberty which has raised us to an elevated rank among the nations of the world, and which has afforded us a greater measure of peace, and security, of wealth and improvement, than ever fell to the lot of any country.

In the name of my country, and by the authority of Government I promise you protection to your persons, property and rights. Remain at your homes; pursue your peaceful and customary avocations, raise not your hands against your brethren. Many of your fathers fought for the freedom and independence we now enjoy. Being children, therefore, of the same family with us, and heirs to the same heritage, the arrival of an army of friends must be hailed by you with a cordial welcome. You will be emancipated from tyranny and oppression, and restored to the dignified station of freemen. Had I any doubt of eventual success, I might ask your assistance, but I do not. I come prepared for every contingency—I have a force which will look down all opposition, and that force is but the vanguard of a much greater. If contrary to your own interests and the just expectations of my country, you should take part in the approaching contest, you will be considered and treated as enemies, and the horrors and calamities of war will stalk before you. If the barbarous and savage policy of Great Britain be pursued, and the savages let loose to murder our citizens, and butcher our women and children, this war will be a war of extermination. The first stroke of the tomahawk, the first attempt with the scalping knife, will be the signal of one indiscriminate scene of desolation! *No white man found fighting by the side of an Indian will be taken prisoner; instant destruction will be his lot.* If the dictates of reason, duty, justice and humanity cannot prevent the employment of a force which respects no right, and knows no wrong, it will be prevented by a severe and relentless system of retaliation. I doubt not your courage and firmness—I will (not) doubt your attachment to liberty. If you tender your services voluntarily, they will be accepted readily. The United States offer you peace, liberty and security—your choice lies between these, and war, slavery and destruction. Choose then, but choose wisely ;· and may He, who knows the justice of our cause, and who holds in His hand the fate of nations, guide you to a result the most compatible with your rights and interest, your peace and happiness.

W. HULL.

By the General,

H.Q. Sandwich,   A. P. Hull,[2]
  July 8th,[1] 1812.   Captain of 13th U.S. Regt.
                                    of Infantry & Aid de Camp.

As every thing relating to General Brock is, or ought to be, of undying interest to the people of Canada, the counter proclamation, issued by that officer, on receipt of intelligence of the course which was being pursued by

---

[1] This proclamation is found in several documentary histories of the war, and all differ in several minor particulars, such as capitalization and punctuation, but the sense of all, however, is the same. The author was, no doubt, Gen. Hull, but after his death the authorship was claimed for Gen. Cass. Hull's grandson, James Freeman Clarke, in his History of the Campaign of 1812, says : "Whenever the proclamation is condemned, Gen. Hull is treated as the author—when it is praised it is said to have been written by Gen. Cass." Anyone acquainted with the various accounts must come to the same conclusion. A copy was sent to Washington and approved by the President ; but the American Commissioners at the Treaty of Ghent declared the proclamation to have been unauthorized and disapproved by the Government. The date has been given as the 12th and as the 13th of July. Hull in his memoirs says the 12th, so does Brannan in his Military and Naval Letters, while the copy from the Archives of Canada given in Vol. 15 of the Michigan Historical Collections is dated the 13th. The date given by Richardson is certainly not correct.

[2] The Aid to Gen. Hull and the signer of this proclamation was his son, Abraham Fuller Hull. The second initial is a misprint that appears in several copies of the proclamation. A. F. Hull was a captain in the 13th U.S. Infantry, taken prisoner with the army at Detroit, Aug. 16th, 1812, and exchanged on Jan. 18th, 1813. He was given a company in the 9th U.S. Infantry, and was killed at its head at the battle of Lundy's Lane on July 25th, 1814. A small stone marks his grave in Lundy's Lane graveyard.

GENERAL WILLIAM HULL.

General Hull, cannot be more appropriately introduced than at this point of the narrative. It is a striking specimen of manly eloquence, and firmness, and compared with that which precedes it, is as sterling gold to tinsel. Both proclamations, as will be seen hereafter, are singularly characteristic of the men who framed them.

PROCLAMATION.

The unprovoked declaration of War, by the United States of America, against the United Kingdom of Great Britain and Ireland and its dependencies has been followed by the actual invasion of this Province, in a remote frontier of the Western District, by a detachment of the armed force of the United States. The Officer Commanding that detachment has thought proper to invite His Majesty's subjects, not merely to a quiet and unresisting submission, but insults them with a call to seek voluntarily the protection of his Government. Without condescending to repeat the illiberal epithets bestowed in this appeal of the American Commander to the people of Upper Canada, on the administration of His Majesty, every inhabitant of the Province is desired to seek the confutation of such indecent slander, in the review of his own particular circumstances; where is the Canadian subject who can truly affirm to himself that he has been injured by the Government in his person, his liberty, or his property? Where is to be found in any part of the world, a growth so rapid in wealth and prosperity, as this colony exhibits? Settled not thirty years by a band of veterans, exiled from their former possessions on account of their loyalty, not a descendant of these brave people is to be found, who, under the fostering liberality of their Sovereign, has not acquired a property and means of enjoyment superior to what were possessed by their ancestors. This unequalled prosperity could not have been attained by the utmost liberality of the Government or the persevering industry of the people, had not the maritime power of the mother country secured to its colonies a safe access to every market where the produce of their labor was in demand.

The unavoidable and immediate consequence of a separation from Great Britain must be the loss of this inestimable advantage; and what is offered you in exchange? to become a territory of the United States, and share with them that exclusion from the ocean which the policy of their present government enforces—you are not even flattered with a participation of their boasted independence, and it is but too obvious that once exchanged from the powerful protection of the United Kingdom, you must be re-annexed to the dominion of France, from which the Provinces of Canada were wrested by the arms of Great Britain, at a vast expense of blood and treasure, from no other motive but to *relieve* her ungrateful children from the oppression of a cruel neighbour; this restitution of Canada to the Empire of France was the stipulated reward for the aid afforded to the revolted colonies, now the United States; the debt is still due, and there can be no doubt but the pledge has been renewed as a consideration for commercial advantages, or rather for an expected relaxation in the tyranny of France over the commercial world. Are you prepared, Inhabitants of Upper Canada, to become willing subjects, or rather slaves, to the Despot who rules the Nations of Europe with a rod of iron?—If not, arise in a body, exert your energies, co-operate cordially with the King's regular forces, to repel the invader, and do not give cause to your children, when groaning under the oppression of a foreign master to reproach you with having too easily parted with the richest inheritance of this Earth—a participation in the name, character, and freedom of Britons.

The same spirit of justice, which will make every reasonable allowance for the unsuccessful efforts of zeal and loyalty, will not fail to punish the defalcation of principle; every Canadian freeholder is, by deliberate choice, bound by the most solemn oaths to defend the monarchy as well as his own property; to shrink from that engagement is a treason not to be forgiven: let no man suppose that if, in this unexpected struggle, His Majesty's arms should be compelled to yield to an overwhelming force, that the Province will be eventually abandoned; the endeared relation of its first settlers, the intrinsic value of its commerce, and the pretensions of its powerful rival to repossess the Canadas, are pledges that no peace will be established between the United States, and Great Britain and Ireland, of which the restoration of these Provinces does not make the most prominent condition.

Be not dismayed at the unjustifiable threat of the

commander of the enemy's forces to refuse quarter should an Indian appear in the ranks. The brave bands of natives which inhabit this colony were, like His Majesty's subjects, punished for their zeal and fidelity, by the loss of their possessions in the late colonies, and rewarded by His Majesty with lands of superior value in this Province ; the faith of the British government has never yet been violated, they feel that the soil they inherit is to them and their posterity protected from the base arts so frequently devised to overreach their simplicity. By what new principle are they to be prevented from defending their property ? If their warfare, from being different from that of the white people, is more terrific to the enemy, let him retrace his steps—they seek him not—and cannot expect to find women and children in an invading army ; but they are men, and have equal rights with all other men to defend themselves and their property when invaded, more especially when they find in the enemy's camp a ferocious and mortal foe, using the warfare which the American commander affects to reprobate.

This inconsistent and unjustifiable threat of refusing quarter for such a cause as being found in arms with a brother sufferer in defence of invaded rights, must be exercised with the certain assurance of retaliation, not only in the limited operations of war in this part of the King's Dominions, but in every quarter of the globe, for the national character of Britain is not less distinguished for humanity than strict retributive justice, which will consider the execution of this inhuman threat as deliberate murder, for which every subject of the offending power must make expiation.

God Save the King.

ISAAC BROCK,[1]
Maj. Gen. and President.

Head Quarters, Fort George, 22nd July, 1812.
By order of His Honor the President,

J. B. Glegg, Capt. A.D.C.

---

[1] "Brock's admirable production is generally believed to have been prepared by Mr. Justice Powell, then Senior Puisne Judge of the Court of King's Bench, of which Court he became Chief Justice in the year 1816."
Sketches of Glengarry in Canada by J. A. Macdonell. p. 188.

The activity with which General Hull commenced his offensive operations gave indication that they would be followed up with vigor, and that, having once effected his landing, he would afford not time for his enemies to collect the few resources they could command, or place themselves in an attitude of defence. The fort of Amherstburg could not have sustained a siege of any duration. Quadrangular in its form, four bastions alone flanked a dry ditch, offering little obstacle to a determined enemy. This passed, a single line of picketing, perforated with loop holes for musketry, and supported by a slight breast work, remained to be carried. A prudent commander would, however, have chosen a less uncertain mode of dislodging the garrison. A few shells properly directed would have answered the purpose, since, with the exception of the magazine, all the buildings within were of wood, and covered with pine shingles of such extreme thinness, as would have been found incapable of resisting missiles of far less weight. The disadvantage of awaiting the enemy in this position, Colonel St. George well knew. He consequently preferred giving him battle with the trifling force he had at his disposition. With this view, the garrison received orders to be under arms at a moment's warning, and the approach of the invader was anxiously awaited. Satisfied, however, with having effected his landing, and deriving no other advantage than that of having his troops quartered on his enemy, the American General appeared to have forgotten altogether the object of his mission. Instead of descending the river Detroit in boats, or attempting to throw a bridge across the Canard, at a point where we had no outpost, he contented himself with despatching workmen, supported by bodies of cavalry and infantry, to repair that already partially destroyed. Repulsed in every attempt, the daily skirmishes which ensued led to no action of a decisive nature.

Here was poured forth the first British blood shed in

the American War, and that in a manner so honorable to the fallen, that it would be, in the highest degree unjust, to omit insertion here of the most flattering official attestation that ever was penned and published, in approval of the heroic conduct of a private soldier of the British Army. Enduring honor to the 41st Regiment to which corps these gallant and devoted fellows belonged. Their names, which, from some unaccountable cause, have not been given in the General Order, were Hancock and Dean, the former killed, the latter taken prisoner,[1] as shown in the following extract from that order dated Quebec, August 6th, 1812.

" The Commander of the Forces takes great pleasure in also announcing to the troops, that the enemy under Brigadier General Hull have been repulsed in three attacks made on the 18th, 19th and 20th of last month, upon part of the Garrison of Amherstburg, on the River Canard, in the neighborhood of that place ; in which attacks His Majesty's 41st Regiment have particularly distinguished themselves. In justice to that corps His Excellency wishes particularly to call the attention of the Troops to the heroism, and self-devotion displayed by two privates, who being left as sentinels when the party to which they belonged had retired, contrived to maintain their station against the whole of the enemy's force, until they both fell, when one of them, whose arm had been broken, again raising himself, opposed with his bayonet those advancing against him, until overwhelmed by numbers. An instance of such firmness and intrepidity deserves to be thus publicly recorded, and His Excellency thinks that it will not fail to animate the Troops under his command with an ardent desire to follow so noble an example, whenever an opportunity shall hereafter be offered them."

Nor, among the very many daring exploits performed at the Canard river, during the brief period of General Hull's occupation of the Western District of Canada, must omission be made of the gallant conduct of 22 War-

---

[1] This event took place on the 16th of July.
Procter to Brock, July 26th, 1812.

riors of the Minoumini [1] tribe of Indians, who defeated and drove in a detachment of 200 Americans, under the command of Major Denny, who had advanced as far as the mutilated bridge, with a view of forcing a passage. The river, as it is called, is not more than three or four rods in width.

While these unimportant events were passing in the neighbourhood of Amherstburg, the small Garrison of St. Josephs, the most remote of our North Western defences, was not idle. Information having been conveyed to Captain Roberts of the 10th Royal Veteran Battalion, commanding that post, that war had been declared by the American Government, that officer lost no time in availing himself of the advantage afforded by the ignorance of the fact, and consequent absence of preparation on the part of the adjacent American Post of Michilimackinac, and marched his disposable force to compel a surrender of that fortress. Captain Roberts' official despatch [2] on the subject has, we believe, never

---

[1] The modern spelling of this name is Menomoni. Their home was along Green Bay, Lake Michigan.

[2] Capt. Charles Roberts to Colonel Baynes :

FORT MICHILIMACKINAC, 17th July, 1812.

SIR,—On the 15th instant I received letters by Express from Major General Brock, with orders to adopt the most prudent measures either of offence or defence which circumstances might point out, and having received intelligence from the best information that large reinforcements were daily expected to be thrown into this garrison, and finding that the Indians who had been collected would soon have abandoned me if I had not made the attempt, with the thorough conviction that my situation at St. Joseph's was totally indefensible, I determined to lose no time in making the meditated attack on this Fort.

On the sixteenth, at Ten o'clock in the morning, I embarked my few men with about one hundred and fifty Canadian Engagues, half of them without arms, about three hundred Indians and two Iron Six-pounders. The boats arrived without the smallest accident at the place of Rendevouz at three o'clock the following morning. By the exertions of the Canadians one of the Guns was brought up to a height commanding the garrison, and ready to act, about Ten o'clock. A summons was then sent in, a copy of

been published, but the following letter from a gentleman connected with the Indian Department, to Colonel Claus, the Superintendent-in-Chief of Indian affairs, sufficiently details the nature of the operations of the little detachment.

which, as well as of the capitulation which followed, I have the honor to enclose. At twelve the American Colors were hauled down and those of His Majesty were hoisted.

A Committee has been appointed to examine into the state of the Public stores. Enclosed also are the Returns of the Ordnance and Military stores found in the Fort, and the strength of the garrison. The greatest praize is due to every individual employed in this expedition. To my own officers I am indebted in particular for their active assistance in carrying all my orders into effect.

The Indians are flocking in from all Quarters, but in a few weeks I shall be left in a great measure to my own resources, and I trust His Excellency the Governor-General will see the necessity of adding to my force.

    I have the honor to be, sir,
      Your most obedient servant,
        CHARLES ROBERTS,
The Adjutant-General,   Captain Commanding.
 &c., &c., &c.

HEIGHTS ABOVE FORT MICHILIMACKINAC,
        17th July, 1812.

CAPITULATION agreed upon between Captain Charles Roberts, commanding His Britannic Majesty's forces on the one part, and Lieutenant Hanks, commanding the forces of the United States of America, on the other.

ARTICLE.

1st. The Fort of Michilimackinac shall be immediately surrendered to the British force.

2nd. The garrison shall march out with the Honours of war, lay down their arms and become prisoners of War, and shall be sent to the United States of America by His Britannic Majesty not to serve this war until regularly exchanged, and for the due performance of this article the officers pledge their word of honour.

3rd. All the merchant's Vessels in the Harbour with their cargoes shall be in possession of their respective owners.

4th. Private property shall be held sacred as far as in my power.

5th. All Citizens of the United States Who shall not take the oath of Allegiance to His Britannic Majesty shall depart with their property from the Island in one month from the date hereof.

Signed   Signed
LIEUT. HANKS   CHARLES ROBERTS
Commanding   Captain commanding
the forces of the   His Britannic Majesty's
United States at   Forces.
Fort Michilimackinac.

Mackinac,[1] 18 July, 1812.

Dear Sir,

I am happy to have it in my power to announce to you that Fort Mackinac capitulated to us on the 17th inst., at 11 o'clock A.M.   Captain Roberts at our head with part of 10th R.V. Battalion.   Mr. Crawford had the command

---

[1] The first mission station in this district was established by Father Marquette in 1670 or 1671. The site of this mission was Point St. Ignace, *north* of the strait.   In 1673 the French built, near the mission church, a palisaded fort which was the *first* Fort Michilimackinac.   When De la Motte Cadillac was in command it was called Fort Buade in honor of Count Frontenac, Governor of New France.   In 1701 Cadillac built Fort Pontchartrain on the Detroit River, and through his influence the garrison from Michilimackinac was withdrawn and the missionaries followed soon afterwards.   In 1714 a post was re-established but the site of this fort was on the peninsula *south* of the strait.   It remained in the hands of the French till 1761, when it was handed over to the British.   It was before this fort on the 4th of June, 1763, that that great game of "ball" was played between the Chippawas and Sacs, which ended in the capture of the fort and the massacre of nearly all the whites,—an incident described in Major Richardson's novel "Wacousta."   For the sake of security a new fort was built on the island of Mackinac, bought from the Chippawas for £5,000.   On July 13th, 1780, this fort was occupied by the British under Captain Patrick Sinclair, who had the title of Lieut.-Governor and Superintendent of the Post.   In 1796 it was handed over to the United States to fulfil a clause in Jay's treaty of 1794 and consequently the British garrison was removed to the Island of St. Joseph.   Captain Charles Roberts, commanding at St. Joseph, invested Fort Michilimackinac or Mackinac on July 17th, 1812, with a force of whites and Indians, and received its surrender from Lieut. Hanks on the same day. It was held till the close of the war, although the United States made strenuous efforts to retake it.   To prevent surprise the old fort was strengthened and a new one built on higher ground farther inland, and named Fort George in honor of the King ; but when the island was again ceded to the United States this new fort was renamed Fort Holmes after Major Andrew Hunter Holmes, second in command of the American force, who had been killed in the attack on it on Aug. 4th, 1814.   On July 18th, 1815, Lieut.-Col. Robert McDouall, the British commander, handed it over to Col. Anthony Butler, representing the United States.   It remained a garrison post until 1895, when it was abandoned and given by Congress to the State of Michigan.

of the Canadians which consisted of about 200 men.
Mr. Dickson 113 Scioux, Fallsowines,[1] & Winnebagoes ;
myself about 130 men, Ottawas and Chippawas : part of
Ottawas of L'Arbre Croche had not arrived. It was a
fortunate circumstance that the Fort capitulated without
firing a single gun, for had they done so, I firmly believe
not a soul of them would have been saved. My Son,
Charles Langlade, Augustin Nolin, and Michel Cadotte,
Junr., have rendered me great service in keeping the
Indians in order, and executing from time to time such
commands as were delivered to me by the Commanding
Officer. I never saw so determined a set of people as the
Chippawas and Ottawas were. Since the Capitulation,
they have not tasted a single drop of liquor, nor even
killed a fowl belonging to any person, a thing never
known before, for they generally destroy everything they
meet with.

The Hon Col. W. Claus,   I am Dear Sir,
&c.   &c.   &c.   Your most o'bt Servant,
Fort George.   (Signed) JOHN ASKIN,[2] Junr.
Store Kr. Dept.

[1] This name is variously spelled as Fallesavonies, Folavoines,
Fallovines, Fallsovines. The word is the French designation of
the Menomoni tribe and should be spelled Folleavoine. Menomoni
and Folleavoine each means the plant called wild oats by the
French and wild rice by the English.

[2] John Askin, Jr., was son of Colonel John Askin, of "Strabane,"
by his first wife, and consequently uncle of Major Richardson. I
believe his descendants live at London, Ontario, where he died
November 15th, 1869.

III

On the 6th of August,[1] information having been conveyed to Colonel Procter, that a body of the enemy were then on their march to convoy a quantity of provisions for the use of the garrison of Detroit, Brevet-Major Muir, with a detachment of about a hundred men of the forty-first regiment, and a few militia, received orders to cross the river and occupy Brownstown, a small village on the American shore, through which they were expected to pass ; and thither we repaired accordingly.

It was on this occasion, that one of these rigid customs peculiar to the Indians was observed. Previous to our arrival at Brownstown a detachment of American troops, consisting of 200 Riflemen of the Ohio Volunteers, under the command of Major Van Horne, had been sent from Detroit to escort the Mail, and to open a communication with Captain Brush who, on his way with a supply of provisions for the army of General Hull, had been compelled to halt at the River Raisin, thirty-six miles below Detroit, his route having been intercepted by the Indians. The spies or scouts of these latter, having given intimation to Tecumseh, who was then at Brownstown at the

---

[1] This should be 5th August. Procter in his despatch of Aug. 11th, 1812, to Brock, says the date of the skirmish at Brownstown was Aug. 5th. Gen. Hull, in his despatch of Aug. 7th, says that Major Van Horne was detached from his army on Aug. 4th ; but as the American army was on the Canadian side of the Detroit river on this date, Van Horne crossed the river on the 4th and encamped that night about eleven miles beyond the Ecorces river. On the 5th they fell into the Indian ambuscade. Both officers in command, therefore, agree as to the date.

head of a small force, of the approach of Major Van Horne, he took with him a party of 24 warriors, and with these formed an ambuscade about three miles from the village, and lining the thick woods on either side of the road which passed through them, as far as his little band would permit, there awaited the advance of the enemy. Major Van Horne, having neglected to throw out skirmishers or an advanced guard of any kind, came suddenly, with the main body of his riflemen chiefly mounted, within reach of the Indians, who opened upon them a most destructive fire, killing many men [1] and horses, and compelling the remainder to wheel about and seek their safety in flight. The Indians rose from their ambush and, uttering fierce yells, pursued them for a considerable distance, but without much subsequent loss to the enemy, the fleetness of whose horses enabled them soon to distance their pursuers.

The only loss sustained by Tecumseh was one man killed, and that by almost the last shot fired, in their confusion, by the enemy. This individual was a young Chief named Logan, who often acted as an interpreter, and who, from partially understanding the English language, and being in frequent communication with them, was nearly as great a favourite with the Officers and men of the Right Division, as he was with his own people. At the close of the action, Logan's dead body was brought in, and placed in a long, low, log building which the Indians chiefly used as a council room. Here the recently engaged warriors now assembled, taking their seats in a circle, with an air of great solemnity, and in profound silence. Up to that moment one prisoner only

[1] The American loss at Brownstown, according to Hull's despatch of Aug. 7th, 1812, was 7 officers and 10 privates killed; the number of wounded, unknown. Major Van Horne, in his evidence at Hull's trial, put his loss at 18 killed, 12 wounded and 70 missing, which may be considered as correct. Colonel Procter, in his letter to Brock on Aug. 11th, 1812, puts the American loss at "about 50 killed." The British loss was not more than stated, as Major Van Horne made scarcely any resistance.

of the American detachment had fallen into their hands.
This poor fellow had been wounded, although not in such
a way as to disable him from walking, and he was made
to take his seat in the circle. Added to the 24 Warriors
selected by Tecumseh, was the eldest son of Colonel
Elliott, the Superintendent of Indian affairs, a very fine
young man who was afterwards killed, (and scalped I
believe) and who, dressed as an Indian throughout the
day, now took his station as one of the war-party, among
his late companions in arms. It chanced that the prisoner
was placed next to him. After having been seated some
little time in this manner, Mr. Elliott, observing the
blood to flow from some part of his neighbor's body,
involuntarily exclaimed—" Good God, you are wounded."
The sound of an English voice operated like magic upon
the unhappy man, and his look of despair was in an
instant changed for one of hope. " Oh Sir," he eagerly
exclaimed, "if you have the power to save me do so."
Mr. Elliott, who related the whole of the above circumstances to us later, stated that he had never experienced
such moments of mental agony as he felt during this
short appeal. Bitterly repenting the indiscretion which
had been the means of exciting an expectation, which he
well knew he had not the slightest power to realize, he
was compelled to reply somewhat harshly that he had no
more voice there than the prisoner himself, which indeed
was the fact. The American said no more ; he bent his
head upon his chest, and remained silent. Soon afterwards a bowl with food was placed before him, evidently
with a view (as the result proved) of diverting his attention. Of this he slightly partook or seemed to partake.
While occupied in this manner, a young warrior, obeying
a signal from one of the elders, rose from his seat, and
coming round and behind the prisoner, struck him one
blow with his tomahawk on the uncovered head, and he
ceased to live. Not a yell, not a sound beside that of the
crashing tomahawk was heard, not a muscle of an Indian

face was moved. The young warrior, replacing his weapon, walked deliberately back, and resumed his seat in the circle. The whole party remained a few minutes longer seated, and then rose to their feet, and silently withdrew—leaving to those who had not been of the war-party, to dispose of the body of the victim. Tecumseh was not present at this scene.

Nor was this the only melancholy sacrifice offered to the *manes* of the lamented and unconscious Logan. On the very morning after this occurrence, as the Officers sat grouped together on the grass, literally imbedded in letters, the contents of the mail from Detroit, which had been captured by the Indians, and which were now being opened for the purpose of ascertaining the intended movements of the enemy, the wild and peculiar yell of several Warriors announced that another captive was being brought in. We immediately rose and advanced toward the low, log building already described, when we beheld several Indians approaching it, preceded by a prisoner whom they had secured by a long leathern thong, made fast to another which confined his hands. He was a finely-proportioned young man, and the air of dejection which clouded his brow, gradually gave way to a more cheerful expression, when, on approaching the encampment, he perceived those from whom he expected protection. Several of the men advanced to meet and converse with him, and the poor fellow had apparently banished all feeling of apprehension for his future fate, when an aged aunt of the deceased issued from her tent, and stole cautiously behind him. Even at the moment when the mind of the prisoner was lulled into confidence, and without any previous admonition, the heartless woman drew a tomahawk from beneath her mantle, and buried its point in the skull of her victim. Stunned but not felled by the wound, the unhappy man—his whole countenance expressing horror and despair—grasped at the first soldier near him for support ; but the blow was repeated so

suddenly, and with such violence, that he soon fell pant-
ing and convulsive to the earth. Fortunately he was
not suffered to linger in his agony. The Indians around
instantly despatched and scalped him, stripping the body
of its clothes, and committing violations on his person in
which the cruel aunt of Logan bore a principal share.
The indignation of the men was excessive ; but any
attempt to interfere, could they even have foreseen the
occurrence in time to render interference effectual, would
not only have cost them several lives, but produced the
most alarming consequences to our cause. Their displeasure was, however, expressed by their murmurs, and
the atrocity of the act became the theme of conversation
throughout the camp. At the moment of its perpetration,
I had myself approached within a few paces of the group,
and became an unwilling spectator of the whole transaction. The wild expression of the sufferer's eye : the sup-
plicating look which spoke through the very distortion of
his features, and the agony which seemed to creep
throughout his every limb, were altogether indescribable.

   In these two several sacrifices of human life, the
motives for action, it will be seen, were wholly different.
In the first case the Indians simply followed up a custom
which had prevailed among them for ages, and indeed, if
proof were required of this fact, it is at once to be found
in the absence of all ferocity, or excitement, or disposition
to insult the prisoner who had already been doomed to
death. The very fact of their having placed food before
him, with the manifest object of absorbing his attention,
and quieting his mind at the very moment of infliction of
the death blow, was an evidence of mercy—not mercy, it
is true, as understood by the Christian—but still mercy—
the mercy of the child of nature, whom the stern habits
of his forefathers have taught the lesson of sanguinary
retribution, yet who, in the midst of its accomplishment,
seeks to spare all unnecessary pang to its victim.

   The features of the second tragedy bore no resemblance

to those which characterized the first. *There*, it was literally a religious immolation to the ashes of the deceased,
whose spirit, it was presumed, could not rest in quietness,
unless an enemy had been offered up as a propitiatory
sacrifice. *Here*, it was a piece of wanton revenge, and
perpetrated under circumstances of peculiar atrocity.
Not a sound of triumph escaped from the band of Warriors met to avenge the death of their recently-fallen
friend and comrade, although they might have been supposed to have been inflamed and excited by the action in
which each had borne so prominent a part, in the early
part of the day—not a look of levity derogated from the
solemnity of their purpose. On the contrary, loud shouts
and yells, and menacing looks and gestures, accompanied
the actions of those, who, taking their tone from the
cruel relative of Logan, scalped and otherwise mutilated
the body of the second prisoner.

The demeanor of the first party was that of a Christian tribunal, which sits in solemn judgment upon a
criminal, and beholds, without emotion, the carrying into
effect of its sentence by the executioner. The bearing of
the second was that of a Christian mob, to whose infuriated passions a loose has been given, and who, once
excited by the sight of blood know not where to set a
bound to the innate and aroused cruelty of their nature.

In justice, however, to the Indians, it must be admitted
these seeming evidences of cruelty were not confined to
them. The American backwoodsmen were in the habit
of scalping also ; and indeed it is singular enough that,
although General Hull's famous, or rather, infamous
proclamation awarded death to any one of the subjects of
Great Britain, found combating at the side of, and therefore, assumed to be a participator in the barbarities attributed to the Indians, the very first scalp should have
been taken by an officer of his own army, and that within
a few days after the proclamation was issued.—James, in
his History of the War, relates—founded on a vague

rumor of the day—that at the action fought at Brownstown, where Major Van Horne was defeated, a letter was
found in the pocket of Captain McCulloch (who was
among the slain on that occasion) addressed to his wife,
and stating that he had shot an Indian near the Canard
bridge, on the 15th of July, and had the pleasure of *tearing off his scalp with his teeth*. Now of the fact itself
there can be very little doubt, for we had one Indian
(and one only) killed and scalped at the Canard. But,
although Captain McCulloch is entitled to all the credit
of this feat, there is reason to infer that James is incorrect in stating this information was obtained from a letter
found in his pocket. In the first instance it is extremely
unlikely that the Indians, in rifling and stripping the
body, would have brought off anything so valueless to
them as a letter, and secondly, it is much more probable
that such communication from McCulloch to his wife,
had been placed in the mail, which the party, to which
he belonged, were escorting from Detroit with the correspondence of General Hull's army, and which, it will
be recollected, was captured by the Indians. The whole
of the letters passed through our hands, and it is highly
probable the disclosure was made in this manner. I
rather think it was, although I have no distinct recollection of the fact. There is another grave error into which
James has fallen, in regard to the defeat of Major Van
Horne's detachment. He states the force under Tecumseh to have amounted to 70 Warriors. As has already
been shown here, there were but 25 including Tecumseh,
and, added to these, young Elliott.

I call it a grave error, not only because it diminishes
the extraordinary merit of the action, but because it de-
tracts from the glory and influence of Tecumseh, the
prestige of whose name and presence as much as anything else, by inspiring the utmost confidence in his little
band of followers, contributed to the signal defeat sustained by the enemy on that memorable occasion. James

has, moreover, fallen into another error, in stating the first British blood shed, to have been spilt at Maguaga. It has already been shown that Hancock, one of the two gallant sentinels forgotten at the Canard by Lieut. Clemow, on withdrawing his picket, was the first British soldier killed in the war. James incidentally alludes to the matter, but writes of both sentinels as having simply been wounded ; whereas Hancock was cut down, while desperately wounded in two places, and on his knees, (on which he had sunk from inability to support himself otherwise) opposing a fruitless resistance to the advance of a body of men, who had not magnanimity enough to spare the life of so valiant and resolute, yet so helpless a foe. But these are not the only objections to James, on the ground of inaccuracy. There is not one action, fought by the Right Division, which he has described with that fidelity that alone can render history of importance to posterity ; and, moreover, he betrays too much of the spirit of partizanship. Instead of adopting the calm and dignified style befitting the historian, half his pages are filled with bitter, though perhaps merited enough, sneers against the one-sided American accounts of the war, and, in his eagerness to refute these, he is often led into the very error he attributes to them—namely, mis-statements of force and circumstance. Of this, numerous instances might be adduced, but as it does not come within the object of this narrative to notice these, I shall not enter upon the enumeration. After these incidental remarks, it may not be unimportant to add, that I never read James' History of the War until the first number of this compilation was completed.

On the morning of Sunday, the 9th, the wild and distant cry of our Indian scouts gave us to understand that the enemy were advancing. In the course of ten minutes afterwards they appeared issuing from the wood, bounding like wild deer chased by the huntsman, and uttering that peculiar shout which is known among themselves as

the *news-cry*. From them we ascertained that a strong
column of the enemy, cavalry and infantry, were on their
march to attack us, but that the difficulty of transporting
their guns rendered it improbable they could reach our
position before night, although then only at a distance of
eight miles.   It being instantly decided on to meet them,
the detachment was speedily under arms, and on its march
for Maguaga, a small Indian village distant about a league.
The road along which we advanced was ankle-deep with
mud, and the dark forest waving its close branches over
our heads, left no egress to the pestilential exhalations
arising from the naked and putrid bodies of horses and
men killed of Major Horne's detachment, which had been
suffered to lie unburied beneath our feet.   No other sound
than the measured step of the troops interrupted the solitude of the scene, rendered more imposing by the wild
appearance of the warriors, whose bodies, stained and
painted in the most frightful manner for the occasion,
glided by us with almost noiseless velocity, without order
and without a chief ; some painted white, some black,
others half black, half red ; half black, half white ; all
with their hair plastered in such a way as to resemble the
bristling quills of the porcupine, with no other covering
than a cloth around their loins, yet armed to the teeth,
with rifles, tomahawks, war-clubs, spears, bows, arrows,
and scalping-knives.   Uttering no sound, and intent only
on reaching the enemy unperceived, they might have
passed for the spectres of those wilds, the ruthless demons
which War had unchained for the punishment and oppression of man.

Having taken up a position about a quarter of a mile
beyond Maguaga, our dispositions of defence were speedily made, the rustling of the leaves alone breaking on the
silence which reigned throughout our line.   Following
the example of the Indians, we lay reclined on the ground,
in order to avoid being perceived, until within a few
yards of the enemy.   While awaiting, in this manner, the

approach of the column, which we knew to be at no great distance advancing upon us, our little force was increased by the arrival of Lieut. Bullock of the 41st Grenadiers who, with a small detachment of twenty men of his own company, twenty Light Infantry, and twenty Battalion men had been urged forward by Gen. Brock, from the Headquarters of the Regiment, then stationed at Fort George, for the purpose of reinforcing the little Garrison of Amherstburg, and who having reached their destination the preceding day, had been despatched by Col. Procter, (lately arrived to assume the command) to strengthen us. Shortly the report of a single shot echoed throughout the wood ; and the instant afterwards the loud and terrific yells of the Indians, followed by a heavy and desultory fire, apprised us that they were engaged. The action then became general along our line, and continued for half an hour, without producing any material advantage ; when unluckily, a body of Indians that had been detached to a small wood about five hundred yards distant from our right, were taken by the troops for a corps of the enemy endeavouring to turn their flank. In vain we called out to them that they were our Indians. The fire which should have been reserved for their foes was turned upon their friends, who, falling into the same error, returned it with equal spirit. The fact was, they had been compelled to retire before a superior force, and the movement made by them, had given rise to the error of the troops. That order and discipline which would have marked their conduct as a body in a plain, was lost sight of, in a great measure, while fighting independently and singly in a wood, where every man, following the example of the enemy, was compelled to shelter his person behind the trees as he could. Closely pressed in front by an almost invisible foe, and on the point of being taken in the rear, as was falsely imagined, the troops were at length compelled to yield to circumstance and numbers.

Although our retreat, in consequence of this unfortunate misapprehension, commenced in some disorder, this was soon restored, when Major Muir, who had been wounded early in the engagement, succeeded in rallying his men, and forming them on the brow of a hill which commanded a short and narrow bridge intersecting the high road, and crossing a morass over which the enemy's guns must necessarily pass. This was about a quarter of a mile in rear of the position we had previously occupied. Here we remained at least fifteen minutes, when finding that the Americans did not make their appearance as expected, Major Muir, whose communication with Tecumseh had been cut off, and who now heard some smart firing in the woods beyond his left, naturally inferred that the enemy were pushing the Indians in that quarter, with a view of turning his flank, gaining the high road in our rear, and thus cutting off our retreat. The order was then given to retire, which we certainly did at the double quick, yet without being followed by the enemy, who suffered us to gain our boats without further molestation.

In this affair, which we never then regarded as anything more than a sharp skirmish, yet to which the Americans have since attached an undue importance, their loss was 18 killed and 63 wounded[1]; ours, one rank and file killed, two Officers, two Sergeants, nineteen

---

[1] Gen. Hull, in his despatch of Aug. 13th, 1812, puts the American loss at 10 non-commissioned officers and privates killed, and 45 wounded of 4th U.S. regiment, 8 killed and 12 wounded of Ohio and Michigan volunteers. He estimates the British loss at—Indians, about 40 killed, number wounded not known ; Major Muir and two subalterns wounded, one since dead ; 15 of the 41st killed and wounded, 4 made prisoners.

Col. Procter, in his letter of Aug. 11th, 1812, says the 41st lost 3 killed, 13 wounded and 2 missing ; the militia 1 killed, 2 wounded ; Indians, 2 killed and 6 wounded. He does not give the American loss, but says it was considerable.

Major Dalliba states the American loss to be 18 killed and 63 wounded, and the British 58 killed and wounded, Indians 102 killed and wounded.

Major Richardson evidently accepted Major Dalliba's report of

rank and file wounded, and two rank and file missing, but afterwards recaptured by the Indians. The wounded officers were Major Muir, and Lieutenant Sutherland. They were near each other when the attack commenced, and Major Muir having observed an American taking a deliberate aim at them, hastily placed a short rifle, which he usually carried with him on these occasions, on the shoulder of his companion, and levelled it at his enemy. Both fired at the same instant. The ball of the American, entering Lieut. Sutherland's cheek, came out at the back of his neck, and passed through one of Major Muir's wings (he commanded the Light Company of the 41st), while the rifleman himself fell dead on the spot, from his adversary's bullet. Major Muir soon afterwards received another ball in the leg, yet without being disabled. Severe as proved the wound of Lieut. Sutherland, (who was borne off the field when the retreat commenced, on the back, if I do not greatly mistake, of one of the Messrs. Caldwell of Amherstburg) he would have recovered had he not imprudently, some ten days afterwards, made premature use of his tooth-brush. This opened the wound, brought on hemorrhage, and before medical assistance could be procured, (the main body of the force being then in occupation of Detroit) he bled to death. Tecumseh was also slightly wounded, by a buckshot, on this occasion.

Here it was that we had first an opportunity of perceiving the extreme disadvantage of opposing regular troops to the enemy in the woods. Accustomed to the use of the rifle from his infancy—dwelling in a measure amid forests with the intricacies of which he is wholly acquainted, and possessing the advantage of a dress

---

the American loss, but gives no authority for his statement of the British loss, which he certainly must have underestimated, as Procter had better means of knowing than any other British officer. The safest guide is to accept the statement of each commanding officer for his own casualties, as they would know more about their own loss than that of their opponents.

which renders him almost undistinguishable to the eye of an European, the American marksman enters with comparative security into a contest with the English soldier, whose glaring habiliment and accoutrements are objects too conspicuous to be missed, while his utter ignorance of a mode of warfare, in which courage and discipline are of no avail, renders the struggle for mastery even more unequal. The principal armies to which the Right Division was opposed during the war, consisted not of regular and well-disciplined troops, but levies of men taken from the forests of Ohio and Kentucky, scarcely inferior as riflemen to the Indians. Dressed in woollen frocks of a gray color, and trained to cover their bodies behind the trees from which they fired, without exposing more of their persons than was absolutely necessary for their aim, they afforded us, on more than one occasion, the most convincing proofs that without the assistance of the Indian Warriors, the defence of so great a portion of Western Canada, as was entrusted to the charge of the numerically feeble Right Division, would have proved a duty of great difficulty and doubt.

I have stated that the Americans subsequently attached an undue importance to the affair of Maguaga. The following is an extract from a most voluminous account, written by Major James Dalliba, and published under the immediate inspection of Gen. (then Colonel) Miller, who on this occasion commanded the American forces which, by their own admission, consisted of the whole of the 4th Regiment of United States Infantry, except one company left at Sandwich to garrison a small fort, built by order of General Hull : a small detachment of the 1st Infantry, and a small number (enough to man two pieces of cannon) of Artillerists from Captain Dyson's company stationed in Fort Detroit. This composed the regular force, in all 300 men. Then there were, according to the same authority, " 60 men of the Michigan Militia, 40 Dragoons and Mounted Spies, and 300 Riflemen of the Ohio Volunteers, making in all 600 men." But now for Major Dalliba's extract.

"The position which the enemy had chosen, lay in an open oak wood, just at the declivity of a rising ground over which the Americans had to pass. He had thrown up breastworks of trees, logs, etc., behind which he lay concealed in force, and in order of battle. His works were thrown up in form of a *courtine* with two flanks. The line of the *courtine* lay across the road and perpendicularly to it. The banks formed an angle with the *courtine* of about 120°. The *courtine* was lined with British regular troops, two deep, of the 41st Regiment of foot, under the command of Major Muir, of that regiment, who had long been in command at Malden. The flank of the *courtine*, on the enemy's right, and American left, was lined with Canadian militia and Indians, commanded by Walk-in-the-water and Marpot. This line was flanked by the river Detroit. Most of the militia were dressed and painted like their 'brethren in arms,' the savages. The left flank of the *courtine* was lined entirely by savages, under the command of the celebrated warrior, Tecumseh, of the Shawanee nation. The number of the British regulars and militia amounted to about 300; about 200 regulars. The Indians amounted to 450; making the enemy's force about 750 men.

"The position and strength of the enemy were entirely unknown to Colonel Miller and to the army, at this time.

"At 12 o'clock, meridian, the detachment arrived at a large opening which contained 4 or 5 Indian houses, gardens and orchards. The army halted to take some refreshment, and bury the man who had been killed; where they lay about one hour. The village was deserted, and nothing left in the houses of consequence.

"The march was again resumed at 1 o'clock P.M. and continued without interruption. The troops marched over the ground on which Major Van Horne had been defeated four days before; and passed the dead bodies of several of the slain, and some dead horses. The body of Captain M'Cullock lay under an Indian bark. The columns having arrived at the oak woods near Brownstown, at half past three, some guns were heard ahead by them. In a few seconds a volley was heard from Captain Snelling's advance guard, and another instantly returned from a great number of pieces. The troops, by this time completely awake, were ordered to halt. Colonel Miller rode towards the centre at full speed, halted, and with a firm voice, ordered the columns to ' form the line of battle,' which was executed with that order, promptness, and zeal, which he had expected : after the first vollies, the firing became incessant in front. Captain Snelling stood his ground till the lines were formed, and moved to his relief. He stood within pistol shot of the enemy's breastworks, in a shower of balls from the regular troops in his front, who shewed themselves after the first fire, and set up the Indian yell. When the first line appeared before the breastwork, they received the fire of the whole front and a part of the flanks : at this instant Colonel Miller discovered that the enemy outflanked him, when the second line and flank guards were brought upon the flanks of the front line, and extended to meet the whole line of the enemy. The savages, in unison with the British troops, set up a horrid yell, and a severe conflict ensued. The incessant firing in the centre ran diverging to the flanks ; from the cracking of individual pieces it changed to alternate vollies ; and at length to one continued sound : and while every thing seemed hushed amidst the wavering roll, the discharge of the six-pounder burst upon the ear. The Americans stood !—At this instant Colonel Miller was thrown from his horse which took fright at the discharge of the artillery ; he was supposed to be shot. Those near him flew to his aid. The savages who saw him fall sprang over the breastwork to take his scalp, but were driven back. Colonel Miller instantly remounted and returned to continue his orders. The fire from the Indians, who were screened by their breastworks, was deadly. The soldiers saw the advantage it gave them, and Colonel Miller, throwing his eye along the line, discovered one or two edging to place themselves behind a tree. He saw the instant must be improved, and ordered '*charge!*' which instantly ran through the line : the men whom he saw edging, with every other, brought down their pieces, struck up a huzza ! and marched directly into the breastworks. The effect of the grape from the six-pounder, and the approach of the bayonet, caused the British line to yield, and then to break, and the troops fled in disorder ! At nearly the same instant the Indians and militia on their right flank, being charged in their work, by the Michigan legion, under Captain De Cant, and a part of the Ohio riflemen turning this flank by the river, fled in confusion. Tecumseh, on the enemy's left flank, stood longer ; some of the Indians under his command, near the extremity of the line, had jumped over the breastworks, in the full assurance of victory : they were driven back, by the point of the bayonet. Tecumseh endeavoured to outflank the American line, and turn their right ; but from the skill and gallantry of the officers, and firmness of the men on that flank, he was foiled in every attempt, and was finally forced to fall back, and take new positions, and fight on the retreat. The British and Indians on their right flank, fled directly down the river, and were pursued by Colonel Miller, with that part of his troops which had opposed them ; and Tecumseh, with his Indians, fled directly from the river, westwardly, into the wilderness and were pursued by that part of the troops which had opposed them overtaking those who were (severely) wounded, and otherwise unable to escape.

"After the British had retreated about one mile, they came into an opening of about half a mile in diameter ; here they endeavoured to form again, but on the precipitate approach of the Americans, they again broke and fled into the woods, down the river. They were pursued to the edge of these woods, when Colonel Miller received information from Major Van Horne, whom he had left in command of the right flank, that Tecumseh had retreated westwardly, that he successively took new positions with his Indians, that they were still fighting, and that it was still doubtful how the conflict would finally terminate in that quarter. On the receipt of this information Colonel Miller ordered the troops under his immediate command, to halt, and form the line. He informed the officers, that it would not do to pursue the enemy any farther, until he had heard again from the right flank. That as Tecumseh had retreated in another direction, the army was now divided, and the two divisions, already out of hearing of each other's musketry. That if Tecumseh was likely to overpower that division, he must send back a reinforcement to their relief, or the Indians would otherwise immediately advance upon the field of battle, and massacre the wounded, destroy the rear guard, and take the ammunition and stores; and finally fall upon his rear.

"Information was at length brought that Tecumseh had finally fled, and that the troops were returning to join that division as soon as possible.

"Colonel Miller immediately ordered the troops to march in further pursuit of the British. They entered the woods, and the cavalry moved ahead at full speed. When they arrived through these woods, which was about half a mile, they came upon the beach of Lake Erie, and discovered the enemy all in boats, steering towards Malden, and out of reach of their shot. They had concealed their boats at this point, when they came over, for this purpose, if they should be defeated. This circumstance, however, could not have been known to Colonel Miller before. He now ordered the troops to return upon the field from whence they had last marched, which was done; and on their arrival, they were joined by the other division, which had returned from the pursuit of Tecumseh and his Indians.

"The cause is now shewn, which has not been generally understood heretofore, why the British were not all captured, when they had been so totally defeated.

"The troops were then formed in line, fronting the field of battle ; when Colonel Miller rode in front of the centre, and addressed them in the following words:

" 'My brave fellows ! you have done well ! every man has done his duty.   I give you my hearty thanks for your conduct on this day ; you have gained my highest esteem ; you have gained fresh honor to yourselves, and to the American arms ; your fellow-soldiers in arms will love you, and your country will reward you.   You will return to the field of battle, to collect those who have gloriously fallen ; your friendly attention to your wounded companions is required.'

"At sunrise the march was resumed, and at 12 o'clock on the 12th of August, the detachment re-entered the town of Detroit, covered with mud from foot to head, their clothes not having been dried in two and a half days.   The sun now cheered them with its influence ; they marched through the street to the encampment.   They were met by their brother soldiers and citizens, with all that sympathy and heartfelt joy which constitutes the soldier's reward for his *hard earned victory.*"

Now, the *courtine*, alluded to by Major Dalliba, could have had no existence except in the heated imagination of a warrior flushed with victory, and magnifying the difficulties which his intrepidity and daring have surmounted. We had no breastwork of any description, and for this simple reason—that when we left Brownstown in the morning to meet the enemy, we knew not at what point we should halt.   When the ground we did occupy was reached, the Americans were not more than a mile, or a mile and a half, in our front, and Major Muir, finding it to be not an unfavorable position for defence, inasmuch as we were covered by the brow of a slightly rising ground,

ordered the men to lie down, and otherwise cover themselves with what logs happened to be in the way. There
had been no previous selection of ground, and, therefore,
no preparation—no precaution beyond that which has just
been stated. Here we had been only a very short time,
before the American advance was engaged with the Indians on our left, thrown forward, and soon the affair,
during which the enemy's grape was very liberally dispensed, became general.—Great, however, as was the disproportion of arm and numbers (for it will be recollected
that even with the reinforcement brought by Lieut. Bullock, ours did not exceed 150 men of the 41st Regiment,
to which might be added some 40 or 50 militia) there is
no reason to infer that the men would not longer have
maintained their ground, had it not been for the certainty
which existed that the enemy were outflanking us. I
perfectly recollect the position, even at this hour, although
I have never passed over the ground since, and I can
understand the alarm which prevailed. Immediately on
our right—and I was on the extreme of that flank—was a
plain of wild high grass, extending about 600 yards, and
at its termination, an open wood, running parallel with
the roads, thro' which, during the heat of the affair, a large
body of men, whom it was impossible to distinguish, were
discovered hastening their movements, with the evident
intention of gaining our rear. Such, indeed, proved to be
their object, but the men, who unluckily had not been
apprised of the fact of a party of Indians having been despatched to the extremity of the wood in question, mistook these (now driven back by the American left) for
the enemy, and commenced firing upon them ; thus re-
lieving the actual enemy from much of the obstacle
which had hitherto been opposed to their advance. The
Indians, probably laboring under the same erroneous impression, or indignant at being assailed in this manner by
their friends, partially returned the fire, and this of
course tended still more to confirm the belief entertained
by the men that they were Americans endeavoring to turn

their flank—nor could the earnest assurances of their officers remove this conviction. The discouraging effect of a panic of this kind is well known. The men hastily retired, carrying off their wounded, however, but the Americans did not pursue farther than the point we had abandoned. As has already been seen, the troops were speedily rallied and reformed, but without further invitation from the enemy to renew the contest.

There is another error in Major Dalliba's very lengthy detail of this affair, a notice of which is only important, because it tends to show, that the *courtine*, which he has so emphatically described, may have originated in the same want of recollection (and he states that he writes from recollection) of the actual condition of the ground where the skirmish commenced. He states, as will be seen in the extract I have given, that before the action commenced, they (the American detachment) passed the spot where Major Van Horne had been defeated a few days before ; and that they, among many dead bodies of men and horses, discovered that of Captain McCulloch placed under an Indian bark. Now this was impossible for we had passed these dead bodies in the morning, and they lay nearly midway between Brownstown and the scene of action. I can well recollect this fact, for such was the stench and the effluvia arising from the disgusting and bloated objects, which had been suffered to fester beneath a scorching sun, during several consecutive days, that, both in the advance, and the retreat, I experienced anything but regret when I had quitted the atmosphere they poisoned with their presence. Major Dalliba must have passed these at a subsequent period of the day, when, as he observes, the Americans came out of the wood near Brownstown, and found that the handful of British had been suffered to effect their retreat without interruption.

It must not be omitted to remark that, on the return of Colonel Miller to Detroit, he was closely followed by a band of about 250 Indians, chiefly Pottawattomies, who hung on the American rear and captured several boats laden with ammunition, and containing their wounded. Among the latter were two privates of the 41st who had been too badly hit to be brought off, and being close to the Americans had fallen into their hands, at the first and feeble attempt made at pursuit.

As I have unconsciously been led into a much more explanatory account of the Maguaga affair than I had originally intended, I cannot take my leave of it without transcribing an anecdote related by the same writer which is so characteristic of the detestation entertained by the Indians for the Americans, and resembles so nearly the conduct of the noble Hancock, who fell at the Canard, that it cannot fail to be read with interest.

" Some time in the evening of the 9th (writes Major Dalliba) Captain Maxwell returned with his spies, having been sent forward to the village of Brownstown, and reported that the village was abandoned, and that no enemy could be discovered. Early next morning, August 10th, detachments were sent out by Colonel Miller, to scour the woods in search of one man who was ascertained to be still missing : he was, however, found dead. While the men were ranging over the woods, one of them was shot dead. A smoke of a piece was discovered at a distance, rising from the ground by the party—they approached the spot, and beheld an Indian lying on the ground wounded, and unable to stand. One arm and one leg were broken, —he had lain there, during the night, by his piece which was loaded when he fell. The cool deliberation with which he died (of course from this we infer the Americans killed the wounded man) proved the native fortitude of the savage to meet death when resistance is useless. Unwilling to endure his pains longer, and die by degrees, he determined to die by the hand of his enemies, and to sell his life as dear to them as possible. He summoned together the little strength which remained, and so steadily levelled his rifle at the approaching American, as to put the ball through his heart."

IV

Meanwhile General Brock, then at York (Toronto) fully sensible of the danger of Amherstburg, threatened as he knew it to be by an overwhelming, and professedly exterminating foe, lost no time in repairing to its assistance. The first detachment of the 41st pushed forward to its relief was, as has been seen, that which joined us at Maguaga—and consisting of sixty men. Forty more were sent to Long Point, for the purpose of collecting the Militia in that neighborhood, and fifty, under Captain Chambers,[1] were despatched into the interior with a view of encouraging and being joined by the Indians. The General himself embarked on the 5th of August,[2] for Fort George and Long Point, doubtless having inwardly matured the daring object which he subsequently accomplished, so much to his own honor, and that of the troops who participated in his glory. Leaving Long Point on the 8th, with no other force than the 40 men of the 41st, who had been previously despatched thither, and about 260 militia, principally volunteers from Toronto, General Brock coasted the shore of Lake Erie, on his route to Amherstburg, which post he reached on the morning of the 13th.

The two subjoined orders, issued on this occasion, are not unworthy of record, not because they are important in themselves, but because they are eminently characteristic

---

[1] Captain Peter Latouche Chambers came to Canada with the 41st Regiment about the year 1800. He was frequently mentioned in despatches during the war and afterward became Lieut.-Colonel of the 41st. His death occurred in 1828.

[2] In Tupper's Life of Brock, p. 241, this date is given as the 6th of August.

of him, who was prudent only where recklessness were a
fault and hazardous only where hesitation were disaster.

> Head Quarters,
> Banks of Lake Erie,
> 15 miles S.W. of Fort Talbot,[1]
> August 11th, 1812, 6 o'clock p.m.

General Orders,

The Troops will hold themselves in readiness, and will
embark in the boats at twelve o'clock this night precisely.

It is Major General Brock's positive order that none of
the boats go ahead of that in which is the Head Quarters,
where a light will be carried during the night.

The Officers commanding the different boats will immediately inspect the arms and ammunition of the men,
and see that they are constantly kept in a state for immediate service, as the troops are now to pass through a
part of the country which is known to have been visited
by the enemy's patroles.

A Captain, with a subaltern and thirty men, will mount
as picquet upon the landing of the boats and a sentry will
be furnished from each boat, who must be regularly
relieved to take charge of the boats and baggage, &c.

A Patrole from the picquet will be sent out on landing
to the distance of a mile from the Encampment.

> By order of the Major Gen.
> J. B. Glegg, Capt., A.D.C.
> J. Macdonell, P.A.D.C.,

> Point Aux Pins,
> Lake Erie, August 12th, 1812.

General Orders.

It is Major General Brock's intention, should the wind
continue fair, to proceed during the night. Officers commanding boats will therefore pay attention to the order of
sailing as directed yesterday. The greatest care and
attention will be requested to prevent the boats from scattering or falling behind.

A great part of the Bank of the Lake when the boats
will this day pass is much more dangerous and difficult of

---

[1] Fort Talbot is a misprint for Port Talbot the home of the Hon.
Col. Thomas Talbot, a man who took a very prominent part in the
settlement of the western district of Upper Canada.

From original photograph in possession of Mr. B. Glegg, Backford Hall, Chester, England.

LIEUTENANT-COLONEL JOHN B. GLEGG.

access than any we have passed. The boat therefore will not land, excepting in the most extreme necessity, and then great care must be taken to choose the best places for landing.

The troops being now in the neighborhood of the enemy, every precaution must be taken to guard against surprise.

By order of the Major-General,

J. B. Glegg, A.D.C.

The arrival of Gen. Brock at Amherstburg was the signal for an offensive demonstration in our turn. The bridge at the Canard—so often the scene and object of contention—had been repaired, immediately after the abandonment of the Western District of Canada, by General Hull, who had recrossed the river, with the whole of his army, during the 7th and 8th, and preparations had already been made for bombarding Detroit. Under the superintendence[1] of Captain Dixon, of the Engineers, and Captain Hall[2] of the Provincial Navy, batteries were already in a train of construction. The Queen Charlotte of twenty guns, and the brig General Hunter of twelve, had moreover been sent up the river for the purpose of covering their operations, and conveying such warlike munitions as were required for the siege. The position chosen for the batteries was an elevated part on the bank of the Detroit, immedi-

[1] These officers were assisted by the Norfolk and Oxford Militia under Captain John Bostwick, First Lieut. George Ryerson and Second Lieut. George Rolph.

Lieut. Ryerson's narrative to Dr. Canniff, published in Belford's Magazine, Toronto, 1877.

[2] Captain George B. Hall was next in command to Hon. Alexander Grant, the Commodore of the government fleet on the Upper Lakes. When the war broke out Commodore Grant was 85 years of age—too old for active service—consequently Captain Hall had charge of the marine department until the arrival of Captain Barclay. He was present at the Miami in May, 1813, and was mentioned in despatches. By order of Captain Barclay he was discontinued in the Provincial Marine. For this act Barclay was reprimanded because he had no authority to annul any appointment. Captain Hall was retained in the service as Superintendent of the dockyard and naval stores at Amherstburg at the same pay as he formerly received.

In 1817 a George B. Hall (in all probability Captain Hall) was elected by Essex, as a member of the Legislative Assembly.

ately opposite to the fort of that name, and on the outskirt of, what has since become, the Village of Windsor. The distance across, at this point, is not quite a mile.

During the morning of the 15th, the batteries being ready to open their fire, General Brock, who had lost no time in repairing to Sandwich, and had ordered all the disposable force in Amherstburg to follow forthwith, despatched a flag, with a summons to the American commander.

Head Quarters, Sandwich, August 15th, 1812.

Sir,—The force at my disposal authorizes me to require of you the immediate surrender of Fort Detroit.—It is far from my inclination to join in a war of extermination, but you must be aware that the numerous body of Indians, who have attached themselves to my troops, will be beyond my control the moment the contest commences. You will find me disposed to enter into such conditions as will satisfy the most scrupulous sense of honor. Lieut.-Colonel Macdonell, and Major Glegg are fully authorized to conclude any arrangement that may lead to prevent the unnecessary effusion of blood.

I have the honor to be,

Sir, your most obdt. Servant,

(Signed) ISAAC BROCK, Major Gen.

His Excellency, Brigadier Gen. Hull,

Commanding at Fort Detroit.

To which the subjoined answer was returned.

Head Quarters, Detroit, August 15th, 1812.

Sir,—I have received your letter of this date. I have no other reply to make, than to inform you that I am prepared to meet any force which may be at your disposal, and any consequences, which may result from any exertion of it you may think proper to make.

I avail myself of this opportunity to inform you that the flag of truce, under the direction of Captain Brown, proceeded contrary to the orders, and without the knowledge of Col. Cass, who commanded the troops which attacked your picket, near the river Canard bridge.

I likewise take this occasion to inform you that Cowie's house was set on fire contrary to my orders, and it did not take place until after the evacuation of the Fort. From the best information I have been able to obtain on the subject, it was set on fire by some of the inhabitants on the other side of the river.

I am, very respectfully.

Your Excellency's most obdt. Servant,

(Signed) W. Hull, Brig. Gen.

His Exc'y. Major Gen. Brock, Comm'g the N.W. Army.
Comm'g His Britannic Majesty's
Forces, Sandwich, Up. Canada.

On this refusal being made known, the batteries, on which were mounted one long eighteen, and two long twelve-pounders, with a couple of mortars, opened a well-directed fire upon the fort, which threw the enemy into evident confusion. Some heavy guns were brought forward by them to the bank to bear upon the batteries, but my impression is, although it may be wrong, as General Brock describes it in his Official Despatch as having been spirited, that their fire was very languidly returned. Certainly it produced no other effect upon the batteries, than to cause them to throw in their shot with increased rapidity and precision.

The refusal to surrender had of course been anticipated, and preparations for crossing, and attempting to carry Detroit by storm, having in the meantime been made—everything was in readiness by daybreak on the following morning. The batteries, which had kept up an irregular fire during the night, renewed it at the first dawn with unabated spirit, and the requisite boats having been provided, the crossing was effected without opposition, under cover of the guns of the Queen Charlotte and General Hunter, which lay anchored about half a mile above Sandwich. A soft August sun was just rising, as we gained the centre of the river, and the view, at the moment, was certainly very animated and exciting, for, amid the little squadron of boats and scows, conveying the troops and artillery, were mixed numerous canoes filled with Indian warriors, decorated in their half-nakedness for the occasion, and uttering yells of mingled defiance of their foes and encouragement of the soldiery.

Above us again were to be seen and heard the flashes and thunder of the artillery from our batteries, which, as on the preceding day, was but feebly replied to by the enemy, while the gay flags of the Queen Charlotte, drooping in the breezeless, yet not oppressive air, and playing on the calm surface of the river, seemed to give earnest of success, and inspirited every bosom.

The point of embarkation was nearly opposite to the low, stone building at Sandwich, which (then a school) is now used as a barrack, and the place of landing was a little above the Spring Wells—not far, indeed, from the spot where now stand the house and grounds of General Schwartz. From this to the fort is about three miles, and the road, occasionally winding, was commanded from the rising ground, which then crowned the immediate entrance to the town on the side by which we approached, but which has since been partially levelled. The whole of the force, including militia and Indians (most of these latter had preceded us during the night of the 15th) having landed, General Brock, who had crossed in one of the leading boats, ordered the reports to be collected, when it was found that there was but 550 men of all arms present. This return appearing extremely weak, Major Glegg assisted by Lieutenant MacLean, Brigade Major to General Procter, was again desired to see if a greater number could not be mustered. These officers finally made out 750 men, including the militia who were employed in rowing the boats, but who were not present upon the ground. I am particular in detailing this fact, because there have been so many versions of our strength, that it is important the correct one should be known.

The column having been formed, we moved forward by sections, at nearly double distance, in order to give to our little force a more imposing appearance. Lieut. Bullock commanded the advanced guard, and immediately in rear of this, and preceding the column, were the light artillery (three six and two three-pounders) with which only we

advanced against the enemy's fortress.[1] Nothing but the
boldness of the enterprize could have ensured its success.
When within a mile and a half from the rising ground to
which I have just alluded, as commanding the approach
to the town, we distinctly saw two long, heavy guns,
(afterwards proved to be twenty-four pounders) planted in
the road, and around them the gunners with their fuses
burning. At each moment we expected that they would
be fired, yet although it was evident the discharge must
literally have swept our small, but dense column, there
was neither halt nor indecision perceptible. This was
fortunate. Had there been the slightest wavering, or
appearance of confusion in the men, the enemy, who were
closely watching us, and who seemed intimidated by the
confidence of our advance, would not have failed to profit
by the discovery; and fearful, in such case, must have
been the havoc; for, moving as we were by the main
road, with the river close upon our right flank, and a
chain of alternate houses and close fences upon our left,
there was not the slightest possibility of deploying. In
this manner, and with our eyes riveted on the guns,

[1] Extract from District General Orders:
Head Quarters, Fort Amherstburg,
Aug. 14th, 1812.

Captains Muir, Tallon and Chambers of 41st Regiment, Captain Glegg, 49th Regiment, Captain Mockler, Newfoundland Regt.,
and Captain Dixon, Royal Engineers, are appointed to the rank of
major so long as the local service on which they are employed continues.

The troops in the Western District will be divided into three
brigades : The First, under Lieut.-Colonel St. George, to consist of
detachments of the Royal Newfoundland Regiment, and of the
Kent and First and Second Regiments Essex Militia.   The Second
under the command of Major Chambers, consisting of 50 men of
the 41st Regiment, and of the whole of the detachments of York,
Lincoln, Oxford and Norfolk Militia.   The Third Brigade, under
the command of Major Tallon, will consist of the remainder of the
41st Regiment.

Colonel Procter will have charge of the whole line, under the
orders of the Major-General.

James Givins, Esquire, late Capt. 5th Regiment, is appointed
Provincial Aid-de-Camp, with the rank of Major in the Militia.
By order of the Major-General.
J. B. Glegg, Major, A.D.C.

which became at each moment more visible, we silently advanced until within about three-quarters of a mile of the formidable battery ; when General Brock, having found this point a position favorable for the formation of the columns of assault, caused the whole to be wheeled to the left, through an open field and orchard, leading to a house about three hundred yards off the road, which he selected as his Headquarters. In this position we were covered.

While this was passing on the right bank of the river, our batteries had been performing good service on the left. The officers in charge had succeeded in getting the true range of their guns, which threw their shot with admirable precision, and in the early part of the morning an eighteen-pound ball had found its way into the fort through an embrasure, and passing into the mess-room, killed four officers (one of whom was Lieut. Hanks, the commandant at Michilimackinac on its recent surrender to Captain Roberts) scattering their brains and blood against the walls of the apartment, and filling the Americans within the fort, as we afterwards understood, with serious dismay. As soon as this circumstance was reported to General Hull, and about the time when the troops were crossing below, he despatched a white flag to the batteries, but Captain Hall, who commanded there, having stated, to the officer who bore it, that General Brock was by that time on his own shore, and was the only person by whom the flag could be received, the bearer immediately returned—the batteries discontinuing their fire, however, in the meantime. This, of course, was during our advance, and it might be reasonable to infer that it was in consequence of this flag being then in the act of passing from one shore to the other that the enemy had not opened his fire from the long twenty-four pounders pointed at our column, were it not that General Cass and others have distinctly stated that they requested the sanction of General Hull to fire, but that such sanction was peremptorily refused, from an apprehension of ulterior consequences. Whatever the cause, we certainly had reason to congratulate ourselves that we had escaped the threatened danger. I confess that I breathed much more freely when we had left the road, which was quite as bad as any *cul-de-sac*, and taken up our position near the farmhouse.

At the moment when the white flag was seen advancing from the point at which the threatening twenty-four pounders—their muzzles turned from the batteries upon us—were yet planted, General Brock had advanced up the brow of the rising ground which concealed us from their view, for the purpose of reconnoitering the fort. He was soon apprized of this new and unexpected feature in the aspect of affairs, and promptly despatched Colonel Macdonell and Major Glegg to meet it. It was the latter officer, if I mistake not, who speedily returned by the main road at full gallop to communicate to the General, who in the meantime had returned to the column, that the object of the flag was to propose a surrender of the fort. Furnished with the instructions of his Chief, Major Glegg rode back at the same speed to the party who were awaiting his return, and all then entered the town for the purpose of arranging the terms of capitulation.

At the termination of an hour, during which the arms of the men who loitered indifferently about, were piled, while such of the Officers as were fortunate enough to be early in their application, were provided with an excellent breakfast by the people of the farm-house, one of the Aids-de-Camp was again descried hurrying from the town at full speed. He brought the gratifying intelligence that the capitulation had been completed; and the order was then given for the troops to advance and form upon the glacis of the fort. The "fall in" was immediately sounded, and we moved as directed, not by the main road, but by the orchards and fields which inter-

vened between our position and the fortress. As we
approached, and beheld the numerous cannon frowning
from their embrasures, it was impossible to avoid feeling
mingled surprise and congratulation that so formidable a
post should have been the fruit, apparently, more of a
party of pleasure than of war.

The glacis gained, the column was halted, and on our
arrival we found that the greatest portion of the regular
troops had marched out of the garrison upon the esplanade, where they were now loitering about as we had a
few minutes before, with piled arms.   A guard of honor,
consisting of an officer and forty men, was immediately
formed to take possession of the fort.   The command of
this devolved upon the officer who had led the advanced
guard—Lieutenant Bullock ; and among those of the
Militia who were attached to his party, and had first the
honor of entering the fortress, were the present Chief
Justice Robinson,[1] Samuel Jarvis,[2] Esquire, Superintendent of Indian affairs, and Colonel William Chisholm,[3] of
Oakville.

---

[1] Sir John Beverley Robinson, Bart., was born in Berthier,
Quebec, July 26th, 1791. He was acting Attorney-General of
Upper Canada, from the death of Col. John Macdonell in 1812,
until the return of Hon. D'Arcy Boulton to Canada in 1815 ; Soli-
citor-General from 1815 to 1818 and Attorney-General from 1818
to 1829 when he was appointed Chief Justice of Upper Canada, an
office he graced till 1862. His death occurred January 31st, 1863.
He was the foremost of "The Fighting Judges," a term applied
to those men who fought for their country, and who afterwards
by their ability rose to the Bench.

[2] Colonel Samuel Peters Jarvis, the eldest son of William Jarvis,
Secretary of Upper Canada from 1792 to 1817, was born at Newark
(Niagara) November 15th, 1792. At Detroit he was attached to
the 41st Regiment and was present as a lieutenant at Queenston
Heights, Stoney Creek and Lundy's Lane. He was Clerk of the
Crown in Chancery and Chief Superintendent of Indian Affairs.
During the rebellion of 1837-38 he raised the "Queen's Rangers."
He died at Toronto, September 6th, 1857.

[3] Colonel William Chisholm was the son of George Chisholm, who
emigrated from Inverness, Scotland, to Nova Scotia, where Colonel
Chisholm was born Oct. 15th, 1788. At the taking of Detroit he
was Lieutenant of No. 1 Flank Company of Lincoln Militia, and

ld medal awarded to Lieut.-Col. John Macdonell, P.A.D.C , to commemorate the capture of Detroit,
now in possession of John Alexander Macdonell, K.C., Alexandria,

An error, which, in many similar circumstances, might have proved a fatal one, occurred on this occasion. The order for the advance of the guard of honor was given prematurely, by some officer of the Staff—whom however I do not now recollect—for no sooner had the head of the guard passed over the drawbridge into the fort, when it found itself almost hemmed in by a host of the Ohio Militia—many of them looking very fierce and very indignant at the surrender—who had not yet been marched out. As the entrance of the guard under these circumstances was a violation of an article of the capitulation, which expressly stipulated that the American Garrison were to march out before the British troops took possession, we were promptly faced to the rear, and marched back again to the glacis—where we waited patiently until the angry-looking riflemen found it convenient to move. We then entered in form, and lowering the American flag, hoisted, in default of the regular British ensign, an Union Jack which a stray blue-jacket had brought with him, tied round his body, and which he very cheer-

---

at Queenston Heights was in command of the flank company of York Militia. He was Colonel of Militia in 1824, and commanded the left wing of the Loyalists at Montgomery's Tavern (Gallow's Hill), Dec. 7th, 1837. For several years he represented the County of Halton in the Legislature, and in 1834 was appointed Collector of Customs at Oakville, where he died May 4th, 1842.

His son, George King Chisholm, was also Colonel of Militia, and took part in the defence of Fort Erie during the Fenian Raid of 1866. He represented Halton for one Parliament, and was for some time Sergeant at Arms of the Parliament of Canada. He died in April, 1874.

Another son Robert Kerr Chisholm succeeded his father as Collector of Customs and was elected to several Municipal offices.

Many of the descendants of Colonel Chisholm reside at Oakville.

Another officer of this name that served on the Niagara frontier during the war was Colonel George Chisholm, who was born at Fort Erie, Sept. 16th, 1792, the youngest son of George Chisholm, a U. E. Loyalist. He took part in the battle of Queenston Heights, and was in command of a company at Lundy's Lane. In 1837 he was made a Lieut.-Col., and Col. in 1838. He was one of the "Men of Gore" that accompanied Sir Allan N. MacNab to Toronto to quell the rebellion. His death occurred in 1872.

D. B. Chisholm, Mayor of Hamilton in 1872, was his youngest son.

fully gave up for the purpose. The sentinels were then planted around the ramparts, and I (at that time a young volunteer armed with a musket taller than myself) had the honor of mounting my first guard at the Flag Staff— not a little elated I confess at the very enviable position in which, as a young Warrior, I conceived myself to be placed on the occasion. Nor was the feeling at all diminished, as strutting most martially to and fro on my post, and, casting my eyes downward upon the esplanade, I saw, or fancied I saw, the American troops looking up with anything but satisfaction at the red-coats who had thus usurped their place.

The articles of capitulation having been finally settled, and the troops—the main body of which had soon followed the guard of honor—in possession of the fort, the first act of General Brock was to enter and liberate, in person, the gallant Dean who had been taken prisoner at the Canard and who then lay confined in the guard-room. Shaking him by the hand in presence of his comrades—while his voice betrayed strong emotion, he warmly approved his conduct, and declared that he was indeed an honor to the profession of a soldier. Such commendation, from such a man, was in all probability the happiest day of poor Dean's existence, and must have amply repaid him for all his sufferings in confinement.

Soon after our occupation of the fort, Lieut. Bullock the officer commanding the guard, discovered the colors of the 4th Regiment of Infantry, which had been left in a room contiguous to that in which the four American officers were killed by the fire from our batteries. When it became known to General Brock that the colors had not been delivered over with the usual formalities, an order was sent to the officer of the guard to take them down to the esplanade where the American prisoners were assembled, and hand them over to the officer in command of the 4th Regt., with a view to their proper delivery. The order was promptly obeyed.   Lieut. Bullock, taking with him a few files of his guard, conveyed the colors to the ground occupied by the 4th, when, on enquiring for the officer commanding that Regiment, he was met by a Captain Cook, who stated that in the absence of Colonel Miller—lying ill with ague at the time—the command had devolved on him.   To this officer Lieut. Bullock communicated his errand.   Captain Cook took from him the colors, and again presented them saying—"Sir! the fortune of war has placed these in your hands—they are yours."   Lieut. Bullock simply bowed, and withdrew.   It was evident that Captain Cook, and those around him felt much chagrin on the occasion.

On the afternoon of the surrender of Detroit the following order was published.

General Order,

Head Quarters, Detroit, 16th August, 1812.

Major-General Brock has every reason to be satisfied with the conduct of the Troops he had the honor to lead this morning against the enemy.   The state of discipline which they so eminently displayed, and the determination they evinced to undertake the most hazardous enterprize, decided the enemy, infinitely more numerous in men and artillery, to propose a capitulation, the terms of which are herewith inserted for the information of the Troops.

The Major-General requests Colonel Procter will accept his best thanks for the assistance he derived from his experience and intelligence.

The steadiness and discipline of the 41st Regiment, and the readiness of the Militia to follow so good an example were highly conspicuous.

The ability manifested by Captain Dixon of the Royal Engineers in the choice and construction of the batteries and the high state of the Royal Artillery under Lieut. Troughton, afforded the Major-General much gratification, and reflect great credit on those officers.

The willing assistance given by Captain Hall and the Marine Department during the whole course of the service has been very conspicuous, and the manner the batteries were served this morning evinced a degree of steadiness highly commendable.

Lieut. Dewar, Dpt. Ass. Qr.-Master-General, afforded strong proof by the local knowledge he had acquired of the country, of an unremitting attention to his duty ; and the care and regularity with which the troops were transported across the river, must in a like degree, be ascribed to his zeal for the service.

To Lieut.-Col. St. George, Majors Tallon and Chambers, who commanded brigades, every degree of praise is due for their unremitting zeal and attention to their respective commands. The detachment of the Royal Newfoundland Regiment, under the command of Major Mockler, is deserving every praise for their steadiness in the field, as well as when embarked in the King's vessels.

The Major-General cannot forego this opportunity of expressing his admiration at the conduct of the several companies of Militia who so handsomely volunteered to undergo the fatigues of a journey of several hundred miles to go to the rescue of an invaded district ; and he requests Major Salmon,[1] Captains Hatt,[2] Heward,[3] Bostwick,[4]

---

[1]Major George C. Salmon was an officer of the 2nd Norfolk Militia. By a militia general order of July 22nd, 1812, Colonel Talbot was commanded to make up a detachment of 200 men from the 1st and 2nd Norfolk, and the Oxford and Middlesex militia, and place it under the command of Major Salmon, who was to proceed with this force to Moraviantown to await the arrival of Major Chambers, of the 41st Regiment, under whose command he was to place himself. It is doubtful whether this order was carried out, as some authorities say he accompanied General Brock. Major Salmon was an excellent officer, and was frequently mentioned in despatches.

Mr. Justice William Salmon, Judge of the County of Norfolk, who died Feb. 8th, 1868, was the second son of Major Salmon. He took an active part in the suppression of the Rebellion of 1837. The father of Judge Salmon and the father of Dr. Rolph emigrated together from near Bristol in England in 1809.

[2]Captain Samuel Hatt was appointed by General Brock to command the flank companies of the 5th and 6th Regiments of Lincoln Militia. At the repulse of General Smyth at Fort Erie, Nov. 28th, 1812, he was commended for his services by Col. Bisshopp.

[3]Major Stephen Heward was in command of a company of the York Militia at Detroit. He was for many years a prominent citizen of York (Toronto).

[4]Colonel John Bostwick served in the war as a captain of the

and Robinson,[1] will assure the officers and men under their respective command, that their services have been duly appreciated and will never be forgotten.

The Major-General is happy to acknowledge the able assistance he has derived from the zeal and local information of Lieut.-Col. Nichol, acting Quarter-Master-General to the Militia.

To his personal Staff the Major-General feels himself under much obligation ; and he requests Lieut.-Colonel Macdonell, Majors Glegg and Givins,[2] will be assured that their zealous exertions have made too deep an impression on his mind ever to be forgotten.

Norfolk militia. His conduct at Fort Erie, November 28th, 1812, where he was slightly wounded, was specially mentioned in the official despatch of that event. He served as colonel during the rebellion of 1837-38.

There was a Lieut.-Col. Henry Bostwick of the Oxford Militia, who served during the war.

[1]Captain William Robinson, an officer in the Norfolk Militia, was born in New Jersey in 1776, his father having emigrated from Yorkshire, England, four years before. In 1802 he came to Upper Canada. His eldest son Richard enlisted at the beginning of the war although but 15 years of age and served till its close. Capt. Robinson died in 1829.

[2]Colonel James Givins came to Canada when a young man as an officer in a British Regiment. For some years he was on the Detroit frontier and among the native tribes of the west picking up a knowledge of several Indian dialects which made his services afterwards so useful to the Lieut.-Governors and the government. In 1792 we find him at Newark (Niagara) as Lieutenant of the Queen's Rangers and afterwards as Aid to Simcoe on his journey to Detroit in February, 1793.

He accompanied Simcoe on his search for a new metropolis of the province, and when the site of Toronto was chosen he took up his residence there and was appointed a Superintendent in the Indian Department, an office which he held till 1842. When the war commenced he entered upon active service which lasted till its close. At the taking of Detroit he was Aid to Brock and Interpreter, and at the defence of Fort Erie, he commanded the Indians. When York was taken by the Americans in April, 1813, he, at the head of 25 Indians and 60 men of the Glengarry Fencibles stubbornly opposed the landing of Major Forsyth. In 1819 he asked to be granted the Gold Medal for Detroit, as a staff officer, his name being left off the list of recommendations by an oversight, but if he received this distinction to which he was justly entitled, I have seen no record of it.

Canon Saltern Givins, Judge Givins, sometime of London, Ontario, and Surgeon Major Givins, of the India Medical Staff, were his sons.

The conduct of the Indians under Col. Elliott, Capt. McKee,[1] and other officers of that department, joined to that of the gallant and brave Chiefs of their respective tribes, has since the commencement of the war been marked with acts of true heroism, and in nothing can they testify more strongly their love to the King, their Great Father, than in following the dictates of honor and humanity, by which they have been hitherto actuated. Two fortifications have already been captured from the enemy without a drop of blood being shed by the hands of the Indians ; the instant the enemy submitted, his life became sacred.

By order of Major-General Brock.
J. B. Glegg, Capt., A. D. C.

From Major-General Brock, to His Excellency, Sir George Prevost.

Head Quarters, Detroit,
Aug. 17th, 1812.

Sir,—I have had the honor of informing your Excellency, that the enemy effected his passage across the Detroit river on the 12th ult. without opposition ; and that, after establishing himself at Sandwich, he had ravaged the country as far as the Moraviantown. Some skirmishes occurred between the troops under Lieut.-Col. St. George and the enemy, upon the River Canard, which uniformly terminated in his being repulsed with loss. The occupation of Sandwich was evidently productive of considerable effect on the minds of a large portion of the inhabitants. The disaffected became more audacious, and the wavering more intimidated. I judged it therefore proper to

---

[1] Captain Thomas McKee, son of Colonel Alexander McKee, was in command of a party of Indians at the taking of Detroit, and in the several subsequent engagements. He was Superintendent of Indian Affairs for many years. The McKee family have occupied prominent positions in the western district since 1775. Colonel Alexander McKee was appointed Deputy Superintendent General of Indian Affairs by Lord Dorchester, who expressed his satisfaction with his conduct. His death on January 14th, 1799, was a distinct loss to the British in their dealings with the Indians. Captain Thomas McKee was elected a member of the Legislative Assembly for Kent in 1796 and for Essex in 1801. Thomas McKee, who so long has honorably filled the office of County Clerk of Essex, is a grandson of Captain Thomas McKee. The present able representative of North Essex in the Ontario Legislature is W. J. McKee, great-grandson of the representative of 100 years ago and son of the present County Clerk.

detach at every risk a force down the River Thames, capable of acting in conjunction with the garrison of Amherstburg offensively, but Captain Chambers, whom I had appointed to direct this detachment, experienced difficulties from the prevalent spirit of the moment that frustrated my intentions.

The intelligence received from that quarter admitting of no delay, Colonel Procter was directed to assume the command, and his force was soon after increased with sixty rank and file of the 41st regiment.

In the meantime, the most strenuous measures were adopted to counteract the machinations of the evil disposed, and I soon experienced the gratification of receiving voluntary offers of service from that portion of the embodied militia the most easily collected. In the attainment of this important point, gentlemen of the first character and influence shewed an example highly creditable to them; and I cannot, on this occasion, avoid mentioning the essential assistance I derived from John Macdonell, Esq., His Majesty's Attorney-General, who, from the beginning of the war, has honored me with his services as my Provincial Aid-de-Camp. A sufficiency of boats being collected at Long Point for the conveyance of 300 men, the embarkation took place on the 8th instant, and in five days we arrived in safety at Amherstburg.

I found that the judicious arrangements which had been adopted immediately upon the arrival of Colonel Procter, had compelled the enemy to retreat, and take shelter under the guns of his fort; that officer commenced operations by sending strong detachments across the river, with a view of cutting off the enemy's communication with his resources.

This produced two smart skirmishes on the 5th and 9th inst., in both of which the enemy's loss was very considerable, whilst ours amounted to 3 killed and 13 wounded; amongst the latter, I have particularly to regret Captain Muir and Lieutenant Sutherland, of the 41st regiment; the former an officer of great experience, and both ardent in His Majesty's service. Batteries had likewise been commenced opposite Fort Detroit, for one 18 pounder, two 12's, and two 5½ inch mortars; all of which opened on the evening of the 15th (having previously summoned Brigadier Gen. Hull to surrender), and although opposed by a well directed fire from seven 24 pounders, such was their construction under the able direction of Captain Dixon of the Royal Engineers, that no injury was sustained from its effect.

The force at my disposal being collected in the course of the 15th in the neighborhood of Sandwich, the embarkation took place a little after day-light on the following morning, and by the able arrangements of Lieutenant Dewar, of the Quarter-Master-General's department, the whole was, in a short time, landed without the smallest confusion at Spring-Well; a good position, three miles west of Detroit. The Indians, who had in the meantime effected their landing two miles below, moved forward and occupied the woods, about a mile and a half on our left.

The force which I instantly directed to march against the enemy consisted of 30 Royal Artillery, 250 41st Regiment, 50 Royal Newfoundland Regiment, 400 militia, and about 600 Indians, to which were attached three 6 pounders and two 3 pounders. The services of Lieutenant Troughton, commanding the Royal Artillery, an active and intelligent officer, being required in the field, the direction of the batteries was intrusted to Captain Hall, and the Marine department, and I cannot withhold my entire approbation of their conduct on this occasion.

I crossed the river, with an intention of waiting in a strong position the effect of our force upon the enemy's Camp, and in hopes of compelling him to meet us in the field; but receiving information upon landing, that Colonel M'Arthur, an officer of high reputation had left the garrison three days before with a detachment of 500 men, and hearing, soon afterwards, that his cavalry had been seen that morning three miles in our rear, I decided on an immediate attack. Accordingly, the troops advanced to within one mile of the fort, and having ascertained that the enemy had taken little or no precaution toward the land side, I resolved on an assault, whilst the Indians penetrated his Camp. Brigadier Gen. Hull, however, prevented this movement, by proposing a cessation of hostilities, for the purpose of preparing terms of capitulation. Lieutenant-Colonel John Macdonell and Captain Glegg were accordingly deputed by me on this mission, and returned within an hour with the conditions, which I have the honor to transmit. Certain considerations

MAJOR-GENERAL SIR ISAAC BROCK.

afterwards induced me to agree to the two supplementary articles.

The force thus surrendered to His Majesty's arms, cannot be estimated at less than 2,500 men. In this estimate, Colonel M'Arthur's detachment is included, as he surrendered, agreeably to the terms of capitulation, in the course of the evening, with the exception of 200 men, whom he left escorting a valuable convoy at some little distance in his rear ; but there can be no doubt the officer commanding will consider himself equally bound by the capitulation.

The enemy's aggregate force was divided into two troops of cavalry ; one company of artillery regulars ; the 4th United States regiment ; detachments of the 1st and 3rd United States regiments, volunteers ; three regiments of the Ohio Militia ; one regiment of the Michigan territory.

Thirty-three pieces of brass and iron ordnance have already been secured.

When this contest commenced, many of the Indian nations were engaged in active warfare with the United States, notwithstanding the constant endeavors of this government to dissuade them from it. Some of the principal chiefs happened to be at Amherstburg, trying to procure a supply of arms and ammunition, which for years had been withheld, agreeably to the instructions received from Sir James Craig, and since repeated by your Excellency.

From that moment they took a most active part, and appeared foremost on every occasion ; they were led yesterday by Colonel Elliot and Captain M'Kee and nothing could exceed their order and steadiness. A few prisoners were taken by them, during the advance, whom they treated with every humanity ; and it affords me much pleasure in assuring your Excellency, that such was their forbearance and attention to what was required of them, that the enemy sustained no other loss in men than what was occasioned by the fire of our batteries.

The high sense I entertain of the abilities and judgment of Lieut.-Col. Myers, induced me to appoint him to the important command at Niagara ; it was with reluctance I deprived myself of his assistance, but had no other expedient ; his duties, as head of the Quarter-Master-General's department, were performed to my satisfaction by Lieut.-Col. Nichol,[1] Quarter-Master-General of the Militia.

Captain Glegg, my Aid-de-Camp will have the honor of delivering this despatch to your Excellency; he is charged with the colors taken at the capture of Fort Detroit, and those of the 4th United States regiment.

Captain Glegg is capable of giving your Excellency every information respecting the state of this province, and I shall esteem myself highly indebted to your Excellency to afford him that protection, to which his merit and length of service give him a powerful claim.

I have the honor to be, with every consideration, &c.,

ISAAC BROCK, Maj.-Gen.

His Excellency,
Lt.-Gen'l. Sir G. Prevost, Bart., Etc.

P. S. I have the honor to enclose a copy of a proclamation, which I have issued immediately on taking possession of this country.

I should have mentioned, in the body of my despatch, the capture of the Adams; she is a fine vessel, and recently repaired, but without arms.

---

[1] Lieutenant-Colonel Robert Nichol, of the 2nd Regiment of Norfolk Militia, was appointed Quartermaster General of Militia at the beginning of the war, and performed the arduous and important duties of that office to the entire satisfaction of the commanding officers. In his young days he worked as clerk for Colonel John Askin, of Detroit, and after leaving this service he established a milling and mercantile business at Port Dover on Lake Erie.

When Brock resolved to go to Detroit, Col. Nichol was entrusted with the arrangements for moving the force by water from Long Point to Amherstburg. This duty was so well performed that it called forth the praises of the General. He directed the crossing of the troops on August 16th, 1812, and after the surrender of Detroit he remained to assist Colonel Procter to establish means of defence. He was present at Fort Erie, Nov. 28th, 1812; and at the battle of Fort George, May 27th, 1813, his horse was killed under him while acting as Aid to Colonel Myers. But the greatest service that Colonel Nichol did for his country during the war was to induce Colonel Bisshopp and afterwards Major-General Vincent to disobey the orders of Sir George Prevost to abandon western Canada. On every important question he was consulted by the officers in command, and his reports, such as on the possibility of building a new fleet on Lake Erie and on the state of affairs on the Detroit frontier—show a thorough knowledge of military matters. He sacrificed a great deal during the war. On May 15th, 1814, his houses, barns, mills and distillery were destroyed

Camp at Detroit, 16th Aug., 1812.

Capitulation for the surrender of Fort Detroit, entered into between Major-General Brock, commanding his Britannic Majesty's forces, on the one part, and Brigadier General Hull, commanding the North-Western army of the United States, on the other part.

1st. Fort Detroit, with all the troops, regulars as well as militia, will be immediately surrendered to the British forces under the command of Major-General Brock, and will be considered prisoners of war, with the exception of such of the militia of the Michigan territory, who have not joined the army.

2d. All public stores, arms, and all public documents, including every thing else of a public nature, will be immediately given up.

3d. Private persons, and property of every description will be respected.

4th. His Excellency, Brigadier-General Hull, having expressed a desire that a detachment from the State of Ohio, on its way to join his army, as well as one sent from Fort Detroit, under the command of Colonel M'Arthur, should be included in the above capitulation, it is accordingly agreed to. It is, however, to be understood, that such part of the Ohio Militia as have not joined the army, will be permitted to return to their homes, on condition that they will not serve during the war; their arms will be delivered up if belonging to the public.

5th. The Garrison will march out at the hour of 12

---

by a marauding party under Colonel Campbell. Notwithstanding his valuable services and losses, his pay and allowances were struck off at the peace. In 1817 he memorialized Earl Bathurst to present his case to the Prince Regent for relief, but I am not aware that he received any compensation for his losses. He received the gold medal for Detroit. On three occasions he was honored by being elected member of the Legislative Assembly for the County of Norfolk-in 1813, 1817 and in 1820. His death was caused by falling over the precipitous bank of the Niagara river between Niagara Falls and Queenston one stormy night at the beginning of May, 1824, his funeral to Stamford cemetery taking place on the 6th. He was married to Theresa Wright on December 21st, 1811. I have not seen any record of the place or date of his birth, or that any of his descendants are living at the present time.

o'clock this day, and the British forces will take immediate possession of the Fort.

J. MACDONELL, Lieut.-Col. militia, P.A.D.C.,

J. B. GLEGG, Major, A.D.C.,

JAMES MILLER, Lieut.-Col. 5th U. S. Infantry,

E. BRUSH,[1] Col. com'g 1st regt. of Michigan Militia,

Approved,

W. HULL, B. Gen'l. Com'g the N. W. Army,

Approved,

ISAAC BROCK, Major-General.

An article supplemental to the articles of Capitulation, concluded at Detroit, the 16th of August, 1812.

It is agreed that the Officers and soldiers of the Ohio Militia and Volunteers shall be permitted to proceed to their respective homes, on this condition, that they are not to serve during the present war, unless they are exchanged.

W. HULL, B. Gen'l. Com'g N. W. Army, U.S.

ISAAC BROCK, Major-General.

An article in addition to the supplemental article of the capitulation, concluded at Detroit, the 16th of August, A.D. 1812.

It is further agreed that the officers and soldiers of the Michigan Militia and Volunteers, under the command of Major Wetherell, shall be placed on the same principles as the Ohio militia and volunteers are placed by the supplemental article of the 16th instant.

W. HULL, B. Gen'l. Com'g N. W. Army, U. S.

ISAAC BROCK, Major-General.

Return of the Ordnance taken in the fort and batteries at Detroit, August 16th, 1812.

Iron Ordnance—nine 24 pounders, eight 12 pounders, five 9 pounders. Brass Ordnance—three 6 pounders, two

---

[1] Colonel Elijah Brush who signed the capitulation was Attorney-General of the North-West Territory, as well as commander of the 1st Regiment of Michigan Militia. In 1802 he married Adelaide Barthe Askin, daughter of Col. John Askin, and was consequently uncle of Major Richardson. Colonel Brush was granted special privileges after the capture of Detroit on the intercession of his Canadian relatives, and, when the fortunes of war inclined to his country after the defeat of Captain Barclay, he had an opportunity to repay this kindness. His letter to Colonel Askin given in the appendix shows how he interceded with Captain Perry for Doctor Richardson.

4 pounders, one 3 pounder, one 8 inch howitzer, one 3½ inch ditto.

Total of Ordnance[1] taken—33.

FELIX TROUGHTON, Lieut. Com. Royal Artillery.

Proclamation by Isaac Brock, Esquire, Major-General commanding His Britannic Majesty's Forces in the Province of Upper Canada, &c.

Whereas the territory of Michigan was this day, by Capitulation, ceded to the Arms of His Britannic Majesty, without any other condition than the protection of private property, and wishing to give an early proof of the moderation and justice of the Government, I do hereby announce to all the inhabitants of the said Territory, that the laws heretofore in existence shall continue in force until His Majesty's pleasure be known, or so long as the peace and safety of the said Territory will admit thereof ; and I do hereby also declare and make known to the said inhabitants, that they shall be protected in the full exercise of their religion, of which all persons both civil and military will take notice, and govern themselves accordingly.

All persons having in their possession, or having any knowledge of, any public property, shall forthwith deliver in the same, or give notice thereof to the officer commanding, or Lieut.-Col. Nichol, who are hereby duly authorised to receive and give proper receipts for the same.

Officers of Militia will be held responsible, that all arms in possession of militia-men be immediately delivered up, and all individuals whatever who have in their possession arms of any kind, will deliver them up without delay.

Given under my hand at Detroit, this 16th day of August, 1812, and in the 52d year of His Majesty's reign.

ISAAC BROCK, Major-General.

---

[1] There is a mistake in this copy of the return of the ordnance. The following is made up from the copy in the Canadian Archives.

Iron Ordnance—Nine 24 pounders, nine 12 pounders, five 9 pounders, four 6 pounders, one 3 9-10 inch howitzer.

Brass Ordnance—Three 6 pounders, two 4 pounders, one 3 pounder, one 8 inch howitzer, one 5½ inch howitzer, three 2 9-10 inch howitzers.

Total, 39.

The 5½ inch howitzer was surrendered at Saratoga by Burgoyne. The 3 pounder was surrendered by Cornwallis at Yorktown.

Four of the 12 pounders were on board the Detroit in the harbor of Fort Erie when it was recaptured by the Americans under Lieut. Jesse D. Elliot and destroyed on the morning of Oct. 9th, 1812.

Explanatory as are the above documents, in relation to the important capitulation of Detroit ; and indicative as they are of the high aspirings of him to whose firmness and decision its fall is alone attributable, the account would be incomplete, were mention not here made of the causes stated to have led to the surrender of so strong a position, by the American Commander. Every particular. relating, not merely to the conquest of Detroit—the first and leading feat performed during the war—but to the Hero, its conqueror, cannot be viewed as being given in any spirit of prolixity. I shall therefore proceed to give, first General Hull's letter of exculpation, addressed to the American Secretary at War ; and secondly a somewhat lengthy document from Colonel Cass, (now the United States Minister at Paris,) highly condemnatory of the conduct of his Chief.

From Brigadier-General Hull to the American Secretary at War.

Fort George, August 26th, 1812.

Sir,—Enclosed are the articles of capitulation, by which the fort of Detroit has been surrendered to Major-General Brock commanding His Britannic Majesty's forces in Upper Canada, and by which the troops have become prisoners of War. My situation, at present, forbids me from detailing the full and particular causes which have led to this unfortunate event. I will, however, generally observe that after the surrender of Michilimackinac, almost every tribe and nation of Indians, excepting a part of the Miamis and Delawares, north from beyond Lake Superior, west from beyond the Mississippi, south from the Ohio and Wabash, and east from every part of Upper Canada, and from all the intermediate country, joined in open hostility, under the British standard, against the army I commanded, contrary to the most solemn assurances of a large portion of them to remain neutral: even the Ottawa chiefs from L'Arbre Croche, who formed the delegation to Washington the last summer, in whose friendship I know you had great confidence, are among the hostile tribes, and several of them distinguished leaders. Among the vast number of chiefs who led the hostile bands, Tecumseh, Marpot, Logan, Walk-in-the-water,

Split-log,[1] &c., are considered the principals. This numerous assemblage of savages, under the entire influence and direction of the British commander, enabled him totally to obstruct the only communication which I had with my country. This communication had been opened from the settlements in the state of Ohio, 200 miles through a wilderness, by the fatigues of the army, which I had marched to the frontier on the river Detroit. The body of the lake being commanded by the British armed ships, and the shores and rivers by gun-boats, the army was totally deprived of all communication by water. On this extensive road it depended for transportation of provisions, military stores, medicine, clothing, and every other supply, on pack-horses—all its operations were successful until its arrival at Detroit, and in a few days it passed into the enemy's country, and all opposition seemed to drop before it. One month it remained in possession of this country, and was fed from its resources. In different directions, detachments penetrated 60 miles in the settled part of the Province and the inhabitants seemed satisfied with the change of situation which appeared to be taking place. The militia from Amherstburg were daily deserting, and the whole country, then under the control of the army, was asking for protection.—The Indians generally, in the first instance, had certainly appeared to be neutralized, and determined to take no part in the contest. The fort of Amherstburg was 18 miles below my encampment. Not a single cannon or mortar was on wheels suitable to carry before this place. I consulted my officers whether it was expedient to make an attempt on it with the bayonet alone, without cannon to make a break in the first instance. The council I called was of the opinion it was not. The greatest industry was exerted in making preparation, and it was not until the 7th of August that two 24 pounders, and three howitzers, were prepared. It was then my intention to have proceeded on the enterprise. While the operations of the army were delayed by these preparations, the clouds of adversity had been for some time, and seemed still thickly to be gathering around me. The surrender of Michilimackinac opened the northern hive of Indians, and they

[1]The Huron chief Split-log and Chief Blackbird who were British allies in 1812 and 1813, went over to the Americans in 1814. Drummond's letter to Prevost, Kingston, May 31st, 1814.

were swarming down in every direction. Reinforcements from Niagara had arrived at Amherstburg, under the command of Col. Procter. The desertion of the militia ceased. Besides the reinforcements that came by water, I received information of a very considerable force under the command of Major Chambers, on the river Le Trench,[1] with four field pieces ; and collecting the militia on his route, evidently destined for Amherstburg. And, in addition to this combination and increase of force, contrary to all my expectations, the Wyandots, Chippewas, Ottawas, Pottawatamies, Munsees, Delawares, &c, with whom I had the most friendly intercourse, at once passed over to Amherstburg, and accepted the tomahawk and scalping knife. There being now a vast number of Indians at the British post, they were sent to the river Huron, Brownstown, and Maguaga to intercept my communication. To open this communication, I detached Major Van Horn of the Ohio volunteers, with 200 men, to proceed as far as the river Raisin, under an expectation he would meet Captain Brush, with 150 men, volunteers from the State of Ohio, and a quantity of provisions for the army. An ambuscade was formed at Brownstown, and Major Van Horn's detachment was defeated, and returned to camp, without effecting the object of the expedition.

In my letter of the 7th instant, you have the particulars of that transaction with a return of the killed and wounded. Under this sudden and unexpected change of things, and having received an express from General Hall, commanding opposite the British shore on the Niagara river, by which it appeared that there was no prospect of any co-operation from that quarter, and the two Senior Officers of the artillery having stated to me an opinion that it would be extremely difficult, if not impossible, to pass the Turkey-river, and river Aux Canard, with the 24 pounders, and that they could not be transported by water as the Queen Charlotte, which carried eighteen 24 pounders lay in the river Detroit above the mouth of the river Aux Canard; and as it appeared indispensably necessary to open the communication to the river Raisin and the Miami, I found myself compelled to suspend the operation against Amherstburg, and concentrate the main force of the army at Detroit. Fully intending at that time, after the communication was opened, to re-

---

[1] Now called Thames.

cross the river, and pursue the object at Amherstburg, and strongly desirous of continuing protection to a very large number of the Inhabitants of Upper Canada, who had voluntarily accepted it under my proclamation, I established a fortress on the banks of the river a little below Detroit, calculated for a garrison of 300 men. On the evening of the 7th, and morning of the 8th instant, the army, excepting the garrison of 200 infantry, and a corps of artillerists, all under the command of Major Denny of the Ohio volunteers, re-crossed the river and encamped at Detroit. In pursuance of the object of opening the communication, on which I considered the existence of the army depending, a detachment of 600 men, under the command of Lieut.-Col. Miller, was immediately ordered. For a particular account of the proceedings of this detachment, and the memorable battle which was fought at Maguaga, which reflects the highest honor on the American arms, I refer you to my letter of the 13th August instant, a duplicate of which is enclosed, marked G. Nothing, however, but honor was acquired by this victory ; and, it is a painful consideration, that the blood of 75 gallant men could only open the communication as far as the points of their bayonets extended. The necessary care of the sick and wounded, and a very severe storm of rain, rendered their return to camp indispensably necessary for their own comfort. Captain Brush with his small detachment, and the provisions being still at the river Raisin, in a situation to be destroyed by the savages, on the 13th instant, in the evening, I permitted Colonels M'Arthur and Cass to select from their regiments 400 of their most effective men, and proceed by an upper route through the woods, which I had sent an express to Captain Brush to take, and had directed the militia of the river Raisin to accompany him as a reinforcement. The force of the enemy continually increasing, and the necessity of opening the communication, and acting on the defensive, becoming more apparent, I had previous to detaching Colonels M'Arthur and Cass on the 11th instant evacuated and destroyed the fort on the opposite bank. On the 13th, in the evening, General Brock arrived at Amherstburg, about the hour Colonels M'Arthur and Cass marched, of which at that time I had received no information. On the 15th I received a summons from him to surrender Fort Detroit of which the paper marked A. is a copy. My answer is marked B. At this time I had received no information from Colonels M'Arthur and Cass. An express was immediately sent, strongly escorted, with orders for them to return. On the 15th as soon as General Brock received my letter his batteries opened on the town and fort, and continued until evening. In the evening, all the British ships of war came nearly as far up the river as Sandwich, three miles below Detroit. At daylight, on the 16th (at which time I had received no information from Colonels M'Arthur and Cass, my expresses, sent the evening before, and in the night, having been prevented from passing by numerous bodies of Indians) the cannonade re-commenced, and in a short time I received information, that the British Army, and Indians, were landing below the Spring-Wells, under the cover of their ships of war.

At this time the whole effective force at my disposal at Detroit did not exceed 800 men. Being new troops, and unaccustomed to camp life; having performed a laborious march; having been engaged in a number of battles and skirmishes, in which many had fallen, and more had received wounds, in addition to which a large number being sick, and unprovided with medicine, and the comforts necessary for their situation, were the general causes by which the strength of the army was thus reduced. The fort at this time was filled with women, children, and the old and decrepit people of the town, and country; they were unsafe in the town, as it was entirely open and exposed to the enemy's batteries. Back of the fort above or below it, there was no safety for them on account of the Indians. In the first instance, the enemy's fire was principally directed against our batteries, towards the close it was directed against the fort alone, and almost every shot and shell had their effect.

It now became necessary either to fight the enemy in the field; collect the whole force in the fort; or propose terms of capitulation. I could not have carried into the field more than 600 men, and left an adequate force in the fort. There were landed at that time of the enemy a regular force of much more than that number, and twice the number of Indians. Considering this great inequality of force, I did not think it expedient to adopt the first measure; the second must have been attended with a great sacrifice of blood, and no possible advantage, because the contest could not have been sustained more than a day for want of powder, and but a very few days for the want of provisions. In addition to this, Colonels M'Arthur and Cass would have been in a most hazardous situation. I feared nothing but the last alternative—I have dared to adopt it—I well know the high responsibility of the measure, and I take the whole of it on myself —it was dictated by a sense of duty, and a full conviction of its expediency. The bands of savages which had then joined the British force, were numerous beyond any former example. Their numbers have since increased, and the history of the barbarians of the north of Europe does not furnish examples of more greedy violence than these savages have exhibited. A large portion of the brave and gallant officers and men I commanded would cheerfully have contested until the last cartridge had been expended, and the bayonets worn to the sockets—I could not consent to the useless sacrifice of such brave men, when I knew it was impossible for me to sustain my situation. It was impossible, in the nature of things that an army could have been furnished with the necessary supplies of provisions, military stores, clothing and comforts for the sick, on pack-horses through a wilderness of 200 miles, filled with hostile savages. It was impossible, sir, that this little army, worn down by fatigue, by sickness, by wounds, and deaths, could have supported itself not only against the collected force of all the Northern Nations of Indians ; but against the united strength of Upper Canada, whose population consists of more than 20 times the number contained in the territory of Michigan, aided by the principal part of the regular forces of the province, and the wealth and influence of the North-West and other trading establishments among the Indians, which have in their employment and under their control more than 2,000 white men. Before I close this despatch, it is a duty I owe my respectable associates in command, Colonels M'Arthur, Findlay, Cass, and Lieutenant-Colonel Miller to express my obligations to them for the prompt and judicious manner they have performed their respective duties. If aught has taken place during the campaign, which is honorable to the army, these Officers are entitled to a large share of it. If the last act should be disapproved, no part of the censure belongs to them. I have likewise to express my obligation to General Taylor, who has performed the duty of quarter-master-general, for his great exertions in procuring every thing in his department, which it was possible to furnish, for the convenience of the army ; likewise to brigade Major Jessup, for the correct and punctual manner in which he has discharged his duty ; and to the army generally for their exertion and the zeal they have manifested for the public interest. The death of Dr. Foster soon after he arrived at Detroit, was a severe misfortune to the army ; it was increased by the capture of the Chachago packet, by which the medicine and hospital stores were lost. He was commencing the best arrangements in the department of which he was the principal, with the very small means he possessed. I was likewise deprived of the necessary services of Captain Partridge by sickness, the only officer of the corps of engineers attached to the army. All the officers and men have gone to their respective homes, excepting the 4th United States regiment, and a small part of the 1st and Captain Dyson's company of Artillery. Captain Dyson's company was left at Amherstburg, and the others are with me prisoners ; they amount to about 340. I have only to solicit an investigation of my conduct, as early as my situation and the state of things will admit ; and to add the further request that the government will not be unmindful of my associates in captivity, and of the families of those brave men who have fallen in the contest.

I have the honor to be very respectfully,
Your Most obedient Servant,
W. HULL, Brig. Gen. Commanding

Hon. W. Eustis, Secretary   N. W. Army, U. S.
of the Department of War.

———

Letter of Col. Cass, of the army late under the command of Brig.-General Wm. Hull to the Secretary of War.

Washington, Sept. 10th, 1812.

SIR,—Having been ordered on to this place by Col. M'Arthur, for the purpose of communicating to the government such particulars respecting the expedition lately commanded by Brig.-Gen. Hull, and its disastrous result, as might enable them correctly to appreciate the conduct of the officers and men, and to develop the causes which produced so foul a stain upon the national character, I have the honor to submit to your consideration the following statement.

When the forces landed in Canada, they landed with an ardent zeal, and stimulated with the hope of conquest. No enemy appeared within view of us, and had an immediate and vigorous attack been made upon Malden, it would doubtless have fallen an easy victory. I knew Gen. Hull, afterwards declared he regretted this attack had not been made, and he had every reason to believe success would have crowned his efforts. The reasons given for delaying operations, was to mount our heavy cannon and to afford to the Canadian militia, time and opportunity to quit an obnoxious service. In the course of two weeks, the number of their militia who were embodied had decreased by desertion from six hundred to one hundred men, and in the course of three weeks, the cannon were mounted, the ammunition, and every preparation made for an immediate investment of the fort. At a council, at which were present all the field officers, and which was held two days before our preparations were completed, it was unanimously agreed to make an immediate attempt to accomplish the object of this expedition. If by waiting two days, we could have the service of our heavy artillery, it was agreed to wait ; if not it was determined to go without it, and to attempt the place by storm. This opinion appeared to correspond with the views of the General, and the day was appointed for commencing our march. He declared to me, that he considered himself pledged to lead the army to Malden. The ammunition was placed in the wagons ; the cannon were embarked on board the floating batteries, and every article was prepared. The spirit and zeal, the order and animation displayed by the officers and men, on learning the near accomplishment of their wishes, were a severe and sacred pledge, that in the hour of trial, they would not be found wanting in duty to their country and themselves. But a change of measures, in opposition to the wishes and opinions of all the officers, was adopted by the General. The plan of attacking Malden was abandoned, and instead of acting offensively, we broke up our camp, evacuated Canada, and re-crossed the river in the night, without even the shadow of an enemy to injure us. We left to the tender mercy of the enemy, the miserable Canadians who had joined us, and the protection we afforded them was but a passport to vengeance. This fatal and unaccountable step dispirited the troops, and destroyed the little confidence which a series of timid, irresolute, and indecisive measures had left in the commanding officer.

About the 10th of August, the enemy received a reinforcement of 400 men. On the 12th, the commanding officers of three of the regiments (the fourth was absent) were informed through a medium which admitted of no doubt, that the General had said, that a capitulation would be necessary. They on the same day addressed to Gov. Meigs, of Ohio, a letter of which the following is an extract.

" Believe all the bearer will tell you. Believe it, however it may astonish you, as much as if told by one of us. Even a c—— is talked of by the ————. The bearer will fill the vacancy."

The doubtful fate of this letter rendered it necessary to use circumspection in its details, and therefore these blanks were left. The word "capitulation" will fill the first and "commanding general" the other. As no enemy was near us, and as the superiority of our force was manifest, we could see no necessity for capitulating, nor any propriety in alluding to it. We therefore determined in the last resort to incur the responsibility of divesting the General of his command. This plan was eventually prevented by two of the commanding officers of regiments being ordered upon detachments.

On the 13th, the British took a position opposite Detroit, and began to throw up works. During that and the two following days, they pursued their object without interruption and established a battery of two 18 pounders, and an 8 inch howitzer. About sunset on the evening of the 14th, a detachment of 350 men from the regiments commanded by Col. M'Arthur and myself, was ordered to march to the river Raisin, to escort the provisions, which had some time remained there, protected by a party under the command of Capt. Brush.

On Saturday the 15th, about one o'clock, a flag of truce arrived from Sandwich, bearing a summons from General Brock, for the surrender of the town and fort of Detroit, stating he could no longer restrain the fury of the savages. To this an immediate and spirited refusal

was returned.   About 4 o'clock their batteries began to
play upon the town.   The fire was returned and continued
without interruption and with little effect until dark.
Their shells were thrown until 11 o'clock.

At daylight the firing on both sides recommenced;
about the same time the enemy began to land troops at
the Spring-Wells, three miles below Detroit, protected by
two of their armed vessels.

Between 6 and 7 o'clock, they had effected their landing and immediately took up their line of march.   They
moved in a close column of platoons, twelve in front,
upon the bank of the river.

The fourth regiment was stationed in the fort; the
Ohio volunteers and a part of the Michigan militia,
behind some pickets, in a situation in which the whole
flank of the enemy would have been exposed.   The
residue of the Michigan militia were in the upper part of
the town to resist the incursions of the savages.   Two 24
pounders loaded with grape shot, were posted upon a
commanding eminence, ready to sweep the advancing
column.   In this situation, the superiority of our position
was apparent, and our troops in the eager expectation of
victory, awaited the approach of the enemy.   Not a
sigh of discontent broke upon the ear; not a look of
cowardice met the eye.   Every man expected a proud
day for his country, and each was anxious that his individual exertion should contribute to the general result.

When the head of their column arrived within about 500
yards of our line, orders were received from Gen. Hull
for the whole to retreat to the fort, and for the 24
pounders not to open upon the enemy.   One universal
burst of indignation was apparent upon the receipt of
this order.   Those whose conviction was the deliberate
result of a dispassionate examination of passing events,
saw the folly and impropriety of crowding 1,100 men into
a little work, which 300 men could fully man, and into
which the shot and shells of the enemy were falling.
The fort was in this manner filled; the men were directed
to stack their arms, and scarcely was an opportunity
afforded of moving.   Shortly after, a white flag was
hung out upon the walls.   A British officer rode up to
inquire the cause.   A communication passed between the
commanding Generals, which ended in the capitulation
submitted to you.   In entering into this capitulation,

the General took counsel from his own feelings only.
Not an officer was consulted. Not one anticipated a
surrender, till he saw the white flag displayed. Even the
women were indignant at so shameful a degradation of
the American character, and all felt as they should have
felt, but he who held in his hands the reins of authority.

Our morning report had that morning made out effective men present fit for duty 1,060, without including the
detachment before alluded to, and without including 300
of the Michigan militia on duty. About dark on Sunday evening, the detachment sent to escort the provisions,
received orders from General Hull, to return with as
much expedition as possible. About 10 o'clock the next
day, they arrived in sight of Detroit. Had a firing been
heard, or any resistance visible, they would have immediately advanced and attacked the rear of the enemy.
The situation in which this detachment was placed,
although the result of accident, was the best for
annoying the enemy and cutting off his retreat, that
could have been selected. With his raw troops enclosed
between two fires, and no hopes of succour, it is hazarding
little to say, that very few would have escaped.

I have been informed by Col. Findlay, who saw the
return of their Quarter-Master-General, the day after the
surrender, that their whole force of every description
white, red and black was 1,030. They had 29 platoons,
12 in a platoon, of men dressed in uniform. Many of
these were evidently Canadian Militia. The rest of their
militia increased their white force to about 700 men.

The number of their Indians could not be ascertained
with any degree of precision ; not many were visible.
And in the event of an attack upon the town and fort, it
was a species of force which could have afforded no
material advantage to the enemy.

In endeavoring to appreciate the motives, and to investigate the causes which led to an event so unexpected and
dishonorable, it is impossible to find any solution in the
relative strength of the contending parties, or in the
measures of resistance in our power. That we were far
superior to the enemy ; that upon any ordinary principles
of calculation, we could have defeated them, the wounded
and indignant feelings of every man there will testify.

A few days before the surrender, I was informed by
Gen. Hull, we had 400 rounds of 24 pound shot fixed and

GENERAL LEWIS CASS.

about 100,000 cartridges made. We surrendered with the fort, 40 barrels of powder and 2,500 stand of arms.

The state of our provisions has not been generally understood. On the day of the surrender we had 15 days' provisions of every kind on hand. Of meat there was plenty in the country, and arrangements had been made for purchasing and grinding the flour. It was calculated we could readily procure three month's provisions, independent of 150 barrels of flour, 1,300 head of cattle which had been forwarded from the State of Ohio, and which remained at the river Raisin under Captain Brush, within reach of the army.

But had we been totally destitute of provisions, our duty and our interest undoubtedly was to fight. The enemy invited us to meet him in the field.

By defeating him, the whole country would have been open to us, and the object of our expedition gloriously and successfully obtained. If we had been defeated we had nothing to do but to retreat to the fort, and make the best defence which circumstances and our situation rendered practicable. But basely to surrender without firing a gun—tamely to submit without raising a bayonet—disgracefully to pass in review before an enemy as inferior in the quality as in the number of his forces, were circumstances, which excited feelings of indignation more easily felt than described. To see the whole of our men flushed with the hope of victory, eagerly awaiting the approaching contest, to see them afterwards dispirited, hopeless, and desponding, at least 500 shedding tears because they were not allowed to meet their country's foe and to fight their country's battles, excited sensations which no American has ever before had cause to feel, and which, I trust in God, will never again be felt while one man remains to defend the standard of the union.

I am expressly authorized to state, that Col. M'Arthur, Col. Finlay and Lieut.-Col. Miller, viewed this transaction in the light which I do. They know and feel, that no circumstance in our situation—none in that of the enemy, can excuse a Capitulation so dishonorable and unjustifiable. This too is the universal sentiment among the troops : and I shall be surprised to learn, that there is one man, who thinks it was necessary to sheath his sword, or lay down his musket.

I was informed by General Hull, the morning after the

Capitulation, that the British forces consisted of 1,800 regulars and that he surrendered to prevent the effusion of human blood. That he magnified their regular force nearly five-fold, there can be no doubt. Whether the philanthropic reason assigned by him is a sufficient justification for surrendering a fortified town, an army and a territory, is for the government to determine.

Confident I am, that had the courage and conduct of the General been equal to the spirit and zeal of the troops, the event would have been as brilliant and successful, as it now is disastrous and dishonorable.

Very respectfully, Sir, I have the honor to be, your most obedient Servant,

Lewis Cass, Col. 3rd Regt. Ohio volunteers.
The Hon. Wm. Eustis,
    Secretary of War.

Although it does not come strictly within the object of this narrative to comment upon the statements of the enemy, it should not be concealed that the apprehension, entertained by General Hull, of the increased danger to his troops, and to the comparatively defenceless town of Detroit, arising from the expected arrival of reinforcements of Indians from the West, was in a great degree well founded, and it was well known at the time, (although a sentiment of shame at the yielding up of a post of such strength as Detroit, has since repudiated the measure,) that this was a sentiment by no means confined to General Hull. Mr. Robert Dickson, a gentleman to whom long intercourse with the Indians had imparted a knowledge of their character, and influence over their minds, which proved highly beneficial to the British cause, was then actively engaged in collecting some of the most warlike tribes; while the present Colonel Askin of London, at that time in the Indian Department, was already within a few days' journey of Detroit, with a body of 270 Indian Warriors, under their Chief Big-gun. This little detachment had set out expressly for the relief of Amherstburg, and, on its passage down in birch canoes, encountered much peril and difficulty, having had to cross Saginaw Bay, nearly fifty miles in extent, and for many hours, in their frail barks, even out of sight of the land.   Such was the celerity of their movements, that they reached Amherstburg in the remarkably short period of six days from their departure from Michilimackinac, and about the same lapse of time from the surrender of Detroit.   Thus it will appear, that General Hull was only wrong in as far as related to the actual position of the Indian reinforcements, on their way from the far West.   Whether, however, this was an excuse for the abandonment of his strong post, without an effort in its defence, is a point of discussion which this narrative does not profess to entertain.   Notwithstanding there are two strong features of dissimilarity between the letters of General Hull and Colonel Cass, to which it is impossible not to refer—namely the eagerness of the one to diminish his own force, and increase that of his adversary—and the not less evident desire of the other to show that, not only in the quantity, but the quality of his troops—in resources, and in means of defence of all kinds, the American General had decidedly the advantage.   In truth, without absolutely adopting the opinion of Col. Cass, as expressed in regard to the inferiority of the British troops engaged on this occasion, the question which suggests itself on reading General Hull's Official declaration, that he had not more than 800 men on the day when General Brock appeared before Detroit naturally is— where were the 2,300 men who had been marched, little more than a month previously, through the State of Michigan, and the sound of whose drums, heard from Brownstown, as they passed through that village, was the first intimation the little garrison of Amherstburg had of the proximity of so formidable a force?   True, 400 men had been detached under Colonel Cass, (those, as it has been seen, were included in the capitulation) but where were the remainder?   Not one hundred suffered at Maguaga.   Certainly not fifty during the whole

of the skirmishing at the Canard ; nor had the defeat of
Major Van Horne cost the Americans more than five and
twenty men—in all, at the very utmost, 200. Here then
was a decrease of 600 men, leaving under the immediate
orders of the American General, 1,700 men ,exclusive of
the troops composing the garrison of Detroit[1] on his arrival, and the Michigan militia. General Hull alludes
to his crowded hospitals. Did these contain, or had he
on his sick list, 900 men ? Impossible. These strictures
are necessary, because the gallant 41st and the equally
gallant and patriotic volunteers who followed General
Brock to the theatre of action, cannot submit to be deprived of the glory which was theirs, under their dis-

---

[1]In 1694 Antoine de la Motte Cadillac, an enthusiastic young
French officer, was rewarded by Frontenac, the Governor of New
France, for his services in Acadia by being appointed to the command of Michilimackinac. He had passed through the Detroit
river, and his quick eye saw its advantages as a site for a new post
to command the trade of the west. When on a visit to France
after his five years of command at Michilimackinac he represented
to Count Pontchartrain, the Colonial Minister, the importance of
building a new post on the Detroit. He was successful in his rep-
resentations, and was given a grant of fifteen acres square of land
anywhere on the Detroit and the commission of Commandant. In
1701 he built a stockade fort containing about three acres, with
log blockhouses at the corners, and named it Fort Pontchartrain
after his patron. Three years afterwards the Indians made an unsuccessful attempt to burn it. In Nov., 1760, Major Robert Rogers
received its surrender to Great Britain. Pontiac besieged it in
1763, and after nearly fifteen months of weary but stubborn resistance the British were relieved. The story of this siege is told in
the novel of "Wacousta" by Major Richardson. In the Fall of
1778 a new fort was laid out some distance farther from the river
than the old stockade fort by Captain Henry Bird, and named
Fort Lernoult after Major Lernoult of the 8th (King's) Regiment,
the officer in command there. It was evacuated by the British in
1796, and the guns and garrison transferred to Fort Amherstburg,
a new fort in the township of Malden on the Canadian side of the
river, eighteen miles farther south. From its evacuation in 1796,
until Procter's retreat in 1813, it appears to have been referred to
simply as Fort Detroit, a name by which it was known when captured by Brock on August 16th, 1812. In the Canadian Archives
a plan of this Fort is given as repaired in 1812, and it is called
"Fort L'Arnaud," evidently an attempt to revive the original
name by someone who knew the sound but not the correct orthog-
raphy of Fort Lernoult. When taken possession of by Gen.
Harrison it was called Fort Shelby in honor of the governor of

tinguished leader, on the occasion of the capture of Detroit. They believed, and with every reason (for they
knew not of the departure of Col. Cass, for the River
Raisin) that they were marching to the conquest of a
post which was defended by at least two thousand men—
and they have an undeniable right to impugn a statement
which, incorrectly and for a sinister purpose, reduces that
force, on paper, by two-thirds of the amount.   Honor to
whom honor is due.

In the capture of Detroit, General Brock has been termed
the saviour of Canada, and most deservedly so.   Had
he not struck the blow he did, and at the time he did, at
the American power in the West, Upper Canada—nay
both the Canadas must have been yielded to the triumphant arms of the United States.   At this period the whole
force of the Province consisted of four Regiments of the

Kentucky, who accompanied Harrison in his victorious campaign.
In 1826 it was given to the city of Detroit, and in the Spring of
1827, the embankments were taken away, the ground levelled and
streets continued over its site.

Major James Dalliba, at the trial of Gen. Hull, gave the following description of the Fort at the time of its surrender in 1812.

"The fort lies on the highest ground in a circumference of
three miles, was a regular half bastion fort, composed of 4 curtains
and 4 half bastions, about 100 yards on each face, not including
the half bastions ; about 75 yards being the extreme length of the
curtain—that the fort was made partly of earth—the parapet
eleven feet in elevation—the thickness of the top of the parapet
about 12 feet, the banquet for Infantry six feet from the foundation or level of the fort, and five feet from the parapet—the
whole width of the rampart at its base 26 feet—at the bottom of the
exterior or slope of the parapet there was a horizontal space of
ground about 2 or 3 feet in width, extending around the whole circumference of the work, the ditch upon an average was from five
to six feet deep, and at the bottom 12 feet wide, beyond the exterior or slope of the ditch anscope, or glacis or esplanade.   There
was formerly a covert way, of which traces were remaining unhurt.
In the bottom of the ditch around the fort there was a row of
pickets of cedar, nearly new, (12) in. diameter and 11 or 12 feet high;
these pickets were fastened together by a rib—The gate was
strongly made of plank with spikes ; over the gate was a look out
house, also strongly built in the fall of 1811—cannon were
mounted in the embrazures, most of which were repaired and put
in good order in 1811, and the fort was, generally, in good order
and in good repair.''

line, namely, the 8th, 41st, 49th, and 100th and, added to
these, the Canadian and Glengarry Fencibles, and a few
companies of Veterans, and of the Royal Newfoundland
Regiment. So insignificant a force could have availed
little against the hordes of American irregular troops
which would have been poured in from the west, along
the Delaware and Burlington routes, and which moving
in rear of the centre and left divisions, must necessarily
have cut off their communication with the interior of the
country, and so straitened their supplies as to have rendered them an eventual conquest. That General Hull
would have recovered from the temporary panic, which
seems to have induced his relinquishment of his position
at Sandwich there can be no manner of doubt ; but even
if he had not done so, and reduced Amherstburg, which was
of vital importance to the American interests, there were
other leaders, and other armies, already on their way to
reinforce him, and the subjugation of the Western District must, on their arrival, have been assured. What
then would have been the result ? Half of the Indians,
already bearing arms on our side, would either have seceded
from a cause which they conceived us too helpless to defend,
or have joined the American flag, while those who were
undecided which party to join, would have thrown their
influence and numbers into the opposite ranks. As General Hull has truly enough stated in his official letter,
most of the Militia of the District—particularly the French
Canadian portion of the population, were daily thinning
our ranks, by returning to their homes, and it required
but some strong and effective demonstration, on the part
of the enemy, to have left the regular troops in the West
to their own unaided exertions. Fortunately it was fated
to be otherwise. General Brock, with that keenness of
perception, and promptitude of action, which was so eminently characteristic of his brief but glorious career, at
once saw the danger, and flew to meet and avert it. He

well knew that, on the destruction or discomfiture of the North Western Army, depended the safety of the Province committed to his charge, and the enterprise, which he himself has termed hazardous, was perilled only after profound reflection and conviction. He justly entertained the belief that while, on the one hand, the slightest delay and incertitude of action, would be fatal to the interests of Great Britain inasmuch as it must have a tendency to discourage, not only the inhabitants of the Province, but our Indian allies, there was, on the other, every probability that an immediate and vigorous attack, upon an enemy, who had already lost so much time in inactivity, and who had abandoned so many advantages, would be crowned with success. It was a bold—an almost dangerous measure ; but the danger of the country was greater, and he resolved to try the issue. He succeeded; from that hour Canada was saved.

Independently of "400 rounds of 24 pound shot, already fixed : about 100,000 cartridges made up : 40 barrels of powder : and 2,500 stand of arms," which had been admitted by General Hull, to Colonel Cass, to have been in the fort on the day of the surrender, there was also a quantity of camp equipage such as tents, waggons, entrenching tools, etc., and moreover in the harbour, a very fine brig, the Adams, then unarmed, but hitherto employed in the transport of stores for the use of the garrison of Detroit. With this vessel a very gallant affair was connected, only a few days after the capitulation. Agreeable to the terms of this, the irregular forces of General Hull were transported by water to Buffalo, there to be disembarked preparatory to their return into their native State, Ohio, while the regular troops, principally the 4th U.S. Infantry, were landed at Fort Erie, with a view of being marched on, as prisoners of war, to Lower Canada.

The armed vessels already named, as having covered

our landing, on the 16th, were put in requisition for this
service, and to these were added the Adams (re-named
the Detroit) and the Caledonia, a fine merchant brig, the
property of Angus MacIntosh, Esquire, of Moy, a few
miles above Windsor.   I do not recollect who was appointed to the command of the Detroit, [1] but the Caledonia
had her own Captain—Mr. Irvine, a young Scotchman of
a peculiarly retiring and amiable disposition and gentlemanly manners, yet endowed with great firmness and
resolution of character.   These two vessels, having
reached their destination for landing the prisoners, were
then lying, wholly unprotected and unsuspicious of danger, in the harbour of (Fort) Erie when, one dark night, they
found themselves assailed by two large boats, filled with
American sailors and troops which had dropped alongside
without being perceived, until it was too late for anything like effectual resistance.   The Detroit was almost
immediately carried, but the young Captain of the Caledonia, which lay a little below her, aroused from his bed

---

[1] The commander of the Detroit on this occasion was Lieutenant
Frederic Rolette, who was born in Quebec in 1783.   At an early
age he enlisted in the British navy, and soon had the honor of
taking part in the two greatest naval battles ever fought, and
under the most illustrious naval officer that ever lived.   At the
Battle of the Nile he received five wounds, and was present at
Trafalgar, where the combined naval power of France and Spain
was annihilated by Nelson.   Soon after this he returned home,
and was appointed a second Lieutenant in the Provincial Marine
on Oct. 4th, 1807, and on April 25th, 1812, was promoted to a first
Lieutenantcy and given command of the brig Hunter on Lake
Erie.   On July 1st, 1812, Gen. Hull put his sick, the officers' baggage and some supplies on board of the Cayahoga or Cayuga
Packet at the rapids of the Miami to be taken to Detroit, but on
passing up the Detroit river this vessel was captured by Lieut.
Rolette on the 3rd of July.   At the battle of the river Raisin,
when the marines acted with land forces, Lieut. Rolette was
wounded on the head.   Robert Reynolds, of Amherstburg, who
was Deputy Assistant-Commissary General, says Rolette's life was
saved by a thick handkerchief tied around his head for the head-
ache.   He was second officer of the Lady Prevost, one of the vessels of Captain Barclay's fleet that was defeated on Sept. 10th,
1813, by the fleet of Captain Perry.   Taken prisoner on this occasion, he remained in captivity till the fall of 1814.   At the close of
the war he was presented with a sword by the people of his native
city.   He died at Quebec on the 17th of March, 1831.

by the confusion on board his consort, prepared for a vigorous, although almost entirely personal, resistance.
Hastily arming himself, and calling on his little and in-
experienced crew (scarcely exceeding a dozen men) to do
the same, he threw himself in the gangway, and discharged a loaded blunderbuss into the first advancing
boat, now dropping from the re-captured Detroit to board
the Caledonia. The enemy were staggered, but still they
pursued their object, and Mr. Irvine had barely time to
discharge a second blunderbuss into the same boat, when
he was felled to the deck by a cutlass-stroke from one of
the crew of the second party which had boarded him on
the opposite gangway. The Caledonia was then secured
by her captors, but the Detroit, having grounded, was destroyed.

The intrepidity and self-devotion of Mr. Irvine, whose
single arm it appeared, had killed and wounded no less
than seven of his assailants, met with that reward it so
richly merited. The heads of the Naval Department,
anxious to secure so gallant an Officer to the service,
tendered to him on his exchange, which took place
shortly after, the commission of a Lieutenant in the Provincial Navy, in which capacity he continued to serve
during the whole of the naval operations connected with
the Right Division. But I shall have occasion again to
refer to the gallant bearing of Mr. Irvine.

The surprise of the Detroit and Caledonia was considered by the Americans, at that time, a very brilliant feat,
and contributed in some degree to dissipate the gloom
which the surrender of General Hull and his army had
occasioned. But without in the slightest way seeking to
impeach the American character for bravery, it is impossible to look on the exploit in the light in which they
would have it considered. Both vessels having been
simply employed in cartel service, were without other
than the commonest means of defence peculiar to mer-

chantmen, while their crews were not only weak in number, but composed of a class of men—French Canadian sailors and voyageurs—who were ill-qualified to compete with two full boat-loads of practised and resolute American sailors and soldiers. Moreover both vessels lay in perfect security, and utter absence of preparation. They did not conceive it necessary to be on the alert, because they imagined that the present pacific character in which they appeared, would have shielded them from all hostile attempt. At the moment of the surprise, both vessels had on board the prisoners with whom they had left the fort of Detroit for the purpose of being landed at Buffalo. However inclined to aggression, the Americans were not justified in violating the sanctity of the flag which, of course, continued to float as long as there were American prisoners on board, remaining to be landed. It is true, it must be admitted that an unusual feeling of exasperation had been induced by the surrender of General Hull and his army, for when the 4th Regiment, with the other broken corps of the American line, were marched from Fort Erie, where they had been landed from the Queen Charlotte, on their route for the Lower Province, and escorted only by a portion of the detachment which had joined us at Maguaga, they were fired upon by stragglers from the masses of men who were seen lining the opposite banks of the Niagara river, remarking with evident displeasure the march of the captured troops, and thus giving vent to their indignation.

An accident, at one time promising results far more serious than any which could spring from the capture of the vessels just named, occurred about the same period. General Brock, anxious to assume the offensive on the Niagara frontier, lost not a moment in returning across the lake, ordering down at the same time, not only the Toronto Militia, but those troops of the 41st, who had preceded and accompanied him to Detroit. The

Queen Charlotte, principally laden with the regulars of the captured army, had sailed on the very evening of the surrender, and General Brock the next day embarked in a very small trading schooner, on board which were about 70 Ohio Riflemen, guarded by a small party of militia rifles, which composed a portion of the volunteers from Toronto. During the passage none of the guard were on any account permitted to go below, either by day or by night, and not more than half a dozen Americans were allowed to be upon deck at the same time—the hatches being secured above the remainder. It was a duty of some fatigue, and requiring the exercise of the utmost vigilance on the part of the little guard. One morning, about day break, when by their reckoning they judged they were close to the harbor of Fort Erie, they found themselves suddenly becalmed, and in the midst of a fog which had commenced during the night. As the sun rose the fog began to disperse, but the calm prevailed, and gradually, as the wreathing mists rolled upward, the guard discovered, to their dismay, that they were close upon the American shore near Buffalo. The danger was imminent, for a number of persons were already assembled, evidently at a loss to discover to what flag the vessel belonged, and wondering what had brought her into a position entirely out of the usual course of navigation. In this emergency, the officer commanding the watch (Lieut. Jarvis, now Superintendent of Indian affairs) hastened below to acquaint General Brock, who was lying on his bed, with the danger which threatened the vessel, which it was impossible, by reason of the calm, to get farther from the shore. General Brock immediately sprang to his feet, and rushing upon deck, saw the situation of the vessel was precisely what has been described. He was extremely angry, and turning to the master of the schooner, said, "You scoundrel, you have betrayed me, let but one shot be fired from the shore and (pointing to it) I will run you up on the instant to that yard-arm." The master, though innocent of all design, was greatly alarmed by the stern threat of the General, and as the only possible means of extricating the vessel from her perilous situation, ordered several of his crew into a small punt, attached to her stern, the only boat belonging to her. In this they attempted to tow her, but made so little progress that one of the guard asked permission of the General to discharge his rifle, in order to attract the attention of the Queen Charlotte, then lying at anchor between point Abino and Fort Erie, to a signal which had been previously hoisted. Apprehensive that the shot might not be heard by their friends, while it might be the means of informing the enemy of their true character, General Brock at first refused his sanction, but as the man seemed confident that the report of his rifle would reach the other shore, he finally assented, and the shot was fired. Soon afterwards the answering signal was run up to the masthead of the Queen Charlotte, and that vessel, seeing the doubtful situation of the schooner, on board which however they were not aware the General had embarked, immediately weighed her anchor, and standing over to the American shore, under a slight breeze which was then beginning to rise hastened to cover the little bark with her battery. Taking her in tow she brought her safely into the harbour of (Fort) Erie, greatly to the joy of those who, aware of the invaluable freight with which the schooner was charged, had, on the weighing of the Queen Charlotte's anchor, entertained the utmost apprehension for the safety of the becalmed vessel, and watched with deep interest the vain attempts of her crew to bring her off.

V

EXPEDITION TO FORT WAYNE

The fall of Detroit having secured the tranquillity of Amherstburg and its contiguous districts, an expedition was projected into the interior of the enemy's country, the object of which was the destruction of Fort Wayne, a post distant several hundred miles, and serving as a depot for stores, from which the various troops of the enemy, pushed forward to the frontier, were supplied. The garrison, according to the intelligence received was closely invested, by the Indians, and consisted merely of a few hundred men, and a few pieces of cannon indifferently mounted. Towards the close of September, a small detachment of troops, a howitzer, and two field pieces, under the command of Brevet Major Muir, were embarked in boats, and proceeded across the lake to the Miami village, situated about fifteen miles beyond the entrance of the river of the same name. Being there joined by the body of Indians destined to form a part of the expedition, the detachment continued its route by land, and along a tract of country bearing no mark of civilization whatever. Our only covering was the canopy of Heaven or rather the arches formed by the intermingling boughs of the forest through which we moved, and not even the wigwam of the savage arose to diversify the monotony of the scene. The difficulty of conveying the guns by land caused their transportation to be a work of much time ; and the river from the point where we had disembarked, was so extremely low as to render the progress of the boats, following the sinuosities of its course, tedious to the last degree. Having at length, after much toil, gained that part of the Miami, where it was intended to disembark the stores, every obstacle appeared to be removed, and the capture of Fort Wayne, then at no great distance, an event looked forward to with confidence. Fate, however, had ordained otherwise. About nine o'clock on the evening of our arrival, the shrill cry of our scouts was heard echoing throughout the forest, and soon afterwards seven Indians issued from the wood on the opposite shore, and, leaping through the river, reached our encampment with the scalps of several Americans. The account they gave of their adventure was to the following effect. At a distance of a few leagues, while advancing cautiously along the road, they observed a party, five in number, in a glen, and seated round a large fire, where they were busily occupied in preparing their food. After a slight consultation they proceeded towards the group, and had approached within a few paces before they were perceived by the Americans, who instantly flew to their arms, and assumed a posture of defence. The Indians, however, held out their hands in token of amity, and were suffered to enter the circle. Here, pretending to be in the American interest, and describing themselves as hunters on their way to one of their villages, they succeeded in lulling the suspicions of the officer, who, in return, communicated to them that the party he commanded were scouts preceding the advanced guard of an army of 2,500 men, then on their march for the Miami village, and only distant a few miles. This disclosure obtained, the Indians, satisfied that they had no time to lose, and throwing off the mask, desired them to deliver up their arms. The astonished party thus entrapped, and unwilling to risk a contest with a superior force, consented to accompany them as their prisoners, but positively refused to relinquish their rifles. They all therefore proceeded in silence towards our encampment, three Indians on each flank of their prisoners, and one in the rear. On the approach of evening, the Americans were again desired to deliver up their rifles, and on refusing to do so, at a signal given by one of the Indians, the whole of his party dropped, one by one, and apparently without premeditation, behind. Each then selected his victim, and four of these unhappy men fell to rise no more. The officer alone, slightly wounded, made an ineffectual attempt to escape, but closely pursued through the intricacies of the forest by two of his foes, he was at length overtaken, and felled to the earth by a blow from a tomahawk. This cruel scene must have taken place at no great distance from our encampment, the shots having been distinctly heard about half an hour before the appearance of the Indians, who, on being questioned, excused their conduct, under the plea of the Americans being nearly equal in numbers to themselves, and obstinately refusing to deliver up their arms—circumstances which rendered their destruction, at the approach of evening, a measure of self-security—especially so, as having been sent in advance four or five days before, they were not aware of our being encamped at so short a distance.

In consequence of the foregoing intelligence, all idea of continuing the expedition against Fort Wayne was abandoned, and the boats were ordered the same evening to descend the river. Major Muir having, however, resolved to await the approach of the enemy, a position was taken up early on the following morning on the heights overlooking the ford at which the Americans were expected to cross. Having passed the whole of the day in the vain expectation of his appearance, it was at length decided on, that the enemy apprised of our vicinity by the view of the bodies of their scouts slain the evening before, had taken a different direction, and instead of traversing the river at the usual ford, had forced their march by a less frequented route on the opposite shore. Such a manœuvre on the part of the American general would necessarily have cut off our retreat, and we must have combated an enemy infinitely superior in numbers, under every disadvantage, in the heart of his own country and, in the event of our boats falling into his hands, destitute of every resource. The detachment was consequently ordered to retire on the old fort of Defiance, situated about half way between the Miama village and the point from whence we commenced our retreat, formerly garrisoned by the British troops, during the celebrated Pontiac war, so fatally waged against us by the confederated tribes of Indians, but then in a state of utter ruin and dilapidation. Having crossed the river at this place, a position was again taken up at a point beyond which the enemy could not effect his passage unperceived. Here, however, we did not long remain. Early on the morning after our arrival, a party of Indians appeared along our line, conducting a prisoner they had found straying in the woods, at a short distance from the enemy's camp. From his account it appeared that the information given by the American officer was perfectly correct. The force of the enemy consisted of 2,500 men, under the command of General Winchester ; and were destined for the Miami, where it was intended to construct a fortification. On arriving at the spot where their slaughtered scouts lay unburied along the road, an alarm was spread throughout their columns, and deeming a numerous enemy to be in their front, it was thought prudent to entrench themselves where they were. For this purpose trees were immediately felled, and in the course of a few hours, with that expedition for which the Western Americans, with whom the axe is almost as indispensable a weapon as the rifle, are remarkable, an enclosure with interstices for musquetry, and sufficiently large to contain their whole force, together with their baggage and waggons, was completed. It being evident from this intelligence, that the object of our enterprise was entirely frustrated, and that an attack on the enemy's entrenchment with our feeble force, if unsuccessful, must necessarily compromise the safety of our own posts, Major Muir decided on returning to Amherstburg, which fortress the detachment at length reached after a fruitless absence of three weeks.

Although little or no mention has ever been made of our retreat from Fort Wayne, before so overwhelming a force as that which we so unexpectedly encountered, and by which we ought to have been annihilated, the utmost praise is due to Major Muir for having accomplished it, not only without the loss of a man of his detachment, but even without the abandonment of any of his guns or stores, which, as has already been stated, were being transported with great toil and difficulty. Every thing was brought off, and at no one moment was our march precipitate. Indeed, of the bold front assumed by the detachment, some idea may be formed from the following brief accounts which appeared in the American papers, even during the time we were retiring upon Amherstburg.

Chillicothe, Oct. 6th, 1812.

Col. James Dunlop, who returned last evening from St. Mary's, reports that an express arrived from that place to General Harrison from General Winchester, urging him to repair immediately to Fort Defiance. That Harrison marched with all expedition at the head of 2,500 or 3,000 mounted rifles. The express stated that General Winchester was at or near Fort Defiance, with about 3,000 Ohio and Kentucky volunteers, and that a body of Indians and British amounting to 2,000 or 3,000 with six pieces of Artillery, lay encamped about three miles from him. Winchester was hourly expecting an attack.

Chillicothe, October 7th, 1812.

The vanguard of the North Western army, under General Winchester, arrived some days ago at Isidonia from Fort Defiance. It was composed of Payne's Brigade of Kentucky Volunteers, Gerrard's troop of Dragoons, and about 400 of the 17th Regiment of regulars.

They advanced to within three miles of Fort Defiance (on which we had retired) and there found 3,000 British and Indians with six pieces of artillery who had fortified themselves in the Fort. Winchester also fortified his camp and waited for reinforcements.

Now as I was on this, as well as every other expedition undertaken by the Right Division, during its military existence, I can, from my own personal knowledge, aver that there were not more than 150 regular troops of every description, (principally the 41st) and the same number of militia, composing the detachment under Major Muir, on this occasion. My impression—and it is a very strong one—is that it did not exceed two-thirds of that number, but as, unfortunately, all official papers connected with the Regiment were lost at the Moravian-town, it has been utterly impossible to ascertain the correct embarkation return of the troops employed on this, as well as on various other similar occasions. If I admit 300 men, I do so, not from a belief that there was so many, but from an apprehension of underrating our actual strength. Our Indian force did not exceed 500 men, and our artillery, as has been stated, consisted of one small howitzer—(the calibre I forget) – and two three-pounders. We did not fortify ourselves in Fort Defiance, but occupied it one day, during the greater part of which we continued on the skirt of the surrounding wood, provoking the enemy to attack us, by the occasional advance and retreat of the Indians. Three days, at different periods, during the time it took us to retire, covering our guns and stores, we halted and formed, in order to give the enemy time to come up, and of the position we had assumed on the very last day, after crossing the Miami at the ford near the Rapids, some idea may be formed, from the following extracts from a report from General Tupper, who commanded the Kentucky riflemen of General Winchester's Division.

General Tupper to General Harrison,
Urbana, Oct. 12th, 1812.

SIR,—On receiving your order of the 4th inst., to proceed to the Rapids, with the whole force of mounted men under my command, whose horses were in a condition to perform the service ; I caused an examination to be immediately had, and found that there still remained 960 men, including officers, in a condition to march, including also Captain Bacon's and one other company which left us the morning following.

*   *   *   *   *   *

I ordered returns to be made so that each man should be furnished with 12 rounds ; this return amounted to 4,500 cartridges for the musket men, exclusive of Major Roper's battalion ; the ammunition of the riflemen having received very little damage. Quarter-Master Bassay called on the Quarter-Master in General Winchester's camp, and returned without a supply. About one o'clock this day, a man belonging to Captain Manary's company of Rangers, was killed and scalped across the Miami, within two hundred yards of our camp. I gave immediate orders to arm, and in five minutes, to horse, but owing to our being compelled to confine our horses during the night, and graze them by day, for want of forage, the greater part, at this moment, were under keepers, nearly one mile from camp up the Auglaise. In the meantime I permitted Major Brush to cross over with about 50 foot, to examine the bank, and see in what direction the Indians had retired, but before he reached the opposite shore, every horseman whose horse was in camp, was mounted to follow over. It was in vain that I made an attempt to keep them back, till they were formed—they broke off in numbers from 20 to 30, mostly without their officers and crossed the woods in every direction ; a party of 15 fell upon the trail of the Indians, and at 7 or 8 miles distance, overtook them, but finding them halted and formed, our men, without waiting for a discharge from the enemy, returned to camp.

*   *   *   *   *   *

When it was found that General Winchester had suspended me in the command, the whole force from Ohio broke off, crossed the Auglaise, and refused to march as directed by General Winchester.

With the then remaining force I proceeded to this

place, where I directed Col. Findlay and Major Roper to discharge such men as had continued to their duty.

Thus, Sir, has terminated an expedition, at one time capable of tearing the British flag from the walls of Detroit, wherein our troops might have returned, with the pleasing reflection of having done their country an essential service.

It is a duty, Sir, I owe to the officers of the Kentucky force, to Colonel Findlay and the officers of the first Battalion, to say that they were zealous in pressing forward the expedition ; while the officers of the second Battalion, commanded by Major Taylor, with a few exceptions, were shrinking from their duty, and shamefully deserting the cause of their country.

The detachment of Colonel Simral's Regiment from our force, stands prominent among the causes of our failure ; already was there panic in some parts of our camp ; the enemy that had retired at General Winchester's approach, had been greatly magnified. The day succeeding the alarm, he drew in one wing of his lines, and strengthened his camp with a breastwork— even this circumstance was noticed and urged as an evidence that he apprehended a force superior to his own. Thus, when imaginary obstacles unite with those that are real, to oppose the movements of a force so insubordinate, as that every man's will is his law, little can be expected by the officers, but a plentiful harvest of mortification and disgrace.

At the period of this expedition, to my young and unpractised military eye, the movements of our little force had appeared scarcely worthy of remark, because we had had no actual fighting, but, of later years, and particularly after having had access to the American accounts of our retreat, my impression of its extreme military tact and judiciousness has been greatly increased. In truth it is the only affair during the whole of the War of 1812, in which anything approaching to manœuvre was displayed, for the simple reason that no other opportunity had ever been afforded. Here however was a ten days' retreat, conducted by the leader of a handful of men, before a vastly superior force of the enemy, to whom battle had been offered on three several occasions during that period, and that in a manner to reflect a credit upon the gallant Major Muir, which should not be lost sight of by the future historian of this country.

James, in his History of the War, despatches the subject of Fort Wayne in a very summary manner. He states that it was contemplated to send an expedition against it, but that the idea was abandoned in consequence of General Brock having communicated to Colonel Procter at Amherstburg, information of the armistice which had been concluded with General Dearborn, by Sir George Prevost, expressing at the same time a desire, that although the armistice did not extend to General Hull's recent command, the Indians should be restrained as much as possible, from the commission of any act of hostility. Now, not only, as it is seen, was the idea not abandoned, but the expedition had penetrated a greater distance (nearly two hundred miles) into the enemy's country, and were longer absent from the garrison, than any other that subsequently left the harbor of Amherstburg.

A day or two before our return from this long and tedious expedition, we saw the prisoner who had been taken by the Indians, soon after we commenced our retrograde movement. He had been with the person alluded to in General Tupper's report to General Harrison, as having been killed and scalped within two hundred yards of their encampment, and to avenge whose death the Kentucky mounted riflemen had evinced so much fruitless alacrity. The captive was already adopted in that tribe of Indians, to which his captors belonged, and was habited after their manner. His head was partly shaved, and covered with a handkerchief, rolled in the form of a turban. His face was painted several colors, and so complete was the metamorphosis, that but for the whiteness of skin visible through several parts of his dress, it would have been difficult to distinguish him from those by whom he was surrounded. At the moment we saw him, he was seated in a tent, sharing the evening meal of his new countrymen, with much appetite and unconcern. He expressed himself as being quite reconciled to his new condition, and spoke with warmth of the kind treatment he had received ; nor did he seem to attach much consequence to the assurance given him that every exertion would be made on our return to obtain his liberation. We saw him some weeks later at Amherstburg; and strange as it may appear, he assured us that he preferred the idle life he had led among the Indians, to a repetition of active service in the American army.

About this period Mr. Robert Dickson arrived at Amherstburg with a number of canoes, filled with warriors of the fiercest character and appearance. Among the most remarkable of these tribes were the Sawkies,[1] a race of men, whose towering height, athletic forms, and nobleness of feature, might recall the idea of the Romans in the earlier stages of their barbarity ; and another tribe whose Indian name I do not recollect, but who were known among ourselves by their assumed appellation of *devoted men*. The costume of the latter was a dress of white leather, extremely pliant, and curiously embroidered with the stained quills of the porcupine, in the preparation of which the natives evince much taste and ingenuity. They were few in number, and, professing to hold death in derision, were looked upon by the other warriors much in the same light that we regard our forlorn hope, the post of danger being reserved for them. One of their chiefs having been invited to breakfast with several officers of the garrison, was at much pains, in the course of the meal, to impress upon the minds of his hosts the particular virtues of his tribe; and in order to demonstrate more fully the extent to which they carried their disregard of pain or death, drew a sharp knife from its sheath,

---

[1] Sacs or Sauks from the vicinity of the Sac River, Missouri.

and, having cut a piece of flesh out of one of his thighs, threw it contemptuously away, exclaiming that "he gave it to the dogs."

The arrival of this reinforcement increased our Indian force to about three thousand warriors. The small detachment of the 41st Regiment not 300 strong, and a company of the Newfoundland Fencibles, composed the whole of our regular force. The latter were, however, employed as Marines on board the different vessels of war, so that the defence of the two fortresses of Detroit and Amherstburg was entrusted to the 41st alone.

Major Muir's report of the Expedition to Fort Wayne is given in the appendix.

VI

BATTLE OF QUEENSTON HEIGHTS

The month of October was marked by an event of the most melancholy and disastrous nature—the death of the noble Brock, who fell a victim to the daring and intrepidity of his character, and in the performance of a duty which should have been executed by a captain of a company.

On his arrival at Fort George, which he reached in eight days from the surrender of Detroit, the General found, to his great dismay, that an armistice had been entered into and concluded, during his absence, between Sir George Prevost and General Dearborn, Commander-in-Chief of the American Army, so that the whole of his plans of operation were deranged, and instead of carrying the American fort of Niagara by an instant *coup de main* as he had proposed, and which was to have been a preliminary to more extended offensive demonstrations, he found himself compelled to sit quietly down in presence of his enemy, and watch, without being enabled to interrupt them, his unremitting preparations for defence. From this state of supineness and mortification he was only first actively aroused on the early morning of the 13th of October by an alarm given by the sentinel stationed at the point above Fort George, that he had seen and heard firing in the direction of Queenstown. In a few minutes the General was on his horse, and, unattended even by an Aid-de-Camp, galloped onward to Queenstown to ascertain the cause of the alarm. On arriving about half-way to Brown's Point, he was met by Lieut. Jarvis, of Captain Cameron's Flank Company of York Militia, which, with Captain Heward's, was sta-

tioned there. This officer had been on guard at what was called the half-moon battery, about mid-way between Queenstown and Niagara, and observing on the water, opposite to the former place, numerous and rapid flashes of fire-arms, had alarmed the officer commanding the detachment, who immediately ordered the two companies under arms. An officer was at the same time despatched to Queenstown, to obtain information. Scarcely had the men been turned out, when an officer, who had passed their own messenger on the road, arrived from Queenstown with intelligence that the Americans were crossing in force, and an order for the detachment at Brown's Point to march up immediately, and assist in opposing their landing. He was moreover directed to desire that the officer commanding should instantly despatch a messenger to Fort George, to apprize General Brock of the movement of the enemy. Lieut. Jarvis, who happened to be the only person mounted, was ordered on this service, and he had galloped about half-way to Fort George, when he met General Brock, wholly unattended, cantering his charger up the Queenstown road. As the day had begun to dawn, Lieut. Jarvis had no difficulty in recognizing the General, but such was the spirit of his horse that he could not rein him in, but was borne past, shouting out to his Chief to stop, as he had most important news to communicate. But the General was too impatient to reach the scene of danger to delay a moment, and beckoning the officer to follow him, he still continued his course. After the lapse of a few minutes Lieut. Jarvis succeeded in reining in, and wheeling his restive horse, and soon gaining the General's side, communicated his information. Without in the slightest degree abating his speed even for an instant, the General listened, and then gave his orders. These were that Lieutenant Jarvis should go with all speed to Fort George, and order up General Sheaffe with the whole of the reserve. He moreover particularly directed that the Indians, a small party of whom were encamped near Fort George, should be thrown out upon the right, to occupy the woods, during the advance of the reserve to his support.

Scarcely had Lieut. Jarvis lost sight of the General, on his way to execute the order he had received, when he was met by Col. Macdonell, who was following after his Chief, and who, in his hurry to overtake him, had left Fort George without even recollecting that he was unprovided with his sword. Having satisfied himself that the General was not far in advance, he begged Lieut. Jarvis to supply the deficiency, stating at the same time where he would find his own sabre, in his quarters at Fort George, and desiring him to appropriate it to his use for the day. The young officer complied with his request, and hurriedly parted with the gallant Colonel, as he had with the General, for ever.

Having given these brief yet interesting particulars, in regard to the two brave men whose ashes now repose under the same monumental stone, on the heights near which they fell, only a few hours later, it is time to pass to the scene of action to which they were hastening.

The Americans, availing themselves of the armistice entered into by Sir George Prevost, had contrived to push forward a large force to their camp at Lewiston, under General Van Rensselaer, with the view of an invasion of Canada, similar to that of General Hull. Their force was a powerful one, and their plan of operation highly judicious, but fortunately it failed, from want of unanimity and ardor in the irregular portion of their troops. General Van Rensselaer having concerted his mode of attack, caused thirteen boats to be collected in the course of the 12th of October, for the purpose of crossing over his army long before the dawn of the following day. James, who seems to be good authority in this matter, states—

"The embarkation was to have taken place as follows: Col. Van Rensselaer, who commanded, with 300 militia and Lieut.-Col. Chrystie with 300 regulars ; Lieut.-Col. Fenwick and Major Mullany to follow with about 550 regular troops ; and some pieces of flying Artillery ; and then the militia. It was intended that the embarkation of the regulars and militia should be simultaneous, as far as the boats would suffice to receive them ; but having to descend the bank by a narrow path which had been cut out of it, the regular troops got possession of the boats to the exclusion of the militia ; and the latter were ordered to follow in the return boats.

"The only British batteries, from which the troops could be annoyed in the passage, were one, mounting an 18 pounder, upon Queenstown Heights (about half way up), and another mounting a 24-pound carronade, situate a little below the town. The river at Queenstown is scarcely a quarter of a mile in width, and the part chosen for crossing was not fully exposed to either of the British batteries ; while the American batteries of two 18, and two 6 pounders, and the two 6 pounder field pieces, brought up by Lieutenant-Colonel Scott, completely commanded every part of the opposite shore, from which musketry could be effectual in opposing a landing. With these important advantages the troops embarked ; but a grape-shot striking the boat in which Lieutenant-Colonel Chrystie was, and wounding him in the hand, the pilot and the boatmen became so alarmed, that they suffered the boat to fall below the point of landing, and were obliged in consequence to put back. Two other boats did the same. The remaining ten with the 225 regulars, besides officers, including the commander of the detachment, Colonel Van Rensselaer, struck the shore ; and, after disembarking the men, returned for more troops.

"The only force at Queenstown (at the landing of the enemy) consisted of the two flank companies of the 49th Regiment and a small detachment of militia ; amounting in all to about 300 rank and file. Of these about 60, taken from the 49th Grenadiers, and Captain Hatt's company of militia, having in charge a 3 pounder, advanced at four o'clock in the morning, with Captain Dennis of the 49th at their head, towards the river, near to which Colonel Van Rensselaer had formed his men, to await the arrival of the next boats. A well-directed and warmly-continued fire killed and wounded several American officers and privates, including, among the wounded

Colonel Van Rensselaer and three Captains, and drove the Americans close to the water's edge. In the meantime a fresh supply of troops had effected a landing ; and remained with the others sheltered behind the bank ; whence they returned the fire of the British, killing one man, and wounding four. The remaining sub-divisions of the 49th Grenadiers and of the militia company had now joined Captain Dennis[1] ; and the 49th Light Infantry under Captain Williams, with Captain Chisholm's company of militia, stationed on the brow of the hill, were firing down upon the invaders.

"Of five or six boats that attempted to land a body of American regulars under Major Mullany, one was destroyed by a shot from the hill-battery commanded by Lieutenant Crowther of the 41st Regiment ; two others were captured, and the remainder, foiled in their object, returned to the American side. Daylight appeared, and at the same instant General Brock arrived at the hill-battery from Fort George. Observing the strong reinforcements that were crossing over, the General instantly ordered Captain Williams to descend the hill and support Captain Dennis. No sooner were Captain Williams and his men seen to depart, than the Americans formed the resolution of gaining the heights. Accordingly 60 American regulars, headed by Captain Wool, and accompanied by Major Lush, a volunteer, also by a Captain, six Lieutenants and an Ensign of the 13th Regiment, ascended a fisherman's path up the rocks, which had been reported to General Brock as impassable, and therefore was not guarded. The Americans were thus enabled, unseen by our troops, to arrive at a brow, about 30 yards in rear of the hill-battery. Reinforcements kept rapidly arriving by the concealed path ; and the whole formed on the brow, with their front towards the Village of Queenstown.

---

[1] Major-General Sir James Dennis, K.C.B., son of John Dennis, an Attorney, was born 1778. He served in the navy as a midshipman, but afterwards joined the 49th Regt. as an ensign, Sept. 2nd, 1796, and rose by promotion through all the grades to a majority in the same regiment on Dec. 1st, 1812.   On June 4th, 1833, he was appointed Lieut.-Col. of the 3rd Regiment, and commanded a division of Infantry at the battle of Maharajpore on Dec. 29th, 1843. For his gallantry on this occasion he was made a K.C.B. on Oct. 30th, 1844 ; and was promoted to the rank of Major-General, Nov. 11th, 1851.   His death took place at Pall Mall, London, on Jan. 14th, 1855.

From a Silhouette in possession of John Alexander Macdonell, K.C., Alexandria.

LIEUTENANT-COLONEL JOHN MACDONELL.

Provincial Aid-de-Camp to Major-General Sir Isaac Brock ; M.P. for Glengarry ;
Attorney-General of Upper Canada.

"The moment General Brock discovered the unexpected advance of the American troops, he, with the 12 men stationed at the battery, retired ; and Captain Wool advancing from the rear with his more than tenfold force, took possession of it. Captain Williams and his detachment of regulars and militia were now recalled ; and General Brock putting himself at the head of this force, amounting in all to about 90 men, advanced to meet a detachment of 150 picked American regulars, which Captain Wool had sent forward to attack him. While animating his little band of regulars and militia to a charge up the heights, General Brock received a mortal wound in the breast, and immediately fell.

"At this moment the two flank companies of the York militia, with Lieutenant-Colonel Macdonell, the General's Provincial Aid-de-Camp at their head, arrived from Brown's Point, three miles distant. By this time also Captain Wool had sent additional reinforcements to Captain Ogilvie ; making the latter's force '320 regulars, supported by a few militia and volunteers,' or on the whole, full 500 men. Colonel Macdonell and his 90 men —more than two-thirds Canadian militia—rushed boldly up the hill, in defiance of the continued stream of musketry pouring down upon them ; compelled the Americans to spike the 18 pounder ; and would have again driven them to the rocks, had not the Colonel and Captain Williams been wounded almost at the same instant ; the former mortally. The loss of their commanders created confusion among the men, and they again retreated. Hearing of the fall of General Brock, Captain Dennis proceeded from the valley, towards the foot of the heights, and mounting the General's horse, rode up, and tried to rally the troops. He succeeded in forming a few ; but the number was so inconsiderable that to persist in a contest would have been madness. A retreat was accordingly ordered, by the ground in the rear of the town ; and the men of the 49th, accompanied by many of the militia, formed in front of Vrooman's battery, there to await the expected reinforcement from Fort George.

"While we had at this period not above 200 unwounded men at Queenstown, the Americans, by their own account, had upwards of 800 and General Van Rensselaer tells us that ' a number of boats now crossed over, unannoyed except by one unsilenced gun,' or that at Vrooman's battery ; consequently more troops were hourly arriving. Brigadier-General Wadsworth was left as commanding officer of the Americans on the Queenstown hill; and General Van Rensselaer, considering the victory as complete, had himself crossed over, in order to give directions about fortifying the camp, which he intended to occupy in the British territory.''

Thus far, then is, lucidly and accurately enough, explained the nature of the contest, and the relative positions of the two forces, up to the moment of the arrival of the reserve from Fort George. It may not, however, be unimportant to add, that among the officers wounded in the repulse, and of whom no mention is made by James, were Captain Dennis of the 49th Grenadiers, and the present Mr. Justice McLean[1] of Toronto, who was then a brother subaltern with Mr. Jarvis, in Captain Cameron's flank company of militia. The latter was very severely wounded, yet brought off by the retreating party. The former had received a ball in his thigh, yet impatient of the delay of a regular treatment, he, with characteristic *sang froid*, stopped the effusion of blood by thrusting his finger into the wound, and in that manner supported his share in the action to the last. The fall of so many brave officers had naturally the effect of dispiriting the men, and the remains of the detachment continued their retreat to Durham's farm, about two miles and a half below Queenstown, where Colonel Macdonell's almost lifeless body was deposited, preparatory to its final removal to the Government House at Fort George, in

[1] Lieut. Archibald McLean, the second son of the Hon. Neil McLean, was born at St. Andrew's, County of Stormont, in 1791. He was present at Ogdensburg in 1813, and at the capture of York carried to a place of safety the colors of the York Volunteers. At the Battle of Lundy's Lane he was taken prisoner and detained until the close of the war. After the war he continued his legal studies, and in 1820 was elected a member of the Legislative Assembly for Stormont, being re-elected on five other occasions, once for the town of Cornwall. For two Parliaments, the eleventh and thirteenth, he was honored by being elected Speaker. He subsequently was appointed Chief Justice of Upper Canada, and afterwards President of the Court of Error and Appeal, an office he d at his death in 1865.

which the gallant officer breathed his last, soon after his arrival. The body of the Hero of Canada had been left behind, in one of the houses in Queenstown, hurriedly covered with a pile of old blankets in order to prevent any recognition by the enemy.

It was about 2 o'clock in the afternoon, when the anxiously-expected reserve, under General Sheaffe, consisting principally of the 41st Regiment, made its appearance at Durham's farm. The whole then moved forward in a westerly direction towards the village of St. David's, for the purpose of gaining the rear of the mountain. Here, as might have been expected, the military tact and *prevoyance* of the fallen leader, in urgently desiring the advance of the Indians, to clear a passage for the troops in their ascent of the heights, was made manifest. The column had been halted at the base of the mountain far to the right of the Queenstown road, and inclining towards that which traverses it from St. David's. Profiting by the suggestion of his late superior, General Sheaffe sent forward the Indians, who rapidly ascended the heights, and so well and so gallantly occupied the American pickets, which had been thrown out in that direction, that the little army was enabled to gain the summit of the mountain, by an oblique movement to the right, almost without opposition, and wholly without loss.

And now had arrived the crisis which was to decide, for a brief season at least, the destinies of Canada, and the honor of the British arms.

The height gained on the flank of the enemy, who were discovered drawn up in preparation for the attack, the British line, not exceeding 800 men, was instantly formed. On the extreme left, and resting on the brow of the hill, were the Indians, and next to these the companies of militia who had already borne so honorable a share in the contest of the morning, and a few others just arrived, with General Sheaffe, from Fort George. The centre was composed of the remnant of the 49th flank companies, and the right of the main body of the 41st Regiment—about 350 bayonets—commanded by Captain Derenzy. At this critical moment, and just as the action was about to commence, Captain Bullock, with the principal portion of the 41st Grenadiers, suddenly made his appearance from Chippawa, followed by Lieut Bullock, of the same company, who hastened from his station opposite Navy Island, with the few men he had under his command, partly grenadiers and partly battalion men. The opportune arrival of these little detachments (numbering together 100 bayonets) which immediately took their proper stations in the line, the extreme right of the grenadiers resting on the road leading to the Falls, was hailed as an earnest of success by the little band, who were animated by the most eager desire to encounter the enemy, and avenge the fall of their noble and lamented Chief. The moment of their triumph at length arrived. Between the extreme flank of the 41st, and the bold precipice of Queenstown Heights, there was a space covered with small trees and stunted pines. Under cover of these, the American left attempted to turn the outer flank of the 41st, but were met by such a warm and destructive fire that they were checked and thrown into confusion. Almost simultaneously with this movement of the enemy, commenced an attack upon their centre, by the light company of the 41st under Lieut. McIntyre, and on their extreme right by the Indians, who were led into action by their Chief Norton[1]—or Teyoninhokorawen—as he is named in the British Army Lists even of the present day. Both these

---

[1]Captain John Norton, along with Captain John Brant, had command of the Indians at Queenston Heights. He was a native of Scotland, his Indian name meaning Pale-faced warrior, or Sadcountenanced warrior. Some time after the war he quarrelled with the Indians, went to the State of Georgia and thence to Mississippi, and finally returned to Scotland with his Indian wife Catharine, to whom he was married at Niagara on July 27th, 1813, by Rev. Robert Addison.

MONUMENT TO BROCK, QUEENSTON HEIGHTS.

parties commenced the action with great spirit, driving
the Americans before them, and when it was perceived
that the attempt of the enemy to turn our right had so
signally failed, a tremendous shout arose from the British troops, which, mingling with the war whoop of the
Indians, staggered the wavering assailants still more. At
that instant the advance was sounded, and the whole line
rushed eagerly forward upon the enemy, who made little
or no resistance, but broke and fled in the utmost consternation, closely followed by the immolating bayonet
and tomahawk. Many, in their panic, threw themselves
over the precipice, and were of course dashed to pieces in
their descent. But quarter having at length been de-
manded by the American commander, this was given, and
900 prisoners, including one General and 72 inferior
officers, in some degree atoned for—it was impossible to
repay—the grievous loss the country had sustained in the
morning of that otherwise glorious day.

The British loss[1] at Queenstown was 11 killed and 60

[1]Return of killed, wounded and missing of the army under the
command of Major-General Isaac Brock, in an action at Queenstown, Niagara, on the 13th October, 1812 :

General staff—2 killed.

Royal Artillery—2 rank and file wounded.

Detachment 41st Regiment—1 sergeant, 1 rank and file killed ; 1
sergeant, 9 rank and file wounded.

Flank Companies, 49th Regiment—8 rank and file killed ; 2 captains, 3 sergeants, 27 rank and file, 1 volunteer wounded ; 5 rank
and file, 1 volunteer missing.

Lincoln Artillery—1 rank and file wounded.

Lincoln Militia—1 adjutant, 1 sergeant, 12 rank and file wounded;
10 rank and file missing.

York Militia—2 rank and file killed ; 1 lieutenant, 1 sergeant, 15
rank and file wounded ; 5 rank and file missing.

Total Loss—1 Major-General, 1 aid-de-camp, 1 sergeant, 9 rank
and file, line, 2 rank and file, militia, killed ; 2 captains, line ; 1
adjutant, 1 lieutenant, militia ; 4 sergeants, line ; 2 sergeants, militia ; 2 rank and file, artillery ; 1 do., militia artillery ; 36 rank
and file, line ; 27 rank and file, militia, wounded ; 5
rank and file, 1 volunteer, line ; 15 rank and file, militia, missing.

General Total—2 general staff, 1 sergeant, 11 rank and file,
killed ; 2 captains, 1 lieutenant, 1 adjutant, 6 sergeants, 66 rank
and file, 1 volunteer, wounded ; 20 rank and file, 1 volunteer, missing.

Officers Killed — Major-General Isaac Brock, commanding ;

wounded of the line and militia; and 5 killed[1] and 9 wounded of the brave Indians. The number[2] of killed and wounded of the Americans is not precisely known. The former has however been admitted by themselves to have been between 90 and 100. Independently of those killed upon the field, and dashed over the precipice, a great number perished in two or three boats sunk by the fire from our batteries.

Again, on this occasion, was the present Chief Justice conspicuous for his zeal and his gallantry. In the absence

---

Lieut.-Colonel Macdonell, Provincial Aid-de-Camp.

Wounded—Captains Dennis and Williams, 49th Regiment, volunteer Shaw, do.; Lieut. McLean, York Light Infantry; Adjutant McIntyre, Lincoln Militia.

Fort George, 15th October, 1812.

THOMAS EVANS, Major of Brigade.

(Canadian Archives.)

Return of killed, wounded and prisoners of war in the action at Queenstown, Niagara, on the 13th October, 1812:

Prisoners of War—1 Brigadier-General, 1 major, aid-de-camp, 5 lieutenant-colonels, 3 majors, 19 captains, 32 lieutenants, 10 ensigns, 1 adjutant, 1 surgeon, 852 non-commissioned officers and privates. Total, 925.

Regulars—Officers, 19; non-commissioned officers and privates, 417.

Militia—Officers, 54; non-commissioned officers and privates, 435. Total, 925.

Estimated loss of the enemy in officers and men killed and wounded, and in wounded sent over during the engagement, 500; supposed total loss, 1,425; acknowledged force engaged, 1,600.

Total British force engaged—Regulars and militia, 800; Indians, 200—1,000.

Fort George, 15th October, 1812.

THOMAS EVANS, Major of Brigade.

(Canadian Archives.)

[1]The names of the Indians killed at Queenston were—

Ayanete and Kayentatirhon, Cayuga Chiefs, Ta Kanentye, an Onondaga Warrior, Kayarawagor and Sakangonguquate, Oneida Warriors.

From Documentary History of the Campaign by Lieut.-Col. Cruikshank.

[2]The number of Americans killed and wounded in this battle has never been very accurately ascertained. The most authentic American sources put the number of killed at 90, the wounded at 82, and 764 prisoners, composed of 386 regulars and 378 militia.

of his Captain (Heward) who was upon leave, he commanded the 2nd flank company during the whole of the day. He consequently bore a prominent part in the engagement, from the moment when he arrived at early dawn from Brown's Point where, it has been seen, he was stationed with No. 1, or Captain Cameron's company, to the late hour in the afternoon, when victory finally perched on the British standard. The officers attached to Lieut. Robinson, were Lieut. Stanton,[1] and Lieut. Samuel P. Jarvis. The subalterns of Captain Cameron's company were Lieut. Jarvie,[2] Lieut. Archibald McLean, and Lieut. Geo. Ridout.[3] Captain Hatt's, and Captain

---

[1]Lieutenant Robert Stanton was the son of a British Naval officer, who saw a great deal of active service at the memorable defence of Gibraltar by General Elliot, and with the fleet on the coast of North America and in the West Indies. About the beginning of the last century he came to York with his father, who held several military and civil offices. On the breaking out of the war he was a Lieut. in Captain Stephen Heward's company of York militia, and took part in the battle of Queenston Heights and in the defence of York in 1813. At the latter engagement he was taken prisoner, but released on parole.

In 1825 he became editor and publisher of the Gazette and King's Printer, and in 1843 gave up the publishing business to become Collector of Customs for the port of Toronto, an office he resigned Nov. 10th, 1849. For a time he was manager of the Western Insurance Company, and latterly Clerk of the Process at Osgoode Hall. His death took place in 1866 at the age of 72.

[2]This is the spelling that is given in the original edition of Richardson. It would be considered merely a typographical error for Lieut. Jarvis but for the fact that in Vol. 1 of the report of the Ontario Historical Society, the roll of Captain Cameron's company of York Militia in 1812 is given ; and the name appears as it does here, Lieut. Jarvie. I am inclined to think that the name should be Jarvis, but which one I am not certain. It is neither Lieut. S. P. Jarvis nor Volunteer G. S. Jarvis who were with other companies. I have not been able to find the name " Jarvie " in any published work on the early history of Toronto.

[3]Lieut. George Ridout was the son of Thomas Ridout, sometime Surveyor-General of Upper Canada. His brother John, who met his death in a duel in 1817, was a midshipman on the Royal George during the war. Another brother, Thomas G. Ridout, was also a Lieutenant and afterwards Deputy Assistant Commissary-General. The part taken during the war by this family is fully set forth by Lady Edgar, a descendant, in " Ten Years of Upper Canada in Peace and War."

Chisholm's companies were the first to oppose the landing of the enemy.

The victory of Queenstown Heights, although fought at a distance from the principal theatre of their service, the Right Division distinctly claim as their own. The main body of the 41st, who later composed that Division, principally sustained the action, and among these were the grenadiers who had already assisted at the capture of Detroit. Moreover there were there the York volunteers who also had participated in that memorable triumph. True, the 49th flank companies, and especially their leaders, had gallantly done their duty in the morning, but nevertheless they were defeated, and driven back, and the Queenstown Heights had been so completely gained that no impediment was offered to the passage of the American troops who, at the moment when the 41st, under Captain Derenzy, and the detachments of the same corps from Chippawa, made their appearance, numbered not less than 1,400 men. Under these circumstances it is that the Right Division claim, and justly, the laurels won on this day.

As no portrait, public or private, of General Brock, seems to have been preserved in the country, it may not be unimportant here to give a slight written sketch of the hero. In person he was tall, stout and inclining to corpulency : he was of fair and florid complexion, had a large forehead, full face, but not prominent features, rather small, greyish-blue eyes, with a very slight cast in one of them—small mouth, with a pleasing smile, and good teeth. In manner he was exceedingly affable and gentlemanly, of a cheerful and social habit, partial to dancing, and although never married, extremely devoted to female society. Of the chivalry of his nature, and the soundness of his judgment, evidence enough has been given in the foregoing pages to render all comment thereon a matter of supererogation.

The following is the Official account of the Action.

From Major General Sheaffe to Sir George Prevost.

Fort George, 13th October, 1812.

SIR,—I have the honor of informing Your Excellency, that the enemy made an attack, with a considerable force this morning, before day-light, on the position of Queenstown. On receiving intelligence of it, Major-General Brock immediately proceeded to that post ; and I am excessively grieved in having to add, that he fell whilst gallantly cheering his troops to an exertion for maintaining it. With him the position was lost : but the enemy was not allowed to retain it long; reinforcements having been sent up from this post, composed of regular troops, militia, and Indians, a movement was made to turn his left, while some artillery, under the able direction of Captain Holcroft, supported by a body of infantry, engaged his attention in front. This operation was aided, too, by the judicious position which Norton and the Indians with him had taken on the woody brow of the high ground above Queenstown. A communication being thus opened with Chippawa, a junction was formed with succours that had been ordered from that post. The enemy was then attacked, and after a short but spirited conflict, was completely defeated. I had the satisfaction of receiving the sword of their commander Brigadier-General Wadsworth, on the field of battle, and many Officers, with 900 men, were made prisoners, and more may yet be expected. A stand of colors and one 6-pounder, were also taken. The action did not terminate till nearly three o'clock in the afternoon, and their loss, in killed and wounded, must have been considerable. Ours, I believe to have been comparatively small in numbers : no officer was killed besides Major-General Brock, one of the most gallant and zealous officers in His Majesty's service whose loss cannot be too much deplored, and Lieutenant-Colonel Macdonell, Provincial Aide-de-Camp, whose gallantry and merit render him worthy of his chief.

Captains Dennis and Williams, commanding the flank companies of the 49th Regiment, who were stationed at Queenstown, were wounded, bravely contending at the head of their men against superior numbers ; but I am glad to have it in my power to add, that Captain Dennis fortunately was able to keep the field, though it was with pain and difficulty ; and Captain Williams's wound is not likely long to deprive me of his services.

I am particularly indebted to Captain Holcroft of the Royal Artillery, for his judicious and skilful co-operation with the guns and howitzers under his immediate superintendence. Their well-directed fire contributed materially to the fortunate result of the day.

Captain Derenzy of the 41st Regiment, brought up the reinforcement of that corps from Fort George, and Captain Bullock led that of the same regiment from Chippawa ; and under their commands those detachments acquitted themselves in such a manner, as to sustain the reputation which the 41st Regiment had already acquired in the vicinity of Detroit.

Major-General Brock, soon after his arrival at Queenstown, had sent down orders for battering the American Fort Niagara. Brigade-Major Evans, who was left in charge of Fort George, directed the operations against it with so much effect, as to silence its fire, and to force the troops to abandon it, and by his prudent precautions, he prevented mischief of a most serious nature, which otherwise might have been effected, the enemy having used heated shot in firing at Fort George. In these services he was most effectually aided by Colonel Claus[1] (who remained in the fort at my desire) and by Captain Vigoreux, of the Royal Engineers. Brigade-Major Evans also mentions the conduct of Captains Powell and Cameron, of the Militia artillery, in terms of commendation.

Lieutenant Crowther, of the 41st Regiment, had charge

---

[1]Lieut.-Col. William Claus, of the 1st Lincoln Militia, was the son of Col. Daniel Claus, who married a daughter of Sir William Johnson, Bart., and who served his country over thirty years in the Military and Indian Departments. From his youth Lieut.-Col. William Claus was an officer in the Indian Department, and at the death of Col. Alexander McKee rose to be Deputy Superintendent-General and Deputy Inspector-General of Indian Affairs. The Indians had an affection for him equal to that which they had for his father and grandfather, and his thorough knowledge of their language and customs made him a valuable public officer. He was Lieut.-Col. of the 1st Lincoln Militia, and on the breaking out of the war was in command of the militia from Niagara to Queenston. His services to his country, particularly his management of the Indians, were highly commended by every officer commanding in Upper Canada. His descendants reside at Niagara.

of two 3-pounders that had accompanied the movement of our little corps, and they were employed with good effect.

Captain Glegg, of the 49th Regiment, Aide-de-Camp to our lamented friend and general, afforded me the most essential assistance ; and I found the services of Lieutenant Fowler, of the 41st Regiment, Assistant-Deputy-Quarter-Master-General, very useful. I derived much aid, too, from the activity and intelligence of Lieutenant Kerr, of the Glengarry Fencibles, whom I employed in communicating with the Indians and other flanking parties.

I was unfortunately deprived of the aid, experience, and ability of Lieutenant-Colonel Myers, Deputy-Quarter-Master-General, who had been sent up to Fort Erie a few days before on duty, which detained him there.

Lieutenant-Colonels Butler[1] and Clark[2] of the Militia; and

---

[1] Lieut.-Col. Thomas Butler first saw active service as a Lieutenant in the corps of Rangers commanded by his father, Colonel John Butler. His service in the war was cut short by his death from disease in Dec., 1812.

[2] Lieut.-Col. Thomas Clark, of the 2nd Lincoln Militia, was appointed at the beginning of the war to command the militia that were guarding the border from Queenston to Fort Erie. He took part in the battle of Queenston Heights, and was an active and energetic officer. At the defence of Fort Erie, Nov. 28th, 1812, he had command of the right wing, and on the 11th of July, 1813, was second in command to Lieut.-Col. Bisshopp in the attack on Black Rock, when the block houses, barracks and navy yard and a schooner were burnt, and valuable stores and ordnance captured. While conducting the retreat he was slightly wounded.

In the despatches describing the engagements in which he took part he was highly commended for the able manner that he led the troops under his command. He was a member of the Legislative Council of Upper Canada for many years.

Another officer of this name, that served throughout the war, was Colonel John Clark, son of a soldier of the 8th (King's) Regt. He was born at Kingston in 1783. His father came to Niagara, and was appointed barrack-master and also Sheriff of Lincoln, an office he held till 1803, when he was succeeded by Major Thomas Merritt. When the war commenced the son was appointed Lieut. and Adjutant of the 1st and 4th Lincoln flank companies. In March, 1813, he was promoted to the rank of Captain and Assistant Adjutant-General of Militia by Gen. Sheaffe, and retained in that office till the end of the war. He took part in several engagements, the principal one being Queenston Heights. He was for many years Collector of Customs at Port Dalhousie, but resigned some years before his death, which took place in 1862. For two terms he represented Lincoln in the Legislative Assembly of Upper Canada, being elected in 1820 and again in 1825.

Captains Hatt, Durand,[1] Rowe,[2] Applegarth, James Crooks,[3]

[1]Captain James Durand, who was in command of a flank company of the 5th Lincoln Militia at Queenston Heights, was born in Monmouthshire, Wales, in 1775, and in 1800 came to Upper Canada. During the war he lived on a farm now the site of the city of Hamilton. In 1814 he was elected a member of the Legislative Assembly of Upper Canada for Niagara, and in 1817 for Wentworth. He died at Hamilton, March 22nd, 1833.

James Durand, who was elected for the County of Halton to the Legislative Assembly in 1835, was Captain Durand's son. Another son, Mr. Charles Durand, Barrister, is at present living in Toronto at an advanced age, having been born on April 9th, 1811. Miss Laura B. Durand, a well-known writer on the editorial staff of the Toronto Globe, is a daughter of the latter.

[2]Captain John Rowe was in command of a company of the 2nd Lincoln. He was an officer in that famous corps, Butler's Rangers, and had seen a great deal of active service in the Revolutionary War. He was killed at the head of his company while gallantly contending against a more numerous force at the Battle of Chippawa, July 5th, 1814.

[3]Captain James Crooks, who commanded a company of the 1st Lincoln Militia at Queenston Heights, was born in Kilmarnock, Scotland, in 1778, and immigrated to Canada in 1791. He engaged in trade and farming, and, soon, by his energy and intelligence combined with his excellence of character, became one of the foremost men of the community. After the war he removed to West Flamboro, and there engaged in milling. Here he built and operated the first paper mill in Upper Canada. In 1820 he was elected to the Legislative Assembly, and afterwards was appointed to the Legislative Council, an office he held till his death in 1860. He married in 1808 Jane Cummings, daughter of Thomas Cummings, a soldier in Butler's Rangers, and raised a large family. The Hon. Adam Crooks, for several years a member of the Ontario Cabinet, was his son. His eldest daughter became the wife of A. N. Bethune, Bishop of Toronto. Two of his grandchildren, Miss Jane Crooks, of the Education Department Library, and Lieut. A. D. Crooks, Barrister, are residents of Toronto.

He wrote a "Reminiscence of the Last War" that appeared in the Niagara Reporter, and afterwards, about the first of the year 1841, in the British Colonist.

Captain William Crooks, although three years older than the preceding, did not come to Upper Canada till a year after his brother. He commanded a company of the 4th Lincoln at Queenston Heights. In 1808 he married Mary Butler, daughter of Colonel John Butler, the celebrated commander of Butler's Rangers.

A younger sister of these two officers, Jean Crooks, was the wife of Lieut. William Procter of the 41st Regt., brother of Gen. Henry Procter; and another sister, Jane, was the wife of Lieut.-Col. William C. Short of the 41st Regt., who was killed at the assault on Fort Stephenson.

It may be interesting to observe here that in the same year that

Cooper,[1] Robert Hamilton,[2] McEwen,[3] Duncan Cameron;[4] and Lieutenants Richardson and Thomas Butler,[5] commanding flank companies of the Lincoln and York Militia, led their men into action with great spirit. Major Merritt,[6]

---

these two brothers were defending their adopted country from invasion another brother, Ramsay Crooks, was making a difficult and perilous journey overland to Astoria at the mouth of the Columbia river, as a partner in the American Fur Company, of which he became the head after the withdrawal of John Jacob Astor. Mr. Crooks wrote a journal of the trip, which appears in the travels of John Bradbury, an English botanist who accompanied the Crooks party to the head waters of the Missouri. A graphic description of the dangers and hardships encountered by these adventurous traders may be found in Washington Irving's Astoria. In 1814 when the Americans sent an expedition to retake Fort Mackinac, Mr. Crooks accompanied the fleet to watch the interests of Mr. Astor. It is said that he concentrated, in his reminiscences, the history of the fur trade in America for forty years. He died in New York in 1859.

[1]Captain Cooper, who commanded a company at this battle, is probably an ancestor of the Coopers now living along the river road in the township of Niagara.

[2]Captain Robert Hamilton was the son of Hon. Robert Hamilton, of Queenston, and was born at Fort Niagara in 1787. He was in command of a company of the 2nd Lincoln during the war, and took part in several engagements, among them Queenston Heights and the defence of Fort Erie, Nov. 28th, 1812. He was elected to the Legislature of Upper Canada by the County of Lincoln in 1820.

[3]Captain John McEwen commanded a flank company of the 1st Lincoln Militia at Queenston Heights.

[4]Captain Duncan Cameron, who commanded a company of the York Militia at Queenston Heights, was for many years a prominent citizen of Toronto. He was appointed a member of the Legislative Council, and for a time was Provincial Secretary of Upper Canada.

[5]Lieut. Thomas Butler was the son of Lieut.-Col. Thomas Butler.

[6]Major Thomas Merritt, who raised the Niagara Dragoons and commanded them at the Battle of Queenston Heights, was born in 1759 in Westchester County, New York. He was educated at Harvard College, and on the breaking out of the Revolution was appointed Cornet in the Queen's Rangers, a corps raised by Major Robert Rogers, and afterward commanded by Colonel John Graves Simcoe —the first Lieut.-Governor of Upper Canada. At the peace he went to New Brunswick, but returned to New York, and eventually took up his residence in the Niagara Peninsula, where he died on May 12th, 1842. His son, William Hamilton Merritt, who served as a Captain in his father's corps, and who was taken prisoner at Lundy's Lane, July 25th, 1814, was well known as a parliamentarian and as the projector of the Welland Canal. The present representative of the family is the grandson and namesake of the latter, Major William Hamilton Merritt, who

commanding the Niagara Dragoons, accompanied me, and gave much assistance with part of his corps. Captain A. Hamilton, belonging to it, was disabled from riding, and attached himself to the guns under Captain Holcroft, who speaks highly of his activity and usefulness. I beg leave to add that Volunteers Shaw,[1] Thompson,[2] and Jarvis,[3] attached to the flank companies of the 49th

served in the Boer war as a Major in Brabant's Horse, and is now second in command of the Second Canadian Mounted Rifles.

Four generations of this family have seen active service in North America in a mounted corps : Thomas, in the command of the Niagara Dragoons in 1812 ; William Hamilton, a Captain in the same corps ; Jedediah, with McGrath's Lancers in 1837 ; and William Hamilton with the Governor-General's Body Guard in the North West Rebellion in 1885.

[1] Volunteer Richard Shaw was the son of Major-General Æneas Shaw, so well known in connection with the early history of Upper Canada. Major-General Shaw served as a Captain in the Queen's Rangers during the Revolutionary War. In the winter of 1791-2 he performed the unparalleled feat of marching a detachment of a new corps, also called the Queen's Rangers, from New Brunswick to Montreal on snowshoes. At the beginning of the War of 1812 he proffered his services to Major-General Brock in any capacity that he might be found useful. He was consequently appointed to command the First Division of Militia, with the rank of Colonel, and afterwards served as Adjutant-General of Militia. The hard work and fatigue proved too much for the General at his age, and caused his death in 1815.

All of his sons served in the army. The eldest, Alexander, was a Captain in the 35th and 69th Regiments, and was present at Alexandria, Maida, Calabria, Naples, Corunna, Walchern, Flushing and Waterloo. Charles was a Lieutenant in the 52nd, John a Captain in the 49th, and Æneas a Lieutenant in the Glengarry Fencibles. Richard and George were Captains in the Militia.

The grandson of Captain Alexander Shaw, Lieut.-Col. George A. Shaw, who was in command of the 10th or Royal Regiment, now Royal Grenadiers, is at present a resident of Toronto.

It may be of some interest to note in this connection that Miss Sophia, daughter of Major-General Shaw, was the fiancee of Major-General Brock.

[2] I have not been able to learn much regarding Volunteer Augustus Thompson. He was well known to, and evidently was a companion of, Volunteer George S. Jarvis, as they were together in the daring affairs with the enemy at Stoney Creek, at Black Rock and at Beaver Dam.

[3] George S. Jarvis was born in Fredericton, N.B., April 21st, 1797, and removed to York (Toronto) in 1808 with his father's family. At Queenston Heights he was attached to the 49th Regt., and at the taking of York was attached to the 8th (King's) Regt. He was present at the battles of Stoney Creek, Beaver Dam and Black Rock, and at the unsuccessful assault of Fort Erie. At

From an original photograph in possession of Miss Ellen F. Sheaffe,
Lausanne, Switzerland, grandniece of Sir Roger.

SIR ROGER HALE SHEAFFE, BART.

Regiment, conducted themselves with great spirit ; the first having been wounded, and the last having been taken prisoner. I beg leave to recommend these young men to Your Excellency's notice. Norton is wounded, but not badly ; he and the Indians particularly distinguished themselves, and I have very great satisfaction in assuring Your Excellency, that the spirit and good conduct of His Majesty's troops, of the militia, and of the other provincial corps, were eminently conspicuous on this occasion.

I have not been able to ascertain yet the number of our troops, or of those of the enemy engaged ; ours, I believe did not exceed the number of the prisoners we have taken : and their advance, which effected a landing, probably amounted to 1,300 or 1,400 men.

I shall do myself the honor of transmitting to Your Excellency further details,[1] when I shall have received the several reports of the occurrences which did not pass under my own observation, with the return of the casualties, and those of the killed and wounded, and of the ordnance taken.

I have the honor to be, &c.

(Signed) R. H. Sheaffe, Maj.-Gen.

To His Excellency Sir George Prevost, Bart., &c.

Lundy's Lane he was a Lieut. of the 8th, and went to England with the second battalion of that regiment in 1815. After the defeat of Napoleon at Waterloo several regiments were disbanded, and among them the second battalion of the 8th. Lieut. Jarvis was then after a short interval of five months appointed to the 104th Regiment. Shortly after, he returned to Canada, took up the study of law, and was sworn in as an Attorney in 1820, called to the bar in 1823. In 1820 he went to Cornwall to practice, and in 1842 was appointed County Judge, and in that year organized the Division Courts of the United Counties of Stormont, Dundas and Glengarry. During the troubles of 1837 he raised and commanded three troops of lancers. His death occurred in 1878. The Rev. Arthur Jarvis, of Napanee, is his son.

[1] In this report Major-General Sheaffe mentions every officer in command but two. In his letter to Sir George Prevost of November 3rd, 1812, the following passage occurs :

I am much mortified to find that I omitted the names of Captain Chisholm commanding a flank company of the York Militia, and of Lieutenant Ball commanding the Militia Artillery attached to the post of Queenstown ; Captain Dennis's report, since transmitted, has partly supplied that omission ; he commends highly both those officers, and in justice to them I have issued an order acknowledging my omission and their merit.

The American accounts of the action have been so much altered from General Van Rensselaer's original despatch, that it is difficult to know which is the correct one. At this moment I have two before me, one by Captain Fay, of the United States Artillery, the other by James. There is evidently so much of the *suppressio veri* if not of the *assertio falsi*, in the former, evidently to cloak the national humiliation, that there can be no hesitation in adopting that given by the latter,[1] who seems to have been at some pains to obtain the correct despatch.

From General Van Rensselaer, to General Dearborn.

Head Quarters, Lewiston, Oct. 14th, 1812.

Sir,—As the movements of this Army under my command, since I had last the honor to address you on the 8th, have been of a very important character, producing consequences serious to many individuals ; establishing facts actually connected with the interest of the service and the safety of the army ; and as I stand prominently responsible for some of these consequences, I beg leave to explain to you, sir, and through you to my country, the situation and circumstances in which I have had to act, and the reasons and motives which governed me, and if the result is not all that might have been wished, it is such that, when the whole ground shall be viewed, I shall cheerfully submit myself to the judgment of my country.

In my letter of the 8th instant, I apprised you that the crisis in this campaign was rapidly advancing ; and that (to repeat the same words) " the blow must be soon struck, or all the toil and expense of the campaign go for nothing and worse than nothing, for the whole will be tinged with dishonor."

---

[1] Richardson has unfortunately selected the most imperfect copy. I do not know from what source James obtained his copy, but whole paragraphs are missing, and names, as usual with him, incorrectly spelled and otherwise disguised—as Fleming for Fenwick and Christie for Chrystie. James makes the error of saying that Van Rensselaer addressed the letter to the American Secretary of War, when every authority within reach says it was addressed to Gen. Dearborn and by him transmitted to the Secretary of War. I have corrected the whole letter and added the omissions of James without making any reference to them in foot notes.

Under such impressions, I had, on the 5th instant, written to Brig.-General Smyth, of the United States forces, requesting an interview with him, Major-General Hall, and the commandants of the United States regiments, for the purpose of conferring upon the subject of future operations. I wrote Major-General Hall to the same purport. On the 11th I had received no answer from General Smyth; but in a note to me on the 10th, General Hall mentioned that General Smyth had not yet then agreed upon any day for the consultation.

In the meantime, the partial success of Lieutenant Elliott at Black Rock (of which however, I have received no official information) began to excite a strong disposition in the troops to act. This was expressed to me through various channels, in the shape of an alternative; that they must have orders to act, or at all hazards they would go home. I forbear here commenting upon the obvious consequences, to me personally, of longer withholding my orders under such circumstances.

I had a conference with Lieutenant-Colonel —————, as to the possibility of getting some person to pass over to Canada, and obtain correct information. On the morning of the 4th, he wrote to me that he had procured the man, who bore his letter to go over. Instructions were given him: he passed over, and obtained such information as warranted an immediate attack. This was confidentially communicated to several of my first officers, and produced great zeal to act; more especially as it might have a controlling effect upon the movements at Detroit, where it was supposed General Brock had gone with all the force he dared spare from the Niagara frontier. The best preparations in my power were therefore made to dislodge the enemy from the heights of Queenstown, and possess ourselves of the village; where the troops might be sheltered from the distressing inclemency of the weather.

Lieutenant-Colonel Fenwick's flying artillery, and a detachment of regular troops under his command, were ordered to be up in season from Fort Niagara. Orders were also sent General Smyth, to send down from Buffalo, such detachments of his brigade as existing circumstances in that vicinity might warrant. The attack was to have been made at 4 o'clock on the morning of the 11th, by crossing over in boats at the old ferry opposite the heights. To avoid any embarrassment in crossing the river, (which is here a sheet of violent eddies,) experienced boatmen were procured to take the boats from the landing below to the place of embarkation. Lieutenant Sim was considered the man of greatest skill for this service ; he went ahead, and, in the extreme darkness, passed the intended place far up the river ; and there, in a most extraordinary manner, fastened his boat to the shore, and abandoned the detachment. In this front boat he had carried nearly every oar, which was prepared for all the boats. In this agonizing dilemma stood officers and men, whose ardor had not been cooled by exposure through the night, to one of the most tremendous north-east storms, which continued unabated for 28 hours, and deluged the whole camp. The approach of daylight extinguished every prospect of success and the detachment returned to camp. Colonel Van Rensselaer was to have commanded the detachment.

After this result, I had hoped the patience of the troops would have continued, until I could submit the plan suggested in my letter of the 8th, that I might act under, and in conformity to, the opinion which might be then expressed. But my hope was idle ; the previously excited ardor seemed to have gained new heat from the late miscarriage ; the brave were mortified to stop short of their object, and the timid thought laurels half-won by an attempt.

On the morning of the 12th, such was the pressure upon me from all quarters, that I became satisfied that my refusal to act might involve me in suspicion, and the service in disgrace.

Viewing affairs at Buffalo as yet unsettled, I had immediately countermanded the march of General Smyth's brigade, upon the failure of the first expedition ; but having now determined to attack Queenstown, I sent new orders to General Smyth to march ; not with the view of his aid in the attack, for I considered the force detached sufficient, but to support the detachment should the conflict be obstinate and long continued.

Lieutenant-Colonel Chrystie, who had just arrived at the Four Mile Creek, and had, late in the night of the first contemplated attack, gallantly offered me his own and his men's service : but he got my permission too late. He now again came forward, had a conference with Colonel

Van Rensselaer,[1] and begged that he might have the honor of a command in the expedition. The arrangement was made, Colonel Van Rensselaer was to command one column of 300 militia; and Lieutenant-Colonel Chrystie a column of the same number of regular troops.

Every precaution was now adopted as to boats, and the most confidential and experienced men to manage them. At an early hour in the night, Lieutenant-Colonel Chrystie marched his detachment by the rear road from Niagara to camp. At 7 in the evening Lieutenant-Colonel Stranahan's regiment moved from Niagara Falls; at 8 o'clock Mead's, and at 9 o'clock Lieutenant-Colonel Bloom's regiment marched from the same place. All were in camp in good season. Agreeably to my orders issued upon this occasion, the two columns were to pass over together; as soon as the heights should be carried Lieutenant-Colonel Fenwick's flying artillery was to pass over; then Major Mullany's detachment of regulars; and the other troops to follow in order.

At dawn of day the boats were in readiness, and the troops commenced embarking, under cover of a commanding battery, mounting two eighteen-pounders and two sixes. The movements were soon discovered, and a brisk fire of musketry was poured from the whole line of the Canadian shore. Our battery then opened to sweep the shore; but it was, for some minutes, too dark to direct much fire with safety. A brisk cannonade was now opened upon the boats from three different batteries. Our battery returned the fire, and occasionally threw grape upon the shore, and was itself served with shells from a small mortar of the enemy's. Colonel Scott, of the Artillery, by hastening his march from Niagara Falls in the night arrived in season to return the enemy's fire with two six-pounders.

The boats were somewhat embarrassed with the eddies, as well as with a shower of shot; but Colonel Van Rensselaer, with about 100 men, soon effected his landing

---

[1]Colonel Solomon Van Rensselaer and Major-General Stephen Van Rensselaer were cousins. The former wrote "A Narrative of the Affair of Queenstown," in which he defends himself and the General from the "strictures on that event in a book entitled 'Notices of the War of 1812,'" by General John Armstrong, who was appointed Secretary of War in January, 1813, but resigned in September, 1814, after the capture of Washington.

amidst a tremendous fire directed upon him from every point ; but to the astonishment of all who witnessed the scene, this van of the column advanced slowly against the fire.   It was a serious misfortune to the van, and indeed to the whole expedition, that in a few minutes after land- ing Colonel Van Rensselaer received four wounds.   A ball passed through his right thigh, entering just below the hip bone ; another shot passed through the same thigh a little below ; the third through the calf of the leg ; and a fourth contused his heel.   This was quite a crisis in the expedition.   Under so severe a fire it was difficult to form raw troops.   By some mismanagement of the boatmen, Lieutenant-Colonel Chrystie did not arrive until some time after this, and was wounded in the hand in passing the river.   Colonel Van Rensselaer was still able to stand and with great presence of mind ordered his officers to proceed with rapidity and storm the fort.   This service was gallantly performed and the enemy driven down the hill in every direction.   Soon after this, both parties were considerably reinforced, and the conflict was renewed in various places.   Many of the enemy took shelter behind a stone guard-house, where a piece of ordnance was now briskly served.   I ordered the fire of our battery to be directed upon the guard-house ; and it was so effectually done, that with eight or ten shot the fire was silenced. The enemy then retreated behind a large store-house ; but in a short time the rout became general, and the enemy's fire was silenced, except from a one-gun battery, so far down the river as to be out of the reach of our heavy ord- nance ; and our light pieces could not silence it.   A num- ber of boats now passed over unannoyed, except from the one unsilenced gun.   For some time after I had passed over, the victory seemed complete ; but in the ex- pectation of further attacks, I was taking measures for fortifying my camp immediately ; the direction of this service I committed to Lieutenant Totten, of the Engi- neers.   But very soon the enemy were reinforced, by a detachment of several hundred Indians from Chippawa ; they commenced a furious attack ; but were promptly met and routed by the rifle and bayonet.   By this time I per- ceived my troops were embarking very slowly.   I passed immediately over to accelerate their movements ; but, to my utter astonishment, I found that at the very moment when complete victory was in our hands, the ardor of the

MAJOR-GENERAL STEPHEN VAN RENSSELAER.

unengaged troops had entirely subsided. I rode in all directions ; urged the men by every consideration to pass over, but in vain. Lieut.-Col. Bloom, who had been wounded in action, returned, mounted his horse and rode through the camp ; as did also Judge Peck, who happened to be here, exhorting the companies to proceed, but all in vain.

At this time a large reinforcement from Fort George was discovered coming up the river. As the battery on the hill was considered an important check against their ascending the heights, measures were immediately taken to send them a fresh supply of ammunition as I learnt there were left only 20 shot for the 18-pounders. The reinforcement, however, obliqued to the right from the road, and formed a junction with the Indians in the rear of the heights. Finding, to my infinite mortification, that no reinforcement would pass over ; seeing that another severe conflict must soon commence ; and knowing that the brave men on the heights were quite exhausted, and nearly out of ammunition ; all I could do was to send them a fresh supply of cartridges. At this critical moment I despatched a note to General Wadsworth acquainting him with our situation ; leaving the course to be pursued much to his own judgment ; with assurance that if he thought best to retreat, I would endeavor to send as many boats as I could command, and cover his retreat by every fire I could safely make. But the boats were dispersed ; many of the boatmen had fled panic struck ; and but few got off. But my note could but little more than have reached General Wadsworth about 4 o'clock, when a most severe and obstinate conflict commenced, and continued for about half an hour, with a tremendous fire of cannon, flying artillery and musketry. The enemy succeeded in re-possessing their battery, and gaining advantage on every side ; the brave men who had gained the victory, exhausted of strength and ammunition, and grieved at the unpardonable neglect of their fellow soldiers, gave up the conflict.

I can only add, that the victory was really won ; but lost for the want of a small reinforcement ; one third part of the idle men might have saved all.

I have been so pressed with the various duties of burying the dead, providing for the wounded, collecting the public property, negotiating an exchange of prisoners, and all the concerns consequent of such a battle that I have not been able to forward this despatch at as early an hour as I could have wished. I shall soon forward you another despatch in which I shall endeavor to point out to you the conduct of some most gallant and deserving officers. But I cannot in justice close this without impressing the very great obligation I am under to Brigadier-General Wadsworth, Colonel Van Rensselaer, Colonel Scott, Lieutenant-Colonels Chrystie and Fenwick and Captain Gibson. Many others have also behaved most gallantly. As I have reason to believe that many of our troops fled to the woods with the hope of crossing the river, I have not been able to learn the probable number of killed, wounded and prisoners. The slaughter of our troops must have been very considerable and the enemy have suffered severely.

General Brock is among their slain, and his Aid-de-Camp mortally wounded.

I have the honor to be yours, &c., &c.,

Stephen Van Rensselaer,

Maj.-Gen. Dearborn.   Maj.-Gen.

The following is the report of the Officer commanding the detachment (the present Colonel Wool) which obtained possession of the battery, by ascending the concealed fisherman's path, in the early part of the day.

From Captain Wool to Colonel Van Rensselaer.

Buffalo, Oct. 23, 1812.

Dear Sir,

I have the honor to communicate to you the circumstances attending the storming of Queenstown battery on the 13th inst.; with those which happened previously you are already well acquainted.

In pursuance of your order, we proceeded round the point and ascended the rocks, which brought us partly in rear of the battery. We took it without much resistance. I immediately formed the troops in rear of the battery, and fronting the village, when I observed General Brock with his troops formed, consisting of four companies of the 49th Regiment, and a few militia, marching for our left flank. I immediately detached a party of 150 men, to take possession of the heights above Queenstown battery and to hold General Brock in check; but in consequence of his superior force they retreated. I sent a reinforcement; notwithstanding which the enemy drove us to the edge of the bank, when with the greatest exertions we brought the troops to a stand, and I ordered the Officers to bring their men to a charge as soon as the ammunition was expended, which was executed with some confusion, and in a few moments the enemy retreated. We pursued them to the edge of the heights, when Col. Macdonell had his horse shot from under him, and was himself mortally wounded. In the interim, General Brock, in attempting to rally his forces, was killed, when the enemy dispersed in every direction. As soon as it was practicable, I formed the troops in a line on the heights fronting the village, and immediately detached flanking parties, which consisted of Captain Machesney, of the 6th Regiment, Lieutenant Smith, and Ensign Grosvenor with a small detachment of riflemen, who had that moment arrived; at the same time, I ordered Lieutenant Gansevoort and Lieutenant Randolph, with a detachment of artillery, to drill out an 18-pounder which had been previously spiked, and if possible to bring it to bear upon the village. The wounded and prisoners I ordered to be collected, and sent to the guard-house. About this time, which was about three or four o'clock in the afternoon, Lieutenant-Col. Chrystie arrived, and took the command. He ordered me across the river to get my wounds dressed. I remained a short time. Our flanking parties had been driven in by the Indians but General Wadsworth and other Officers arriving, we had a short skirmish with them, and they retreated, and I crossed the river.

The Officers engaged in storming the battery, were Captains Wool and Ogilvie; Lieutenants Kearney, Hugunin, Carr, and Sammons, of the 43rd Regiment; Lieutenant Gansevoort and Randolph of the Light Artillery, and Major Lush of the Militia.

I recommend to your particular notice Lieuts. Randolph, Carr, and Kearney, for their brave conduct exhibited during the whole of the action.

I have the honor to be,
Your most obedient humble Servant
John E. Wool, Capt. 13th Regt. Inft.

Colonel Van Rensselaer.

VII

THE BATTLE OF FRENCHTOWN

Towards the close of the autumn, General Winchester, having established himself at that point of the Miami, whither General Tupper had, on the occasion of Major Muir's retreat from Fort Wayne, been ordered to dislodge us ; and thrown up on the right bank of the river a strong fortification to which, in compliment to the Governor of the State of Ohio, the name of Fort Meigs had been given, a detachment, consisting of about 50 men under the command of Major Reynolds of the Essex Militia, with a three-pounder, and 200 Indians were sent to Frenchtown[1] on the River Raisin, distant eighteen miles from Amherstburg, to watch his movements. Here this little party continued unmolested until the afternoon of the 18th of January, 1813, when Colonel Lewis, who had been detached from General Winchester's division, with an advanced guard of nearly 800 men suddenly fell upon them, and notwithstanding a very gallant resistance, in the course of which, efficient service was rendered by the three-pounder under Bombardier Kitson of the Royal Artillery, aided simply by a few militia acting as gunners, compelled them to retire across some intermediate open ground to a wood, distant nearly a mile from their original position. Here the enemy were kept in check not only by the fire from the three-pounder, but by a

---

[1]Frenchtown, now the city of Monroe, was so called because a number of French families settled upon the banks of the river, and built their houses near together, as was usual with this nationality. The stream was called Sturgeon river by the Indians, because that fish was found there in large numbers, but Riviere aux Raisins by the French, because, it is said, grapes grew in abundance on its banks.

running fusillade from the Militia, and Indians, chiefly of the Pottawattomi tribe. After the conflict had continued at this point upwards of half an hour, Major Reynolds,[1] finding himself closely pressed by very superior numbers, gave up the contest, the Americans suffering him to effect his retreat without further interruption. In this little affair the British loss was 1 Militia man and 3 Indians killed. That of the enemy was much more severe, they themselves admitting 12 killed and 55 wounded. Colonel Lewis having established himself in the position, sent immediate notice of his success to General Winchester, who quitting Fort Meigs with the main body of his army, pushed forward with all expedition, and effected a junction with Colonel Lewis on the 20th.

The account of the repulse of Major Reynolds having reached Amherstburg in the course of the night of the 18th, Colonel Procter, with a promptness and decision which it is to be regretted had not marked his subsequent operations, resolved on an instant advance upon the captured position, before the enemy could have time to fortify it. Accordingly the whole disposable force of the garrison was ordered upon this service, and early on the 19th, leaving a handful of men to occupy the fort, he crossed the Detroit river opposite Amherstburg, with

---

[1] Major Ebenezer Reynolds, the commander of the Essex Militia, was the son of a Commissary officer to the British troops at Fort Detroit when it was a British possession. In the autumn of 1812 he occupied Frenchtown with two companies of militia, but on the advance of Col. Lewis with a superior force was obliged to retire. He took part in all the engagements of the Right Division.

From Sept. 10th, 1833, till the 7th of August, 1837, Major Reynolds was Sheriff of the Western District.

His brother, Robert Reynolds, Deputy Assistant-Commissary-General, followed the fortunes of the army of the Right Division, and escaped when that army was defeated at Moravian-town on Oct. 5th, 1813. He was born in Detroit in 1781, and lived to an advanced age on his farm on the banks of the Detroit near Amherstburg. His narrative of the events of the war is given by Coffin in " 1812; The War and its Moral," p. 195.

a body of 500 troops and militia, 800 Indians under the Chief Roundhead, (Tecumseh being absent collecting reinforcements) and 3 three-pounders. The different vessels being laid up for the season, parts of their crews were ordered to serve with the artillery, and the two companies of the Newfoundland Fencibles attached to the brigade. No sight could be more beautiful than the departure of this little army from Amherstburg. It was the depth of winter ; and the river at the point we crossed being four miles in breadth, the deep rumbling noise of the guns prolonging their reverberations like the roar of distant thunder, as they moved along the ice, mingled with the wild cries of the Indians, seemed to threaten some convulsion of nature ; while the appearance of the troops winding along the road, now lost behind some cliff of rugged ice, now emerging into view, their polished arms glittering in the sunbeams, gave an air of romantic grandeur to the scene.

On the night of the 21st, we halted and bivouacked in the open air, about five miles from the enemy's position, with no other protection from the cold than our great coats, and the fires which were kindled at our feet. Two hours before dawn, and we were again upon the advance to the River Raisin, and on the 22nd, before daybreak, came within sight of the enemy, occupying the position lately held by Major Reynolds. Such was their security and negligence that they had not thrown out a single picket, and our line was actually half formed within musket shot of their defences, before they were aware even of our presence.

The conduct of Colonel Procter on this occasion has ever been a matter of astonishment to me, and on no one principle that I am aware of, can it be satisfactorily accounted for. The Americans were lying in their beds undressed and unarmed, and a prompt and forward movement of the line, either would have enabled us to have taken them with the bayonet at advantage, or to have seized the intermediate close fence, forming a parapet from which they shortly afterwards so severely annoyed us. Instead of this, he commenced firing his three-pounders in answer to the alarm of the sentinels who, at length perceiving us, had rapidly discharged their muskets—thus affording them time and facility for arming and occupying the only position from which they could seriously check our advance. Resting their rifles on the breastwork by which they were covered, the Americans fought under every advantage, the dark line of troops before them serving as a point of direction, which could not fail to be perceived along the field of snow by which they were surrounded. Much execution was done among the artillery and seamen. Placed in front of the line, and singled out by their marksmen, the officers and men of those departments were particularly exposed, and many of the guns were abandoned from want of hands to work them. The fire of the enemy was not less galling to the troops, yet although falling at every step, they continued to advance with the utmost resolution and gallantry. The action had continued about an hour, when the American right, being entirely broken by the Militia and Indians, a movement was made to occupy the ground they had abandoned, and to take them in flank. This manœuvre succeeding, a corps of Americans, to the number of four hundred, threw themselves into the strong block-houses they had already constructed since their arrival, where they continued to make an obstinate defence. Meanwhile their right, and part of the centre, closely followed across the ice by the Indians, fell almost unresisting victims to the wrath of their pursuers : and for nearly two miles along the road by which they passed, the snow was covered with the blood and bodies of the slain. Among the fugitives was General Winchester himself, who, falling into the hands of the Wyandot Chief Roundhead, was conducted, together with his son—a handsome youth of sixteen—to our rear.

Here, being informed of the state of the action, he immediately wrote an order in pencil to the officer commanding the block-houses desiring him to surrender what troops were under him as prisoners of war. This being conveyed to Colonel Procter who was then in advance with the left wing, which was fast establishing itself on the flank of the enemy's position, the fire from our line was discontinued, and an officer despatched with a flag and the document in question. The result of this was the surrender of a considerable body of men, who dreading to fall into the hands of the Indians had resolved to sell their lives at the dearest possible rate, and who could not, without great difficulty, have been expelled from their formidable position. In this manner was the whole of the American force annihilated—150 men only of those who had been routed early in the day, contriving to effect their escape into Fort Meigs, the post so recently established on the banks of the Miami. So complete was the surprise of the enemy, that General Winchester, when brought in, had no other covering than the dress in which he slept.

In this affair which, if properly conducted, would have been attended by little loss to the assailants, we had 24 rank and file killed and 11 officers and 158 rank and file wounded, exclusive of sergeants whose number is not recorded. Colonel St. George, particularly distinguished by his valor and exertions, received five wounds (the despatch states four) several of them severe—and had a horse shot under him. No officer was killed ; but among the wounded were Ensign Kerr of the Royal Newfoundland Regiment, who was shot through the lungs, and died a few days afterwards, Captain Tallon and Lieut. Clemow of the 41st, Lieut. Troughton of the Artillery, and Lieuts. Rolette and Irvine of the Navy. The conduct of this latter officer, whose gallantry at the capture of the Caledonia has already been described, was marked

General James Winchester.

on this occasion by the same coolness and resolution. In a forward movement made upon the enemy in the heat of the action, but in which we had been checked by the desperate fire of their riflemen, one of the three-pounders had been abandoned not twenty yards from the fence. The Americans eagerly sought to obtain possession of this, and leaped the breastwork for the purpose of dragging it immediately under cover of their own fire. Their object, however, was seen and frustrated by the British line, which had not retired many yards before it again halted and renewed the contest, compelling the Americans to retire behind their breastwork. Lieutenant Irvine saw the peril of the gun, and, under cover of a heavy fire which was thrown into the enemy at that moment, he advanced, seized the drag rope, and bore it off. This daring feat, performed in presence of, and between, the two armies, was not without its penalty. Mr. Irvine received a wound immediately in the centre of his heel, the ball entering and saturating his boot, which was with some difficulty removed, with blood ; and from the effect of this he suffered for some time. The ball was never found.

Another individual who deserves honorable mention here was a young midshipman, a brother[1] of the writer of this narrative, and the son of a medical officer who had long served in the country. This youth, then only fourteen years of age, had ever been anxious to find himself engaged in an affair with the enemy, but no opportunity having presented itself on the lake, he had resolved to seize the first favorable occasion on land. Disobeying the positive order given him to remain behind, he joined the division during the bivouac of the night preceding

---

[1] This was Robert Richardson, the next and favorite brother of the author, born at Queenston, Sept. 10th, 1798, died June 7th, 1819.

For a description of this battle see the letter of the author, written to his uncle after the return of the army to Amherstburg.

the action, and attaching himself to his department, was among the number of those singled out by the enemy's marksmen.   While in the act of applying a match to one of the guns, he was struck by a ball, which shattered his right leg and felled him to the earth.   Doctor Richardson had been called on, in his medical capacity, to attend the expedition, and was then with the staff in the rear.   The first care of this gallant and excellent boy was to conceal his wound from his father ; and he begged those who bore him from the field to convey him to a position re- mote from that occupied by the staff, and to request the surgeon of the 41st to attend him, which was accordingly done.   After having suffered intensely, but with manly and enduring courage, for six months, he was at length enabled to remove to Quebec, where, his conduct being generally known, he was taken into favor by the Com- mander-in-Chief, who gave him the commission of a lieu- tenant in one of the provincial corps.   Sir John Harvey and Sir George Murray, then Colonels in the service, and filling the important offices of Adjutant-General and Quarter-Master-General to the army in Canada, were also forward in affording the most flattering testimony of their esteem ; and this spirited youth had the cheering consolation to know that, although afflicted with a wound which eventually cost him his life, the noble ardor devel- oped at so early a stage of his existence was not without its reward, in the approval of men whose high military rank and character invested their individual regard with a ten-fold value.

The following extract from a letter from the first-named gallant Officer, dated November, 1839, contains so flatter- ing a reminiscence of the devoted boy that it would be an injustice to his memory to withhold it.   '' I am favored with your very interesting communication of the 22nd inst. by which I learn that you are the brother of two youths, whose gallantry and merits—and with regard to one of them, his sufferings—during the late war, excited my warmest admiration and sympathies; and (continues Sir John, under an erroneous impression that his young *protegé* had been subsequently married) I will add, that the desire I felt to serve the father will be found to extend itself to the son, if your nephew should ever find himself under circumstances to require from me any service which it may be within my limited power to render him.''

In the same engagement Mr. William Caldwell[1] of Amherstburg, who was attached to the Indians, had a very narrow escape. Among the number of those of the enemy who first broke and fled across the ice, was an officer who, overtaken by an Indian, and in the act of being tomahawked, was saved by the interposition of this gentleman. As he was conducting him toward the principal scene of action, the American officer drew his knife, at a moment when Mr. Caldwell was off his guard, and springing upon his deliverer, made an incision along his throat, nearly from ear to ear. The wound fortunately was not deep, and Mr. Caldwell, who was an extremely powerful and active person, with great presence of mind,

---

[1]Col. William Caldwell, of Amherstburg, was a native of Ireland, and immigrated to the southern colonies of America before the Revolutionary War. When the colonies rebelled he took the Loyalist side, and was appointed an officer in one of the colonial regiments, but was transferred to that celebrated corps, Butler's Rangers, in which he held the rank of Captain. He took part in all the battles, raids and forays of this corps, and after the war settled in the township of Malden. On the breaking out of the War of 1812 he was appointed Quarter-Master-General of the militia on the western frontier. His influence with the Wyandots was such as to secure their aid for the British in the war. He and his four sons took part in all the engagements of the Right Division. William, Jr., was a Captain in the 1st Essex Militia, and Thomas and Francis, Lieutenants, in the same regiment. The latter was wounded seven times during the war. Another son, James, served through the war.

Francis Caldwell was elected a member of the Legislative Assembly, for the County of Essex in 1835, and re-elected in 1840.

Edwin Caldwell was Collector of Customs at Amherstburg from 1831 till 1857.

caught the arm which had attempted his destruction, and drawing forth a dagger, with which he was provided, thrust it repeatedly into the body of his assailant until death had freed him from all further apprehension—Mr. Caldwell's wound was soon healed.

The appearance of the American prisoners captured at Frenchtown was miserable to the last degree. They had the air of men to whom cleanliness was a virtue unknown, and their squalid bodies were covered by habiliments that had evidently undergone every change of season, and were arrived at the last stage of repair. It has already been remarked that it was the depth of winter; but scarcely an individual was in possession of a great coat or cloak, and few of them wore garments of wool of any description. They still retained their summer dress, consisting of cotton stuff of various colors, shaped into frocks, and descending to the knee: their trowsers were of the same material. They were covered with slouched hats, worn bare by constant use, beneath which their long hair fell matted and uncombed over their cheeks; and these, together with the dirty blankets wrapped around their loins to protect them against the inclemency of the season, and fastened by broad leathern belts, into which were thrust axes and knives of an enormous length, gave them an air of wildness and savageness, which in Italy would have caused them to pass for brigands of the Apennines. The only distinction between the garb of the officer and that of the soldier was, that the one, in addition to his sword, carried a short rifle instead of a long one, while a dagger, often curiously worked and of some value, supplied the place of the knife. This description may be considered as applicable to the various hordes of irregular troops sent forth throughout the war from the States of Ohio and Kentucky. The equipment was ever the same, and differing only inasmuch as their opportunities of preserving or renewing it were more or less frequent.

During the short period the American prisoners remained in Amherstburg, I had an opportunity of rendering a slight service to General Winchester, for which he appeared particularly grateful. This was replied to, moreover, by a request that I would accept a very handsomely-mounted pair of pistols which were with his baggage. The Indians however had forestalled me in the possession, and I believe the General never recovered a single article even of wearing apparel.

The following is the British Official Report of the battle of the River Raisin. Those of General Winchester and of General Harrison will be found succeeding it.

From Colonel Procter to Major-General Sheaffe,

Sandwich, January 25, 1813.

MY DEAR GENERAL,—In my last despatch I acquainted you, that the enemy was in the Michigan territory, marching upon Detroit. I therefore deemed it requisite that he should be attacked without delay, and with all and every description of force within my reach. Early in the morning, on the 19th, I was informed of his being in possession of Frenchtown, on the River Raisin, 26 miles from Detroit, after experiencing every resistance that Major Reynolds, of the Essex militia, had it in his power to make, with a 3-pounder, well served and directed by bombardier Kitson of the Royal Artillery, and the militiamen, whom he had well trained to the use of it. The retreat of the gun was covered by a brave band of Indians, who made the enemy pay dearly for what he obtained. The Indians fell back, 18 miles to Brown's Town, the settlement of the brave Wyandots, where I directed my force to assemble. On the 21st instant, I advanced 12 miles to Swan Creek, whence we marched to the enemy, and attacked him at break of day, on the 22nd instant, and after experiencing, for our numbers, a considerable loss, about half of the enemy's force, posted in houses and enclosures, and which, in dread of falling into the hands of the Indians, they most obstinately defended, at last surrendered at discretion ; the other part of their force, in attempting to return whence they came, were, I believe, all, or perhaps excepting a very few, killed by the Indians. Brigadier-General Winchester was taken in the pursuit by the

Wyandot Chief Roundhead. He was cut off from those who were posted, and whom he afterwards surrendered.

I had much difficulty in bringing the Indians to consent to the sparing of their lives.

You will perceive that I have lost no time ; indeed, there was none to spare, as they would have been joined by Mr. Harrison in a few days, and the people of Detroit had already begun to show themselves. The troops, the marine, and the militia displayed great bravery ; all behaved well. Where so much zeal and spirit were displayed by all it would be unjust to attempt to particularize: I shall only venture to mention some of the wounded. Lieut.-Col. St. George, who received four wounds in a gallant attempt to occupy a building favorably situated for the enemy's annoyance ; Ensign Kerr, of the Royal Newfoundland Regiment, who, I fear, is very dangerously wounded. The zeal and courage of the Indian Department were never more conspicuous than on this occasion. The Indian warriors displayed their usual courage. I am much indebted to the different departments, the troops having been well and timely supplied with every requisite the district can afford.

We feel the insufficiency of surgical assistance. If the Indians had not appeared quite so soon in the enemy's rear, which deterred them from quitting their fastness, scarcely a man could have escaped death. I send my A.D.C., Lieutenant McLean,[1] with this despatch. He will be able to answer any question respecting the affair of Frenchtown that you may be desirous of asking, or concerning our situation here generally. I have decided to the best of my judgment respecting the prisoners, which is to send them by the River Thames, to be passed

[1] Lieut. A. H. McLean, of the 41st Regiment, who was A.D.C. to Colonel Procter, was the son of *Donald McLean, Clerk of the Legislative Assembly, who was killed while bravely opposing the landing of the Americans at York on April 27th, 1813. He was a zealous and painstaking officer, and was in every engagement in the west, and also the battle of Moraviantown. After the close of the war he went to England with his regiment, and thence to India, where he took part in the severe fighting of the first Burmese war. When he retired from the army he came to Canada, and lived on a farm in the township of Scarborough, a few miles east of Toronto. Here he still kept a connection with military affairs, and was appointed Colonel, and was in command during the troubles of 1837. His narrative of the battle of Moraviantown was used by Coffin in that writer's description of the event.

over on your frontier. The reasons for not sending them back the route by which they came are so obvious that I shall not, except required, obtrude them on you ; indeed, I see no option or arrangement that could be made but the one directed.

I, fortunately, have not been deprived of the services of Lieutenant Troughton of the Royal Artillery, and acting in the Quarter-Master-General's Department, although he was wounded. I am indebted much to his zeal and unwearied exertions. I could wish his continuance in the Quarter-Master-General's Department. Were it not unjust to particularize any corps, where all did their utmost, I would mention the zeal and courage of the Royal Artillery. Each officer is deserving of being named, could I do it within the compass of a despatch.

I enclose a list of the killed and wounded. I lament there having been so many of both ; but of the latter a large proportion will return to duty, and most of them before long. Before this reduction of my force, I had too few for the defence of this frontier. May I not hope that you will send me a company of the 41st Regiment ? You are aware of the insufficiency of my means. I also send a return of the arms, ammunition, etc., taken on the 22nd inst., likewise of the prisoners, who you will perceive to be equal to my utmost force, exclusive of the Indians, who, though a powerful aid, are an uncertain one, being dependent on success, and which would have strongly appeared had I failed on the 22nd instant, nor could I have been sure of the militia in the event of any disaster. I have not heard it officially, but I believe that a party of the enemy, one hundred, bringing 500 hogs for General Winchester's force, has been completely cut off. I shall defer until the next opportunity, which shall be in a few days, saying anything more, having already detained Lieut. McLean too long, of whose courage and exertions displayed on the 22nd inst. I would speak, did I think it just to attempt particularizing anyone, especially when I may be supposed partial.

I remain, my dear General, faithfully yours,

Henry Procter, Colonel Commanding.

Major-General Sheaffe,
    Fort George.

To Major-General Sheaffe, &c., &c., &c.

 Fort George.

Return of prisoners taken after the action at Riviere au Raisin, on the 22nd day of January, 1813.

1 Brigadier-general; 1 colonel; 1 major; 9 captains; 6 lieutenants; 10 ensigns; 1 brigade-major; 1 adjutant; 1 quartermaster; 2 surgeons; 27 sergeants; 435 rank and file.—total, 495.

N.B.—The Indians have brought in and delivered up several prisoners since the above return was taken; they continue to do so this morning, so that this return is not perfectly correct, nor can a correct one be procured until they arrive at Sandwich.

   Felix Troughton, R.A.

    Act. Dep. Assist. Quarter-Master-Gen.

Return of the killed and wounded in the action at Riviere au Raisin, 22nd January, 1813.

Royal Artillery;—1 sergeant, 1 gunner, killed; 1 lieutenant, 1 corporal, 1 bombardier, 5 gunners, wounded.

10th Royal Veteran Battalion;—2 privates wounded.

41st Foot;—15 privates, killed; 1 captain, 1 lieutenant, 3 sergeants, 1 corporal, 91 privates, wounded.

Royal Newfoundland Regiment;—1 private killed; 1 ensign, 1 sergeant, 3 corporals, 13 privates, wounded.

Marine Department;—1 seaman, killed; 2 lieutenants, 1 midshipman, 1 gunner, 12 seamen wounded.

1st Essex Militia;—2 privates, killed; 1 captain, 2 lieutenants, 2 sergeants, 7 privates, wounded.

2nd Essex Militia;—3 privates, killed; 1 ensign, 3 privates, wounded.

Staff;—1 lieutenant-colonel, wounded.

Total;—1 sergeant, 1 gunner, 21 privates, 1 seaman, killed; 1 lieutenant-colonel, 2 captains, 6 lieutenants, 2 ensigns, 1 midshipman, 6 sergeants, 5 corporals, 1 bombardier, 6 gunners, 116 privates, 12 seamen, wounded.

General total:—24 killed; 158 wounded.

Names of the Officers wounded.

Royal Artillery;—Lieutenant Troughton.

41st foot;—Captain Tallon and Lieutenant Clemow.

Royal Newfoundland Regiment;—Ensign Kerr (since dead).

Marine Department;—Lieutenants Rolette and Irvine, and Midshipman Richardson.

1st Essex Militia ;—Captain Mills, and Lieutenants McCormick and Gordon.

2nd ditto ;—Ensign Claude Garvin.

Staff ;—Lieut.-Colonel Thomas B. St. George, I.F.O. Militia.

Felix Troughton, Lt. R. A.
Act. Dep. Assist. Quarter-Master-Gen.

From Brigadier-General Winchester to the American Secretary of War.

Malden, January 23rd, 1813.

SIR,—A detachment from the left wing of the North-Western Army under my command at Frenchtown, on the river Raisin, was attacked on the 22nd instant by a force greatly superior in number, aided by several pieces of artillery. The action commenced at the dawn of day ; the picquet guards were driven in, and a heavy fire opened on the whole line, by which a part thereof was thrown into disorder ; and being ordered to retire a small distance in order to form on more advantageous ground, I found the enemy doubling our flank with force and rapidity.

A destructive fire was sustained for some time ; at length borne down by numbers, the few of us that remained with the party that retired from the lines, submitted. The remainder of our force, in number about 400, continued to defend themselves with great gallantry, in an unequal contest against small arms and artillery, until I was brought in as a prisoner to that part of the field occupied by the enemy.

At this latter place, I understood that our troops were defending themselves in a state of desperation ; and was informed by the commanding officer of the enemy, that he would afford them an opportunity of surrendering themselves prisoners of war ; to which I acceded. I was the more ready to make the surrender from being assured, that unless done quickly, the buildings adjacent would be immediately set on fire, and that no responsibility would be taken for the conduct of the savages, who were then assembled in great numbers.

In this critical situation, being desirous to preserve the lives of a number of our brave fellows who still held out, I sent a flag to them, and agreed with the commanding officer of the enemy, that they should be surrendered prisoners of war, on condition of being protected from the savages, allowed to retain their private property, and having their side-arms returned to them. It is impossible for me to ascertain, with certainty, the loss we have sustained in this action, from the impracticability of knowing the number who have made their escape.

Thirty-five officers, and about 487 non-commissioned officers, and privates, are prisoners of war. A list of the names of the officers is herewith enclosed to you. Our loss in killed is considerable.

However unfortunate may seem the affair of yesterday, I am flattered by a belief, that no material error is chargeable upon myself, and that still less censure is deserved by the troops I had the honor of commanding.

With the exception of that portion of our force which was thrown into disorder, no troops have ever behaved with more determined intrepidity.

I have the honor to be, with high respect
Your obedient Servant,
James Winchester,
Brig.-Gen. U.S. Army.

Hon. Secretary at War.

N.B.—The Indians have still a few prisoners in their possession, which I have reason to hope will be given up to Colonel Procter, at Sandwich.

James Winchester, Brig.-Gen.

———

From Major-General Harrison, to Governor Shelby.
Camp on Carrying Rock, 15 miles from the Rapids, January 24th, 1813.

My dear Sir,

I send Colonel Wells to you, to communicate the particulars (as far as we are acquainted with them) of an event that will overwhelm your mind with grief, and fill your whole State with mourning.

The greater part of Colonel Wells's regiment, United States Infantry, and the 1st and 5th regiments Kentucky Infantry, and Allen's rifle regiment, under the immediate orders of General Winchester have been cut to pieces by the enemy, or taken prisoners. Great as the calamity is, I still hope that, as far as it relates to the objects of the campaign, it is not irreparable. As soon as I was informed of the attack upon General Winchester, about 12 o'clock on the 22nd instant, I set out, to overtake the detachment of Kentucky troops, that I had sent that morning to reinforce him, and I directed the only regiment that I had with me to follow. I overtook Major Robb's detachment at the distance of 6 miles ; but before the troops in the rear could get up, certain information was received of General Winchester's total defeat.

A council of war was called, and it was the unanimous opinion of the Generals Payne and Perkins, and all the field officers, that there was no motive that could authorize an advance but that of attacking the enemy and that success was not to be expected after a forced march of 40 miles against an enemy superior in number, and well provided with artillery. Strong detachments of the most active men were, however, sent forward on all the roads, to assist and bring in such of our men as had escaped. The whole number that reached our camp does not exceed 30, amongst whom were Major McClanehan and Captain Claves.

Having a large train of heavy artillery, and stores coming on this road from W. Sandusky under an escort of four companies, it was thought advisable to fall back to this place, for the purpose of securing them. A part of it arrived last evening, and the rest is within 30 miles. As soon as it arrives, and a reinforcement of three regiments from the Virginia and Pennsylvania brigades, I shall again advance, and give the enemy an opportunity of measuring their strength with us once more.

Colonel Wells will communicate some circumstances, which, while they afflict and surprise, will convince you that Kentucky has lost none of her reputation for valor, for which she is famed. The detachment to the River Raisin was made without my knowledge or consent, and in direct opposition to my plans. Having been made, however, I did everything in my power to reinforce them, and a force exceeding by 300 men that which General Winchester deemed necessary was on its way to join him, and a fine battalion within 14 miles of its destination.

After the success of Colonel Lewis, I was in great hopes that the post could be maintained. Colonel Wells will communicate my future views to you, much better than I can do in writing at this time.

I am, dear Sir, &c.,
W. H. Harrison.

His Excellency Governor Shelby.

VIII

Far from being discouraged by the discomfiture of their armies under Generals Hull and Winchester, the Americans despatched a third and more formidable, under one of their most experienced commanders, General Harrison, who reaching Fort Meigs shortly subsequent to the affair at Frenchtown, directed his attention to the construction of works which rendered his position in some measure impregnable. Determined if possible to thwart the views of the enemy, and give a finishing stroke to his movements in that quarter, General Procter (lately promoted) ordered an expedition to be in readiness to move for the Miami. Accordingly, towards the close of April, a detachment of the 41st, some militia, and 1,500 Indians, accompanied by a train of battering artillery, and attended by two gunboats, proceeded up that river, and established themselves on the left bank, at the distance of a mile from the site selected for our batteries. The season was unusually wet, yet, in defiance of every obstacle, they were erected the same night in front of the American fortress, and the guns transported along a road in which the axle-trees of the carriages were frequently buried in mud. Among other battering pieces, were two 24-pounders—splendid guns which we had captured at Detroit—in the transportation of which 200 men with several oxen, were employed from nine o'clock at night until daybreak in the morning. At length every preparation having been made, a shot from one of the gun-boats was the signal for their opening, and early on the morning of the 1st of May, a heavy fire was commenced, and continued for four days without intermission, during which period every one

148

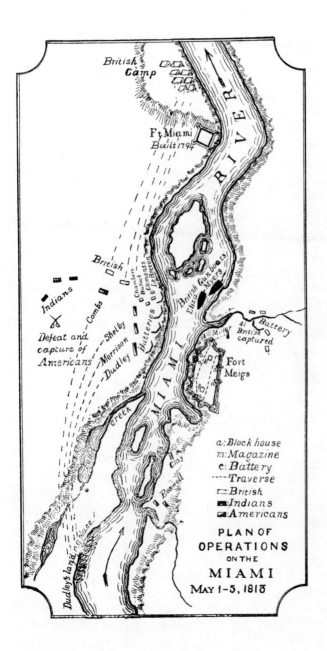

British Camp

Ft Miami Built 1794

RIVER

British

Indians

Defeat and capture of Americans

Combs
Shelby
Morrison
Dudley

Chambers
Bullocks
Clements
Le Breton

Batteries

British Gunboats

Elliot Myers

41 British captured

Battery

Miller

Fort Meigs

MIAMI

Creek

Floyd

Boswell

Clay

Dudley's landing place.

a: Block house
m: Magazine
c: Battery
----- Traverse
□ British
■ Indians
▨ Americans

PLAN OF
OPERATIONS
ON THE
MIAMI
MAY 1-5, 1813

of the enemy's batteries, within our range, was silenced and dismantled. The fire of the 24-pounder battery was principally directed against the powder magazine, which the besieged were busily occupied in covering and protecting from our hot shot. It was impossible to have artillery better served; every ball that was fired sank into the roof of the magazine, scattering the earth to a considerable distance, and burying many of the workmen in its bed, from whence we could distinctly perceive the survivors dragging forth the bodies of their slaughtered comrades. The officers, whom duty or curiosity drew to the ground—often pointed the guns—a favor on the part of the artillerymen, which was generally repaid by a glass of rum or whiskey, both which liquors were extremely scarce with us and were prized accordingly. Meanwhile the flank companies of the 41st, with a few Indians, had been detached to the opposite shore, within a few hundred yards of the enemy's works, and had constructed a battery, from which a galling cross-fire was maintained. Dismayed at the success of our operations, General Harrison, already apprized before our arrival of the approach of a reinforcement of 1,500 men, then descending the Miami under General Clay, contrived to despatch a courier on the evening of the 4th, with an order for that officer to land immediately, and possess himself of our batteries on the left bank, while he (General Harrison) sallied forth to carry those on the right. Accordingly, at eight o'clock on the morning of the 5th, General Clay pushed forward the whole of his force, and meeting with no opposition at the batteries, which were entirely unsupported, proceeded to spike the guns in conformity with his instructions; but elated with his success, and disobeying the positive order of his chief, which was to retire the instant his object was effected, he continued to occupy the position. In the meantime the flying artillerymen had given the alarm, and three companies of the

41st, several of militia, and a body of Indians, the latter
under Tecumseh, were ordered to move on the instant,
and repossess themselves of the works. The rain, which
had commenced early in the morning, continued to fall
with violence, and the road, as has already been described,
was knee-deep with mud, yet the men advanced to the
assault with the utmost alacrity and determination. The
main body of our small detachment, under Major Muir, advanced against the American left and centre which had de-
ployed into the woods, while Major Chambers, an officer
whose gallantry in the field was ever remarkable, boldly
attacked their right then occupying the principal battery.
On approaching the position he threw away his sword,
and seizing the accoutrements and musket of a soldier of
his own company who had been shot dead a moment before, called out in a voice and manner which was characteristic of the man, and which rather denoted indignation
that the enemy should have had the presumption to carry
the position than anything else, '' Who'll follow me and
retake that battery?'' I was immediately behind him at
the time, and as enthusiastically replied (excited no doubt
by the example before me) that I would. Lieutenant
Bullock, who had been wounded over the left eye
a day or two before, on the opposite side of the river,
yet who, when apprized of the capture of the batteries,
had left his tent for the purpose of aiding in their recovery, together with Lieutenant Clements (of the 41st also)
were a few paces in the rear, and these officers, followed
by not more than a dozen men who happened to be near at
the time, pressed eagerly forward in compliance with the
invitation of our dashing leader. It is a matter of perfect
surprise to me, even at this hour, that our little force,
which I have rather overrated, had not been annihilated to
a man ; for the Americans were in strength, and of
course perfectly under shelter, and the easy conquest we.
obtained (for they fled as we drew near to the battery)
can only be attributed to the fact that their centre and

left were being sorely pressed by the detachment under Major Muir, and the Indians under Tecumseh. In an account of this action, recently published by Captain Le Breton, residing near Bytown,[1] and then a Lieut. in the Newfoundland Regiment, that officer states himself to have been one of those who entered the battery with Major Chambers. Of course this is the fact, although my recollection does not embrace any other officers than those I have named, as being present on the occasion.

Driven from the batteries, the enemy in vain sought for safety in the woods. The murderous fire of the Indians, which had already dispersed their main body, drove them back upon their pursuers, until in the end there was no possibility of escape, and their army was wholly destroyed. A vast number were killed, and independently of the prisoners taken by the Indians, 450, with their second in command, fell into our hands. A somewhat curious and characteristic anecdote may be related of a soldier (an Irishman) of the 41st, who being in a position in the woods, isolated from his own party, contrived to disarm and make prisoners of three Americans who were opposed to him. On joining his company towards the close of the affair, preceded by his prizes, and sweating beneath the weight of arms, he declared with great *naïveté* and indifference that he had with great difficulty surrounded, and made them his prisoners.

Of the whole of the division under General Clay, not more than 150 men effected their escape, and among the fugitives was that officer himself. The sortie made, by order of General Harrison, on the right bank of the river had

---

[1] Bytown was the name by which the present city of Ottawa was known before it was selected as the permanent seat of the government of Canada. Bytown took its name from Lieut.-Col. By of the Royal Engineers, who constructed the Rideau canal from the present site of the city of Ottawa to Kingston. This canal was projected for the purpose of providing a safer route for the forwarding of troops and supplies to the Upper Lakes, than that offered by the St. Lawrence, in the event of another war with the United States.

a different result. The detachment supporting the battery already described were driven from their position and two officers (Lieutenants McIntyre and Hailes), and thirty men were made prisoners. Meanwhile, it having been discovered that the guns on the left bank, owing to some error on the part of the enemy, had been spiked with the ramrods of their muskets, instead of the usual instruments, they were speedily rendered serviceable, and the fire from the batteries was renewed. At this moment a white flag was observed waving on the ramparts of the fort, and the courage and perseverance of the troops appeared at length as if about to be crowned by the surrender of a fortress, the siege of which had cost them so much trouble and privation. Such, however, was far from being the intention of General Harrison. Availing himself of the cessation of hostilities which necessarily ensued, he caused the officers and men just captured to be sent across the river for the purpose of being exchanged;[1] but this was only a feint for the accomplishment of a

---

[1] An agreement for the exchange of prisoners, made between Brig.-Genl. Procter, Commanding His Britannic Majesty's Forces in the Miamis, and Maj.-Genl. Harrison, Commanding the North Western Army of the United States.

The prisoners of the Kentucky Militia, now in possession of General Procter, to be sent to the River Huron, upon the condition of not serving against Great Britain or her allies during the war between that power and the United States. Captain Price, of the First Regiment, United States Light Artillery, and twenty regulars of the United States Army, now in possession of General Procter, will be considered as exchanged, and permitted to serve after the termination of one month.

Lieuts. McIntyre and Hailes, of the 41st Regiment, and thirty-nine privates, are also to be exchanged, but are not to serve, except in garrison duty, until the expiration of one month.

A return of prisoners, released on each side, to be furnished to the respective commissaries of each nation, and the surplusage to be accounted for in a future settlement of the account of prisoners, agreeably to the tariff of exchange, heretofore established.

Headquarters Camp, Miamis, 9th May, 1813.

HENRY PROCTER, Col., Commanding His Britannic Majesty's Forces on the Miamis.

WM. HY. HARRISON, Maj.-Genl., Commanding the North Western Army of the United States.

more important object.   Drawing up his whole force, both of cavalry and infantry, on the plain beneath the fortress, he caused such of the boats of General Clay's division as were laden with ammunition, of which the garrison stood much in need, to be dropped under the works, and the stores to be immediately disembarked. All this took place during the period occupied in the exchange of prisoners.   The remaining boats, containing the baggage and private stores of the division, fell into the hands of the Indians, still engaged in the pursuit of the fugitives, and the plunder they acquired was immense. General Harrison having secured his stores, and received the officers and men exchanged for his captives, withdrew into the garrison, and the bombardment was re-commenced.

The victory obtained at the Miami[1] was such as to reflect credit on every branch of the service ; but the satisfaction arising from the conviction was deeply embittered by an act of cruelty, which, as the writer of an impartial memoir, it becomes my painful duty to record.   In the heat of the action a strong corps of the enemy, who had thrown down their arms, and surrendered themselves prisoners of war, were immediately despatched, under an escort of fifty men, for the purpose of being embarked in the gun-boats, where it was presumed they would be safe from the attacks of the Indians.   This measure, however, although dictated by the purest humanity, and apparently offering the most probable means of security, proved one of fatal import to several of the prisoners. On gaining our encampment, then entirely deserted by the troops, they were assailed by a few cowardly and treacherous Indians, who had borne no share in the action, yet who now, guided by the savage instinct of their nature, forced the British guard, and, selecting their victims, commenced the work of blood.   In vain did the harassed

[1] For this victory the 41st Regiment bears on its colors the word, Miami.

and indignant escort attempt to save them from the fury of their destroyers; the frenzy of these wretches knew no bounds, and an old and excellent soldier of the name of Russell, of the 41st, was shot through the heart while endeavoring to wrest a victim from the grasp of his assailant. Forty of these unhappy men had already fallen beneath the steel of the infuriated party, when Tecumseh, apprized of what was doing, rode up at full speed, and raising his tomahawk, threatened to destroy the first man who resisted his injunction to desist. Even on those lawless people, to whom the language of coercion had hitherto been unknown, the threats and tone of the exasperated chieftain produced an instantaneous effect, and they retired at once humiliated and confounded. Never did Tecumseh shine more truly himself than on this occasion; and nought of the savage could be distinguished save the color and the garb. Ever merciful and magnanimous as he was ardent and courageous, the voice of the supplicant seldom reached him in vain; and although war was his idol, the element in which he lived, his heart was formed to glow with all the nobler and more generous impulses of the warrior; nor was his high character less esteemed by ourselves than reverenced by the various tribes over which, in his quality of brother to the Prophet, he invariably presided. In any other country, and governing any other men, Tecumseh would have been a hero; at the head of this uncivilized and untractable people he was a savage; but a savage such as civilization herself might not blush to acknowledge for her child. Constantly opposed to the encroachments of the Americans for a series of years previous to their rupture with England, he had combatted their armies on the banks of the Wabash with success, and given their leaders proofs of a skill and judgment in defence of his native soil, which would not have disgraced the earlier stages of military science in Europe. General Harrison himself, a commander with whom he had often disputed the palm of victory, with the generous candor of the soldier, subsequently ascribed to him virtues as a man, and abilities as a warrior, commanding at once the attention and admiration of his enemies.

The survivors of this melancholy catastrophe were immediately conveyed on board the gun-boats moored in the river ; and every precaution having been taken to prevent a renewal of the scene, the escorting party proceeded to the interment of the victims, to whom the rites of sepulture were afforded even before those of our own men who had fallen in the action. Colonel Dudley, second in command of General Clay's division, was among the number of the slain.

In alluding to the painful occurrence above detailed James states that "Tecumseh buried his tomahawk in the head of a Chippeway Chief whom he found actively engaged in massacring some of Colonel Dudley's men." He furthermore shows, that Colonel Dudley fell in an ambuscade prepared by a body of Indians, stationed in the woods. Neither of these statements is correct— Colonel Dudley was taken prisoner and subsequently massacred in the manner just detailed, while Tecumseh was spared the necessity of inflicting the punishment attributed to him by an instant compliance with his will, on the part of the insubordinate and guilty, but excited Indians.

In bright relief to this piece of treachery and atrocity on the part of the Chippeways, (well known to be the most degenerate of the Indian race) let me hasten to record the noble conduct of a warrior of a very different tribe.

Metoss, the head chief of the Sacs, was a tall, handsome man about six feet in height, and with features (as is peculiar indeed with the whole of this nation) essentially classic and Roman. When dressed, or rather undressed for battle, his body and limbs fantastically painted, and his head ornamented with a handsome circlet of feathers, his tall and commanding figure presented the very *beau ideal* of an Indian warrior. He was a resolute man, and although by no means gifted with the eloquence or intellect of Tecumseh, was a sagacious and active leader—firm in his attachment to British interests, and a most determined foe of the Americans, for whom he had conceived a hatred almost as powerful as that which actuated the noble being who has just been named. The injuries inflicted upon his red brethren rankled at his heart, and appeared to be ever present to his recollection. Still he could forgive an individual wrong, even when perpetrated by those whom he had so much reason to abhor—in proof of which, and to redeem the grossly maligned Indian character, the following touching circumstances may be related.

During the early part of the siege, Metoss with his warriors frequently passed over from the left to the right bank of the river, (where the 41st flank companies were stationed, in support of the small battery which had been constructed there) with a view of picking off such of the enemy as showed themselves above or without the ramparts of the fort. In these excursions the Sacs were generally successful, and the enemy seldom went to the river for water, for themselves or horses, without a shot from a lurking Indian. Metoss himself killed several in this way. One he contrived to make his prisoner, whom he kept in his wigwam, well secured. On the day following this capture, a favorite son of the chief—a fine lad of about thirteen—insisted on accompanying his father, notwithstanding all entreaty to the contrary. By this time the enemy had become so annoyed by the temerity of the Indians who, under cover of the night, used to creep close under the fort, that upon the appearance of any of them on the skirt of the surrounding forest, a shower of grape was instantly poured forth. Unhappily, on this occasion, the American telescopes discovered Metoss and his son in ambuscade, when a discharge of grape

followed, and the poor boy was struck dead, dreadfully
mangled in his bowels. Almost frantic with grief, the
chief raised up the dead body, conveyed it to his canoe,
and recrossing the river, hastened to his wigwam, with
the stern determination of sacrificing his prisoner to the
manes of the deceased. Fortunately Mr. Robert Dickson,
who had brought the Sacs with him from the Mississippi,
and whose influence over the Indians has already been
shown to have been great, heard of the circumstance in
time to intercept Metoss on his way to his wigwam, and
to entreat that he would not destroy his prisoner, assuring
him, at the same time, that if he did so, instead of surrendering him to himself as he proposed he should, His
Great Father, the King, would hear of his refusal with
unfeigned sorrow. Metoss, who had torn off the gay
head-dress with which he ever went into battle, at length
yielded, and going to his wigwam, whither his son's body
had already been conveyed, he went up to the American,
and severing with his knife the thongs by which he was
fastened, took him by the hand, and led him to Mr.
Dickson, saying in a mournful voice, "You tell me that
my Great Father wishes it—take him," and this noble-
hearted Indian, no longer able to suppress the feelings of
his bereaved heart, wept like a child. The gaudy colors
with which he was painted were soon replaced with black,
and many months passed away before he was again seen
to smile.

The body of the young Indian was buried the next
day, and, out of respect to the father, with all military
honors. The funeral party, which was commanded by
Lieut. Bullock, proceeded to the wigwam of Metoss, where
the body of the young Chief was laid out—his little rifle,
with some powder and ball, and a supply of provisions,
according to Indian usage, being placed at his side.
About a dozen of the Sac tribe, all painted black, were
dancing what seemed to be a solemn war-dance around
the body, when suddenly Metoss rushed frantically into

the midst of the group, and exhibited every painful evidence of the most violent and ungovernable grief. With difficulty he was removed from the body of his child, when the corpse was taken up, and the party proceeded towards the grave which had been dug in the midst of our encampment, on the left bank of the Miami. The black-painted Indians slowly followed, and after the British party had fired the customary three rounds, they discharged their rifles several times as fast as they could load. The fierce wild air of the warriors, whose countenances evinced the strong desire they entertained of avenging the untimely death of the fallen youth, the originality of their costume, markedly contrasting as it did with that of the officers and soldiers present at the ceremony, and the sombre silence which prevailed, heightened in effect by the deep gloom of the forest in which they were assembled, composed a wild and romantic picture, in which melancholy grandeur shone principally conspicuous.

When the expedition subsequently returned to Amherstburg, Metoss, who had embarked in General Procter's boat, was frequently observed to be in tears. He later conceived a strong attachment for Lieut. Bullock, principally by reason of that officer having commanded the funeral party of his son. He made him a chief of his tribe, and requested, as a great favor, that he would assent to an exchange of names. This was of course cheerfully complied with, for it was impossible not to esteem and like the untutored warrior who had so nobly, and in so affecting a manner, departed from the fierce Indian law which, not only authorizes, but enjoins the sacrifice of life for life.

On the evening of the second day after this event, I accompanied Major Muir of the 41st, in a ramble throughout the encampment of the Indians, distant a few hundred yards from our own. The spectacle there offered o our view was at once of the most ludicrous and revolting nature. In various directions were lying the trunks and boxes taken in the boats of Gen. Clay's division, and the plunderers were busily occupied in displaying their riches, carefully examining each article, and attempting to divine its use. Several were decked out in the uniforms of the officers ; and although embarrassed to the last degree in their movements, and dragging with difficulty the heavy military boots with which their legs were for the first time covered, strutted forth much to the admiration of their less fortunate comrades. Some were habited in plain clothes ; others had their bodies clad in clean white shirts, contrasting in no ordinary manner with the swarthiness of their skins ; all wore some article of decoration, and their tents were ornamented with saddles, bridles, rifles, daggers, swords, and pistols, many of which were handsomely mounted and of curious workmanship. Such was the ridiculous part of the picture ; but mingled with these, and in various directions, were to be seen the scalps of the slain drying in the sun, stained on the fleshy side with vermilion dyes, and dangling in the air, as they hung suspended from the poles to which they were attached ; together with hoops of various sizes, on which were stretched portions of human skin taken from various parts of the body, principally the hand and foot, and yet covered with the nails of those parts ; while, scattered along the ground, were visible the members from which they had been separated, and serving as nutriment to the wolf-dogs by which the Indians were accompanied.

Since the action of the 5th the enemy continued to keep themselves shut up within their works, and the bombardment, although followed up with vigor, had effected no practicable breach. From the report made by the officers captured during the sortie from the fort, it appeared that, with a toil and perseverance peculiar to themselves, the Americans had constructed subterranean passages to protect them from the annoyance of our shells, which sinking into beds of clay, softened by the incessant rains that had fallen, instead of exploding, were immediately extinguished. Impatient of longer privation, and anxious to return to their families and occupations, the militia[1] gradually withdrew themselves in small bodies, while the Indians, enriched by plunder, and languishing under the tediousness of a mode of warfare so different from their own, with less ceremony and caution, left us to prosecute the siege alone. Tecumseh at the head of his own tribe (the Shawnees) and a few others, in all not exceeding four hundred warriors, continued to remain. The troops also were worn down by constant fatigue, for here, as in every other expedition undertaken against the enemy, few even of the officers had tents to shield them from the weather. A few slips of bark torn from the surrounding trees, and covering the skeleton of a hut, was their only habitation, and they were merely separated from the damp earth by a few scattered leaves, over which was generally

---

[1]The following is the statement of the Militia Captains to Lieut.-Col. Warburton, Inspecting Field Officer of Militia :—

Camp Miamis, 6th May, 1813.

Sir,—We, the undersigned officers of the first and second Regiments of Essex and Kent Militia, beg leave to state to you, as head of the Militia, our opinion on the present circumstances of the Militia-men, and of the District in general.

From the situation of our district last fall but very short crops of grain were put in the ground, and these, small as they were, will be rendered still less by the unfavorableness of last winter. Under these unfavorable appearances the farmer had only the resource left of putting in crops of spring wheat, and should they be kept here any longer, that of corn will also be out of their power, and the consequence must be a famine next winter. Indeed, the men are now detained with the greatest reluctance, some have already gone, and we are apprehensive that it will not be in our power to detain them much longer.

We have the honor to be

Your obedient humble servants,

Wm. Shaw, Captain, Kent Militia.
Wm. Caldwell, Captain, 1st Regt., Essex.
Geo. Jacob, Captain, Kent Militia.
Wm. Buchanan, Captain, 1st Essex Militia.
John Dolson, Captain, Kent Riflemen.
Wm. Elliott, Captain, Essex Militia.
Wm. Sterling, Captain, Kent Militia.
Jas. Askin, Captain, 2nd Essex Militia.

spread a great coat or blanket by the men, and a cloak by the officers. Hence frequently arose dysentery, ague, and the various other ills to which an army, encamped in a wet and unhealthy position is invariably subject ; and fortunate was he who possessed the skin of the bear or the buffalo, whereon to repose his weary limbs, after many consecutive hours of toil and privation which those only, who have acquired practical experience in the wild warfare peculiar to the country at that period, can fully understand.

Such was the position of the contending armies towards the middle of May, when General Procter (very naturally) despairing to effect the reduction of Fort Meigs, caused preparations to be made for raising the siege. Accordingly the gun-boats ascended the river, and anchored as near to the batteries as the lowness of the water would permit. Here the battering ordnance was embarked under a feeble fire from the enemy, and the whole having been secured, the expedition returned to Amherstburg, the Americans remaining tranquil spectators of our departure, nor offering further molestation.

It is a circumstance perhaps not unworthy of remark here that in 1840, after a lapse of twenty-seven years (during three and twenty of which I had been absent from the country), I alone of the force engaged at the siege of Fort Meigs, should have met with General Harrison on the very spot which he so vigorously defended against us in 1813 ; and, yet more remarkable, that the occasion of such meeting should have been the commemoration of the events of that important period. It was during the great delegation, or convention, which preceded the gallant old General's elevation to the Presidential chair, and when introduced to him by the Governor of Michigan, as one who had borne arms against him during that siege, and had later become his prisoner, I was received in that spirit of true and generous courtesy which is ever characteristic of the soldier. It is but an act of justice to the memory of General Harrison to record here that, although the great object of the meeting—at which were present from fifty to sixty thousand persons—deputed from almost every state in the Union —was to honor him by celebrating his *asserted* triumph over the British arms, there was, in his address to the hushed multitude, when referring to his past services, less of allusion to those of the War of 1812, than to those of the revolution.

The following is General Procter's official account of the action.

Upper Canada, Sandwich, May 14th, 1813.

SIR,—The usual communication being interrupted by the capital of the Province being in the possession of the enemy, I have judged it expedient to make a direct report to your Excellency of our operations and present state in this district.

In the expectation of being able to reach the enemy, who had taken post near the foot of the Rapids of the Miami, before the reinforcement and supplies could arrive, for which only he waited to commence active operations against us, I determined to attack him without delay, and with every means in my power; but from the necessary preparations and some untoward circumstances, it was not in my power to reach him within three weeks of the period I had proposed, and at which he might have been captured or destroyed.

From the incessant and heavy rains we experienced, and during which our batteries were constructed, it was not until the morning of the 1st inst., the fifth day after our arrival at the mouth of the river, twelve miles from the enemy, that our batteries could be opened. Illness from successive fatigue deprived me of the services early of the only Artillery officer, on an occasion when three would have found ample employment.

The enemy who occupied several acres of commanding ground, strongly defended by block-houses, and batteries well furnished with ordnance, had, during our approach, so completely entrenched and covered himself, as to render unavailing every effort of our artillery, though well served, and in batteries most judiciously placed and constructed under the able direction of Captain Dixon, of the Royal Engineers, of whose ability and unwearied zeal, shown particularly on this occasion, I cannot speak too highly.

Though our attack had not answered fully the purpose intended, I have the satisfaction to inform your Excellency of the fortunate result of an attack of the enemy, aided by a sally of most of their garrison, made on the morning of the 5th inst., by a reinforcement which descended the river a considerable distance in a very short time ; consisting of two corps of Kentucky Militia, Dudley's and Boswell's, amounting to 1,300 men, under the command of Brigadier-General Green Clay.   The attack was very sudden, and on both sides of the river.   The enemy were for a few minutes in possession of our batteries, and took some prisoners.   After a severe contest, though not of long continuance, the enemy gave way, and excepting the body of those who sallied from the fort, must have been mostly killed or taken.

In this decisive affair, the officers and men of the 41st Regt., who charged and routed the enemy near the batteries, well maintained the long-established reputation of the corps.   Where all deserve praise it is difficult to distinguish.   Captain Muir, an old officer, who has seen much service, had the good fortune to be in the immediate command of these branches.   Besides my obligations to Captain Chambers, for his unwearied exertions preparatory to, and on the expedition, as Deputy-Assistant-Quarter-Master-General, I have to notice his gallant conduct in the attack of the enemy near the batteries at the point of the bayonet ; a service in which he was well supported by Lieut. Bullock of the 41st Regt. and Lieut. Le Breton of the Royal Newfoundland Regt.   The courage and activity displayed through the whole scene of action by the Indian chiefs and warriors contributed largely to our success.   I have not been able to ascertain the amount of the prisoners in possession of the Indians.   I have sent off agreeable to the agreement, near 500 prisoners to the river Huron, near Sandusky.

I have proposed an exchange, which is referred to the American Government.

I could not ascertain the amount of the enemy's loss in killed, from the extent of the scene of action, and mostly in the woods.   I conceive his loss to have been between 1,000 and 1,200 men in killed and prisoners.

These unfortunate people were not volunteers and complete Kentucky's quota.   If the enemy had been permitted to receive his reinforcements and supplies undisturbed, I should have had at this critical juncture to contend with him for Detroit, or perhaps on this shore.

I had not the option of retaining my situation on the Miami if it had appeared to me a judicious measure. The mode in which the militia turned out raised hopes and expectations that were very far from being realized in the sequel. The day after the enclosed letter was received half of the militia had left us and the remainder declared their determination not to remain longer. I also received a deputation from the Indian chiefs, counselling me to return, as they could not prevent their people, as was their custom after any battle of consequence, returning to their villages with their wounded, their prisoners, and plunder, of which they had taken a considerable quantity in the boats of the enemy.

Before the ordnance could be withdrawn from the batteries, I was left with Tecumseh, and less than twenty chiefs and warriors, (?) a circumstance which strongly proves that, under present circumstances at least, our Indian force is not a disposable one, or permanent, though occasionally a most powerful aid.   I have, however, brought off all the ordnance ; and, indeed, have not left anything behind ;   part of the ordnance was embarked under the fire of the enemy.

The service on which we have been employed has been, though short, a very severe one ; and too much praise cannot be given to the officers and men, for the cheerfulness with which, on every occasion, they met the service. To Lieut.-Colonel Warburton I feel many obligations for the aid he zealously afforded me on every occasion. From my Brigade-Major, Lieut. McLean, I received the same zealous assistance as on former occasions.   To Captain Mockler, Royal Newfoundland Regt., who acted as my Aide-de-Camp, I am much indebted for the assistance afforded me.

Lieut. Le Breton, of the Royal Newfoundland Regt., assistant engineer, by his unwearied exertions, rendered essential service, as did also Lieut. Gardiner, of the 41st Regt., from his science in artillery. The Royal Artillery, in the laborious duties they performed, displayed their usual unwearied zeal, and were well assisted by the Royal Newfoundland, (under Lieut. Garden) as additional gunners. The laborious duties which the marine, under the command of Commodore Hall, have performed, have been most cheerfully met, and the most essential service rendered.

I have the honor to send an embarkation return of the force that served under my command at the Miami, exclusive of the Indians, who may be stated at 1,200.

I also enclose a return of our killed, wounded, and prisoners, who have, however, been exchanged.

I had taken upon me to give the rank of major to the six captains of the line, as militia were employed on the same service with them ; some of them are old officers ; all of them deserving ; any mark of your Excellency's approbation of them would be extremely grateful to me.

I beg leave to mention the four volunteers of the 41st Regt., Wilkinson, Richardson, Laing, and Procter, as deserving of promotion.

Your Excellency will perceive that the reinforcement you intended I should have long since received has not been sent ; nor do I expect to receive any whilst any circumstance may seem to justify their detention. I had only half the 41st Regt. before the late action. Daily experience more strongly proves that a regular force is absolutely requisite to ensure the safety of this district, and which may be endangered by the detention of the intended reinforcement. My Brigade Major, Lieut. McLean, who is the bearer of my reports, will be able to give your Excellency any further information relative to this district or our late movements that may be required. I hope by sending him, and by the only service route at present, will meet with your Excellency's approbation.

I have the honor to be, &c.,

(Signed)   Henry Procter,
Brigadier-General, Comg.

I beg to acknowledge the indefatigable exertions of the Commissariat.   (Signed)   Henry Procter.
To His Excellency Lieut.-General ⎱
  Sir G. Prevost, Bart., &c.   ⎰

Embarkation return of the Western Army commanded by Brigadier-General Procter, on an expedition to the Miami.

Amherstburg, April 23, 1813.

General Staff,—1 general, 1 lieut.-colonel, 1 dep. asst-. qr.-mr.-general, 1 brigade major, 1 staff adjutant.

Royal Artillery,—1 lieut., 1 serjeant, 1 surgeon, 1 drummer, 27 rank and file.

Royal Engineers,—1 captain.

10th Royal Veteran Battalion,—5.

41st Regiment,—3 captains, 7 lieutenants, 1 assistant surgeon, 22 serjeants, 6 drummers and buglers, 374 rank and file.

Royal Newfoundland Regt.—1 captain, 2 lieutenants, 3 serjeants, 2 drummers, 55 rank and file.

Commissariat,—1 dep. asst.-commissary-general, 1 assistant to do., 1 issuer.

Field Train,—1 clerk of stores, 1 conductor.

Militia,—1 major, 12 captains, 11 lieutenants, 8 ensigns, 1 adjt., 1 quarter-master, 22 serjeants, 406 rank and file.

(Signed)   Peter L. Chambers, Major.

Capt. 41st Regt., Dep. Asst.-Qr.-Mr.-General.

Return of killed, wounded, missing and prisoners, of the Army under the command of Brig.-Gen. Procter, at the battle fought at the Miami, May 5th, 1813.

Royal Artillery,—1 serjeant, 1 rank and file wounded, 2 rank and file prisoners.

41st Regiment,—11 rank and file killed, 1 lieutenant, 3 serjeants, 35 rank and file wounded, 2 lieutenants, 1 serjeant, 1 drummer, 33 rank and file prisoners.

Royal Newfoundland Regt.—1 drummer, 2 rank and file killed, 1 rank and file wounded, 1 rank and file prisoner.

Militia,—1 captain, 4 rank and file wounded, 1 rank and file prisoner.

Total,—1 drummer, 13 rank and file killed, 1 capt., 1 lieut., 4 serjeants, 41 rank and file wounded, 2 lieuts., 1 serjeant, 1 drummer, 37 rank and file prisoners.

Names of officers wounded and prisoners.

41st Regiment.—Lieut. Bullock wounded on the 3rd inst. Lieuts. McIntyre and Hailes prisoners.

Militia,—Captain Bondy, since dead.

(Signed)   Peter L. Chambers,

&c, &c, &c.

Return of Officers, Non-Commissioned Officers and privates taken prisoners from the enemy on the 5th May, 1813, at the battle fought at the Miami.

United States Regulars,—1 captain, 21 rank and file.

10th and 13th detachment Kentucky Militia,—2 majors,

1 brigade inspector, 8 captains, 9 lieutenants, 6 ensigns,
1 adjutant, 1 paymaster, 1 surgeon, 1 asst. surgeon, 26
serjeants, 3 drummers, 373 rank and file.

Prisoners since delivered up } 1 ensign, 1 asst. surgeon,
by the Indians.   }   12 rank and file.

Grand Total, 468.

N.B. There are a number of prisoners not yet come
in, who are in the possession of the Indians, but they are
bringing them in daily.

(Signed)   Peter L. Chambers,
                   &c,   &c,   &c.

May 17th,—Since the above return, 28 prisoners have
been given up by the Indians.

(Signed)   A. H. McLean,
                   Brigade Major.

In reference to the closing paragraph[1] of the despatch,
in which, as it will be perceived, the Volunteers of the
41st are for the first, and only time named, I cannot
forbear a passing comment. I had the honor of being
particularly named, in Major Chambers' report[2] to General Procter of the action of the 5th of May, as having
been the only one of the volunteers who chanced to have
been engaged in the storming of the batteries. Yet the
Official despatch includes the names of all, without any
regard to their particular service. Messrs. Laing and
Wilkinson were on the right bank of the river with the
defeated party, who of course did their duty, but of
whom no particular mention is made, while the General's
son never once quitted the encampment during the day,
or was at any period, either then or heretofore, suffered
to be exposed to the enemy's fire. This remark would
not have been recorded but for the very glaring injustice

[1] Richardson evidently copied Procter's report as given by James,
who appears to have taken unwarranted liberties with the original. The closing paragraph of the report is omitted by James and
consequently does not appear in Richardson. The reference here
is to the next to the closing paragraph.

[2] Major Chambers in a letter to Noah Freer, Military Secretary,
gives a concise account of the events of each day from April 24th
to the close of the action on May 5th. No person is particularly
mentioned in his report of the action of May 5th. I have not seen
Major Chambers' report to General Procter.

which, in bestowing commendation in so general and un-distinguishable a manner, would aim at depriving a sol-dier of that distinct claim to approbation, admitted by his immediate commanding officer to have been won from him on the field. In the course of this narrative of mili-tary events, in which, it must be borne in mind by the reader, I was a constant participator, I have endeavored, as much as possible, to avoid any personal allusion to myself ; but this is a case where the injustice is too marked to be passed silently by. I had never seen Gen-eral Procter's despatch, until this narrative was com-menced, but had always understood it to have embraced the particular report made by Major Chambers, which, however, seems to have been suppressed.

Copy of a despatch from Gen. Harrison (No. 1) to the Secretary of War dated

Head-Quarters, Camp Meigs, 9th May, 1813.

Sir,—I have the honor to inform you, that the enemy, having been several days making preparations for raising the siege of this post, accomplished this day the removal of their artillery, from the opposite bank, and about 12 o'clock left their encampment below, were soon em-barked, and out of sight.—I have the honor to enclose you an agreement entered into between Gen. Procter and myself, for the discharge of the prisoners of the Ken-tucky militia, in his possession, and for the exchange of the Officers and men of the regular troops, which were respectively possessed by us. My anxiety to get the Kentucky troops released as early as possible induced me to agree to the dismission of all the prisoners I had, although there was not as many of ours in Gen. Procter's possession ; the surplusage is to be accounted for, and an equal number of ours released from their parole, whenever the government may think proper to direct it.

The two actions on this side of the river, on the 5th, were infinitely more important and more honorable to our arms, than I had at first conceived. In the sortie made upon the left flank, Capt. Waring's company of the 19th regiment, a detachment of 12 months' volunteers, under Major Alexander, and three companies of Kentucky militia, under Colonel Boswell, defeated at least double the number of Indians and British militia. The sortie on the right was still more glorious. The British batteries, in that direction, were defended by the grenadier and light infantry companies, of the 41st regiment, amounting to 200 effectives, and two companies of militia, flanked by a host of Indians. The detachment sent to attack these, consisted of all the men off duty, belonging to the companies of Croghan and Bradford, of the 17th regiment, Langham's, Elliott's, (late Graham's,) and Waring's, of the 19th, about 80 of Major Alexander's volunteers, and a single company of Kentucky militia, under Captain Sebree, amounting, in the whole, to not more than 340. Yet the event of the action was not a moment doubtful ; and, had not the British troops been covered in their retreat by their *allies*, the whole of them would have been taken.

It is not possible for troops to behave better than ours did, throughout ; all the officers exerted themselves to execute my orders, and the enemy, who had a full view of our operations, from the opposite shore, declared that they had never seen so much work performed in so short a time.

To all the commandants of corps, I feel particular obligations ; these were Col. Miller, of the 19th infantry, Col. Mills, of the Ohio militia, Major Stoddart, of the artillery, Major Ball, of the dragoons, and Major Johnson, of the Kentucky militia.

Captain Gratiot, of the engineers, having been, for a long time, much indisposed, the task of fortifying this post devolved on Captain Wood ; it could not have been placed in better hands. Permit me to recommend him to the President, and to assure you that any mark of his approbation, bestowed on Captain Wood, would be highly gratifying to the whole of the troops, who witnessed his arduous exertions.

From Major Hukill, Acting Inspector-General, my aid-de-camp, Major Graham, Lieutenant O'Fallon, who has done the duty of Assistant Adjutant-General in the absence of Major Adams, and my volunteer aid-de-camp, John Johnson, Esq., I received the most useful assistance.

I have the honor to enclose you a list of the killed and wounded, during the siege, and in the two sorties ; those of the latter were much greater than I had at first expected.

Want of sleep, and exposure to the continued rains which have fallen almost every day, for some time past, render me incapable of mentioning many interesting particulars ; amongst others, a most extraordinary proposition of General Procter's, on the subject of the Indians, within our boundary ; this shall form the subject of a communication, to be made to-morrow or next day, and for which I will provide a safer conveyance than that which carries this.

All the prisoners and deserters agree in saying, that the information given to Major Stoddart, by Ryland, of the British having launched a sloop of war this spring, is incorrect; and the most of them say, that the one which is now building will not be launched for many weeks.

I am, &c.

W. H. HARRISON.

Hon. J. Armstrong.

P.S. Captain Price, of the Regiment Light Artillery; and the 20 Regulars, prisoners with General Procter, were taken on the northwestern side of the river, with the Kentucky militia. We had no prisoners taken on this side during the siege.

In the siege, and the several sorties of the 5th instant, there was 81 killed, and 189 wounded—total, killed and wounded, 270.

———

Copy of a Despatch, from Maj. General William H. Harrison (No. 2) to the Secretary of War, dated

Headquarters, Lower Sandusky, May 13, 1813.

SIR,—Having ascertained that the enemy (Indians as well as British,) had entirely abandoned the neighborhood of the Rapids, I left the command of camp Meigs with General Clay, and came here last night. It is with the greatest satisfaction I inform you, Sir, that the loss of the Kentucky troops, in killed, on the north side of the river, does not exceed fifty. On the 10th and 11th inst. I caused the ground, which was the scene of action, and its environs, to be carefully examined ; and, after the most diligent search, 45 bodies only, of our men, were discovered ; amongst them was the leader of the detachment, Col. Dudley. No other officer of note fell in the action. I have strong reason to believe that a considerable number of Kentuckians effected their retreat up the river, to Fort Winchester. General Procter did not furnish me with a return of the prisoners in his possession, although repeatedly promised.

His retreat was as precipitate as it could possibly be, leaving a number of cannon balls, a new elegant sling carriage for cannon, and other valuable articles. The night before his departure, two persons that were employed in the British gun-boats (Americans by birth), deserted to us—the information they gave me was very interesting ; they say that the Indians, of which there were from 1,600 to 2,000, left the British, the day before their departure, in a high state of dissatisfaction, from the great loss which they had sustained in the several engagements of the 5th, and the failure of the British, in accomplishing their promise, of taking the post at the Rapids. From the account given by these men, my opinion is confirmed of the great superiority of the enemy, which were defeated by our troops in the two sallies made on the 5th instant. That, led by Col. Miller, did not exceed 350 men ; and it is very certain that they defeated 200 British regulars, 150 militia men, and 400 or 500 Indians. That American regulars, (although they were raw recruits), and such men as compose the Pittsburg, Penn., and Petersburg, Va., volunteers, should behave well is not to be wondered at ; but, that a company of militia should maintain its ground, against four times its number, as did Captain Sebree's, of the Kentucky, is truly astonishing. These brave fellows were at length, however, entirely surrounded by Indians, and would have been cut off, but for the gallantry of Lieut. Gwynne, of the 19th regiment, who, with a part of Captain Elliott's company, charged the enemy, and released the Kentuckians. I enclose you a list of the killed and wounded during the whole siege ;—it is considerably larger than I supposed it would be, when I last wrote you—but it is satisfactory to know that they did not bleed uselessly, but in the course of successful exertions. The return does not embrace those who fell on the Northwestern side of the Miami.—You will also receive, herewith, a monthly return of the troops, at camp Meigs, for the last month ; the communication with the other posts being cut off, the returns were not received. A copy of Gen. Clay's report to me, of the manner of his executing my order, for the attack on the enemy's batteries, is likewise forwarded, by which it will be seen that my intentions were perfectly understood ; and the great facility with which they might have been executed is apparent to every individual who witnessed the scene ; indeed, the cannon might have been spiked and the carriages cut to pieces, the magazine destroyed, and the retreat effected to the boats, without the loss of a man, as none were killed in taking the batteries—so complete was the surprise.

An extensive open plain intervenes between the river and the hill, upon which the batteries of the enemy were placed ; this plain was raked by 4 of our 18 pounders, a 12, and a 6 ; the enemy, even before their guns were spiked, could not have brought one to bear upon it. So perfectly secured was their retreat, that the 150 men, who came off, effected it without loss, and brought off some of the wounded, one of them upon the back of his comrade. The Indians followed them to the woods, but dared not enter into the plain.

I am unable to form a correct estimate of the enemy's force. The prisoners varied much in their accounts ; those who made them least, stated the regulars at 560, and the militia at 800; but the number of Indians were beyond comparison greater than have ever been brought into the field before ; numbers arrived after the siege commenced. I have caused their camps, on the S. E. side of the river, to be particularly examined, and the general opinion is, that there could not have been fewer on that side than 1,000 or 1,200. They were, indeed, the efficient force of the enemy.

I have the honor to acknowledge the receipt of your favors of the 14th, 18th, and 28th ultimo, and 5th inst.

I am sorry to inform you, that Major Stoddard died the night before I left the Rapids, of a lock-jaw, produced by a slight wound from a fragment of a shell, which struck him on the thigh ; several have died in this way, from their great and unavoidable exposure to the cold ; but, perhaps there were never so many instances of desperate wounds likely to do well. The gallant Captain Bradford will recover.

I shall go from here to Upper Sandusky, and shall take my station at Delaware, or Franklinton, until the troops are assembled. Gen. Clay, who commands at the Rapids, is a man of capacity, and entirely to be relied upon.

I have the honor, &c.

Wm. H. Harrison.

Hon. J. Armstrong, Sec. War.

Killed, 81—wounded, 189, in the siege of Camp Meigs and the several sorties of the 5th of May, 1813.

Copy of a letter from Gen. Clay, to Gen. Harrison.

Camp at Fort Meigs, May 13th, 1813.

Sir,—On the 5th instant, about 8 o'clock, A.M., descending the Miami of the lake, about midway of the Rapids, with 1,200 of the Kentucky troops, in the eighteen flat-bottomed boats, I was met by Captain Hamilton and a subaltern, who delivered me (as he said) the orders of Major-Gen. Harrison to the following effect :

" You must detach about 800 men from your brigade, who will land at a point I will show, about one, or one and a half miles above the fort, and I will conduct them to the British batteries, on the left bank of the river— they must take possession of the enemy's cannon, spike them, cut down the carriages, and return to their boats," observing that the British force at their large batteries was inconsiderable ; but that their main force was at the old garrison, about one and a half miles below, on the same side of the river, that the Indian forces were chiefly on the right bank of the river—" the balance of the men under your command must land on the right bank, opposite to the first landing, and will fight their way through the Indians to the fort,"—observing that the route thus to be taken, would be shown by a subaltern officer there, in company with Captain Hamilton, who would land the perogue at the point on the right bank, at which the boats would land.

The order of descending the river in boats was the same as the order of march, in line of battle, in solid column, each officer taking position according to his rank. Col. Dudley, the eldest colonel, led the van, and in this order the river had been descended. As soon as Captain Hamilton had delivered these orders, being in the thirteenth boat from the front, I directed him to proceed immediately to Col. Dudley, and order him to take the men in the 12 front boats, and execute Gen. Harrison's orders, on the left bank of the river; and to post his (Capt. Hamilton's) subaltern on the right bank, to conduct myself, with the men in the six boats, to the fort. I ordered the five boats in the rear to fall in a line, and follow me. High winds, and the rapidity of the current, drove four of the rear boats ashore, in the attempt to follow on according to order, where they remained a short time ; sufficient, however, to detain them one-half, or three-fourths of a mile to the rear.—To land, according to order, I kept close along the right bank, until opposite Col Dudley's landing ; there I found no guide left to conduct me to the fort, as Captain Hamilton promised. I then made an attempt to cross the river, and join Col. Dudley ; but, from the rapid current on the falls, I was unable to land on the point with him. Being nearly half way across the river, and the waves running too high to risk the boats then driving down the current sidewise, veered about the boat, and rowed the best way we could, to save our boat. My attempt to cross the river, to Col. Dudley, occasioned all the boats, (I presume in the rear of me), and which were then out of hailing distance, to cross over, and land with Col. Dudley. Having been defeated in landing on the left, we then endeavored to effect one on the right, even without a guide ; but before a landing could be effected, we received a brisk fire from the enemy on shore, which was returned, and kept up on both sides ; and I was in this unavoidable situation, compelled to make to Fort Meigs ,with no other force than about 50 men on board, (the other boats being still in the rear) and to receive the enemy's fire, until we arrived under the protection of the fort. Col. Boswell's command (except the men in my boat,) having landed, to join Col. Dudley, were, as I have been informed, ordered by Captain Hamilton, immediately to embark, and land on the right hand shore, about a mile above the fort, and prepare to fight his way through to the garrison. The Colonel embarked, landed, as he conceived, at the proper point, pursuant to Captain Hamilton's order, and was forming his men in order of battle, when he was met by Captain Shaw, and ordered to march into the garrison, at open order, the safest route.

When my own boat landed, we were met by two men, who took charge of the boat, as we understood, to bring her under the protection of the fort batteries ; believing our baggage to be thus made safe, we forbid our servants to carry any portion of it ; but loaded them with cannon balls, which they bore to the fort. Our baggage was, however, taken by the Indians, in a very short time after we left the boat. Upon receiving the orders of Capt. Hamilton, I asked if he had brought spikes, to spike the enemy's cannon ? to which he replied, that he had plenty. Capt. Hamilton, on delivering the orders of General Harrison, observed, that the object of landing, and marching a portion of the troops on the right bank, was to draw the attention of the Indians ; and, by thus engaging them, afford an opportunity to the garrison to make a sally ; and, by a circuitous route, surprise and carry the batteries and cannon of the enemy, below the fort, on the right bank.

I am, respectfully, &c.,

GREEN CLAY, Brig.-Gen.

His Ex. Maj.-Gen. Harrison.

The following General Order, issued by Brigadier Green Clay to his troops, preparatory to their departure for the Miami, is so amusingly in contrast with the report made by him of his defeat, that, although suppressed by the American historians of the war, it would be an unpardonable omission not to record it here. It will be remarked that this corps met with precisely the same fate with their *butchered* brethren of the River Raisin, they were hastening to avenge. The words emphasized are such as they appear in the original document.

CINCINNATI, April 7, 1813.

General Orders.

SOLDIERS, You are now about to leave the shores of Kentucky—Many of you can boast that she gave you birth—She is indeed dear to us all.

KENTUCKIANS *stand high in the estimation of our common country*. Our brothers in arms, who have gone before us to the scene of action, have acquired a fame, which should never be forgotten by you—a fame worthy your emulation.

I feel conscious you would rather see your country no more, than return to it, under the impression, that by an act of yours, the high character of Kentucky had fallen.

To support this reputation, purchased by valor and by blood, you must with fortitude meet the hardships, and discharge the duties of soldiers. Discipline and subordination mark the real soldier—and are indeed the soul of an army.

In every situation, therefore, the most perfect subordination—the most rigid discharge of duty, will be expected from all. Partiality or injustice shall be shown to none.

I have the most perfect confidence in your attachment and support through every difficulty we may encounter.

It is upon you—it is upon your subordination and discipline I rely, for a successful issue of the present campaign. Without this confidence and support, we shall achieve nothing honorable or useful.

The same destiny awaits us both. That which exalts or sinks you in the estimation of your country, will produce to me her approbation or condemnation.

Feeling this same common interest, the first wishes of my heart are, that the present campaign should prove honorable to all, and useful to the country.

Should we encounter the enemy—REMEMBER THE DREADFUL FATE OF OUR BUTCHERED BROTHERS AT THE RIVER RAISIN—*that British treachery produced their slaughter*.

The justice of our cause—with the aid of an approving Providence, will be sure guarantees to our success.

GREEN CLAY,
Brigadier-General.

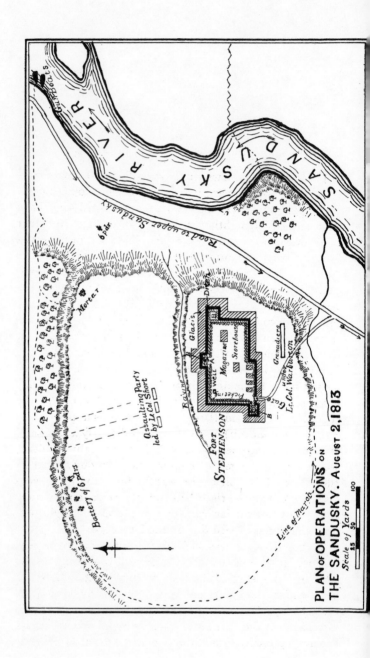

PLAN of OPERATIONS on
THE SANDUSKY. August 2, 1813

Scale of Yards

25   50   100

IX

THE ATTACK ON FORT STEPHENSON

The Right Division were not long suffered to remain inactive—Like Sir Thomas Picton's famous division in Spain, they might, on a much more modest and limited scale, have been termed the fighting division of Canada. No other corps was so incessantly in the field—no other corps achieved such important and beneficial results to the country, and when it is considered that this force comprised scarcely more than a single regiment of the line, the repeated claims made upon its energies and exertions, becomes even more remarkable. Late in July, at the earnest instance of Tecumseh, who had formed a plan for the reduction of Fort Meigs, which he conceived would be crowned with the fullest success, a second expedition, consisting of the main body of the 41st, (Captain Derenzy having recently joined with those detachments of the regiment which had borne so conspicuous a part in the Battle of Queenston) a few militia, and nearly a thousand Indians, accompanied by a few pieces of light artillery, was undertaken against this fortress. On our arrival in the Miami the whole of the regular force and guns were disembarked on the right bank of the river, out of view of the fort, yet not far from the point where our light batteries had been carried during the late siege.

Tecumseh's plan was as follows. Immediately in rear of Fort Meigs, and at right angles with the river, ran the road to Sandusky, (distant about thirty miles) upon, or near, which the chief had been apprized by his scouts that General Harrison, who with a large portion of his force had left the fort soon after its relief from General Procter's presence, was at that moment encamped. Having landed some miles lower down the river, the whole of the Indian force was to march through the woods, and gain, unperceived by the troops in the fort, the Sandusky road where a sham engagement was to take place, leading the garrison to believe a corps hastening to their relief had been encountered and attacked by the Indians, and inducing them to make a sortie for their rescue. The moment they had crossed the open ground, intervening between their position and the skirt of the wood, we were to rise from our ambuscade, and take them in the rear, making at the same time a rush for the fort, before the enemy could have time effectually to close his gates.

All the preliminary features in this plan, (which certainly was one that gave every fair promise of success) had been completed, and we were waiting with some interest and impatience the result, when the heavy firing of two distinct parties suddenly commenced on the Sandusky road. We were all instantly, although noiselessly, upon the alert, but in vain did we look for any movement in the fort. Many of the garrison lined the ramparts in the rear, and seemed to look out anxiously in the direction of the firing, but they gave not the slightest indication of a design to leave the fort, even when the musketry had become so animated and heavy, that we were half in doubt ourselves whether the battle was a sham one or a real. Either they had obtained information of our presence, or they suspected the nature and object of the *ruse*, and we had the mortification to find ourselves utterly foiled in the grand design of the expedition. Annoyed at the failure of his cherished scheme, Tecumseh urged upon General Procter, the necessity of doing something before our return, and it being found out of all question to attempt the reduction of Fort Meigs with the light guns (6-pounders) which accompanied us, it was determined to change the theatre of operation to Sandusky. Thither the main body of Indians proceeded by land, while we re-embarked in our boats, and descending again the Miami, gained Lake Erie, and thence the Sandusky river, on which the fort of that name[1] is built.

The expedition having reached the Sandusky river early on the 1st of August, a landing was effected on the same day, and within range of the enemy's guns, several ineffectual discharges from which passed over us, as we traversed a plain several hundred yards in extent in order to gain the wood, on the skirt of which it was intended to plant the batteries. These being immediately erected, at daybreak on the following morning our fire was opened, and continued until three o'clock in the afternoon of the 2nd, when, it being evident that no breach could be effected on the stockade work, General Procter resolved to attempt it by assault. Accordingly at four o'clock the troops divided into three columns of about 120 men each, were put in motion, and advancing through the plain, in double quick time, were suffered to approach within fifty yards, before they were met by the destructive fire of the enemy. The strong line of picketing, constituting their defence, was surrounded by a ditch flanked by batteries, and beyond the ditch was a deep ravine covered with brushwood, and more or less approximate to the place, according to its windings. Far from being checked by the severe fire of the Americans, the divisions redoubled their exertions, and vying with each other to take the lead, dashed down the ravine, and clambering up the opposite steep, were soon beneath the walls of the fort. Not a fascine, however, had been provided ; and although axes had been distributed among a body of men selected for the purpose, they were so blunted by constant use, that it would have been the work of hours

---

[1]The proper name of this fort is Fort Stephenson, and was situated in the centre of what is now the city of Fremont, called Lower Sandusky previous to 1846. It is at the head of navigation on the Sandusky river and about 20 miles from Sandusky bay. The fort was a simple stockade, skirted by a ditch about 9 feet wide and 6 feet deep. It was erected in the summer of 1812, and strengthened by blockhouses the following summer.

to cut through the double line of pickets, even if an enemy had not been there to interrupt its progress. In defiance of this difficulty, the axe-men leaped without hesitation into the ditch, and attempted to acquit themselves of their duty; but they were speedily swept away by the guns from the batteries, charged with musket balls and slugs and directed with fatal precision. The troops had established themselves on the edge of the ditch, but it was impossible to scale without the aid of ladders or fascines; and within a few paces of the enemy only, they saw their comrades fall on every hand with no hope of avenging their deaths. The second division had only two officers attached to it. Brevet Lieutenant-Colonel Short,[1] of the 41st, was killed while descending the ravine at the head of his column, when, the command devolving on Lieutenant Gordon of the same regiment, that officer encouraging his men, and calling on them to follow his example, was one of the first in the ditch, and was in the act of cutting the picketing with his sabre, when a ball, fired from a wall-piece, struck him in the breast. Although dangerously wounded, he refused to abandon his post, and continued to animate his men by his example, until a second ball, fired from the same piece, and lodging in his brain, left the division without an officer. The action had continued nearly two hours without producing the slightest impression on the enemy, when the bugles sounded the "cease-firing," and the men were ordered to lie flat on the ground on the edge of the ravine. The first division were so near the enemy, that they could distinctly hear the various orders given in the fort, and the faint voices of the wounded and dying in the ditch, calling out for water, which the enemy had the humanity to lower to them on the instant. After

---

[1] Lieut.-Col. William Charles Short, who was killed in this assault, came to Canada with the 41st Regiment. While stationed at Fort George his first wife died and was buried on Aug. 15th, 1805. On July 30th, 1809, he married Jane Crooks, an elder sister of Hon. James Crooks. They had one son, James Symington Short.

continuing in this position until nine o'clock, the columns received an order to effect their retreat in silence, which was done accordingly, the enemy merely firing a few volleys of musketry, producing however no material effect. The troops having been re-embarked the same night, the expedition descended the river, and returned to Amherstburg. Our loss in this affair was severe—3 officers, 1 sergeant, 22 rank and file killed ; 3 officers, 2 sergeants, 36 rank and file wounded ; and 1 sergeant, 28 rank and file missing. Of this number, the proportion of the 1st division alone, consisting principally of the light company of the 41st, which had attacked the strongest point of the position, was five and thirty men.

During the assault, no assistance whatever was afforded by the Indians, who, unaccustomed to this mode of warfare, contented themselves with remaining quiet spectators of the scene. The "devoted men" alone, to whom I have before alluded, followed close in the rear of one of the columns, but they had not long witnessed the effect of the enemy's fire on the divisions, when they retreated to the wood with a precipitation, that with any other people, would be attributed to cowardice, but with the natives it could only be considered as the effect of habit. They expressed much astonishment at the coolness and intrepidity with which the men supported the fire of the enemy, without returning it until arrived at the edge of the ditch; and concluded by saying that they had ever hitherto deemed themselves the bravest nation in the world, but were now willing to concede that distinction to the warriors of their Great Father.

The garrison of Sandusky when attacked, consisted of a force inferior in number to that of the assailing columns, and was commanded by Major Croghan of the line, a promising officer, only nineteen[1] years of age. The gal-

---

[1] Major George Croghan (pronounced Crawn) was born at Locust-Grove, Ohio, on Nov. 15th, 1791, and was consequently more than 21 years of age.

lant defence made by him on this occasion met with the highest encomia from his countrymen, and he was immediately promoted to the rank of lieutenant-colonel ; neither was his conduct without its reward in the approbation of a sex, whose favor and encouragement seldom fail to act as incentives to the acquisition of military glory. The ladies of Ohio (the State in which Colonel Croghan was born) subscribed a considerable sum, with which a handsome sword was purchased and presented by themselves.   It is but just to record an act of great courtesy on the part of this gentleman.   An officer having been despatched to Sandusky with a flag, some days subsequent to the assault, in order to obtain an exchange of the prisoners, who were chiefly wounded, was received with much politeness by the commandant, who at the moment of departure drew from his secretary a pair of pistols, which had been lost in the brushwood of the ravine during our retreat at night.   Presuming from the workmanship and style, that they might be, what in fact they actually were, old family arms, and naturally imagining that their loss must be regretted by their possessor, he begged the officer in question to take charge of, and present them to the individual to whom they belonged. It is unnecessary to add that they were gratefully received. They were my own, and had been lent to the gallant Lieutenant Gordon.

It is somewhat singular that General Procter's report[1] of the second expedition to the Miami is nowhere to be found.   It could not fail to prove a document of some interest to the public, desirous of knowing in what manner he had accounted for his unpardonable neglect of all necessary precaution, to ensure the successful issue of an attack which ought, in no way, to have been rashly undertaken.   The only British document, referring to the matter at all, is the following brief notice by Sir George

[1] General Procter's report, as found in the Canadian Archives, is given at the end of this chapter.

Prevost, on the subject ; evidently founded on a more detailed communication from General Procter, which it has been expedient to suppress.

General Order.

Head Quarters, Kingston,

Adjutant-General's Office, 3rd Sept., 1813.

His Excellency the commander of the Forces, has received a despatch from Major-General Procter reporting the circumstances of an attack, made by a small portion of regular troops, and a body of Indian Warriors, on the 2nd of August on the American Fort of Lower Sandusky, which owing to the strength of the enemy's works, which resisted the fire of the light field guns brought against it —so that a practicable breach could not be effected—as also from the want of sufficient co-operation on the part of the Indian Warriors, unused to that mode of warfare, the assault was not attended with that brilliant success which has so uniformly signalized the gallant exertions of the Right Division.   The Major-General extols the intrepid bravery displayed by the detachment under Brevet Lieutenant-Colonel Short, in endeavoring to force a passage into the enemy's fort, and laments the loss of the brave soldiers who have fallen in this gallant, although unsuccessful assault.

Return of killed and wounded.

1 brevet lieut.-col., 2 lieutenants, 1 sergeant, 1 drummer, 21 rank and file killed. 1 sergeant and 28 rank and file missing. 2 captains, 1 lieutenant, 2 sergeants, 1 drummer, 35 rank and file wounded.

Killed, Brevet Lieut.-Col. Short, Lt. Gordon, 41st Regt., Lt. Laussaussiege, Indian Department.

Wounded, Captain Dixon, Royal Engineers, Capt. Muir and Lieut. McIntyre, 41st Regt., all slightly.

By His Excellency's command,

Edward Baynes, Adjutant-General.

Copy of a letter from Major Croghan, to Gen. Harrison dated

Lower Sandusky, August 5, 1813.

Dear Sir—I have the honor to inform you, that the combined force of the enemy, amounting to, at least 500 regulars, and 700 or 800 Indians, under the immediate command of Gen. Procter, made its appearance before this place, early on Sunday evening last; and, so soon as the General had made such disposition of his troops, as would cut off my retreat, (should I be disposed to make one), he sent Col. Elliott, accompanied by Major Chambers, with a flag, to demand the surrender of the fort, as he was anxious to spare the effusion of blood; which he should probably not have in his power to do, should he be reduced to the necessity of taking the place by storm. My answer to the summons was, that I was determined to defend the place to the last extremity; and that no force, however large, should induce me to surrender it. So soon as the flag had returned, a brisk fire was opened upon us, from the gun-boats in the river, and from a five and a-half inch howitzer, on shore, which was kept up with little intermission throughout the night. At an early hour, the next morning, three sixes, (which had been placed, during the night, within 250 yards of the pickets), began to play upon us—but with little effect. About 4 o'clock, P.M., discovering that the fire, from all his guns, was concentrated against the north-western angle of the fort, I became confident that his object was to make a breach, and attempt to storm the works at that point: I, therefore, ordered out as many men, as could be employed, for the purpose of strengthening that front—which was so effectually secured, by means of bags of flour, sand, &c., that the picketing suffered little or no injury. Notwithstanding which, the enemy, about 5 o'clock, having formed in close column, advanced to assail our works, at the expected point; at the same time making two feints at the front of Captain Hunter's lines. The column, which advanced against the North-Western angle, consisting of about 350 men, was so completely enveloped in smoke, as not to be discovered, until it had approached within 15 or 20 paces of the lines; but, the men being all at their posts, and ready to receive it, commenced so heavy and galling a fire, as to throw the column a little into confusion. Being quickly rallied, it advanced to the outer works, and began to leap into the ditch. Just at that moment, a fire of grape was opened, from our 6-pounder (which had been previously arranged, so as to rake in that direction),which, together with the musketry,threw them into such confusion, that they were compelled to retire, precipitately, to the woods. During the assault, which lasted about half an hour, an incessant fire was kept up by the enemy's artillery, (which consisted of five sixes, and a howitzer), but without effect. My whole loss, during the siege, was one killed, and seven wounded slightly. The loss of the enemy in killed, wounded and prisoners, must exceed 150. One Lieut.-Colonel, a Lieutenant, and 50 rank and file, were found in and about the ditch ; those of the remainder, who were not able to escape, were taken off, during the night, by the Indians. Seventy stand of arms, and several brace of pistols, have been collected near the works. About 3, in the morning, the enemy sailed down the river, leaving behind them a boat, containing clothing, and considerable military stores.

Too much praise cannot be bestowed on the officers, non-commissioned officers, and privates, under my command, for their gallantry, and good conduct, during the siege.

Yours, with respect,

G. CROGHAN, Maj. 17th U.S. Inf. comg.

MAJOR-GENERAL HARRISON,
Comg. N.W. Army.

The following is Procter's report referred to on page 182 :

Sandwich, Aug. 9th, 1813.

Sir,—It being absolutely requisite, for several urgent reasons, that my Indian force should not remain unemployed, and being well aware that it would not be movable except accompanied by a regular force, I resolved, notwithstanding the smallness of that force, to move, and where we might be fed at the expense of the enemy. I had, however, the mortification to find that instead of the Indian force being a disposable one, or under my direction, our movements should be subject to the caprices and prejudices of the Indian body, to the degree in which my regular force was disproportionate to their numbers. For several days after the arrival of Mr. R. Dickson his Indians were restrainable, and tractable to a degree that I could not have conceived possible. I am sorry to add that they have been contaminated by the other Indians. I was, very contrary to my judgment, necessitated to go to the Miami, in the vicinity of the enemy's fort, where I remained a few days, in the hope that General Harrison might come to the relief of the fort, which was invested, in the Indian mode, when finding that the Indians were returning to Detroit and Amherstburg I moved to Lower Sandusky, where, however, we could not muster more hundreds of Indians, than I might reasonably have expected thousands. The neighborhood of the Sandusky, and the settlement on the Huron River, eight miles below it, could have afforded cattle sufficient to have fed my whole Indian force for some time, had they been induced to accompany us. Sandusky is nearly fifty miles by water from Lake Erie ; and nearly forty from several points whence strong reinforcements might be expected ; I could not therefore with my very small force remain more than two days, from the probability of being cut off, and of being deserted by the few Indians who had not already done so. The fort at Sandusky is composed of blockhouses connected by picketing which they flank, and is calculated for a garrison of five or 'six hundred men. On viewing the fort I formed an opinion entirely different from any person under my command. The general idea being that the garrison did not exceed fifty men, and that the fort could be easily 'carried by assault. On the morning of the 2nd instant the gentlemen of the Indian department who have the direction of it, declared formally their decided opinion that unless the fort was stormed we should never be able to bring an Indian warrior into the field with us, and that they proposed, and were ready to storm one face of the fort, if we attempt another. I have also to observe, that in this instance, my judgment had not that weight with the troops, I hope might reasonably have been expected. If I had withdrawn without having permitted the assault, as my judgment certainly dictated, much dissatisfaction would have followed me, and I could scarcely have continued to direct their movements. I thus, with all the responsibility resting on me, was obliged to yield to circumstances I could not possibly have prevented. The troops, after the artillery had been used for some hours, attacked two faces, and, impossibilities being attempted, failed. The fort from which the severest fire, I ever saw, was maintained during the attack, was well defended. The troops displayed the greatest bravery, the much greater part of whom reached the fort and made every effort to enter ; but the Indians who had proposed the assault, and had it not been assented to, would have ever stigmatized the British character, scarcely came into fire before they ran off out of its reach. A more than adequate sacrifice having been made to Indian opinion, I drew off the brave assailants who had been carried away by a high sense of honor to urge too strongly the attack. I enclose a disembarkation return which will show how small my disposable force was. The enemy had a six pounder and a smaller one in the fort. I also enclose a return of the killed, wounded, and missing. Our loss, though severe, and much to be regretted, is less, everything considered, than could have been expected. You will perceive that the Indian force is seldom a disposable one, never to be relied on, in the hour of need, and only to be found useful in proportion as we are independent of it.

Ten Indians were surprised on a plain near Sandusky and were cut to pieces. The Indians have always had a dread of cavalry, of which the enemy have a considerable number. A troop of the 19th would be of the greatest service here, in the confidence they would give to our mounted Indians. I have experienced much deficiency in my artillery, another officer at least is absolutely required, and one of science and experience. The enemy's defences are composed of wood. If we knew how to burn them, as they did ours at Fort George, Mr. Harrison's army must have been destroyed long since. The enemy's army vessels are out of Presque Isle harbor, and so decidedly stronger than ours, that Captain Barclay has been necessitated to return to Amherstburg, and with all haste to get the new vessel ready for sea, which she will be in eight or ten days at farthest, and then only want hands. Whatever may happen to be regretted, may be fairly attributed to the delays in sending here the force Your Excellency directed should be sent. Had it been sent at once, it could have been used to the greatest advantage, but it arrived in such small portions, and with such delays that the opportunities have been lost. The enemy are in great numbers at Presque Isle, and have been already reinforced at Fort Meigs. General Harrison's headquarters are near Lower Sandusky, where he arrived on the 3rd instant. I must now look for the enemy from two quarters, and will have to meet them with my small force divided, for the Indians will make no stand without us. You will probably hear of the enemy's landing shortly at Long Point, whence they may gain the rear of the Centre Division, and also affect my supplies. A hundred and fifty sailors would have effectually obviated this evil. I apprehend the enemy's rapid advance to the River Raisin in force and establish himself there, which he can do surprisingly soon. If I had the means I would establish a post at that river, but not having two or three hundred to send there it is not in my power. I must entreat your Excellency to send me more troops, even the second battalion of the 41st Regt., though weak, would be extremely acceptable. If the enemy should be able to establish themselves in the territory it will operate strongly against us with our Indian allies. Your Excellency may rely on my best endeavors, but I rely on the troops alone, and they are but few, and I am necessitated to man the vessels with them. I have never desponded, nor do I now, but I conceive it my duty to state to Your Excellency the inadequateness of my force.

I have the honor to be, with much respect,

Your Excellency's obedient servant,

HENRY PROCTER,

Brigr.-General, Comg.

His Excellency,

Lt.-General Sir George Prevost, Bt.

X

The period was now fast approaching when the fruits of so much toil and privation were to be wrested from our grasp, and the extensive line of territory, both original and acquired, so gallantly defended by a single regiment against the repeated invasions of the enemy during a period of fifteen months, was to fall beneath the efforts of numerical strength. Since the capture of. Detroit, the Americans had been indefatigable in their exertions to establish a superiority of naval force, on which, they well knew, depended the ultimate success of their arms. Buffalo was the harbor selected[1] for the construction of their flotilla, which, under the hands of numerous workmen, soon presented a formidable appearance, and was deemed more than sufficient to ensure their ascendancy on the lake. Manned by experienced seamen taken from several frigates then blockaded in their sea-ports, and commanded by able and intelligent officers, these vessels put forth towards the close of August, and continued cruising off the harbor of Amherstburg, in which our fleet lay, awaiting the completion of the Detroit, a vessel of twenty guns then on the stocks, and the arrival of seamen long promised and vainly expected from Lake Ontario. Captain Barclay had arrived some time previous to take the command, and with him several officers and forty men : but notwithstanding every remonstrance on the subject made by the commanding officer of the division, no further assistance was afforded. The remaining part of the crews were provincial sailors, willing and anxious, it is true, to do their duty, but without that perfection and experience in their profession, which are so indispensably

---

[1] Five vessels of Perry's fleet were built at Presque Isle (Erie) harbor.

necessary to the insurance of success in a combat at sea.
In defiance of this disadvantage, the enemy had no sooner
made his appearance, than the Detroit was launched in her
rough and unfinished state, and armed, in default of other
guns, with long battering pieces taken from the ramparts. Every calibre was employed—sixes, nines, twelves,
eighteens and even the two twenty-four pounders which
had been so successfully used at the Miami. The early part
of September was employed in getting in her masts and
rigging, and in a few days the fleet was ready to sail.
Our position at this period had become exceedingly critical. The want of provisions began to be seriously felt,
and the ultimate possession of the garrison depended
wholly on the result of the naval conflict, for which both
parties were preparing. In the event of the enemy being
successful, not only must we be open to the incursions of
the large forces, then collected in several quarters, and
ready to overwhelm us at the moment that the command of
the lake would afford them facility of movement, but the
means of obtaining supplies from Fort Erie must be en-
tirély cut off. The quantity of provisions already con-
sumed had been enormous; for independently of the
wanton destruction of cattle by the Indians, who
often shot or stabbed them merely to possess themselves
of the horns, in which they secured their powder, leaving
the carcasses to putrify in the sun, ten thousand rations
were daily issued to the warriors and their families : the
latter apparently increasing in numbers, as our means of
supplying them became more contracted.

Such was the situation of the garrison, reduced in its
regular force to a handful of men, by the losses sustained
in the various engagements herein detailed, when Captain
Barclay, who had hoisted his flag on board the Detroit,
made the signal, early in the morning of the 9th, to
weigh anchor and bear across the lake. The little fleet,
consisting of six sail, were, at daylight on the 10th, perceived by the enemy, then lying among a cluster of

islands at some leagues distance, who immediately bore
up under a light side-wind, favorable at that moment to
the approach of the two squadrons.   At one o'clock[1] the
engagement commenced.   The Detroit leading into
action, was opposed to the Lawrence, mounting eighteen thirty-two pounders, and commanded by the American Commodore ; and such was the effect of the long
guns, that the latter vessel was soon compelled to strike
her flag, having only twenty serviceable men left.   The
Detroit and Queen Charlotte had, however, suffered
severely in their sails and rigging from the fire of the
enemy's gun-boats ; and not only every one of their
boats had been so severely wounded as to render it impossible to take possession of the prize ; but the united and
unceasing exertions of their crews could not prevent
them from running foul of each other.   Availing himself
of this unfortunate accident, Commodore Perry, who had
shifted his flag to the Niagara, a vessel of equal force
with the Lawrence, bore up and discharged his broadside with murderous effect.   Waring immediately, a
second and equally destructive followed, and in this
manner was the action continued, rendering resistance
almost hopeless.   The other smaller vessels, already
warmly engaged, could afford no aid, and the guns of the
unfortunate wrecks were at length nearly all unservice-
able,—those, at least, of the only batteries which could
be brought to bear upon the enemy.   Almost every
officer had been compelled to leave the deck, and the
helplessness of the crews could only be exceeded by their
despair, when after two hours and a half of incessant
cannonading, the British flag was replaced by the Eagle
of America.

The anxiety with which the issue of the combat was
awaited at Amherstburg, where the firing was distinctly
heard, may easily be conceived.   From the heights overhanging the lake, and nearly opposite to the islands, the

[1] Barclay says, a quarter to twelve.

first encounter of the fleets was clearly observed, but the
thick columns of smoke in which they were speedily
enveloped, precluded all possibility of following the progress of the contest ; nor was it until the thunder of the
artillery had been some time discontinued, that the clouds
of vapour gradually dispelling, presented the melancholy
picture of our vessels, several of them crippled and dis-
masted, following in the track of the American fleet, then
directing its course towards the bay of Sandusky.

In this affair, so unfavorable in its result to our already
precarious cause, the enemy had the most decided advantage, not only in respect to superiority of seamen, but in
number of ships, and in weight of metal.[1] Their fleet
consisted of nine sail, of which the two principal, the
Lawrence and Niagara, mounted eighteen thirty-two
pounders. Four others were armed with a long gun of
the same calibre, and keeping aloof during the action,
were enabled by the calm state of the lake to do much
execution among our principal vessels, which were com-

---

[1]The most carefully-prepared and the fairest account of this action
is given by Theodore Roosevelt in "The Naval War of 1812."
Anyone who would desire to get an honest summing up of all the
evidence bearing on the contest should read the narration given
in this work. Both commanders and their crews were equally
brave and about equally skilful; Perry's line, however, was not so
well formed as Barclay's, the Niagara not coming to close action
until Perry took command. There could be no other ending to
the battle. Victory must rest with the stronger force, everything
else being practically equal. Perry's fame should rest chiefly upon
the indomitable energy and ability he displayed in preparing for
the contest, with the inadequate means at his command. In this
respect he far surpassed both Barclay and Procter. Although the
British officers were wretchedly provided with everything for
building and equipping vessels, yet they might have done more
with the material they had. Had Barclay shown the same vigilance subsequently to the 2nd of August as he had before that date,
Perry could not have got his largest and most formidable vessels
over the bar at the entrance to Presque Isle (Erie) harbor without
considerable trouble, and here his superior force would have been
at a great disadvantage.
    The following is a table describing the two squadrons on the
day of the battle. The number of the guns is taken from Barclay's letter to Prevost and the tonnage and crews from Roosevelt's
estimate. I take Barclay's account of the guns because he gives
his squadron a slightly greater long-gun armament than Roosevelt, and the two accounts of Perry's armament about coincide.

pletely raked by their destructive fire. The vessels composing Captain Barclay's force were—the Detroit, twenty guns; Queen Charlotte, twenty guns; Lady Prevost, twelve guns; General Hunter, six guns; and

BARCLAY'S SQUADRON.

Vessel.	Tons.	Crew.	Broadside in lbs.	Long guns.	Calibre	Short guns.	Calibre
Detroit	490	150	138	2 1 6 8	24 18 12 9	1 1	24 18
Queen Charlotte ...	400	126	192	3	12	14	24
Lady Prevost	230	86	78	3	9	10	12
Hunter...........	80	45	28	2 4 2	6 4 2	2	12
Little Belt.........	90	18	21	1 2	9 6		
Chippeway	70	15	9	1	9		
	1360	440	466	35		28	

PERRY'S SQUADRON.

Vessel.	Tons.	Crew.	Broadside in lbs.	Long guns.	Calibre	Short guns.	Calibre
Lawrence	480	136	300	2	12	18	32
Niagara	480	155	300	2	12	18	32
Caledonia	180	53	80	2	24	1	32
Ariel	112	36	48	4	12		
Somers	94	30	56	1	24	1	32
Scorpion...........	86	35	56	1 1	32 24		
Porcupine	83	25	32	1	32		
Tigress	96	27	32	1	32		
Trippe	60	35	24	1	24		
	1671	532	928	16		38	

In the table Perry's crew is given as 532, but sickness reduced his effectives to 416. Barclay probably had more than 440 men, but as some were unfit for duty, his effectives were about the same or probably a few less than Perry's. During the action the Lawrence and Niagara each fought a long 12 instead of one of the carronades on the engaged side, making a broadside of 888 lbs., 312 lbs. being from long guns. Barclay's vessels threw a broadside of at least 466 lbs., 202 lbs. of which was from long guns, but, as will be observed, from guns of small calibre.

two small craft, one of which mounted a mortar, the other a long eighteen-pounder ; and the whole weight of metal did not amount to 1,100 pounds : while that of the enemy, exclusive of the three remaining vessels of their flotilla each mounting several guns, was 1,280 : and when it is taken into consideration that the accident which occurred early in the engagement to the two principal ships, prevented all possibility of bringing a second broadside to bear, while the enemy, on the contrary, were enabled to avail themselves of their whole metal, the disproportion will appear even more enormous. Notwithstanding the disparity of force, however, a different result might have been expected, had the unceasing applications made for sailors been attended to by the naval commander on Lake Ontario, to whose unwillingness to part with men, who might very well have been spared for the occasion, must be attributed the sacrifice of the gallant Barclay and his fleet, and eventually that of the Right Division. The necessity of having regular and experienced seamen was never more cruelly exemplified than on the present occasion ; since, in all probability, had they been present, the accident which left the Detroit and Queen Charlotte entirely at the mercy of the enemy, would either have been prevented, or remedied in time. All that courage and perseverance could effect was done : but against the decree of Providence who may successfully oppose himself ? Captain Barclay, who had already lost one limb while fighting the battles of his country, was so severely wounded in his only remaining arm as to be compelled to leave the deck early in the action. Captain Finnis, commanding the Queen Charlotte, was killed by a round shot soon afterwards, and the same ball carried off Lieutenant Garden, a promising young officer of the Newfoundland Regiment, mingling the blood of the one and the brains of the other, on the bulwark, in one melancholy and undistinguishable mass. I had subsequently an opportunity of witnessing the devastation of this sanguinary day. The decks were literally filled with the wounded ; and such was the crippled state of the Detroit, that not a mast was left standing : almost all the guns were dismounted, and it was impossible to place a hand on that side which had been exposed to the enemy's fire, without covering part of a wound, either from grape, canister, or round shot.

Subjoined is Captain Barclay's account of the action.

Head Quarters, Montreal, Nov. 25th, 1813.

My Lord,

I have the honor to transmit to Your Lordship copy of a letter from Commodore Sir James Yeo, together with Captain Barclay's official account of the action on Lake Erie, referred to in my despatches to your Lordship, No. 90 of the date of the 22nd September, and No. 91 of 8th October last.

The loss sustained on that occasion Your Lordship will find subjoined to the general order also herewith transmitted, which I have felt it my duty to issue in consequence of the recent events in this command.

I am happy to be able to add, that Captain Barclay is recovering of his wounds, and that there is a prospect of his valuable life and services being preserved for the benefit of his country.

I have the honor to be, &c.,

George Prevost.

The Right Hon. Earl Bathurst,

His Majesty's Ship Wolfe,
. at Kingston, Nov. 15th, 1813.

Sir,—I yesterday received Captain Barclay's official statement of the ill-fated action on Lake Erie, and as Your Excellency must wish to be informed of every particular, I have the honor to enclose the same.

It appears to me that though His Majesty's Squadron were very deficient in seamen, weight of metal, and particularly long guns, yet the greatest misfortune was the loss of every officer, particularly Captain Finnis, whose life, had it been spared, would, in my opinion, have saved the squadron.

I have honor to be, &c.,

James Lucas Yeo, Commodore.

His Excellency Sir George Prevost, Bart.
Governor and General in Chief.

His Majesty's late Ship Detroit,
    Put-in Bay, Lake Erie, Sept. 12th, 1813.

Sir,—The last letter I had the honor of writing to you, dated the 6th instant, I informed you, that unless certain intimation was received of more seamen being on their way to Amherstburg, I should be obliged to sail with the squadron deplorably manned as it was, to fight the enemy (who blockaded the port), to enable us to get supplies of provisions and stores of every description ; so perfectly destitute of provisions was the port, that there was not a day's flour in store, and the crews of the squadron under my command were on half allowance of many things, and when that was done there was no more. Such were the motives which induced Major-General Procter (whom by your instructions I was directed to consult, and whose wishes I was enjoined to execute, as far as relates to the good of the country), to concur in the necessity of a battle being risked under the many disadvantages which I labored, and it now remains for me, the most melancholy task to relate to you the unfortunate issue of the battle, as well as the many untoward circumstances that led to that event.

No intelligence of seamen having arrived, I sailed on the 9th inst. fully expecting to meet the enemy next morning, as they had been seen among the islands ; nor was I mistaken ; soon after daylight they were seen in motion in Put-in Bay, the wind then at south-west and light, giving us the weather-gage. I bore up for them, in hopes of bringing them to action among the islands, but that intention was soon frustrated, by the wind suddenly shifting to the south-east, which brought the enemy directly to windward. The line was formed according to a given plan, so that each ship might be supported against the superior force of the two brigs opposed to them. About ten the enemy had cleared the islands, and immediately bore up, under easy sail, in a line abreast, each brig being also supported by the small vessels. At a quarter before twelve I commenced the action, by firing a few long guns ; about a quarter past, the American Commodore, also supported by two schooners, one carrying four long twelve-pounders, the other a long 32 and 24-pounder, came to close action with the Detroit ; the other brig of the enemy, apparently destined to engage the Queen Charlotte, supported in like manner by two schooners, kept so far to windward as to render the Queen Charlotte's 24-pounder carronades useless, while she was, with the Lady Prevost, exposed to the heavy and destructive fire of the Caledonia, and four other schooners, armed with long and heavy guns, like those I have already described.

Too soon, alas! was I deprived of the services of the noble and intrepid Captain Finnis, who soon after the commencement of the action fell, and with him fell my greatest support; soon after, Lieutenant Stokoe, of the Queen Charlotte, was struck senseless by a splinter, which deprived the country of his services at this very critical period. As I perceived, the Detroit had enough. to contend with, without the prospect of a fresh brig. Provincial Lieutenant Irvine, who then had charge of the Queen Charlotte, behaved with great courage, but his experience was much too limited to supply the place of such an officer as Captain Finnis, hence she proved of far less assistance than I expected.

The action continued with great fury until half past two, when I perceived my opponent drop astern, and a boat passing from him to the Niagara (which vessel was at this time perfectly fresh); the American Commodore seeing, that as yet the day was against him (his vessel having struck soon after he left her), and also the very defenceless state of the Detroit, which ship was now a perfect wreck, principally from the raking fire of the gun boats, and also that the Queen Charlotte was in such a situation, that I could receive very little assistance from her, and the Lady Prevost being at this time too far to leeward, from her rudder being injured, made a noble, and alas! too successful an effort to regain it, for he bore up, and supported by his small vessels, passed within pistol shot, and took a raking position on our bow, nor could I prevent it, as the unfortunate situation of the Queen Charlotte prevented us from wearing; in attempting it we fell on board her; my gallant first Lieutenant Garland was now mortally wounded, and myself so severely, that I was obliged to quit the deck.

Manned as the squadron was, with not more than fifty British seamen, the rest a mixed crew of Canadians and soldiers, and who were totally unacquainted with such service, rendered the loss of officers more sensibly felt, and never in any action was the loss more severe; every officer commanding vessels, and their seconds, were either killed or wounded so severely, as to be unable to keep the deck.

Lieut. Buchan, in the Lady Prevost, behaved most nobly, and did everything that a brave and experienced officer could do in a vessel armed with 12-pounder carronades, against vessels carrying long guns. I regret to state that he was very severely wounded. Lieut. Bignall of the Dover, commanding the Hunter, displayed the greatest intrepidity ; but his guns being small, (two, four and six pounders) he could be of much less service than he wished.

Every officer in the Detroit behaved in the most exemplary manner. Lieut. Inglis showed such calm intrepidity, that I was fully convinced that, on leaving the deck, I left the ship in excellent hands ; and for an account of the battle, after that, I refer you to his letter which he wrote me, for your information. Mr. Hoffmeister, purser of the Detroit, nobly volunteered his services on deck, and behaved in a manner that reflects the highest honor on him. I regret to add that he is very severely wounded in the knee. Provincial Lieut. Purvis, and the military officers, Lieuts. Garden, of the Royal Newfoundland Regt., and O'Keefe, of the 41st Regt., behaved in a manner which excited my warmest admiration ; the few British seamen I had behaved with their usual intrepidity, and as long as I was on deck, the troops behaved with a calmness and courage, worthy of a more fortunate issue to their exertions.

The weather-gage gave the enemy a prodigious advantage, as it enabled them not only to choose their position, but their distance also, which they did in such a manner as to prevent the carronades of the Queen Charlotte and Lady Prevost from having much effect ; while their long guns did great execution, particularly against the Queen Charlotte.

Capt. Perry has behaved in a most humane and attentive manner, not only to myself and officers, but to all the wounded. I trust that although unsuccessful, you will approve of the motives that induced me to sail under so many disadvantages, and that it may be hereafter proved that, under such circumstances, the honor of His

Majesty's flag has not been tarnished.   I enclose the list of killed and wounded.

I have the honor to be, &c.,
(Signed)   R. H. Barclay, Commander,
and late Senior Officer.
To Commodore
Sir James L. Yeo, Bt., &c.

His Majesty's late ship Detroit,
Sept. 10th, 1813.

Sir,—I have the honor to transmit to you an account of the termination of the late unfortunate action with the enemy's squadron.

On coming on the quarter-deck after your being wounded, the enemy's second brig, at that time on our weather-beam, shortly afterwards took a position on our weather-bow to rake us ; to prevent which, in attempting to wear, to get our starboard broadside to bear upon her, a number of the guns of the larboard broadside being at this time disabled, fell on board the Queen Charlotte, at this time running up to leeward of us.   In this situation the two ships remained for some time.   As soon as we got clear of her, I ordered the Queen Charlotte to shoot ahead of us if possible ; and attempted to back our fore-topsail to get astern, but the ship laying completely unmanageable, every brace cut away, the mizzen top-mast and gaff down, all the other masts badly wounded, not a stay left forward, hull shattered very much, a number of the guns disabled, and the enemy's squadron raking both ships ahead and astern, none of our own in a situation to support us, I was under the painful necessity of answering the enemy, to say we had struck, the Queen Charlotte having previously done so.

I have the honor to be, &c.,
(Signed)   George Inglis.
To Capt. Barclay,
&c., &c., &c.

A list of killed and wounded in His Majesty's ships and vessels in an action with the American squadron on Lake Erie, the 10th September, 1813.

3 officers and 38 men, killed ; 9 officers, 85 men, wounded.

Total—41 killed ; 94 wounded.

Names of officers killed and wounded—Lieut. James Garden, Royal Newfoundland Regiment, killed; Detroit, killed : First Lieut. John Garland ; wounded : Captain R. H. Barclay, dangerously ; J. R. Hoffmeister, purser, dangerously ; Queen Charlotte, killed : Captain Robert Finnis ; wounded : First Lieut. James Stokoe, severely ; James Foster, midshipman, slightly ; Lady Prevost, wounded : Lieut. Edward Buchan, commanding, dangerously ; First Lieut. F. Rolette, severely ; Hunter, wounded : Lieut. George Bignall, commanding, severely; Henry Gateshill, master's mate, slightly ; Chippeway, wounded : master's mate, J. Campbell, commanding, slightly.

(Signed)   R. H. Barclay, Commander, and late Senior Officer.

The annexed is Commander Perry's Official account of the action.

U.S. Schr. Ariel, Put-in Bay, 13th Sept., 1813.

Sir,—In my last, I informed you that we had captured the enemy's fleet on this lake. I have now the honor to give you the most important particulars of the action :—On the morning of the 10th instant, at sun-rise, they were discovered from Put-in Bay, when I lay at anchor, with the squadron under my command. We got under weigh, the wind light at south-west, and stood for them. At 10 a.m. the wind hauled to south-east, and brought us to windward ; formed the line, and bore up. At 15 minutes before 12, the enemy commenced firing ; at 5 minutes before 12, the action commenced on our part. Finding their fire very destructive, owing to their long guns, and it being mostly directed at the Lawrence, I made sail, and directed the other vessels to follow, for the purpose of closing with the enemy—every brace and bow line being soon shot away, she became unmanageable, notwithstanding the great exertions of the sailing master. In this situation, she sustained the action upwards of two hours, within canister distance, until every gun was rendered useless, and the greater part of her crew either killed or wounded. Finding she could no longer annoy the enemy, I left her in charge of Lieut. Yarnall, who, I was convinced, from the bravery already displayed by him, would do what would comport with the honor of

Oliver Hazard Perry.

the flag. At half past two, the wind springing up, Captain Elliott was enabled to bring his vessel, the Niagara, gallantly into close action ; I immediately went on board of her, when he anticipated my wish, by volunteering to bring the schooner, which had been kept astern by the lightness of the wind, into close action.

It was with unspeakable pain that I saw, soon after I got on board the Niagara, the flag of the Lawrence come down; although I was perfectly sensible that she had been defended to the last, and that to have continued to make a show of resistance, would have been a wanton sacrifice of the remains of her brave crew. But the enemy was not able to take possession of her, and circumstances soon permitted her flag again to be hoisted. At 45 minutes past two, the signal was made for "close action"; the Niagara being very little injured, I determined to pass through the enemy's line—bore up and passed ahead of their two ships, and a brig, giving a raking fire to them, from the starboard guns and to a large schooner and sloop from the larboard side, at half pistol-shot distance. The smaller vessels, at this time, having got within grape and canister distance, under the direction of Capt. Elliott, and keeping up a well-directed fire, the two ships, a brig, and a schooner surrendered, a schooner and sloop making a vain attempt to escape.

Those officers and men, who were immediately under my observation, evinced the greatest gallantry ; and, I have no doubt that all others conducted themselves as became American officers and seamen. Lieut. Yarnall, 1st of the Lawrence, although several times wounded, refused to quit the deck. Midshipman Forrest, (doing duty as Lieutenant), and sailing master Taylor, were of great assistance to me. I have great pain, in stating to you the death of Lieut. Brooks, of the marines, and Midshipman Laub, both of the Lawrence, and Midshipman John Clark, of the Scorpion ; they were valuable and promising officers. Mr. Hambleton, purser, who volunteered his services on deck, was severely wounded, late in the action. Midshipmen Claxton and Swartwout, of the Lawrence, were severely wounded. On board the Niagara, Lieutenants Smith and Edwards, and Midshipman Webster, (doing duty as sailing master), behaved in a very handsome manner. Captain Brevoort, of the army, who acted as a volunteer, in the capacity of a marine officer, on board that vessel, is an excellent and brave officer; and, with his musketry, did great execution. Lieut. Turner, commanding the Caledonia, brought that vessel into action in the most able manner, and is an officer, in all situations, that may be relied on.

The Ariel, Lieut. Packett, and Scorpion, sailing master Champlin, were enabled to get early into action, and were of great service. Captain Elliott speaks in the highest terms of Mr. Magrath, purser, who had been dispatched in a boat, on service, previous to my getting on board the Niagara; and, being a seaman, since the action has rendered essential service in taking charge of one of the prizes.

Of Captain Elliott, already so well known to the government, it would be almost superfluous to speak:—in this action, he evinced his characteristic bravery and judgment; and, since the close of the action, has given me the most able and essential assistance.

I have the honor to enclose you a return of the killed and wounded, together with a statement of the relative force of the squadrons. The Captain and 1st Lieutenant of the Queen Charlotte, and 1st Lieut. of the Detroit, were killed. Captain Barclay, senior officer, and the commander of the Lady Prevost, severely wounded. The commanders of the Hunter and Chippeway, slightly wounded. Their loss, in killed and wounded, I have not been able to ascertain; it must, however, have been very great.

I have caused the prisoners, taken on the 10th inst., to be landed at Sandusky; and have requested Gen. Harrison to have them marched to Chillicothe, and there wait, until your pleasure shall be known respecting them.

The Lawrence has been so entirely cut up, it is absolutely necessary she should go into a safe harbor; I have, therefore, directed Lieut. Yarnall to proceed to Erie, in her, with the wounded of the fleet; and dismantle, and get her over the bar, as soon as possible.

The two ships, in a heavy sea, this day at anchor, lost their masts, being much injured in the action. I shall haul them into the inner bay, at this place, and moor them for the present. The Detroit is a remarkably fine ship; sails well and is very strongly built;—the Queen Charlotte is a much superior vessel to what has been represented;—the Lady Prevost is a large, fine schooner.

PERRY'S STATUE, CLEVELAND, OHIO.

I also beg your instructions, respecting the wounded ; I am satisfied, sir, that whatever steps I might take, governed by humanity, would meet your approbation ;— under this impression, I have taken upon myself to promise Capt. Barclay, who is very dangerously wounded, that he shall be landed as near Lake Ontario as possible ; and, I had no doubt, you would allow me to parole him ; he is under the impression, that nothing but leaving this part of the country will save his life. There is also a number of Canadians among the prisoners—many who have families.

I have the honor, &c.,
O. H. Perry.

Hon. W. Jones, Sec. Navy.

The Return above alluded to by Commodore Perry,[1] admits the American loss to have been 27 killed, and 96 wounded—total 123.[2]

---

[1] Perry was not a Commodore, neither was Barclay. The Commodore of the Americans was Isaac Chauncey, and of the British Sir James Lucas Yeo. James Fenimore Cooper says: "Perry was not made a Captain until after the Battle of Lake Erie, his commission being dated Sept. 10th, 1813, the day of his victory."

[2] These casualties were distributed in the following manner,—

VESSEL.	KILLED.	WOUNDED.	TOTAL.
Lawrence	22	61	83
Niagara	2	25	27
Caledonia	0	3	3
Somers	0	2	2
Ariel	1	3	4
Trippe	0	2	2
Scorpion	2	0	2
Total	27	96	123

XI

THE BATTLE OF MORAVIANTOWN

With the loss of our fleet vanished every hope of maintaining our positions against the enemy, who, already assembled in the neighborhood of Forts Sandusky and Meigs, to the number of ten thousand men, only awaited the result of the action to decide on their future movements. A vast number of boats had been collected for the purpose of transporting them across the lake, under cover of their squadron, whose recent success leaving them undisputed masters of that element, necessarily precluded all probability of effectual opposition. A council was accordingly assembled, and the various chieftains summoned to attend. After a brief exposition of the defenceless state of the garrison, the almost utter impossibility of preventing the landing of the enemy, and the alarming destitution into which the magazines of provision had fallen, General Procter proposed that the forts of Detroit and Amherstburg, together with the various public buildings, should be destroyed, and that the troops and Indians should retire on the Centre Division at Niagara. This proposal was met by the chieftains with divided sentiments; but Tecumseh, whose gallant and impetuous spirit could ill brook the idea of retiring before his enemies, had no sooner heard the conclusion, than he arose, and, in a speech of much length, and accompanied by powerful energy and gesticulation, protested against the infamy of abandoning the position without first using every exertion for its defence. He addressed the commanding officer in the severest terms; accused him of cowardice; and after having compared his conduct with that of Captain Barclay, whose noble defence had inspired him with an enthusiasm surpassed only by the regret he entertained at his failure, concluded by declaring it to be his fixed determination to remain with his warriors and defend the place himself.

"Father,—(he thundered), Listen to your children! You see them now all before you. The war before this, our British father gave the hatchet to his red children when our old chiefs were alive. They are now all dead. In that war, our father was thrown on his back by the Americans, and our father took them by the hand without our knowledge, and we are afraid our father will do so again at this time.

Summer before last, when I came forward with my red brethren, and was ready to take up the hatchet in favor of our British father, we were told not to be in a hurry—that he had not yet determined to fight the Americans.

Listen! When war was declared, our father stood up and gave us the tomahawk, and told us that he was now ready to strike the Americans—that he wanted our assistance; and that he would certainly get us our lands back, which the Americans had taken from us.

Listen! You told us at that time to bring forward our families to this place—we did so, and you promised to take care of them, and that they should want for nothing, while the men would go and fight the enemy—that we were not to trouble ourselves with the enemy's garrisons—that we knew nothing about them, and that our father would attend to that part of the business. You also told your red children that you would take good care of their garrison here, which made our hearts glad.

Listen! When we last went to the Rapids, it is true we gave you little assistance. It is hard to fight people who live like ground-hogs.

Father—Listen! Our fleet has gone out; we know they have fought; we have heard the great guns; but know nothing of what has happened to our father with one arm.[1] Our ships have gone one way, and we are

---

[1] The allusion here is to Captain Robert Herriott Barclay, R.N., who arrived from England in May, 1813, and after some service on Lake Ontario was assigned the command on Lake Erie about the first of July. He served with Nelson at Trafalgar, where he lost an arm. A court-martial was held upon him for the loss of the fleet on Lake Erie, which decided that he was "fully and honorably acquitted." After returning to Great Britain he lived in Edinburgh. The inscription on his tombstone, in Greyfriar's churchyard, states that he died on the 8th of May, 1837, aged 52 years.

much astonished to see our father tying up everything and preparing to run away the other, without letting his red children know what his intentions are. You always told us to remain here and take care of our lands; it made our hearts glad to hear that was your wish. Our great father, the king, is the head, and you represent him. You always told us you would never draw your foot off British ground; but now, father, we see you are drawing back, and we are sorry to see our father doing so without seeing the enemy. We must compare our father's conduct to a fat animal, that carries its tail upon its back, but when affrighted, it drops it between its legs and runs off.

Listen, father! The Americans have not yet defeated us by land; neither are we sure that they have done so by water; we therefore wish to remain here, and fight our enemy, should they make their appearance. If they defeat us, we will then retreat with our father.

At the battle of the Rapids, last war, the Americans certainly defeated us; and when we retreated to our father's fort at that place, the gates were shut against us. We were afraid that it would now be the case; but instead of that we now see our British father preparing to march out of his garrison.

Father! You have got the arms and ammunition which our great father sent for his red children. If you have any idea of going away, give them to us, and you may go in welcome, for us. Our lives are in the hands of the Great Spirit. We are determined to defend our lands, and if it is his will, we wish to leave our bones upon them.''

No sooner had the last words of this startling speech[1] died away upon his lips, than the various chieftains started up to a man, and brandishing their tomahawks in the most menacing manner, vociferated their approbation of his sentiments. The scene altogether was of the most imposing character. The council room was a large, lofty building, the vaulted roof of which echoed back the wild yell of the Indians; while the threatening attitude and

[1] This speech was delivered on September 18th, 1813.
In the yard of Mr. Simon Fraser, ex-mayor of Amherstburg, is preserved a large boulder upon which Tecumseh used to stand when addressing his braves.

diversified costume of these latter formed a striking contrast with the calm demeanor and military garb of the officers grouped around the walls. The most prominent feature in the picture, however, was Tecumseh. Habited in a close leather dress, his athletic proportions were admirably delineated, while a large plume of white ostrich feathers, by which he was generally distinguished, overshadowing his brow, and contrasting with the darkness of his complexion and the brilliancy of his black and piercing eye, gave a singularly wild and terrific expression to his features. It was evident that he could be terrible. Tranquillity being at length restored, General Procter, through the medium of his interpreters, entered into a more detailed account of the motives by which he was influenced, and finally succeeded in prevailing on the warrior to assent to a second proposal, which was to retire on the Moravian village, distant nearly halfway between Amherstburg and the outposts of the Centre Division, and there await the approach of the enemy.

It having been resolved to move without loss of time, the troops were immediately employed in razing the fortifications, and committing such stores as it was found impossible to remove to the flames, kindled in the various public buildings ; and the ports of Detroit and Amherstburg for some days previous to our departure presented a scene of cruel desolation. At length, the baggage waggons and boats having been sent in advance, the troops of the latter garrison commenced their march early in the last week of September, and being joined by those of Detroit, proceeded up the mouth of the Thames, a river navigable for small craft, and separated from that of Detroit by the Lake St. Clair, into which it empties itself. Our movements were extremely dilatory ; and although the bridge near Amherstburg, already described in the early part of this narrative, had been destroyed by our rear-guard, it was speedily repaired by the American

general who, on the third day after our departure from
Amherstburg, crossed the lake in boats ; and hastening
to overtake us with a corps of five thousand men, was
within a few leagues at the moment we approached the
position where it was originally intended the little army
should entrench itself.

The Moravian village, situated in a small plain, offered
every facility of defence, being bounded on one flank by
a thick wood, highly favorable to the operations of the
Indians, and on the other, by the river Thames, while
immediately in front, a deep ravine, covered with brushwood, and commanded by our guns, presented an
obstacle peculiarly unfavorable to the passage of cavalry,
of which, we were sufficiently informed, a large portion
of the advancing columns consisted. Yet, notwithstanding the excellence of the position, from some singularly
selfish motive, the project was entirely abandoned. On
the evening of the 4th, the enemy had captured our
boats and, with them, the guard by which they were accompanied. Lieut. Holmes, of the Provincial Dragoons,
an active and enterprising officer, who, with a small detachment of men, was of great service to the army during
its retreat, also fell into the hands of the enemy on this
day, having been taken while in the act of swimming his
horse across the Chatham river,[1] on his return from destroying some bridges. On the 5th, at one o'clock in the
afternoon, we were within two miles of the Moravian village, but in defiance of that repeated experience which
should have taught us the hopelessness of combating a
concealed enemy, the troops were ordered to defile into
the heart of a wood, not very close it is true, yet through
the interstices of which it was impossible for the view to
extend itself beyond a distance of twenty paces, much
less to discover objects bearing so close a resemblance to
the bark and foliage of the trees and bushes as the cos-

---

[1]McGregor's Creek, which debouches into the Thames about
the centre of the present city of Chatham.

tume of the Americans; whereas, on the contrary, the glaring red of the troops formed a point of relief on which the eye could not fail to dwell. In this position we continued to remain during two hours, our left wing extending to the road, in which a solitary six pounder was posted, and the right flanked by the Indians to the number of 1,000 under Tecumseh; when the bugles of the enemy sounding at length to the attack, the engagement commenced. The result of an affair, against a body of such numerical superiority, and under such circumstances, may easily be anticipated. Closely pressed on every hand, and principally by a strong corps of mounted riflemen, the troops were finally compelled to give way, and completely hemmed in by their assailants, had no other alternative than to lay down their arms—about fifty men only, with a single officer of the regiment, (Lieut. Bullock), contriving, when all was lost, to effect their escape through the wood. General Procter, mounted on an excellent charger, and accompanied by his personal staff, sought safety in flight at the very commencement of the action, and being pursued for some hours by a detachment of mounted Kentucky riflemen, was in imminent danger of falling into their hands.

In this affair, I had an opportunity of witnessing the cruel dexterity and despatch with which the Indians use the tomahawk and scalping knife. A Kentucky rifleman, who had been dismounted within a few yards of the spot where I stood,—and the light company, to which I was attached, touched the left flank of the Indians—was fired at by three warriors of the Delaware tribe. The unfortunate man received their several balls in his body, yet, although faint from loss of blood, he made every exertion to save himself. Never was fear so strongly depicted on the human countenance, and the man's hair (for he was uncovered) absolutely seemed to me to stand on end, as he attempted to double a large fallen tree, in order to elude the weapons of his enemies. The foremost of his pursuers was a tall powerful man—a chief whom I well knew, having, only a few days before we commenced our retreat, obtained from him a saddle in exchange for a regimental coat, purchased at the sale of the effects of Lieut. Sutherland, wounded at Maguaga. When within twelve or fifteen paces of the rifleman, he raised and threw his tomahawk, and with such precision and force, that it immediately opened the skull, and extended him motionless on the earth. Laying down his rifle, he drew forth his knife, and after having removed the hatchet from the brain, proceeded to make a circular incision throughout the scalp. This done, he grasped the bloody instrument between his teeth, and placing his knees on the back of his victim, while at the same time he fastened his fingers in the hair, the scalp was torn off without much apparent difficulty and thrust, still bleeding, into his bosom. The warrior then arose, and after having wiped his knife on the clothes of the unhappy man, returned it to its sheath, grasping at the same time the arms he had abandoned, and hastening to rejoin his comrades. All this was the work of a few minutes.

While this brief scene was enacting, the main body of the enemy, who had by this time succeeded in breaking through our centre, and had wheeled up, in order to take the Indians in flank, moved rapidly upon us in every direction ; so that the resistance the light company had hitherto opposed, was now utterly hopeless of any successful result. Persuaded moreover, from the sudden cessation of the firing in that direction, that our centre and left (for the wood intercepted them from our view), had been overcome, we, at the suggestion and command of Lieutenant Hailes, the only officer with us, prepared to make good our retreat, but, instead of going deeper into the wood as we purposed, we mistook our way, and found ourselves unexpectedly in the road ; when, on glancing to the right, we beheld, at a distance of about five hundred yards, the main body of our men disarmed

—grouped together, and surrounded by American troops. On turning to the left, as we instinctively did, we saw a strong body of cavalry coming toward us, evidently returning from some short pursuit, and slowly walking their horses. At the head of these, and dressed like his men, in Kentucky hunting frocks, was a stout elderly officer whom we subsequently knew to be Governor Shelby, and who the moment he beheld us emerging from the wood, galloped forward and brandishing his sword over his head, cried out with stentorian lungs "Surrender surrender, it's no use resisting, all your people are taken, and you had better surrender." There was no alternative. The channel to escape had been closed by the horsemen in the wood, as well as those in the road, and a surrender was unavoidable. We accordingly moved down to join our captured comrades, as directed by Governor Shelby, yet I well recollect burying my musket in the mud, which was very deep, in order to avoid giving it up to the enemy. Perfectly also do I recollect the remark made by a tall Kentuckian as I passed by him to the group—"Well I guess now, you tarnation little Britisher, who'd calculate to see such a bit of a chap as you here?" But I heeded not the sneer of the Kentuckian. My eye had fallen and rested upon a body of American Indians, about fifty in number, from some one of whose tomahawks, I apprehended the death-blow—I had seen their weapons too often exercised (and indeed, as has been seen, only a few minutes before) to feel anything like security. But my fear was without foundation. As I watched them more narrowly, I found that their countenances wore an expression of concern, and that, so far from seeking to injure us, they seemed rather to regret our fate. Nor is this at all unlikely, as it was well known that the greater portion of the warriors who had taken up the hatchet in favor of the United States, had been induced to do so from compulsion alone. This little anecdote, otherwise too personal per-

Drawn by F. Brigden.

TECUMSEH.

haps, affords another in support of the many striking evidences of the strong attachment of the Indians for the British.

The most serious loss we sustained on this occasion was that of the noble and unfortunate Tecumseh. Only a few minutes before the clang of the American bugles was heard ringing through the forest, and inspiriting to action, the haughty Chieftain had passed along our line, pleased with the manner in which his left was supported, and seemingly sanguine of success. He was dressed in his usual deer skin dress, which admirably displayed his light yet sinewy figure, and in his handkerchief, rolled as a turban over his brow, was placed a handsome white ostrich feather, which had been given to him by a near relation of the writer of this narrative, and on which he was ever fond of decorating himself, either for the Hall of Council or the battle field. He pressed the hand of each officer as he passed, made some remark in Shawnee, appropriate to the occasion, which was sufficiently understood by the expressive signs accompanying them, and then passed away forever from our view. Towards the close of the engagement, he had been personally opposed to Colonel Johnson, commanding the American mounted riflemen, and having severely wounded that officer with a ball from his rifle, was in the act of springing upon him with his tomahawk, when his adversary drew a pistol from his belt, and shot him dead on the spot. It has since been denied by the Americans that the hero met his death from the hand of Colonel Johnson. Such was the statement on the day of the action, nor was it ever contradicted at that period. There is every reason to infer then that the merit (if any merit could attach to the destruction of all that was noble and generous in savage life), of having killed Tecumseh, rests with Colonel Johnson. The merit of having flayed the body of the fallen brave, and made razor strops of his skin, rests with his immediate followers. This too has been denied, but

denial is vain. On the night of the engagement, when seated around a fire kindled in the forest, partaking, on the very battle ground, of the meat which Gen. Harrison's aids-de-camp were considerately and hospitably toasting for us on long pointed sticks, or skewers, and which, half-famished as we were, we greedily ate without the accompaniment of either salt or bread, the painful subject was discussed, and it is not less an eulogy to the memory of the high-minded Tecumseh, than a justice to that of General Harrison to add, that that officer was the first to deplore his death ; while the sentiments he expressed, when the circumstance and manner of his fall were made known, were such as to reflect credit on himself, both as a man, a Christian, and a soldier.

Doubts as to the fact of Tecumseh having fallen at all at the Moraviantown, have, in the same spirit of party which has denied to Colonel Johnson the act of having shot him, been entertained ; and it has even been asserted that the mutilated remains which were supposed to have been his, were in reality those of another Chief. Would for the honor of humanity it had been so : but this is incorrect. Several of the officers of the 41st, on being apprized of his fall, went, accompanied by some of General Harrison's Staff, to visit the spot where Tecumseh lay, and there they identified (for they knew well) in the mangled corpse before them, all that remained of the late powerful and intelligent chieftain. Of the pain with which the sight was viewed, and the deep regret with which his death was regarded, no stronger evidence can be given than in the fact that there was scarcely an officer of the captured Division who, as he reposed his head upon the rude log, affording him the only pillow that night, did not wholly lose sight of his own unfortunate position in the more lively emotion produced by the untimely fate of the lamented and noble Indian. It has ever been a source of profound regret to me that I was not present at this inspection, for although the sight of the mutilated hero could not have failed to inflict upon my heart pain of the most poignant kind, it would have been at least a consolation to have seen the last of his remains on earth : and this not more from the reverence and honor in which I had, and have, ever held the Warrior, than from the opportunity I should now possess of bearing attestation to the fact and manner of his fall, from my own positive and personal observation. I was not, however, aware of the purposed visit until the party had returned, and made it the subject of conversation, in presence of General Harrison, as already stated. Nor was there time afforded for remedying the unintentional omission.

But the battle of the Moraviantown (if indeed battle it can be called) embracing as it does an important portion of Canadian History, and involving the honor of the British arms, is not thus briefly to be dismissed. The Right Division has been grossly vilified for its conduct on the occasion, and that vilification stands on public record. The proud—the honorable—the gratifying task of refuting the unmerited aspersion has devolved on the young, and humble, and comparatively unnoticed volunteer, who had the advantage of tracking it throughout its whole course of unceasing service, and whose lot it seems to be to have been nursed in the regiment, chiefly to become, at this distant day, the impartial chronicler of its deeds, and the vindicator of its unjustly sullied name.

First on the list of calumny stands the general order issued by Sir George Prevost—a commander whose marked imbecility and want of resolution, on more than one occasion, (reflecting the deepest disgrace on the British arms), had doubtless been ordained as a fitting punishment for his arrogant censure of the conduct of a corps, whose general excellence he was incompetent to appreciate, and whose only positive crime was that of its weakness, its physical disorganization, and its utter destitution. Here is the insulting and most uncalled for document, and who, on perusing it, after having traced the regiment through its previous course of glory will fail to entertain a sentiment of deep indignation at its injustice?

General Order,
Head Quarters, Montreal, Nov. 24th, 1813.

His Excellency the Commander of the Forces has received an Official report from Major-General Procter of the affair which took place on the 5th October, near the Moravian village, and he has in vain sought in it, for grounds to palliate the report made to His Excellency by Staff Adjutant Reiffenstein, upon which the General Order of the 18th October was founded—on the contrary that statement remains confirmed in all the principal events which marked that disgraceful day; the precipitancy with which the Staff Adjutant retreated from the field of action, prevented his ascertaining the loss sustained by the division on that occasion; it also led him most grossly to exaggerate the enemy's force, and to misrepresent the conduct of the Indian Warriors who instead of retreating towards Machedash, as he had stated, gallantly maintained the conflict, under their brave Chief Tecumseh, and in their turn harassed the American Army on its retreat to Detroit.

The subjoined return states the loss the Right Division has sustained in the action of the fleet on Lake Erie on the 10th Sept., and in the affair of the 5th October near the Moravian village. In the latter but very few appear to have been rescued by an honorable death, from the ignominy of passing under the American yoke, nor are there many whose wounds plead in mitigation of this reproach. The Right Division appears to have been encumbered with an unmanageable load of unnecessary, and forbidden private baggage—while the requisite arrangements for the expeditious, and certain conveyance of the ammunition, and provisions, the sole objects worthy of consideration, appear to have been totally neglected, as well as all those ordinary measures resorted to by officers of intelligence, to retard and impede the advance of a pursuing enemy. The result affords but too fatal a proof of this unjustifiable neglect. The Right Division had quitted Sandwich in its retreat on the 26th September, having had ample time, for every previous arrangement, to facilitate and secure that movement ; on the 2nd October following, the enemy pursued by the same route, and on the 4th succeeded in capturing all the stores of the division, and on the following day attacked and defeated it almost without a struggle.

With heart-felt pride and satisfaction the Commander of the Forces had lavished on the Right Division of this army, that tribute of praise which was so justly due to its former gallantry and steady discipline. It is with poignant grief and mortification that he now beholds its well-earned laurels tarnished, and its conduct calls loudly for reproach and censure.

The Commander of the Forces appeals to the genuine feelings of the British soldier from whom he neither conceals the extent of the loss the army has suffered, nor the far more to be lamented injury it has sustained in its wounded honor, confident that but one sentiment will animate every breast, and that zealous to wash out the stain, which by a most extraordinary and unaccountable infatuation, has fallen on a formerly deserving portion of the army, all will vie to emulate the glorious achievements recently performed, by a small but highly spirited and well-disciplined division, led by officers possessed of enterprise, intelligence, and gallantry, nobly evincing what British soldiers can perform, when susceptible of no fear, but that of failing in the discharge of their duty.

His Excellency considers it an act of justice, to exonerate most honorably from this censure the brave soldiers who were serving as marines on board the squadron on Lake Erie, the Commander of the Forces having received the official report of Capt. Barclay of the action which took place on Lake Erie on the 10th September when that gallant officer, from circumstances of imperious necessity was compelled to seek the superior force of the enemy, and to maintain an arduous and long-contested action under circumstances of accumulating ill fortune.

Captain Barclay represents, that the wind, which was favorable early in the day, suddenly changed, giving the enemy the weather-gage, and that this important advantage was, shortly after the commencement of the engagement, heightened by the fall of Captain Finnis, the commander of the Queen Charlotte. In the death of that intrepid and intelligent officer, Capt. Barclay laments the loss of his main support. The fall of Capt. Finnis was soon followed by that of Lieut. Stokoe, whose country was deprived of his services at this very critical period leaving the command of the Queen Charlotte to Provincial Lieutenant Irvine, who conducted himself with great courage, but was too limited in experience to supply the place of such an officer as Capt. Finnis, and in consequence this vessel proved of far less assistance than might be expected.

The action commenced at about a quarter before 12 o'clock, and continued with great fury until half-past 2, when the American Commodore quitted his ship, which struck shortly after, to that commanded by Capt. Barclay (the Detroit.) Hitherto the determined valor displayed by the British squadron, had surmounted every disadvantage, and the day was in our favor ; but the contest had arrived at that period when valor alone was unavailing—the Detroit and Queen Charlotte were perfect wrecks, and required the utmost skill of seamanship, while the commanders and second officers, of every vessel, were either killed or wounded : not more than fifty British seamen were dispersed in the crews of the squadron, and of these a great proportion had fallen in the conflict.

The American Commodore made a gallant, and but too successful an effort to regain the day. His second largest vessel, the Niagara, had suffered little, and his numerous gun-boats which had proved the greatest source of annoyance during the action, were all uninjured.

Lieutenant Garland, First Lieutenant of the Detroit, being mortally wounded, previous to the wounds of Captain Barclay obliging him to quit the deck, it fell to the lot of Lieutenant Inglis, to whose intrepidity and conduct the highest praise is given, to surrender His Majesty's Ship, when all further resistance had become unavailing.

The enemy, by having the weather-gage, were enabled to choose their distance and thereby avail themselves of the great advantage they derived in a superiority of heavy long guns, but Captain Barclay attributes the result of the day, to the unprecedented fall of every Commander, and second in command, and the very small number of able seamen left in the squadron, at a moment when the judgment of the officer, and skilful exertions of the sailor were most immediately called for.

To the British seamen, Captain Barclay bestows the highest praise—*that they behaved like British seamen*. From the officers and soldiers of the regular force serving as marines, Captain Barclay experienced every support within their power, and states that their conduct has excited his warmest thanks and admiration.

Deprived of the palm of victory, when almost within his grasp, by an overwhelming force which the enemy possessed in reserve, aided by an accumulation of unfortunate circumstances, Captain Barclay and his brave crew have, by their gallant daring, and self-devotion to their country's cause, rescued its honor and their own, even in defeat.   EDWARD BAYNES,
                                        Adjutant-General.

Return of the Right Division of the Army of Upper Canada :

Detachment serving as marines on board the squadron in action on 10th September, 1813.

Killed—1 lieutenant, 1 sergeant, 21 rank and file.

Wounded—3 sergeants, 46 rank and file.

Prisoners—2 lieutenants, 1 asst. surgeon, 4 sergeants, 4 drummers, 167 rank and file.

Killed, wounded, and missing in the retreat and in the action of the 5th October, 1813 :

1 inspecting field officer, 1 dep. asst. qr.-master-general, 1 fort adjutant, 1 hospital mate, 1 lieutenant-col., 6 captains, 12 lieutenants, 3 ensigns, 1 paymaster, 1 asst. surgeon, 34 sergeants, 13 drummers, 559 rank and file, 46 horses.

Assembled at Ancaster on the 17th October, 1813 :

1 major-general, 1 major of brigade, 1 aid-de-camp, 1 staff adjutant, 3 captains, 5 lieutenants, 2 ensigns, 1 adjutant, 1 quarter-master, 2 asst. surgeons, 15 sergeants, 9 drummers, 204 rank and file, 53 horses.

Total strength of the Right Division on the 10th September, 1813 :

1 major-general, 1 inspecting field officer, 1 major of brigade, 1 dep. asst. q.m. gen., 1 aid-de-camp, 1 staff adjutant, 1 fort adjutant, 1 hospital mate, 1 lieutenant-colonel, 9 captains, 20 lieutenants, 5 ensigns, 1 paymaster, 1 adjutant, 1 quarter-master, 4 assistant surgeons, 57 sergeants, 26 drummers, 997 rank and file, 99 horses.

Killed—Lieut. Garden, Royal Newfoundland Regt.
                                        EDWARD BAYNES,
                                        Adjutant-General.

Well timed indeed, and with a befitting grace does the insulting censure, contained in the opening of the above order, emanate from the man who had previously made a descent upon Sackett's Harbor, with a view of destroying the enemy's naval and military works, and who at the very moment of accomplishment of the object of the expedition, and when the Americans were retreating, turned and fled with precipitation to his boats, presenting to the troops, who were unwilling sharers in his disgrace, the monstrous yet ludicrous anomaly of two hostile armies fleeing from each other at the same time. Well does it become the leader who, at Plattsburg, covered the British army with shame, and himself with enduring infamy, by retiring at the head of 15,000 men—chiefly the flower of the Duke of Wellington's army—before a force of Americans not exceeding as many hundreds ; and this even at the moment when the commander of these latter was preparing to surrender his trust without a struggle. Well does it proceed from him, who through timidity and vacillation alone, at an earlier period of the war, entered into a disgraceful armistice with the enemy at the very moment when General Brock was preparing to follow up his successes on the western frontier, by sweeping the whole southern border of the St. Lawrence. Happily was it devised by the authority to whose culpable inattention and neglect alone was owing the loss of the gallant Barclay's fleet, and the consequent helplessness of that very Right Division he has hesitated not to condemn for a disaster attributable to himself alone. Nay, well and most consistently does the sting issue from the Commander of the Forces, who, on the occasion of the capture of Detroit, and the victory obtained at the River Raisin, ordered royal salutes to be fired in honor of conquests which had been achieved principally by the 41st Regiment, and whose remarks, even on the occasion of their unavoidable repulse at Sandusky, convey rather a compliment than dispraise.

That Sir George Prevost had been induced to issue this order, on the gross misrepresentation of General Procter, who, in order to shield himself from the consequences of his incapacity, scrupled not to sacrifice the reputation of the regiment, which had so often repaired, by their valor, what his marked inefficiency had endangered, there can be no question. It is only necessary to refer to an earlier memorandum on the subject to be fully satisfied of the fact. But this does not the more exonerate Sir George, whose duty it was, before publishing a document, the tendency of which was to cast odium on a corps which he himself admits to have previously won his warmest admiration, to possess himself of the true facts of the action ; nor, by any exercise of undue severity, to have provoked commentaries on his own conduct of a far more humiliating character. But posterity will judge of the Right Division, not by the sweeping and unfounded denunciations of an angry and misjudging Governor, but by its universally admitted gallantry on all former occasions.

Who on looking over the state of the 41st Regiment, which ostentatiously appears at the close of the General Order, would not infer that, in the action of the Moraviantown, they mustered at least 1,000 men, including non-commissioned officers ? Even General Harrison, in his most voluminous despatch, enumerates the prisoners taken by him in such a way as to create the impression that his (admitted) force of 3,000 had been opposed by 600 British regulars, present in action. This is not worthy of General Harrison, who must have known that our actual force in the field was, according to the state of the adjutant of the regiment—the original of which is before me at this moment—1 lieut.-colonel, 6 captains, 9 lieuts., 3 ensigns, 3 staff, 26 sergeants, 18 corporals, 4 drummers, and 297 rank and file—and these divided into two open, and irregular lines. The remainder of the 600, captured by General Harrison, many of them sick and wounded men, had been taken, without a possibility of opposition, in the boats conveying stores, during the early morning of the action, and on the preceding day. Yet the American general seriously claims the palm of " superior bravery " for his force of 3,000 men, opposed in their native woods (wherein he himself admits in his despatch they " can ride better than any other people ") to not as many hundreds, and these almost wholly unaccustomed to them. It is impossible to entertain a feeling of disrespect for General Harrison, but there is something so absurd in this remark, that the reader cannot forbear a smile. Nor can it be pretended that the Indians are to be considered as having formed any portion of our force during the first advance of the enemy, for General Harrison has distinctly stated that he formed his assailing columns in such manner as to direct them wholly upon the 41st, leaving the Indians unmolested, until he should be enabled to break through our feeble and extended line, and *then* turn their position. This plan was acted upon. What then was there in this defeat to justify Sir George Prevost, in the sweeping and splenetic denunciation cast upon a corps who had done so much for the country, and had only now been overcome through the incompetency of their chief ? But let us turn to General Procter.

That officer has stated in his specious defence before the court-martial which tried him for general misconduct in the retreat, that he had drawn up his men in a position the most favorable for a successful stand against the enemy's cavalry, and that he had expected a result which the want of firmness manifested by the regiment alone had denied to him. Who will second General Procter in this view of the subject? Who, with him, will aver that the proper place for British troops to engage an enemy is the woods, and that he was justified in the selection, when, not two miles in his rear, were numerous houses in which to throw his men, a wood on his right flank, and the river on his left, while immediately in front ran a ravine difficult of access by cavalry, and capable of being swept by his guns, which, singularly enough, had already been stationed there without the slightest use or service in the battle planned by him to be waged. On what does General Procter ground his claim to be considered as competent to decide upon the success which ought to attend his military movements? Is it on his dispositions at the River Raisin, where, instead of attacking an unprepared enemy sword in hand, he absurdly and unaccountably apprized them of their danger, giving them ample opportunity to arm and cripple his own force, in such a manner as to render victory for a period doubtful? Is it on his arrangements at the Miami, where he suffered an important line of batteries to be left without the support of even a single company? Is it on his attack upon Sandusky, where he ordered his men to storm before any breach had been effected, without a fascine or scaling ladder, and with axes so blunt that he might have been suspected of treason in suffering them to be placed in the hands of the unfortunate men who perished while fruitlessly wielding them? Yet this man, whose brows the 41st Regiment covered in these several instances with glory, when they rather should have been bowed to the earth in shame, turns upon his gallant supporters in the moment of their misfortune, and, in his base attempt to redeem his own blighted military reputation, scruples not to charge them with misconduct in the field. Where was this misconduct? In what did it consist? It has been seen that 3,000 men, 1,500 of whom were mounted riflemen, dashed through the front line, composed of something less than 200 men, receiving the only two volleys there was time to pour in before they had completely surrounded them. Was it possible to make a more lengthened defence against an enemy who thus overwhelmed them *en masse*? The true matter for surprise is, not that the force yielded so soon, but that it had ever made a stand at all ; for the strong conviction on the mind of

every officer and man present, was that General Procter
was making a wanton sacrifice of their lives, for the sole
purpose of covering the departure of his family and personal effects from the Moraviantown ; and that it was for
this reason also that he had drawn them up in the heart
of a wood, in preference to occupying a position which
all had been previously informed was susceptible of the
best defence against the expected cavalry.

I have said that only two volleys were fired by the men
before they were overwhelmed by the American force.
This was I believe the case on the centre and left, upon
which the main attack of the enemy was directed. On
the right, and near Tecumseh's flank, where the horsemen opposed to us were less numerous, the action was of
at least twenty minutes' duration, and in this time much
desultory firing took place. The instance I have already
given of the shooting, tomahawking, and scalping of an
American rifleman, who had been dismounted in the
action, is an evidence that the engagement was not so
speedily brought to a close as General Procter sought to
make it appear. But I will relate another fact in cor-
roboration. Only a few minutes before this scene was
enacted before our eyes, a mounted rifleman was in the
act of taking aim at one of the light company, who was
moving quickly at the time, and whom therefore he could
not conveniently cover. My attention was called to this
man by Lieut. Hailes (since commanding the 28th Regiment), who was near me at the time, and who suggested
that I should fire at him. I raised my musket, supporting it against a tree, and before the American, who was
still following his object with his eye and weapon, could
find what he deemed a favorable moment for discharging
it, I fired, when his rifle tumbled from his shoulder to
the ground, and he sank over his horse's side.

Now if, as General Procter states, the line " had discharged their pieces without orders, had given way, and
had dispersed in a manner to preclude all hope of their

being again formed," there could have been no time for these two deliberate actions.   When a few minutes afterwards, we, from a consciousness of having been cut off from our main body, attempted a retreat, we were not so sorely pressed as to have failed in our object, had we taken the proper direction.   We had continued firing to the close, and it was only on emerging from the wood into the road, and beholding our captured comrades, that we found resistance to be hopeless.   Including Lieut. Hailes we were then about twenty in number.

I have already stated that General Procter was without the confidence of his army.   This is strictly correct.   So far from their having the slightest knowledge of the object of his movements, or of his intentions, not even his second in command was consulted on any one occasion during the retreat.   As for the expression of surprise, contained in the defence, that Dover had not been fortified it is perfectly ridiculous.   Independently of its peculiar unfitness for that purpose, no such instructions had ever been left with Colonel Warburton, who, when repeatedly asked by the officers of the Division what was purposed to be done, or to what tended General Procter's unaccountable conduct, could only shrug his shoulders, and in a manner indicative of mingled mortification and contempt, reply that they knew as much of the matter as he did.   How, indeed, and under what direction was Dover to be fortified, when, as General Procter himself admits, he had taken with him to the Moraviantown the only officer of Engineers (Captain Dixon) who was attached to the Division ?

Such was the general feeling of distrust, produced by General Procter's continued absence from, and in advance of the army, at a moment when the enemy were known to be near us, and when the second in command was left wholly in the dark, as to the course it was expected of him to pursue, that serious intentions were formed of depriving that officer of his authority, and investing

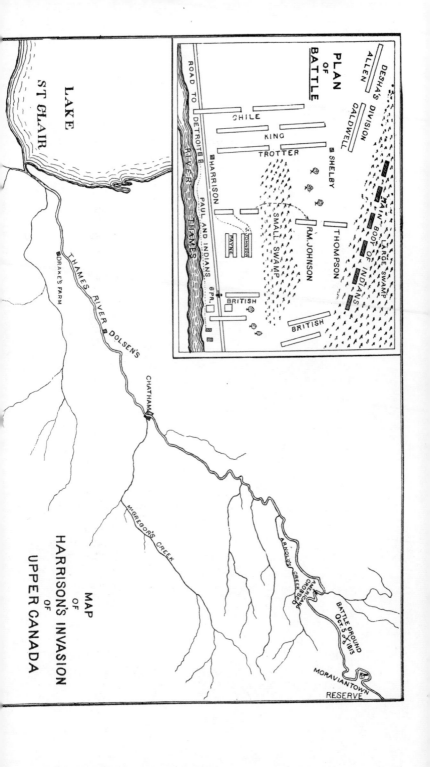

PLAN OF BATTLE

DESHA'S DIVISION
ALLEN
CALDWELL

CHILE
KING
TROTTER

ROAD TO DETROIT &

SHELBY

MAIN BODY OF INDIANS

LARGE SWAMP

THOMPSON

R.M. JOHNSON

SMALL SWAMP

HARRISON

RIVER THAMES

PAUL AND INDIANS

PAYNE
JOHNSON
6 Pr.

BRITISH

BRITISH

LAKE ST CLAIR

THAMES RIVER
DRAKE'S FARM
DOLSEN'S
CHATHAM
McGREGOR'S CREEK
ARNOLD'S CREEK
CROSSING
MAIN CROSSING
BATTLE GROUND Oct. 5 1813
MORAVIANTOWN
RESERVE

MAP
OF
HARRISON'S INVASION
OF
UPPER CANADA

Colonel Warburton with it.   This indeed was only not
done, because it was assumed that any disaster which
might, in consequence of the extraordinary delay and
want of military capacity hitherto manifested in its conduct, occur to the Division, would be gladly seized hold
of by the General, with a view to exonerate himself from
the heavy responsibility he was already so fearfully incurring.   Of the sentiments entertained by all, a tolerably
correct estimate may be formed from the following mem-
oranda at the time by an officer of the regiment.

" 3rd Oct., Dolsen's.   A report of the Americans being
within two or three miles of us. ' Our dragoons fell in
with their advanced guard.   The General at Moraviantown, 26 miles from Dolsen's or Dover.   Marched from
this place 2½ miles ; halted and formed on the bank of
the river in expectation of the enemy every instant.
Marched a few miles further and halted for the night.
Col. Warburton did not appear to know how to act, the
General not having left any directions, but he decided on
falling in with the wishes of the Indians.

4th Oct.   This morning the Indians thought it advisable to proceed at once to Moraviantown.   We accordingly marched : at dusk the rear guard halted at Richardson's ; the remainder proceeded about a mile farther,
within five miles of Moraviantown.

5th Oct.   This day we proceeded towards Moraviantown, and when within a mile and a half of it, were halted
and marched back a few paces, when we halted a second
time : no person appeared to have any idea of what was
going to be done.   A report came in of the Americans
being within a very short distance of us, and that they
had taken all our boats, in which was most of our baggage and the whole of the ammunition, except what the
men had in their pouches.   After having halted for
nearly an hour, we were suddenly ordered to form in
the midst of a very thick wood apparently without any
previous arrangement and in such a manner that the
Grenadiers were nearly in the centre of the line, and the
light company towards the right—a second order came
for the Grenadiers and No. 1 company to march to the
rear as a reserve, which was done.   The men were
formed at extended order, and the enemy, it was said,

were strong in cavalry and mounted riflemen.   N.B. No
brushwood to prevent the cavalry acting.   About four
o'clock the enemy attacked us, and succeeded in driving
us from our ground.   The company I commanded had
not received their provisions for the two last days, until
the very moment before we received the order to march :
the consequence was that those men who had time to do
so, cut off a slice of the raw beef and ate it uncooked.
The rest had none at all.

Mem.—While at Dolsen's was told by G——e that a
council of war was going to assemble immediately, in
order to decide whether or not the command should be
taken from the G.   The day before the action Captain
Muir remarked to me that the G. ought to be hanged for
being away, and that Col. W. ought to be hanged for not
assuming the command.   A few moments before the
action Captain D. said it was downright murder if we attempted to make a stand where we were—Colonel Elliott
told me that the day the G. went to the Moraviantown,
the Prophet (Tecumseh's brother) asked him, Col. Elliott,
where the G. was going, and on being informed remarked
that he had a great mind to take the epaulettes off his
shoulders, for he was not worthy to wear them.''

General Procter furthermore asserts in his defence, that
his original intention was to fortify a position on the
Thames, for the two-fold purpose of protecting the Centre
Division, and conciliating the Indians.   I am not prepared, at this distant day, to state with exactness what
was the original proposal made to the Indians in the celebrated council, but my strong impression has ever been
(and I was present during the whole of the debate) that
it was only in consequence of the deep and unconcealed
indignation, manifested by Tecumseh and many of the
inferior Chiefs, on his intimating the necessity which
existed for a retreat upon the Centre Division, that he was
compelled to yield to the will of the Indians, and to name
the Moraviantown as the understood termination of his
proposed march.   Even this proposal was received by
Tecumseh with mingled regret and disdain, for he was
desirous of meeting the Americans at the moment of their

landing, and trying the chances of battle before incurring the odium of a retreat; but on the inexpediency of defending a fortress which had been wholly deprived of its heavy guns for the purpose of arming the fleet, being further discussed and pointed out to him, he finally assented, and in a second short speech, which does not appear to have been placed on record, consented to retire as far as the Moraviantown, declaring however, at the same time, that at that place he was fully determined to conquer or lay down his life. Had the retreat been commenced from that moment, and the Moraviantown fortified, as it ought to have been, no matter how imperfectly, none of the subsequent disasters would have occurred. It is insincere in General Procter to state that his march was delayed in order to afford the Indians time to remove their effects, and cross the Detroit river. Those who understand the manners and active habits of the red-men of the forest must be aware that twenty-four hours were quite sufficient with them for any purpose of the sort; neither is there less absurdity in the assertion that it was necessary to linger on the road, in order to enable them to overtake us. The Indians could march, in a single day, more than we did in five, and even if they had not overtaken us, it was our object to be in position to cover them, if pursued by the enemy, and to be enabled to oppose to these latter something like a respectable attitude of defence. All this might, and should, have been done, and on whom can the onus of neglect fall, if not on General Procter?

There are yet two points in the defence to which it is essential to advert. General Procter very gravely complains that the gun placed in the road on the left of the line, in the affair of the Moraviantown, and on which he so much depended, had been deserted "without an effort." What will be thought of the general conduct of the retreat, when it is known that there was not a single round of ammunition for the gun, it having by some unfortunate accident been left behind, on resuming our march in the morning! It is true General Procter cannot be held individually responsible for this omission, but had the only officer of artillery, attached to the Division, been where he ought to have been—in the action—instead of posting himself, by the direction of his Chief, with the reserve guns at the Moraviantown, his sagacity and forethought would have prevented this difficulty. That there was fault with those who had immediate charge of the field-piece there can be no question, but it is unjust to the last degree that such fault should be visited by a general condemnation of the conduct of the troops engaged. Yet even had the gun been supplied with ammunition the result must have been nearly the same. One discharge might have temporarily checked the advance of the enemy upon the road, but as this was open only a few hundred yards in front, the range commanded was necessarily so limited, that the American cavalry might have dashed in upon it, before the Artillery men could have time to load and fire again; moreover there was the certainty of its being turned through the wood. General Procter alludes to twenty Provincial Dragoons of Lieut. Holmes' command (that officer then, it has been seen, a prisoner with the enemy), as having been posted by him in support of the gun, and confesses disappointment that they had not maintained their trust. What could be expected from so mere a handful of men against the masses that were opposed to them? And how absurd to suppose that they could have offered the slightest resistance.

Again, General Procter adverts to an attempt made by him to rally the broken line, and in a manner to show that his prosecutors had admitted such attempt, although they denied its efficacy. How this admission (if made) was wrung from them, it is difficult to understand, unless that it had been made inadvertently. General Procter had stationed himself in rear of the second line, and he made no attempt, at any one period of the brief action, to pass it. When the first line retreated upon the second, and the latter opened its fire upon the advancing cavalry, he fled precipitately, accompanied by the whole of his personal staff, leaving the Division to maintain the unequal conflict in the best manner they could. This has been asserted by an officer who was near him during the whole of the affair.

Of the impression created by the cruel and ungenerous order, issued by Sir George Prevost on this occasion, a tolerable estimate may be formed from the following communication, addressed to Lieut. Bullock by Major Friend, then in command of the 2nd Battalion of the regiment. In the reply will be found so full an explanation that beyond it, it will not be necessary to pursue the subject.

Barton Heights, 30th Nov., 1813.

Sir,—I request you will, with as little delay as the nature of the report will admit, furnish me with every circumstance within your knowledge, and that you may have heard from undoubted authority, relative to the late unfortunate affair that took place between General Harrison's army and the 1st Battalion 41st Regiment at Moraviantown on the 5th October last, for the purpose of transmitting it to Lieut.-Gen. Champagne. As you are the senior and only officer of the regiment who has escaped from the field, that was in the ranks, it is highly incumbent on you to state most minutely the nature of the ground on which the regiment were formed for action, the manner in which it was formed, the number then of the regiment actually in the field, the number of the enemy opposed to you, and of what they consisted, and what resistance was made by the regiment previous to its defeat—if it had received provisions regularly, was complete in ammunition, and could have got supplies when required, and in short every circumstance that happened from the commencement of the retreat from Amherstburg relative to the regiment. You cannot be too particular in your statement, as I am sorry to say there are reports afloat disgraceful in the extreme to the regiment, and every individual with it that day. I think it but proper to inform you that I saw Major-General

Procter's official report which highly censures the conduct of the regiment, and in which he says, that he never went into action more confident of success.

I have the honor to be, &c.

Your very obed't. humble serv't.

Richard Friend,

Major Commg. 41st Regt.

Lieut. Bullock,

41st Regiment.

Cross Roads, Barton Heights,
6th Dec., 1813.

Sir,—The following report is made, in compliance with your orders to me in a letter dated 30th Nov. last, in which you request I would furnish you with every circumstance within my knowledge, and what I may have heard from undoubted authority, relative to the late unfortunate affair which took place between the American army under Gen. Harrison, and the 1st Bat. 41st Regt. near Moraviantown, on the 5th October last, the nature of the ground on which it was formed, the number of men of the Regt. actually in the field, the number of the enemy in the field opposed to it, of what they consisted, and what resistance was made by the Regiment previous to its defeat; if it had received provisions regularly, was complete in ammunition, and could have got supplies when required, and in short every circumstance that happened from the commencement of the retreat from Amherstburg relative to the Regiment. As a platoon officer I cannot positively say whether the whole regiment was complete with ammunition or not, but this I can say, that a number of the men who escaped from the enemy that day, were not complete before the action commenced; and this I am inclined to believe was the case with many of those killed or taken, and in the event of expending the ammunition in their pouches they could not have received a fresh supply, the whole of the spare ammunition being taken by the enemy some hours before the action, which circumstance was known to many of the regiment. I now proceed to give every other information required in your letter, as correctly as my rank, and situation on various occasions, enabled me to observe.

The force under Major Gen. Procter consisting of the 1st Bat. 41st Regiment, a few of the 10th Veterans,

(about 18 or 20) some Artillery, and a body of Indians
retreated from Amherstburg on — Sept. last to Sandwich,
from whence we retired on the 27th of the same month
to the River Thames, the banks of which, at a place
called Chatham (54 miles from Sandwich, and 70 from
Amherstburg) Gen. Procter had promised the Indians to
fortify, with a view to await the enemy.   On this retreat
I commanded the grenadier company.   We arrived
within three miles of Chatham, at a place called Dolsen's
on the 1st Oct.   On the 3rd Gen. Procter was at Moraviantown, 26 miles from us, on the road leading to the
head of Lake Ontario; when information was received
that the enemy was within 4 or 5 miles of us, and we retired 1½ a mile by order of Lieut.-Col. Warburton,
second in command, and formed on the bank of the river
in expectation of an attack.   At the expiration of half an
hour we retired to Chatham.   The Indians were encamped on the opposite bank of the river, and on our
arrival, sent to say to me, that we should not proceed
beyond the ground we then occupied—that Gen. Procter
had promised them to await the enemy on that ground
and fight them ; and had also promised to erect fortifications there.   After endeavoring to reason with them,
Lieut.-Col. Warburton was compelled to remain there for
the night, and informed the Indians, through Col. Elliott
of the Indian Department, that whatever had been promised by Gen. Procter should be fulfilled, as far as he
(Lieut.-Col. Warburton) had it in his power.   I was then
ordered on picquet with the Grenadier company, and at
the same time received such particular instructions from
Lieut.-Cols. Warburton and Evans, that I have no doubt
they expected the enemy that night.   Capt. Chambers of
the Qr.-Mr.-Gen. Department, accompanied me and pointed
out the ground my picquet was to occupy, which was one
mile and a half in advance, towards the enemy.   Early
next morning the picquet was called in.   On arriving at
Chatham, where the rest of the regiment had passed the
night, provisions were issued ; the meat was raw, and before it could be divided, we were ordered to march, in
consequence of the approach of the enemy.   We retired
about 6 miles when we were joined by Gen. Procter, on
his return from Moraviantown.   We marched all
day, the roads were excessively bad; about eight o'clock
in the evening Capt. Muir's Company was halted at

Richardson's, six miles from Moraviantown, and the Grenadier company was left with it, to support in the event of an attack; the remainder proceeded on, the advance being at a house called Shearman's, one mile from where the rear guard had halted. At daybreak next morning (the 5th) the rear guard and Grenadier company moved to Shearman's, where the whole regiment collected. At this place, after having halted some time, a few head of cattle were shot, but before the meat could be divided, the enemy were reported to be close at hand, and we were ordered to march. We proceeded to Moraviantown, and when within 1½ miles of it, were ordered to halt. After halting about 5 minutes, we were ordered to face to the right about, and advanced towards the enemy in files, at which the men were in great spirits. Having advanced about 50 or 60 paces we were halted a second time, at which the men appeared dissatisfied, and overhearing some of those nearest to me express themselves to the following effect, ''that they were ready and willing to fight for their knapsacks: wished to meet the enemy, but did not like to be knocked about in that manner, doing neither one thing nor the other,'' I immediately checked them, and they were silent. About this time several of the Regiment came up without arms or accoutrements, who had escaped from boats cut off by the enemy's cavalry. From these men we learnt that the enemy was within a mile of us, and had a large force of cavalry. We had halted about half an hour, when the Indian alarm was given that the enemy was advancing : most of our men were sitting on the logs and fallen trees by the side of the road. On the alarm being given we were suddenly ordered to form across the road. From the suddenness of the order, apparently without any previous arrangement, the manner in which we were situated when it was given, the way in which it was given, which was '' form up across the road,'' and from the nature of the ground, the formation was made in the greatest confusion ; so much so, that the Grenadier company was nearly in the centre of the line and the Light company on the right. A second order, as sudden as the first, was given for the Grenadiers and No. 1 to march to the rear and form a reserve. The Grenadiers and part of Capt. Muir's company accordingly formed a second line, about 200 yards in rear of the first, under command of Lieut.-Col. Warburton ; the left of it about 8 or 10 yards to the left of the road, and extending to the right into the woods, formed at extended order, the men placing themselves behind trees, and consequently much separated. The 1st line I could not distinguish, but from what I have been informed by Lt. Gardiner, 41st Regt., commanding a six-pounder, it was formed in the following manner— a six-pounder was placed in the road, having a range of 50 yards, the 41st Regt. drawn up on its right, extending in the wood ; on each side of the limber of the 6-pounder were some of the Canadian Light Dragoons. From the men of the Regiment, who escaped from that line, I understand they were not formed at regular extended order, but in clusters and in confusion. To the left of the road in which the 6-pounder was placed, and parallel to it, ran the River Thames. To the right and left of the road was a remarkably thick forest, and on the right, where we were formed, free from brushwood for several hundred yards, and where cavalry could act to advantage. My position at this time, (being on the right of the 2nd line) and the thickness of the forest precluded me from noticing the manner in which the enemy attacked the 1st line. The attack commenced about two hours after the order was given to form up across the road. I heard a heavy firing of musketry, and shortly after saw our dragoons retreating together with the limber of the 6-pounder—placed on the left of the 1st line. About a minute afterwards I observed that line retreating in confusion, followed closely by the enemy's cavalry, who were galloping down the road. That portion of the 1st line which had escaped the enemy's cavalry, retreated behind the 2nd line, which stood fast, and fired an irregular volley obliquing to the right and left, which appeared to check the enemy. The line having commenced firing, my attention was directed to that part of the enemy moving down directly in my front. Hearing the fire slacken, I turned towards the line and found myself remaining with 3 non-commissioned officers of the Grenadier company. The enemy's cavalry had advanced so close, before the reserve could commence firing, from the number of trees, that before a third round could be fired they broke through the left, and the rest not being formed in a manner to repel cavalry, were compelled to retreat. The number of the Regiment actually in the field were one Lieut.-Col., 6 captains, 9 lieutenants, 3 ensigns, 3 staff, 26 sergeants, 18 corporals, 4 drummers, 297 rank and file. In what manner the rest of the Regiment was distributed you will be made acquainted with by the enclosed state signed by the Adjutant of the Regiment. The number of Indians we had in the field was 800. The number of the enemy I cannot positively affirm, but from the information obtained from individuals of the regiment taken prisoners on that day, and who afterwards escaped, the number could not have been less than 6,000; of which 1,200 or 1,500 were cavalry and mounted riflemen. The number of our dragoons did not exceed 20. Our loss on this occasion was 3 sergeants, and 9 rank and file killed, and 36 wounded, that of the enemy 15 killed, and from 40 to 50 wounded. Having been thus far particular in stating everything to which I was an eye witness, and which has come to my knowledge, I beg leave to remark that, from the well-known character of the Regiment, any observations emanating from those whose interest it is to cast a direct or indirect reflection upon its conduct, cannot be received with too much distrust.

I have the honor to be, sir,

Major Friend,   Your very obed't humble serv't, &c.
Comm'g 2nd Batt.   Richard Bullock,
   41st Regiment.   Lieut. 41st Grenadiers.

The following is the American General's very prolix account of the affair of the Moraviantown.

Copy of a letter from Maj.-General Harrison, to the Secretary of War, dated

Head-Quarters, Detroit, Oct. 9th, 1813.

SIR,—In my last letter from Sandwich, of the 30th ult., I did myself the honor to inform you, that I was preparing to pursue the enemy the following day. From various causes, however, I was unable to put the troops in motion until the morning of the 2nd instant; and then to take with me only about 140 of the regular troops, Johnson's mounted regiment, and such of Gov. Shelby's volunteers as were fit for a rapid march; the whole amounting to about 3,500 men. To Gen. McArthur, (with about 700 effectives), the protection of this place, and the sick was committed. Gen. Cass's brigade, and the corps of Lieut.-Col. Ball, were left at Sandwich, with

MAJOR-GENERAL WILLIAM HENRY HARRISON.

orders to follow me as soon as the men received their knapsacks and blankets, which had been left on an Island, in Lake Erie.

The unavoidable delay at Sandwich was attended with no disadvantage to us ; General Procter had posted himself at Dolsen's, on the right bank of the River Thames, (or Trench) 56 miles from this place, where, I was informed, he intended to fortify, and to receive me. He must have believed, however, that I had no disposition to follow him, or that he had secured my continuance here by the reports that were circulated, that the Indians would attack and destroy this place, upon the advance of the army—as he neglected the breaking up of the bridges, until the night of the 2nd instant. On that night, our army reached the river, which is 25 miles from Sandwich, and is one of four streams, crossing our route, over all of which are bridges ; and, being deep and muddy, are unfordable for a considerable distance into the country : the bridge, here, was found entire ; and, in the morning, I proceeded with Johnson's regiment, to save, if possible, the others. At the second bridge, over a branch of the River Thames, we were fortunate enough to capture a Lieutenant of Dragoons and 11 privates, who had been sent by General Procter to destroy them. From the prisoners, I learned that the third bridge was broken up, and that the enemy had no certain information of our advance; —the bridge, having been imperfectly destroyed, was soon repaired, and the army encamped at Drake's farm, 4 miles below Dolsen's. The River Thames, along the bank of which our route lay, is a fine deep stream, navigable for vessels of considerable burthen ; after the passage of the bar, at its mouth, over which there is six and a-half feet of water.

The baggage of the army was brought from Detroit in boats, protected by three gun-boats which Commodore Perry had furnished for the purpose, as well as to cover the passage of the army over the Thames itself, or the mouths of its tributary streams ; the banks being low, and the country generally open, (prairies), as high as Dolsen's, these vessels were well calculated for the purpose. Above Dolsen's, however, the character of the river and adjacent country is considerably changed ; the former, though still deep, is very narrow, and its banks high and woody.

The Commodore and myself, therefore, agreed upon the propriety of leaving the boats under a guard of 150 infantry ; and I determined to trust to fortune, and the bravery of my troops, to effect the passage of the river.   Below a place called Chatham, and 4 miles above Dolsen's is the third unfordable branch of the Thames ; the bridge over its mouth had been taken up by the Indians, as well as that at McGregor's mills, one mile above.   Several hundred of the Indians remained to dispute our passage, and upon the arrival of the advanced guard, commenced a heavy fire from the opposite bank of the creek, as well as that of the river.   Believing that the whole force of the enemy was there, I halted the army, formed in order of battle ; and brought up our two 6-pounders, to cover the party that were ordered to repair the bridge ; a few shot, from those pieces, soon drove off the Indians, and enabled us, in 2 hours, to repair the bridge, and cross the troops.   Col. Johnson's mounted regiment, being upon the right of the army, had seized the remains of the bridge at the mills, under a heavy fire from the Indians.   Our loss upon this occasion was 2 killed, and 3 or 4 wounded —that of the enemy was ascertained to be considerably greater.   A house, near the bridge, containing a very considerable number of muskets, had been set on fire ; but it was extinguished by our troops, and the arms saved.   At the first farm, above the bridge we found one of the enemy's vessels[1] on fire, loaded with arms and ordnance stores ; and learned that they were a few miles ahead of us, still on the right bank of the river, with a great body of the Indians.   At Bowles' farm, 4 miles from the bridge, we halted for the night ; found two other vessels, and a large distillery, filled with ordnance and other valuable stores, to an immense amount, in flames ; it was impossible to put out the fire—two 24-pounders, with their carriages, were taken, and a large quantity of ball and shell of various sizes.

---

[1]This vessel sank at the place it was burnt, in about 12 feet of water, and its presence was forgotten. In the summer of 1900 two fishers for sunken timber accidentally found it, and the presence of cannon balls determined the nature of the timbers. In the early spring of 1901 the sunken hull was raised, taken down the river to Tecumseh Park in the city of Chatham and placed high and dry on a fitting foundation. The gunboat is supposed to be the General Myers that was used at the siege of Fort Meigs. About two tons of cannon balls of various sizes, several bayonets and muskets of American manufacture, and an Indian rifle were found in it. The position of the two other boats that were burnt have also been located.

The army was put in motion early on the morning of the 5th. I pushed on, in advance, with the mounted regiment, and requested Gov. Shelby to follow, as expeditiously as possible, with the infantry ; the Governor's zeal, and that of his men, enabled them to keep up with the cavalry ; and, by nine o'clock we were at Arnold's mills, having taken, in the course of the morning, two gun boats, and several batteaux, loaded with provisions and ammunition. A rapid, at the river at Arnold's mills, affords the only fording to be met with for a very considerable distance ; but, upon examination, it was found too deep for the infantry. Having, however, fortunately, taken two or three boats, and some Indian canoes, on the spot, and obliging the horsemen to take a footman behind each, the whole were safely crossed by 12 o'clock. Eight miles from the crossing, we passed a farm where a part of the British troops had encamped the night before, under the command of Col: Warburton ; the detachment, with General Procter, had arrived the day before, at the Moraviantown, four miles higher up. Being now certainly near the enemy, I directed the advance of Johnson's regiment to accelerate their march, for the purpose of procuring intelligence ; the officer commanding it, in a short time, sent to inform me that his progress was stopped by the enemy, who were formed across our line of march : one of the enemy's waggoners being also taken prisoner, from the information received from him, and my own observation, assisted by some of my officers, I soon ascertained enough of their position, and order of battle, to determine that, which it was proper for me to adopt.

I have the honor, herewith, to enclose you my general order, of the 27th ult., prescribing the order of march, and of battle, when the whole army should act together ; but, as the number and description of the troops had been essentially changed, since the issuing of the order, it became necessary to make a corresponding alteration in their disposition.

From the place where our army was last halted, to the Moraviantown, a distance of about three and a-half miles, the road passes through a beech forest, without any clearing ; and, for the first two miles, near to the bank of the river ; at from 200 to 300 yards from the river, a swamp extends parallel to it, throughout the whole distance ; the intermediate ground is dry, and, although the trees are tolerably thick, it is in many places clear of underbrush ; across this strip of land, its left *appuyed* upon the river, supported by artillery, placed in the wood ; their right in the swamp, covered by the whole of their Indian force—the British troops were drawn up.

The troops at my disposal consisted of about 120 regulars of the 27th regiment, five brigades of Kentucky volunteer militia infantry, under His Excellency Governor Shelby, averaging less than 500 men ; and Col. Johnson's regiment of mounted infantry, making, in the whole, an aggregate of something above 3,000. No disposition of an army opposed to an Indian force, can be safe, unless it is secured on the flanks, and in the rear ; I had, therefore, no difficulty in arranging the infantry, conformably to my general order of battle. Gen. Trotter's brigade, of 500 men, formed the front line ; his right upon the road —his left upon the swamp ; Gen. King's brigade as a second line, 150 yards in the rear of Trotter's ; and Chiles' brigade, as a corps of reserve, in the rear of it— these three brigades formed the command of Major-General Henry ; the whole of Gen. Desha's division, consisting of two brigades, were formed, *en potence*, upon the left of Trotter.

Whilst I was engaged in forming the infantry, I had directed Col. Johnson's regiment, which was still in front, to be formed in two lines opposite to the enemy ; and upon the advance of the infantry, to take the ground to the left ; and, forming upon the flank, to endeavor to turn the right of the Indians.

A moment's reflection, however, convinced me, that from the thickness of the woods, and swampiness of the ground, they would be unable to do anything on horseback—and there was no time to dismount them, and place their horses in security ; I, therefore, determined to refuse my left to the Indians, and to break the British lines, at once, by a charge of the mounted infantry. The measure was not sanctioned by anything that I had seen or heard of, but I was fully convinced that it would succeed. The American backwoodsmen ride better in the woods than any other people ; a musket or rifle is no impediment to them, being accustomed to carry them, on horseback, from their earliest youth. I was persuaded, too, that the enemy would be quite unprepared for the shock, and that they could not resist it. Conformably to this idea,

I directed the regiment to be drawn up in close column with its right at the distance of 50 yards upon the road, (that it might be, in some measure, protected by the trees, from the artillery), its left upon the swamp, and to charge at full speed, as soon as the enemy delivered their fire. The few regular troops of the 27th Regiment, under the command of their Colonel (Paul), occupied, in columns of sections of four, the small space between the road and the river, for the purpose of seizing the enemy's artillery; and some 10 or 12 friendly Indians were directed to move under the bank. The *crotchet* formed by the front line, and General Desha's division, was an important point ; at that place the venerable Governor of Kentucky was posted, who at the age of 66, preserves all the vigor of youth—the ardent zeal, which distinguished him in the revolutionary war—and the undaunted bravery which he manifested at King's Mountain. With my aids-de-camp, the acting assistant Adjutant-General Capt. Buttler; my gallant friend, Com. Perry, who did me the honor to serve as my volunteer aid-de-camp, and Brig.-Gen. Cass, who, having no command, tendered me his assistance—I placed myself at the head of the front line of infantry, to direct the movements of the cavalry, and give them the necessary support. The army had moved on, in this order, but a short distance, when the mounted men received the fire of the British line, and were ordered to charge : the horses in the front of the column, recoiled from the fire ; another was given by the enemy, and our column, at length getting in motion, broke through the enemy with irresistible force. In one minute the contest, in front, was over. The British officers, seeing no hopes of reducing their disordered ranks to order, and our mounted men wheeling upon them, and pouring in a destructive fire, immediately surrendered. It is certain that three only, of our troops, were wounded in this charge. Upon the left, however, the contest was more severe with the Indians : Col. Johnson, who commanded on that flank of his regiment, received a most galling fire from them, which was returned with great effect. The Indians, still further to the right, advanced, and fell in with our front line of Infantry, near its junction with Desha's division, and, for a moment, made an impression upon it. His Excellency, Gov. Shelby, however, brought up a regiment to its support ; and the enemy, receiving a severe fire in front, and a part of Johnson's regiment having gained their rear, retreated with precipitation.   Their loss was very considerable in the action, and many were killed in their retreat.

I can give no satisfactory information of the number of Indians that were in the action ; but they must have been considerably upwards of one thousand.   From the documents in my possession (Gen. Procter's official letters, all of which were taken), and from the information of respectable inhabitants of this territory, the Indians, kept in pay by the British, were much more numerous than has been generally supposed.   In a letter to Gen. De Rottenburg, of the 27th ulto. Gen. Procter speaks of having prevailed upon most of the Indians to accompany him ; of these, it is certain that 50 or 60 Wyandot warriors abandoned him.

The number of our troops was certainly greater than that of the enemy ; but when it is recollected that they had chosen a position, that effectually secured their flank, which it was impossible for us to turn ; and that we could not present to them a line more extended than their own, it will not be considered arrogant to claim, for my troops, the palm of superior bravery.

In communicating to the President, through you, sir, my opinion of the conduct of the officers, who served under my command, I am at a loss how to mention that of Gov. Shelby, being convinced that no eulogium of mine can reach his merits ; the Governor of an independent state—greatly my superior in years, in experience, and in military character—he placed himself under my command ; and was not more remarkable for his zeal and activity, than for the promptitude and cheerfulness with which he obeyed my orders.

The Major-Generals, Henry and Desha, and the Brigadiers, Allen, Caldwell, King, Chiles, and Trotter, all of the Kentucky volunteers, manifested great zeal and activity.

Of Governor Shelby's staff, his Adjutant-General, Colonel Walker, rendered great service, as did his aids-de-camp, Gen. Adair, and Majors Barry and Crittenden. The military skill of the former was of great service to us, and the activity of the two latter gentlemen could not be surpassed.   Illness deprived me of the talents of my

ISAAC SHELBY.

First Governor of Kentucky.

Adjutant-General Colonel Gaines, who was left at Sandwich. His duties were, however, ably performed by the acting assistant Adjutant-General, Captain Buttler. My aids-de-camp, Lieutenant O'Fallon and Captain Todd, of the line and my volunteer aids John Speed Smith and John Chambers, Esquires, have rendered me the most important services from the opening of the campaign. I have already stated that General Cass and Commodore Perry assisted me in forming the troops for the action. The former is an officer of the highest merit, and the appearance of the brave Commodore cheered and animated every breast.

It would be useless, sir, after stating the circumstances of the action, to pass encomiums upon Col. Johnson and his regiment. Veterans could not have manifested more firmness. The Colonel's numerous wounds prove that he was in the post of danger. Lieut.-Col. James Johnson, and the Majors Payne and Thompson, were equally active, though more fortunate. Maj. Wood, of the engineers, already distinguished, by his conduct at Fort Meigs, attended the army with two 6-pounders; having no use for them in the action, he joined in the pursuit of the enemy; and, with Major Payne of the mounted regiment, two of my aids-de-camp, Todd and Chambers, and three privates, continued it for several miles after the rest of the troops had halted, and made many prisoners.

I left the army before an official return of the prisoners, or that of the killed and wounded, was made out; it was, however, ascertained that the former amounted to 601 regulars, including 25 officers. Our loss is seven killed and 22 wounded, five of which have since died. Of the British troops, 12 killed and 22 wounded; the Indians suffered most—33 of them having been found upon the ground, besides those killed on the retreat.

On the day of the action, six pieces of brass artillery were taken, and 2 iron 24 pounders the day before;—several others were discovered in the river, and can be easily procured. Of the brass pieces, 3 are the trophies of our revolutionary war, that were taken at Saratoga and York, and surrendered by Gen. Hull. The number of small arms, taken by us, and destroyed by the enemy, must amount to upwards of 5,000; most of them had been ours, and taken by the enemy at the surrender of

Detroit, at the River Raisin, and at Col. Dudley's defeat. I believe that the enemy retain no other military trophy of their victories, than the standard of the 4th regiment ; they were not magnanimous enough to bring that of the 41st regiment into the field, or it would have been taken. You have been informed, sir, of the conduct of the troops under my command in action ; it gives me great pleasure to inform you that they merit, also, the approbation of their country, for their conduct in submitting to the greatest privations with the utmost cheerfulness.

The infantry were entirely without tents ; and, for several days, the whole army subsisted upon fresh beef, without bread or salt.

I have the honor, &c.,

William H. Harrison.

Hon. J. Armstrong, Sec. War.

P.S.—Gen. Procter escaped by the fleetness of his horse, escorted by 40 dragoons, and a number of mounted Indians.

On the 22nd September, Harrison's army rendezvoused at Put-in Bay Island, and on the evening of the 25th took up a position on the Middle Sister Island, about twenty miles from Amherstburg. A storm delayed them here till the 27th, when they again embarked and landed near Bar Point, about three miles from the Fort at Amherstburg. Harrison, it is said, made an attempt to land in Colchester township, but was prevented from doing so by John Naudee, the Chippeway chief and his Indians. On the 27th, Amherstburg was in their possession, but the army encamped that night on the farm now owned by Edward Honor, where their temporary earthwork fortifications may still be seen. There is a tradition that some horses of the American officers were stampeded and captured by the Canadians and Indians. Among them was a fine Arab stallion, that was hidden by one Drouillard until the war was over. Many of the horses in the vicinity show the Arab strain, and tradition points to this horse as their progenitor. If the above has any fact as a basis, the horses must have been captured about the 1st October near Sandwich, as Harrison had no horses until Col. Johnson's mounted corps crossed the Detroit at that town. On the 28th, the invading army passed the Canard and encamped two miles beyond it, and at 2 o'clock the next day entered Sandwich. On the 2nd October everything was ready for the pursuit, which was continued as outlined in the despatches given.

Harrison had as one of his guides Matthew Dolsen, who, with a wife and five children, lived near Chatham in 1812. At the beginning of the war he was drafted into the militia, but deserted to Hull, and after the capture of Detroit escaped and joined Harrison's army. Meanwhile his wife and family enjoyed the protection of the Canadian Government until after Procter's defeat, when they moved to Detroit.

From the original daguerreotype in possession of G. Mills McClurg, Toronto.

JOHN NAUDEE.

(OSHAWAHNAH)

Second in command of the Indians at the Battle of Moraviantown.

XII

Although, with the capture of the Right Division, ceases all military operations of any consequence in the West, as its imprisonment and detention as hostages form no inconsiderable feature in the historical occurrences of that period, I have, under the impression that the narrative would be imperfect without it, decided on detailing the several vicissitudes to which, principally in their character of hostages, the captured troops were subjected. From this it will be seen, that the feeling of dislike and jealousy entertained by the Americans for everything English, was precisely in 1812 what it is at the present day. (1842).

On reaching Detroit, after having traversed for the last time, as prisoners, that soil which, almost unaided, a single Regiment had for fifteen months defended against the efforts of successive powerful armies sent to wrest it from their grasp, we found that Fort Meigs was the route through which the Division was to be marched into the State of Ohio. The majority of the officers, having pledged their parole to General Harrison, were suffered to take the advance, mounted on pack horses provided by the American Government. A few only, desirous of taking the Sandusky route across the lake, were embarked in the Ariel gun-boat, and conveyed to Put-in-Bay island, where the shattered fleets were then lying. Here indeed was to be seen evidence of a most sanguinary conflict, especially in Captain Barclay's ship. Every mast of this latter had been carried away—more than half her long guns had been dismounted—and the bulwarks were in fragments, while it was impossible to place a hand upon that broadside which had been exposed to the enemy's fire, without covering some portion of a wound, either from grape, round, canister, or chain-shot. The decks of all were moreover filled with wounded, and, on being introduced into Captain Barclay's cabin, we found that gallant officer in bed, presenting a most helpless picture of mutilation. Pain and disappointment were upon his brow, and the ruddy hue of health, for which he had ever been remarkable, had deserted him. In short, of his former self there then seemed to be little left besides his untainted honor. The scene altogether was one of a most melancholy and impressive character.

On the second morning of our arrival at this island, after having taken on board such of the naval officers as were not prevented by the severity of their wounds from performing the journey, we continued our course for Sandusky Bay. We had nearly made the spot intended for our disembarkation, when one of those dangerous and sudden hurricanes, peculiar to the lakes of Canada during the autumnal months, drove us back under bare poles, and along the sheet of foam with which the broad expanse of water was literally covered, to the port we had just quitted. At length we finally separated from our companions in misfortune, and after a few hours' sail were enabled to cast anchor in the bay, where, being immediately landed, we were conducted to the fort of Sandusky.

During our stay at this place we had full leisure for examining not only the defences of the fortress, but the various positions occupied by our troops during the assault; and the result of our observation was, that an attack on a stockade work of this description, without the aid of ladders must inevitably entail discomfiture. The nature of the fortification, and the manner in which the enemy were protected from our fire, may be judged of from the fact of their having had only one man killed in the affair.

That which most excited my own immediate attention

was the ground occupied by the left column of attack, consisting chiefly of the light company of the 41st, to which I was then attached, and which having forced their way to the very batteries of the fort had consequently sustained the greatest loss. My escape from the ravine, where we had continued so many hours, was truly providential. When the order for retiring was, in order to deceive the enemy, given in the Indian language, it was immediately explained by one or two interpreters present with the grenadier column on the right, and conveyed by them in a low voice to the remaining divisions. Covered by the brow of the opposite eminence, they followed the course of the ravine in safety, until they emerged from the defile, at a distance sufficient to admit of their forming unperceived by the enemy. Nearly all the men of the light column, having received the order, had retired with the main body ; but those on the extreme left, having been separated from the line by the brushwood and other obstacles they had encountered in the ascent, remained in utter ignorance of what was passing on the right ; and such was the caution observed in retiring, that neither the enemy in the fort nor ourselves could distinguish the slightest sound to justify the supposition. It was now half-past nine o'clock. We had continued since half-past five lying extended on the wet ground, where the mud was ankle-deep, and most of the men were chilled with cold. At this moment we heard, though indistinctly, various orders given in the direction of our encampment, and then only did we surmise the fact of the troops having been withdrawn. In this belief we were speedily confirmed, by hearing a command issued in a suppressed tone of voice in the fort, to open the sallyports. Perceiving that no time was to be lost, I proposed in a whisper, which the rising ground prevented being overheard by the enemy, that we should brave every risk, and attempt our immediate retreat. The men, however, refused to move, until the moon, which was

then in the first quarter, and reflecting its beams every-
where but in the bed of the ravine, was set, or should be
obscured by some passing cloud. Leaving them to their
fate, I therefore prepared to effect my escape alone, and
immediately in front of the fortress ; but notwithstanding all my caution, I had not advanced many paces, when
I stumbled over the dead body of a soldier, who, after
having received a mortal wound, had evidently crawled
on his hands and knees to rest his bleeding form against
a clump of bushes, and had died in that singular position. The noise occasioned by my fall put the enemy
once more on the alert ; and as the moonbeams reflected
on my arms and regimentals, I had no sooner ascended
the opposite side of the ravine, than the whole front of
the fort was lighted up with their fire. Not an individual,
save myself, was exposed to their aim, and the distance
did not exceed fifty paces; yet, although the balls
whistled round my ears in every direction, and hissed
through the long grass with which the plain was covered,
I did not sustain the slightest injury, even though a
second volley was fired after the interval of half a minute. On reaching the spot where the columns had been
originally formed for the assault, I found that my retreat
had been well-timed, for the troops were already in
motion towards the boats, the guns having been previously embarked. In that which contained my provision-
basket, I discovered a few bottles of port wine, which
had arrived that very morning from Amherstburg. This
was indeed a luxury that I would not at the moment
have exchanged for a throne ; and so thoroughly exhausted was I with hunger, thirst and fatigue, that placing a bottle to my parched lips, I did not abandon it until
the whole of its contents had been emptied at a draught.
The effect was instantaneous, and I lay in the bottom of
the boat all night enjoying the most delicious moments of
repose I recollect ever having experienced. When I awoke

at a late hour on the following morning, a mild September[1] sun was glancing its golden rays along the tranquil bosom of Lake Erie, in the centre of which our boats were all assembled, and gliding along its surface with a speed proportioned to the vigorous efforts of the rowers—the men alternately singing and indulging in rude jests, reckless of the comrades whose dying groans had assailed their ears a few hours before, and evidently without care or thought for the future. Every individual of those who had refused to accompany me on that occasion was taken prisoner by the American party despatched through the sallyport.

Some difficulty was experienced at Sandusky in procuring the means of conveyance; at length, however, on the morning of the third day, mounted on miserable pack horses, scarcely able to sustain their own weight, and tottering at every step beneath their additional burden, we commenced our route for Chillicothe, the place selected for our detention. A single officer of infantry composed our escort, and he had been appointed to the service chiefly with a view to protect us from insult, and to procure lodgings and other accommodations on the road. To describe the fatigue and privation which we endured during this tedious journey would require more time and space than it can be necessary to bestow upon this part of the narrative. The rainy season had already set in, and scarcely a single day passed by without our being literally wet to the skin. Our route lay through an inhospitable tract of country, consisting alternately of gloomy forest and extensive savannah, the latter often intersected by streams fed from the distant mountains, and swollen by the unceasing rains. Sometimes a solitary hut, vying in filthiness with the beings by whom it was tenanted, afforded us shelter for the night, but more frequently we found that repose which absolute fatigue

[1]This happened on the 3rd of August.

and exhaustion ensure to the traveller, near the fires we were compelled to kindle in the forest. At length our jaded animals, slipping at every step, and threatening to sink beneath their efforts, brought us to Fort Wayne. Here we were provided with other horses, but of the same miserable description : their backs cruelly galled by the ill-stuffed saddles, and their ribs almost protruding from beneath their hair-divested hides. The appearance of these unfortunate animals was pitiable in the extreme ; and few of us, on leaving Fort Wayne, entertained the slightest doubt of their sinking successively beneath us, before our destination could be gained. The rain still continued to fall, and during the latter part of October and the commencement of November we never once beheld the sun. Many of the officers were without great-coats, having been plundered of everything, as well by the followers of the division as by the enemy themselves ; and, although we each possessed a change of linen, during the whole journey we had no opportunity of having anything washed, so that in a short time we were infested by vermin, which gave the finishing stroke to our calamities. Still we proceeded on our journey, and through a country of the same character with that we had previously traversed. On one occasion we found ourselves stopped by a stream of considerable depth, the bridge over which had been broken down by the torrent. No other alternative remained than to swim our horses across, or run the risk of their breaking their legs in the interstices of the bridge, which had partly sunk beneath the surface of the water. The former course was, after due deliberation, adopted ; and lots having been drawn, the first attempt devolved on Lieutenant Stokoe of the Royal Navy. Spurring his horse into the current, this officer with much difficulty reached the opposite bank ; but, unable to effect a landing, was thrown from his seat in consequence of the violent struggles made by the animal, and, with one foot fastened in the stirrup, lay for some moments in imminent danger of perishing. At length, after much exertion, he succeeded in disengaging himself, when clambering up the steep, he soon drew his horse after him. This experiment being considered too dangerous for repetition, we decided on effecting our passage across the bridge ; and owing to the caution we observed, no accident occurred to the horses—a circumstance peculiarly fortunate, since we could have found no means of supplying our loss. After several weeks of tedious travelling through this dreary region some few traces of civilization and cultivation were perceptible, and we finally beheld the banks of the Scioto. On the opposite shore of this small river stands the town of Chillicothe; and after having for the last time committed our steeds and persons to the water, in default of a bridge, we found ourselves at the termination of our journey, overcome with lassitude, and in a state which might have caused us to pass for anything rather than British officers. The party which had taken the route of Fort Meigs was already arrived, and with it the troops of the division.

At Chillicothe I was singularly fortunate in meeting with a gentleman who exercised the rites of hospitality in my favor to the fullest extent. An apartment in his house was appropriated to my service, a cover daily laid at his table, and his horses declared at my command. In short, no individual in the character of a prisoner of war had ever less reason to inveigh against his destiny. This ray of sunshine was, however, of short duration. Soon after the arrival of the Sandusky party at Chillicothe, the officers captured at the Moravian village were, in consequence of an order from the American government, despatched to Frankfort, the capital of Kentucky—those of the naval service alone being suffered to remain, and, through the influence used by my kind host, my name was included in the list of the latter. At the moment when we began to reconcile ourselves to our situation, and to appreciate the attention paid us by the more respectable inhabitants, an order suddenly arrived for our close imprisonment. This unexpected measure owed its origin to the following circumstance. Among the prisoners taken at the affair in which the lamented General Brock lost his life, twenty-three men, recognized as deserters from the various regiments in Canada, had been sent to England, and subsequently tried and convicted. The execution of the sentence, had, however, been deferred. The American government was no sooner apprized of their impending fate, than, acting on that system of naturalization which, in defiance of every principle of equity, would preclude the hitherto undisputed right of nations to punish their criminal subjects, they caused an equal number of British soldiers to be kept closely confined, to answer as hostages for the safety of the convicted deserters. This unjustifiable proceeding was followed by the seclusion of twenty-three commissioned, and an equal number of non-commissioned American officers, and retaliated by them in a similar manner ; so that finally nearly all the officers of both parties were deprived of their liberty, and liable at any moment to answer with their lives for the apostasy of three and twenty individuals America should have blushed to claim as subjects of her republic.

With a view to the thorough comprehension of the subject by the reader, and to exhibit in its true light the extraordinary course pursued by the United States, it will be important here to annex, not only the remonstrance of the British Government, as conveyed through two distinct general orders issued by Sir George Prevost, under the direction of His Royal Highness the Prince Regent, but the particular instructions, for the close confinement of the officers of the Right Division in the Penitentiary of Frankfort, transmitted by the American Secretary of State to the Governor of Kentucky.

Headquarters, Montreal, Oct. 27, 1813.

His Excellency the Governor-General and Commander of the Forces, having transmitted to His Majesty's Government a letter from Major-Gen. Dearborn, stating that the American Commissary of Prisoners in London had made it known to his Government, that twenty-three soldiers of the 1st, 6th and 13th Regiments of United States Infantry, made prisoners, had been sent to England and held in close confinement as British subjects, and that Major-Gen. Dearborn had received instructions from his Government, to put into close confinement twenty-three British soldiers, to be kept as hostages for the safe keeping and restoration in exchange of the soldiers of the United States, who had been sent as above stated to England ;—in obedience to which instructions, he had put twenty-three British soldiers into close confinement to be kept as hostages ; and the persons referred to in Major-Gen. Dearborn's letter being soldiers serving in the American army, taken prisoners at Queenstown, who had declared themselves to be British-born subjects, and were held in custody in England there to undergo a legal trial.

His Excellency, the Commander of the Forces, has received the commands of His Royal Highness the Prince Regent, through the Right Honorable the Earl Bathurst, Secretary of State, to lose no time in communicating to Major-Gen. Dearborn, that he has transmitted a copy of his letter, and that he is in consequence instructed, distinctly to state to Major-Gen. Dearborn, that His Excellency has received the commands of His Royal Highness the Prince Regent, forthwith to put in close confinement, forty-six American officers and non-commissioned officers, to be held as hostages for the safe keeping of the twenty-three British soldiers stated to have been put in close confinement by order of the American Government.

And he is at the same time to apprise him that if any of the said British soldiers shall suffer death, by reason that the soldiers now under confinement in England have been found guilty, and that the known law, not only of Great Britain, but of every independent state under similar circumstances, has been in consequence executed, he has been instructed to select out of the American officers and non-commissioned officers put into confinement as many as may double the number of British soldiers who shall have been so unwarrantably put to death, and cause such officers and non-commissioned officers to suffer death immediately.

And His Excellency is further instructed to notify to Major-Gen. Dearborn that the commanders of His Majesty's armies and fleets on the coast of America have received instructions to prosecute the war with unmitigated severity against all Cities, Towns and Villages belonging to the United States, and against the inhabitants thereof, if after this communication shall have been duly made to Major-Gen. Dearborn, and a reasonable time given for its being transmitted to the American Government, that Government shall unhappily not be deterred from putting to death any of the soldiers who now are, or who may hereafter be, kept as hostages for the purposes stated in the letter from Major-Gen. Dearborn.

His Excellency the Commander of the Forces, in announcing to the Troops the commands of His Royal Highness the Prince Regent, is confident that they will feel sensible, of the paternal solicitude which his Royal Highness has evinced for the protection of the person and honor of the British soldier thus grossly outraged in contempt of justice, humanity, and the Law of Nations, in the persons of twenty-three soldiers placed in close confinement, as hostages for an equal number of traitors who had been guilty of the base and unnatural crime of raising their parricidal arms against that country which gave them birth, and who have been delivered over for legal trial to the just laws of their offended country.

The British soldier will feel this unprincipled outrage, added to the galling insults and cruel barbarities that are daily wantonly inflicted on many of his unfortunate comrades, who have fallen into the enemy's hands, as additional motives to excite his determined resolution never to resign his liberty but with his life, to a foe so regardless of all sense of honor, justice and the rights of war.

(Signed) Edward Baynes, Adj't-Gen.

Extract from a letter from the Secretary of State to the Governor of Kentucky.

Nov. 27, 1813.

Sir,—The British Government seems to have given to this war every degree of savage barbarity and cruelty which it may be able to inflict. In the close of the late campaign, the British commanders at Quebec seized and sent to England, twenty-three of our soldiers who had been prisoners, to be tried for treason, on the pretence that they were British subjects. For so unjust and outrageous an act, the President was bound to confine a like number of British prisoners in the United States, which he did in the expectation that the British Government, seeing the inevitable consequence of the first measure, would relax from it, or at least leave the affair in the state in which it had thus been placed for accommodation by treaty. More recently, however, a measure of still greater injustice has been adopted. The Prince Regent has ordered into close confinement forty-six officers of the United States upon the principle, as he says, of retaliation, expecting, by the violence of the proceeding, to intimidate this government into a submission to the extravagant and unfounded claims of the British Government. The President has met this measure with equal decision, by ordering into like confinement forty-six British officers, as a pledge for the safety of those on whom the British Government seems disposed to wreak its vengeance.

These officers are ordered to be conveyed to Frankfort, in Kentucky, to be confined there in the penitentiary of that State, which is represented to be a building affording the two-fold advantage of *good* and *safe* accommodations.

This step is taken in the full confidence that every facility will be afforded to its complete execution, by Your Excellency, that may be expected from a character so strongly attached to the union, and decided in the support of all the necessary measures to secure success to the just war in which we are engaged.

———

General Order, Adjutant General's Office,
Headquarters, Montreal, 12th December, 1813.

His Excellency the Governor-in-Chief and Commander of the Forces has to announce to the troops under his command, that he has received a communication from Major-General Wilkinson, commanding a division of the army of the United States of America, by order of his government, of which the following is an extract :

" The Government of the United States adhering unalterably to the principle and purpose declared in the communication of Gen. Dearborn to you, on the subject of the twenty-three American soldiers, prisoners of war, sent to England to be tried as criminals ; and the confinement of a like number of British soldiers, prisoners of war, selected to abide the fate of the former; has in consequence of the step taken by the British Government, as now communicated, ordered forty-six British officers into close confinement, and that they will not be discharged from their confinement until it shall be known that the forty-six American officers and non-commissioned officers in question are no longer confined."

It would be superfluous to use any argument to refute an assumption so extravagant, unjust, and unprecedented as to deny the right of a free nation to bring to legal trial, in a due course of law, her own natural-born subjects taken in the actual commission of the most heinous offence that man can commit against his king, his country, and his God; that of raising his parricidal arm against his allegiance to his countrymen, by leaguing with their enemies; a crime held in such abhorrence by every civilized nation in Europe, that summary death by the law martial is its avowed reward, and is inflicted with unrelenting severity by France, the ally of the United States. This pretention must appear to every unprejudiced and upright mind as iniquitous and unjust, as is the retaliation which the Government of the United States has adopted, by placing in close confinement three and twenty British soldiers, as hostages for an equal number of infamous wretches, the unworthy offspring of Great Britain, who, when drawn from the ranks of the enemy, solicited to be suffered to expiate their treason by turning their arms against their employers. These Rebels have (with the contempt they merit) been consigned to the infamy and punishment that await them from the just laws of their offended country, while the Government of the United States does not blush to claim these outcast traitors as their own, and outrage the custom of civilized war, in the persons of honorable men, by placing them on a par with Rebels and Deserters.

No alternative remains to the Commander of the Forces, in the discharge of his duty to his king, his country, and his fellow-soldiers, but to order all the American officers, prisoners of war, without exception of rank, to be immediately placed in close confinement as hostages for the forty-six British officers so confined, by the express command of the supreme authority in that country, until the number of forty-six be completed, over and above those now in confinement.

His Excellency directs that this General Order together with that issued on the 27th of October, be read to the troops, that the British soldier may be sensible of the terms on which America has determined to wage this war ; confident that he will meet them with proper spirit and indignation ; for should he become the prisoner of a foe so regardless of those laws, which for ages have governed civilized nations in war, he would be doomed to a rigorous confinement, and that only preparatory to a more savage scene.

(Signed)   Edward Baynes, Adj.-Gen.
North America.

But more than either of the foregoing documents, does the following statement, copied from the Salem Gazette, prove the nature and consequences of this cruel system of retaliation, as carried on between the two countries.

" TREATMENT OF BRITISH PRISONERS OF WAR IN THE UNITED STATES.—It is time that the public should be correctly informed on the subject of the unfortunate prisoners at Ipswich.   Seventeen of our fellow-beings have been immured in dungeons in our own neighborhood, three months, and the public attention has not been called to their sufferings.   The following we believe to be a correct statement of this affair.

" On the seventh day of October, 1813, James Prince, Esq., Marshal of this District, issued his mandate directed.

" ' To the keeper of the gaol of the United States at Ipswich, within the District aforesaid—Greeting '—requiring him ' to receive into his custody, and safely keep in dungeons in the gaol aforesaid, the bodies of Thomas Cooper, John Clark, Adam Kirby, Samuel Thorp, Thomas Hewes, John Bendow, James Onion, Richard How, Daniel Dowland, and James Humphries,' in retaliation for cruelties ' said to be ' ' exercised ' on certain persons at Halifax, ' and also as hostages to respond for any acts of violence which may be inflicted on them.'

" By similar orders dated Oct. 11th, 12th, 13th, and Nov. 2nd, he also directs the under keeper to confine in dungeons the bodies of Wm. Nickerson, Elkanah Clements, R. Kirkland Black, Wm. Owen, Benj. Johnson, and James Ross in retaliation for ' cruelties ' said to be committed on other American prisoners of war in Halifax.

"By another order dated Oct. 12th, the Marshal directs the gaoler to receive and detain in his custody the body of Peter H. Diedale, a maritime prisoner of war, without alleging any other cause, and he has been confined in a dungeon with the rest.

"These men have ever since been kept in dungeons as dreary as Mr. Madison could desire. The gaol is a gloomy stone building. The dungeons are seven feet by ten on the ground floor, of rough stone at top, bottom, and on all sides. There are loop holes or narrow openings of two or three inches wide through the upper part of the stone walls, to admit the little light and air which these unfortunate victims are allowed to enjoy. In damp weather, the water runs down the walls and drops from the stone ceiling over the floors. These dungeons were never intended for any other purpose, than to punish the worst of convicts by a few days' solitary imprisonment, and it is believed have never been used even for that purpose. Yet in these places have innocent men been languishing for three months, sixteen of them, four in a dungeon, and the other (Captain Ross) in a dungeon by himself. A few days since ten of them were removed to the cells in the second story, appropriated to criminals. These cells are larger than the dungeons, but extremely cold and uncomfortable. So far have these unfortunate prisoners been 'released' (as had been asserted in another American paper), and no farther. Seven, viz. Capt. Clements, Lieuts. Owen, Black, and Nickerson, and two seamen, it is understood, are still confined in two dungeons, and on some of the late cold nights several were past recovery, notwithstanding they had received a supply of warm clothing from some charitable individuals; and medical aid was necessarily called in to restore the perishing; and it is only by this charitable relief and the attention of the gaoler's family, unwarranted by the orders of Government, that these poor prisoners are not dead! They must have perished, if left to the care of Government! Such is the situation of these prisoners, and this is the 'retaliation' that is called 'Christian'!"

That the threat of retaliation would have been carried into effect by the American government, it is scarcely possible to believe, since, exclusively of the blot such a proceeding must have imprinted on their character, the disproportion of prisoners was greatly in our favor, as well in regard to rank as numbers; but we had too much reason to apprehend, from the unqualified hatred manifested towards us by the populace in the States of Ohio and Kentucky, that the will of their rulers would have had little effect in restraining the ebullition of their rage, had the original sentence been carried into execution. Let it not be imagined that this idea arose simply from surmise, or had its being in the vague apprehension of men who, more immediately interested in the result, might be deemed ready to admit the agency of fancy in their impressions of impending evil. Several gentlemen, estimable for their rank and character in these States, warned us during their occasional visits of the fact, and with every opportunity of ascertaining the public feeling, communicated circumstances which left us no reason to infer that their fears for the result should be disregarded. Our sensations in consequence were not, it will be imagined, of the most pleasing or enviable description. The common gaol of the town had been fixed on for our abode, and we were distributed into two small rooms in an upper story, communicating with each other, and containing each ten persons. During the day they were left open, but carefully locked and bolted at night, and sentinels were posted in the corridor into which they opened. The height was upwards of sixty feet from the ground; and through the strong bars with which the windows were furnished, we beheld others pacing to and fro, and exercising their vigilance so far as to direct their attention repeatedly to our rooms. Thus guarded, and unprovided with instruments of any description whatever, we had no hope of effecting an escape; while, to crown our misery, fortune had thrown us into the hands of a gaoler of the most ruffianlike character. On one occasion, in consequence of some trifling misunderstanding with an interpreter who had been confined in the adjoining room —a man remarkable for the mildness and forbearance of his nature,—the wretch inflicted so severe a wound on his head with a ponderous key, as to cause the blood to gush forth with extreme violence. When visited by the officer of the guard, a complaint was preferred by the injured man; but the liberal republican, with true patriotic feeling, justified the act of his countryman, and concluded by threatening a repetition of the punishment.

We had now been some time in this disagreeable situation, when a project was formed which promised to throw a more favorable coloring over our destiny. The whole of the captive division, including the seamen, were confined in a fortified camp, erected for the purpose on the skirt of a wood adjoining one of the suburbs of the town, and were guarded by a considerable detachment of regular infantry. These noble fellows were no sooner apprized of the ignominious fate with which their officers were threatened, than with the generous devotedness characteristic of their respective professions, they deputed two sergeants who had been suffered to communicate with us on subjects relative to the clothing of the men, to express their determination to effect our liberation, or perish in the attempt. Accordingly, the following plan was adopted, and fixed on for execution at a certain day. At midnight, the men were to rise and overpower the guard, and having secured them, and possessed themselves of their arms, to separate into three distinct parties. The first of these, headed by one of the deputies, were to advance on the prison, and having effected our liberation, to hasten to the boats on the river, which the second division was to have secured; while the third, patrolling the streets in silence, were to prevent the inhabitants from assembling and impeding the operations of the first. The plan, hastily adopted, from the circumstances in which we found ourselves placed, was at best a wild one, since, had it succeeded in all its primary stages, we must have been eventually destroyed in descending the narrow river of the Scioto, by the fire from the numerous riflemen the enemy would have collected, on the first intimation of our departure. We were then, however, sanguine of success, and none paused to consider the difficulties that awaited us after our liberation, in the heart of an enemy's country, where ammunition and provisions were alike beyond our reach. We spoke of our descent of the Mississippi from the Scioto, and the Ohio, and our final reception on board the English fleet we knew to be cruising off New Orleans, as a matter of course, and discussed our meditated movements with all the confidence of the soldier, but certainly with little of the prudence or foresight of the general. Such was the plan decided on for our escape; but, while awaiting the completion of the necessary preparations, a circumstance, ludicrous in itself, yet alarming in our actual position, threatened to blight every hope by which we had lately been sustained. One morning about daybreak, the noise of workmen was distinctly heard beneath the windows of the room in which, covered with a solitary blanket, and huddled together without order or ceremony, we contrived to enjoy a few moments of repose. One of the party immediately jumped up, and running to the window, beheld a number of men engaged in the erection of a scaffold. The exclamation wrung from him by the sight, drew us all to the spot, and then, indeed, we might be said to have experienced the sensations of men who behold for the first time, and without a hope of reprieve, the gloomy preparations for an ignominious end. The predominent sentiment with us was, however, less regret for the existence we considered ourselves about to forfeit, than rage at the idea of having surrendered ourselves prisoners of war to an enemy capable of violating every principle of justice, for the sake of shielding a few perjured and despicable criminals from the laws of their offended country. In this state of cruel suspense, we continued until nine o'clock, the hour at which the bolts of our prison were withdrawn for the day, when the explanation given by the gaoler dissipated our alarm. The scaffolding was being erected for the purpose of sinking a pump for the use of the prison ; and the indistinct view we had obtained of the construction through our bars had given rise to the error.

At length the much-wished-for day fixed on for the execution of our enterprise arrived, and we arose, as we fully hoped, from our couch of misery, for the last time. To persons in our situation, it may easily be imagined, the hours appeared to move on leaden wings, yet we doubted not an instant of a favorable result. Fate had, however, ordained otherwise. At four in the afternoon, while yet partaking of our wretched meal, the trampling of horses' feet, and a confused sound of drums and voices, drew us suddenly to the window, and in a few minutes we beheld Governor Shelby literally armed to the teeth, a rifle on his shoulder, and accompanied by a numerous staff, riding up at full speed. We were for some time lost in astonishment and unable to account for this singular appearance ; but a clue to the mystery was soon afforded by the entrance of an American officer, who, leaving his guard in the corridor, advanced into the outer room, accompanied by a formidable cyclop, bearing certain insignia of his trade, with which we could very willingly have dispensed.

For the better insurance of success in our enterprise, it had been found necessary to admit two individuals in the town into our confidence—certain essential and preliminary arrangements remaining to be effected. These gentlemen were of the federal party, and entered into our views with a willingness which gave very fair promise of a favorable issue. We had been rather intimately known to them prior to our confinement, and with their sentiments, both political and private, we were well acquainted. The measures necessary to forward our undertaking were faithfully executed by them, and on the morning of the night which was to give us to liberty, as we fondly imagined, nothing of a preparatory nature remained to be done. Seized, however, by a sudden panic, and anti-

cipating the consequences of a discovery of co-operation
with the enemies of their country, they resolved to elude
the danger they feared, by a voluntary and unreserved
disclosure of our intentions to the Governor of the State,
who resided in Chillicothe. This was accordingly done,
and the active and precautionary measures consequent on
this alarming intelligence, had given rise to the bustle
and tumult which assailed our ears from without, and
carried disappointment and despair to our hearts.

This latter information was conveyed to us by our new
visitor, Lieutenant Harrison, of the 19th Infantry (a
gentleman whose name I feel peculiar pleasure in record-
ing), who now proceeded to communicate the disagreeable duty with which he was charged, and which the
equipment of his forbidding attendant, armed with a
hammer, anvil, and about twenty pairs of hand-cuffs,
sufficiently explained. With a tearful eye and in a falter-
ing tone, did this gentleman entreat us to lose sight of
the man in the subordinate, and to believe how much it
pained him to be the instrument selected for the purpose.
Such an indignity, he said, he deplored being compelled
to offer to British officers ; but he trusted that with men
to whom the rigor of military duty was familiar, the public act would be forgotten in the expression of private
feeling. The delicacy of such conduct was felt by all,
and we hastened to assure him of our grateful sentiments
in return. He then desired the man to proceed to the
execution of his office ; and in less than an hour the
hands of the whole party, myself alone excepted, were
fettered with irons, which the rough and malignant-look-
ing son of Vulcan seemed to feel no little satisfaction in
applying. On inquiry, I learned that I had been excepted
at the express desire of Colonel Campbell, commanding
the troops at Chillicothe, from whom the order had emanated. For this favor I felt that I was indebted to my
kind friend Mr. Brush, but as I had little inclination to
be exempted from a participation in the fate of my com-

panions, I expressed myself to that effect to Lieutenant
Harrison, requesting at the same time that he would
impart to the Commandant, who was the colonel of
his own regiment, the utter disinclination I entertained
to owe him any thing in the shape of obligation, while
my brother officers were manacled as felons.

On the departure of the officers we had full leisure to
reflect on the hopelessness of our situation, and we in-
veighed not a little against the defection of our American
friends, though, in fact, our own folly alone was to be
taxed in having made the subjects of a country so interested in our detention accessory to the design. These
reflections, however, finally yielded to a feeling of mirth
excited by the ludicrous appearance we exhibited, stalk-
ing about the room like spectres, and deprived of the
usage of our arms ; and we began to enjoy the panic
partly visible to our eyes, and principally ascertained
from our gaoler, from whose account it appeared large
bodies of the inhabitants were already assembling to the
sounds of the alarm drums and bugles. The guards and
sentinels of our prison had been doubled at the first
rumor, and the militia of the adjacent country were
flocking in to strengthen the troops intrusted with the
security of the men. It was not until a late hour in the
night, that these warlike preparations appeared to be
completed, the rolling of the drums frequently breaking
on our ears, as we lay extended on our blankets, to
which, after a close examination of our apartments by
the gaoler, followed by an unusually careful application
of bolts and keys, we had long since consigned our
aching limbs.

In the state of utter helplessness to which my companions were reduced, we found the advantage of the exception made in my favor, since I was thus enabled to perform many little offices which the brutality and remiss-
ness of the gaoler left us no hope would be attended to
by him. Three days had now elapsed since the visit of

Lieutenant Harrison, when the situation of the sufferers had become irksome to a degree. Not once, during that period, had they been permitted to throw off their clothes, or perform their customary ablutions; and when they descended to the court, which was rarely and but for a few minutes, a sentinel followed with his bayonet extended, and within a foot of the prisoner. Their hands and wrists had also become extremely swollen by the compresssion of the irons, and the extremities of the fingers of several were discolored with the quantity of blood propelled to those parts. Under these circumstances I wrote a polite note to Colonel Campbell, detailing the several inconveniences sustained by my brother officers, and requesting that he would cause the fetters to be removed under the inspection of an officer, and merely for the time requisite to clean their persons and change their linen. To this communication I received a negative reply, couched in the most positive and unfeeling terms. I immediately wrote a second, expressive of our united sentiments in respect to his conduct, which I had no doubt would have brought down the wrath of the generous commandant on my head; but no notice whatever was taken of the letter. Finding it vain to expect any relief from this quarter, we adopted an expedient which answered all the intention proposed. With the aid of an old knife, we contrived to divide the nails by which the irons were riveted around the wrists, and substitute others of lead, a small quantity of which article one of the midshipmen happened to have in his haversack. The relief afforded by the removal of the fetters, which was only effected by stealth, and at those moments when we considered ourselves free from interruption, was grateful to all, although the fingers were so cramped by the extended position in which they had been kept, as to render it difficult and painful to move them. The leaden pins had been blackened to imitate iron, and as the sleeves were carefully drawn over, the deception could only be discovered on a minute examination. Thus were the officers enabled not only to enjoy some little cessation from suffering, but to attend to the comfort and cleanliness of their persons, an advantage for which they certainly were not much indebted to the humanity of the public authorities of Chillicothe.

Nearly ten days had succeeded to the detection of our plan of escape, when, one evening at a late hour, we received intimation to prepare for our removal to the penitentiary of Frankfort in Kentucky, and accordingly the next day, about two o'clock in the afternoon, we were conducted to the front of the prison, where a detachment of regular infantry was drawn up with their ranks facing inwards, and at extended order. Between these ranks we were placed two abreast, and the detachment being ordered to face to the right and left, we moved on, thus escorted or rather enfiladed, from the gloomy walls of our prison. As if to humiliate us to the last degree, and add insult to misfortune, we were paraded through the principal streets of the town, though such a route was at once circuitous and unnecessary. The taunts and hisses of the populace who had assembled at an early hour to witness our departure, and were now with difficulty kept back by the guard, followed us throughout ; but the clamorous ebullition of their hate gave us far less concern than the sombre countenances of the more respectable inhabitants, collected to view the passing scene. Those with whom we had lately associated, and who had exercised the courtesies of hospitality in our favor, now gazed upon us with various expression —some in a triumphant disdain originating in a false rumor, which had been industriously circulated of a design to fire the town—others with evident interest and concern, arising from a conviction of the injustice of such a charge. Friends and foes were, however, alike to us at that moment, and the proud indifference of our looks rested on all with the same cold expression ; for we felt that the ignominious treatment to which we were then being subjected, reflected, not on us, who had attempted the fulfilment of a duty we owed both to our country and to ourselves, but on those who thus abused their power over us as defenceless captives. At length when it was presumed that the good inhabitants of Chillicothe had sated themselves with a view of the "incendiary English" we were conducted to a large boat on the river, already manned with soldiers, and awaiting our arrival.

It was with a feeling of real pleasure that we found Lieutenant Harrison to be the officer in command of the detachment to whose charge we were here given over ; and as we took our places, the boat was pushed off from the shore, and quickly glided down the Scioto, amid the continued hootings of the rabble, collected at the point of embarkation on its banks. Impressed with various reflections arising from the preceding scene, few of the party were disposed for conversation, and an almost uninterrupted silence had prevailed some hours, when, towards the close of the day, the boat struck against a " sawyer," or trunk of a tree carried off from the land during the floods, and frequently stationary in the beds of rivers, from whence, when acted on by the tide and current, it rises suddenly to the surface in a perpendicular direction, preserving a state of reaction, and threatening destruction even to the largest boats used in the navigation of the Ohio and Mississippi. The concussion we experienced gave rise to serious apprehensions for our safety ; and in an instant the leaden pins of the handcuffs were removed, but yet with sufficient precaution to escape the attention of the guard. Lieutenant Harrison, however, caused the boat to be directed towards the shore, and having expressed his intention to pass the night in an old deserted building, which stood at the distance of some few hundred paces, we were accordingly disembarked. When arrived at the spot indicated for our temporary sojourn, the American officer, evidently impressed with a full sense of

our recent danger, declared it to be his determination to
remove the fetters from our hands, provided we would
pledge our words to him, as British officers, that no attempt at escape should be made. This step, he observed,
had not in any way the sanction of his superiors, but he
was willing to take the responsibility upon himself, satisfied that our parole once engaged, no ultimate risk could
be incurred. This circumstance, however grateful in
fact, placed the manacled officers in a rather awkward
dilemma, since it was evident that in removing the irons,
which had been replaced the instant the danger was
passed, the deception must be discovered. We had, however, formed too just an estimate of the character of
Lieutenant Harrison to hesitate long in the avowal of a
subterfuge to which we had been driven by suffering and
necessity. Our promise was then given, and the whole
party once more enjoyed the unrestrained use of their
limbs. At an early hour on the following morning we
again embarked, and a few hours brought us to the point
of confluence with the majestic waters of the Ohio. The
strong current of this expansive river carried us rapidly
forward, and we soon found ourselves at Cincinnati, the
capital of the State.

After leaving Cincinnati, and passing the boundary
line which separates the States of Ohio and Kentucky,
the direction of our course was changed, and we
ascended a small river intersecting the latter state
and leading in the line of the capital. Our progress here was slow and difficult. A thick and apparently impervious wood skirted its banks, and occasionally interweaving its protruding tops, threw a chilling
gloom over the scene, while the close underwood, reaching to the very margin of the waters, seemed to preclude
all possibility of a landing. At length a more open space
was perceptible, and at this point our journey by water,
owing to the increasing difficulty of movement, was discontinued. Horses were procured in the adjacent country ;

and, escorted by Lieutenant Harrison, who left his detachment in the boat, we continued our route towards Frankfort, then at no great distance. After travelling through a wild and thinly-inhabited country, and along paths which no other than American horses could have trod with safety, a range of lofty and gloomy hills, by which that capital is nearly surrounded, announced the proximity of what we were to consider as our future home. The morning was cold and rainy, and as we wound round the base of a hill which intercepted our view, the towering walls of the penitentiary, situated in that extremity of the town by which we approached, fell suddenly on our gaze. A few minutes brought us in a line with its principal entrance ; and as we glanced upwards at the low and narrow windows we beheld our companions thrusting their handkerchiefs through the bars, and saluting us as they could. They were the party that had preceded us from Chillicothe, and consisted chiefly of the officers taken at the Moraviantown. It was a melancholy moment for recognition, and our feelings had imbibed much of the sombre character of the season, as we moved on to the spot appointed for our delivery into the hands of the Marshal of Kentucky. This duty performed, Lieutenant Harrison bade us adieu, with a friendly warmth which every individual in our party fully appreciated and returned. He was in truth a noble fellow.

On entering the prison of the penitentiary, we found our friends distributed into two small rooms little larger than common cells, and crowded together in a distressing manner ; but many had reconciled themselves to their situations, and enjoyed a temporary distraction in studying the trades carried on by the convicts in the court, who cheerfully initiated them into the rudiments of their respective arts. The following is a correct list, taken from an American paper, of the names and rank of the several officers assembled within its walls.

Lieut.-Col. Warburton—Major Chambers, D.A.Q.M.
G.—Major Muir, 41st—Captain Derenzy, do—Capt.
McCoy, do—Capt. Hill, do—Capt. Tallon, do—Capt.
Dixon, Royal Engineers—Lieut. Hailes, 41st—Lieut.
Watson, do—Lieut. Linn, do—Lieut. Jeboult, do—Lieut.
O'Keefe, do—Lieut. Gale, do—Lieut. Purvis, Royal
Navy—Lieut. Stokoe, do—Lieut. Bremner, Provincial
do—Lieut. Rolette, do. do—Lieut. Irvine, do. do—Lieut.
Holmes, Light Dragoons—Ensign Mompesson, 41st—
Ensign Cochran, do—Ensign Jones, do—A. B. Garden,
Gent. Volunteer, Royal Newfoundland Regt.—J. Rich-
ardson, do. 41st—James Laing, do—J. Campbell, Master's
Mate, R.P.N.—G. Collins, do—J. Fortier, do—R. Nelson,
Midshipman.

The whole number of prisoners were about 900, including those taken on the lake.

Our residence in the penitentiary was, however, too
limited to admit of perfection in our new occupations.
At this period a strong sensation was produced in
America by the intelligence of Napoleon's unexpected
reverses in Russia. A termination of the war between
Great Britain and France might now be anticipated as an
event of no very remote occurrence, and the ability thus
afforded to the former power of sending a more formidable
army to oppose that of the United States would place the
struggle between the two countries on a very different
footing. Under this view of the case, and as one of the
measures consequent on the altered aspect of the war,
the affair of the hostages was gradually suffered to die
away. The first step, however, was only an amelioration
of our condition, which was effected by our removal from
the penitentiary to the town. The principal hotel in
Frankfort, to which was attached an extensive garden,
surrounded by a low wall, was the place selected for our
residence, with the express prohibition, however, of out-
stepping its limits. Here on the score of personal comfort we had no reason to complain. Three shillings a

day was the allowance granted by the American government to each officer, and the sick were entitled to twice that amount. One room was occupied by two prisoners, and our table was abundantly supplied with excellent food. Tea, coffee, eggs, cold meat, and the various "sweet sauces" to which the Americans are so partial, composed our breakfast; while at dinner we generally found ourselves seated before meats of every description, and succeeded by a plentiful dessert. Tea, coffee and hot cakes composed our evening repast. A number of black slaves were also at our orders, and the preparation of our linen was included in the moderate charge. Such was the revolution effected in our position, and but for the restraint imposed on our liberty, our chains would have been light.

At length, in consequence of an order from the seat of Government, we were once more placed on parole, and permission was accorded to such of the prisoners as chose to pay their own expenses, and provide their own horses, to repair to the Canadian frontier. This offer was eagerly embraced by the field officers and such others as the state of their finances would permit. The remainder were compelled to await the issue of the arrangements then in agitation for an exchange of prisoners, hoping that the shackles of captivity, which had at the outset promised to be of long continuance, would speedily be removed; and we availed ourselves of the liberty once more accorded. Several gentlemen of the highest respectability in the place were forward in offering attention; and among the first of these was Major Madison. This officer had been himself a prisoner in Lower Canada, from whence he was only recently returned, and, impressed with a grateful sense of the treatment he had received, hastened to evince it by various acts of hospitality and courtesy towards ourselves. We became welcome visitors in his family, and frequently accompanied him in excursions to several delightful country seats at some distance from the town. Permission was frequently obtained for us to visit places at the distance of twenty miles without any escort whatever ; and as our purses had been replenished by the kindness of Mr. Sproule, a Frankfort banker, without any other guarantee for future payment than our simple bills, these excursions were not few. A good understanding was, however, only maintained with a very small portion of the inhabitants. By the rest we were regarded with an eye of jealousy and detestation, and whenever opportunities did present themselves, these feelings were undisguisedly manifested. One instance must suffice.

As a slight return for the attentions of Major Madison, Lieutenant Irvine of the Navy, the person so honorably alluded to in the first part of this narrative, had, with an ingenuity for which he was remarkable, constructed a vessel in miniature for the daughter of that gentleman. To many of the inhabitants of Kentucky the model even of a frigate complete in all her parts was a novel sight, and the present was thankfully received. Anxious to tender a similar offering, though in a different quarter, a young midshipman named Campbell, occupying one of the upper rooms, had undertaken a similar task, and devoting himself with all the anxiety and ardor of his years to the completion of his vessel, soon had the satisfaction of seeing it in a state of great forwardness. Most unfortunately for him, however, he had forgotten that an English flag, even on a bark of those Lilliputian dimensions, is ever an offensive image to an American eye ; and decked in this fatal ornament, it now lay exposed in one of the windows of his apartment, and was distinctly visible from the street. On the morning of its exhibition, a crowd of persons, delighted at having what they conceived a pretext for insult, rushed in a body up the stairs, uttering imprecations and threats. Having reached the spot where the object of their fury was lying, they seized the luckless ship, and dashed it on the pavement of the street, where it was shattered in a thousand fragments, the leader of the party exclaiming, "You British rascals, if you show your tarnation colors here again, we'll throw you after them." This noble feat being accomplished, they retired, swearing at us all in true Kentucky style, and leaving poor Campbell to brood at leisure over his misfortune.

Shortly after this event, arrived the agreeable intelligence that the whole of the prisoners were to be marched to the frontier for the purpose of an immediate exchange. Those alone who have experienced the miseries and restraints attendant on a state of captivity, especially under such circumstances as those by which that of the officers of the Right Division was marked, can enter into the feelings by which we were all more or less actuated. By many the news, although long expected, of our exchange being actually effected, had been received as a pleasing dream or illusion, from which the mind dreaded to be awakened ; and until the moment of actual departure, that restlessness of impatience which is the offspring of uncertainty seemed to predominate in every breast. A thousand things unlikely to occur, but still within the pale of possibility, presented themselves to imaginations more disposed to the expectation of gloomy than of agreeable events. The order for our departure might be repealed —the negotiation for the exchange broken off altogether —and to crown all, the cruel subject of the hostages renewed. Pleasurable anticipations belong only to those who have basked in the unbroken sunshine of Fortune— those who have been tutored in the school of Adversity are less sanguine in their hopes, and temper the glow of generous confidence with the steady calm of warning experience.

That we were not wrong, indeed, in apprehending interruption to the negotiations, then pending between the two Governments, will be seen from the following important General Orders issued by Sir George Prevost, embracing the correspondence between Adjt.-General Baynes, and General Winder, to whom had been confided the delicate task of entering on the subject of the exchange of hostages.

General Order,

Headquarters, Montreal,

16th April, 1814.

His Excellency the Governor in Chief, and Commander of the Forces, announces to the troops under his command, that he was pleased to sanction and confirm, on the 15th inst., Articles of a Convention entered into by Colonel Baynes, Adjutant-General of the Forces, and Brigadier-General Winder of the army of the United States of America, for the mutual release of all prisoners of war, Hostages or others, with the exception of the forty-six American officers and non-commissioned officers placed in close confinement as Hostages, in conformity to the General Order of the 27th of October last, in retaliation for twenty-three British Soldiers, confined by the Government of the United States as hostages for twenty-three British-born subjects, taken from the ranks of the enemy, and sent to England for legal trial.

By this agreement it is stipulated that all prisoners of war (the above mentioned alone excepted) shall be mutually exchanged, and delivered at such places as shall be agreed on, with all convenient expedition, and shall be declared, respectively and severally, to be released, and free to carry arms and serve on the 15th day of May next, the same as if they had never been prisoners of war : and it has been further provided, that whatever balance shall appear on the returns of prisoners of war, respectively exchanged or given up on parole, by either party since the commencement of Hostilities, the number of Prisoners for which an equivalent has not been returned, shall be withheld from all military service, until exchanged.

It is with proud satisfaction that the Commander of the Forces feels confident, that this provisional clause can never apply to the Army in Canada, from the immense disparity in the number and rank of the prisoners it has restored to the enemy.

All officers, non-commissioned officers and soldiers, being prisoners of war, who are not prevented in conse-

From a painting in possession of Mr. O Hara Baynes, Montreal.

ADJUTANT-GENERAL EDWARD BAYNES.

quence of their wounds, are commanded to join their respective corps and stations on the 15th day of May next, and to resume their military duties.

(Signed) Edward Baynes, Adjt.-Gen.

General Order,
Headquarters, Camp at Chambly,
July 2nd, 1814.

Several officers of this army having returned from the United States, where they had been held in close confinement as hostages, and having on their release signed a conditional parole containing a pledge on their part, to return to their captivity at the expiration of a limited period, unless previously exchanged : His Excellency the Governor in Chief, and Commander of the Forces, considering such parole to be inconsistent with the provisions of a convention for the exchange of prisoners which was entered into by persons duly empowered for that purpose by the Government of the United States, and His Excellency respectively, and has already been carried into complete execution on his part, and has also been in part executed by the American Government,—is pleased to declare that all those officers, whether of the Line or Militia are absolved from their parole, under and by virtue of the before-mentioned convention :—that they are released and free to serve as if they had never been Prisoners of War and are all and severally included in the General Order of the 16th of April, directing all Prisoners of War after the 15th of May to repair to their respective corps and stations, and to resume their military duties.

To destroy any doubts which may by possibility be entertained with regard to the complete execution of the Convention above mentioned ; to satisfy the nice and scrupulous sensibility with which a British soldier must ever view and examine an act, professing to release him from an obligation in which his honor is implicated, and to remove every apprehension from the minds of those who may come within the scope of the present General Order, His Excellency is pleased to authorize the communication to the army under his command, of the principal circumstances attending the commencement, progress, and final conclusion of the Convention to which allusion has above been made.

At the solicitation of the Government of the United States, conveyed in a letter from their Secretary of State of the 19th of March, and not less induced by his anxious desire to alleviate the unnecessary severity which the system of retaliation had introduced into the conduct of this war, the Commander of the Forces did not hesitate in acceding to a proposal which seemed to promise the attainment of an object so desirable. In that spirit, and with that view, His Excellency consented to the exchange of Brigadier-General Winder, (a Hostage) in consequence of that officer having been selected by the President of the United States, as an agent, vested with full powers to negotiate for an exchange of prisoners of war, as well Hostages as others. His Excellency was also pleased to nominate Colonel Baynes as an Agent vested with similar powers, on the part of the British army.

The negotiation commenced under the most favorable auspices. The basis and conditions of the convention being left to the discretion of the two officers above mentioned, it was agreed that all prisoners of war, Hostages or others (with the sole exception of the British subjects taken from the ranks of the enemy and sent to England for legal trial) should be released in conformity to the regulations of the cartel, General Winder pledging himself that his Government entertained the most liberal sentiments, and that the great disparity of prisoners, both with respect to rank and numbers, which the United States would receive, and for which they had no equivalent to return, should be withheld from service on parole, until duly exchanged.

This agreement was on the point of being ratified, when a despatch from the American Secretary of State, dated Washington, the 22nd March, was received by Brigadier-General Winder, and was verbally represented by him to convey a positive prohibition to his consenting to the release of the twenty-three British soldiers held in confinement as Hostages for the British subjects sent to England for trial, unless it was stipulated that they also should be released, and sent to the United States.

This proposition was instantly answered by a note informing Brigadier-General Winder, that as a new basis had been substituted by the Secretary of State, inadmissible in principle, the negotiation was in consequence at an end, and that his partial exchange as a preliminary measure was also void, and of no effect as emanating from an act which had from the conduct of the proposing party become a nullity.

The introduction of this new pretension on the part of the Government of the United States had arrested the progress of the negotiation, when a note from Brigadier-General Winder came (No. 3) which was acceded to by Colonel Baynes as the basis of a convention (No. 4).

To ascertain the existence of the power of final ratification on the part of Brigadier-General Winder, the Commander of the Forces was pleased to direct Colonel Baynes to address to that officer the note (No. 5) and although the answer of Brigadier-General Winder, as contained in note (No. 6) did not completely accord with the spirit of candor professed by him, and manifested by His Excellency, nevertheless the fair construction of it was such as to carry to his mind the conviction which it must impress on every honorable man who peruses it, that Brigadier-General Winder possessed the power of finally ratifying any new agreement for the exchange of prisoners into which he might think proper to enter.

Under this impression the Commander of the Forces was pleased to declare his assent to the immediate release and exchange of Brigadier-General Winder; the negotiation for the exchange of prisoners, on the contracted basis imposed by Brigadier-General Winder, was re-commenced, and the conditions being arranged, a convention was concluded on the 15th April last, and ratified by the contracting parties.

It is under this convention, so begun and ratified, and carried into effect according to the tenor of it, with promptitude and good faith on the part of the Commander of the Forces, and to which no objection has been specified by the American Government, in any of their communications to His Excellency, since the conclusion of it, but which, on the contrary, must have been accepted, since it has been in part executed by that Government, that His Excellency, the Commander of the Forces, has been pleased thus publicly to absolve all the officers and others who have recently returned from the United States from a parole which His Excellency conceives to be inconsistent with the terms of that convention, and which he considers to have been enacted by persons ignorant of its existence, or misconceiving its conditions.

By His Excellency's Command,
Edward Baynes, Adj.-General,
British North America.

No. 1.

Montreal, 10th April, 1814.

Colonel Baynes has communicated to His Excellency the Commander of the Forces the purport and extent of the alterations explained by Brigadier-General Winder to exist, between the instructions of the 19th March, addressed to him by the Secretary of State, and those of the 22nd, of the same date received yesterday, and that the omission of the same in the first copy was owing to an error in transcribing it.

His Excellency, however, on reference to the letter of the Secretary of State of the 19th March, addressed to him, as it is stated, "with the view, and in the sincere desire to restore to the mildest practice of civilized nations the treatment of prisoners on both sides," and authorizing Brigadier-General Winder, on the part of the United States Government, to conclude an arrangement which may embrace the exchange, as well as those held as hostages, as of other prisoners ; and His Excellency learning from that officer that his instructions fully comported with the unqualified tenor of the proposal made in the Secretary of State's letter to him, did not hesitate a moment in acceding to the other arrangements therein suggested, and was prepared to waive just grounds which he conceived he had of complaint against the Government of the United States, on the subject of the exchange of prisoners of war, in the hopes of promoting an arrangement so desirable for the cause of humanity and the honor of both nations ; and he is much disappointed to find his hopes frustrated by the introduction, at this period of the negotiation, of a claim so totally inadmissible, that had the Secretary of State's letter borne the most distant allusion to it, His Excellency would have felt himself, as he now does, prohibited from proceeding any further on the subject.

The British view the confinement of twenty-three soldiers as the first act of aggression : for the undoubted right which every free nation possesses of investigating and punishing the crimes committed by her own natural-born subjects, in a due course of law, is too self-evident to require a comment, nor can it, by any distortion of sense or justice, be construed into a just ground for an act of fair retaliation exercised on twenty-three British soldiers : the latter are characterized by their patriotism and loyalty, the former stigmatized for their treason and rebellion.

It would be wasting time to enter into any further discussion on this subject. Great Britain has successfully maintained her national rights unsullied for twenty years against the whole world combined : it is not to be supposed that it is reserved for the United States to stop the course of justice, and to dictate to England what procedure she shall observe towards her own natural-born subjects, in her own courts of civil judicature, arrested in her own territories, in the commission of acts of treason and rebellion.

It is to be remarked, that as the exchange of prisoners of war now proposed by the United States no longer has the general character that was at first proposed, but is specifically to restore quota for quota, it becomes on this ground, incumbent on the part of the British Government, to demand, as a preliminary step, a detailed statement of about three thousand prisoners of war, of which the third were of the United States' regular service, captured in Canada during the first campaign, and given up in good faith to the United States, who at that period had no British prisoners,—and as all subsequent exchanges on the part of the United States, have been acquitted by an equivalent number of prisoners simultaneously exchanged, it is insisted that the American Government is bound by honor and good faith to make full and complete satisfaction for the above debt, in conformity to the 14th article of the cartel, before she can in justice retain, or ask an equivalent for a single British prisoner now in her possession ; and for this purpose returns will be prepared, not only of the number of prisoners remaining unexchanged in the possession of either power, but of those given up in good faith by the British Government to the United States, and for which no return has yet been made, or satisfaction offered ; and as it appears from the documents now transmitted, that the United States are adding to the number of prisoners placed in restraint as Hostages, His Excellency is left no alternative, and is under the imperious necessity of ordering into close confinement, all the American officers remaining in his possession, not heretofore considered as Hostages.

If the instructions of the Secretary of State leave to the discretion of Brigadier-General Winder no latitude on the subject of the twenty-three British soldiers considered by Great Britain as the sole just origin of the system of retaliation, the further prosecution of this negotiation, for an exchange of prisoners, must be unavailing, as His Excellency, although prepared to waive all minor considerations, to meet the American Government on a fair and liberal basis, is at the same time unalterably firm in his determination not to compromise in the slightest degree, that principle of justice and equity upon which the measures of his Government have been framed.

On a former occasion, Colonel Baynes communicated to Major Melville that if the prisoners of war in Canada were not exchanged previous to the arrival of the transports expected early in the Spring, it would become a necessary measure to relieve the Canadas of that charge, and that they would be sent to England ; and on the opening of the river navigation, the prisoners now at Montreal will be sent to Quebec for that purpose.

(Signed) Edward Baynes,
Colonel, and Adjt.-General.

No. 2.

Brigadier-General Winder has received Colonel Baynes' note of this morning, and has read it with close and profound attention, not without considerable surprise and the deepest regret—surprise because it seems to have been expected that the discussions depending between Colonel Baynes and himself were in fact to have settled and adjusted a principal question which will no doubt occupy the Congress at Gottenburg—regret because he fears that the beneficial consequences which would result from making exchanges, as far as was practicable under the powers held by General Winder, must be defeated by persisting in the views held out by the note of Colonel Baynes—exchanges which would restore to liberty so many brave and honorable men of both nations, who may otherwise linger out a tedious protracted confinement, finally to be terminated by an inglorious death, and which beside, would have left untouched in the fullest extent, the pretentions of Great Britain, on the question from whence the system of retaliation has arisen.

It appears to Brigadier-General Winder, from the note of Colonel Baynes, that he considered an exchange made under the restriction in Brigadier-General Winder's power, as an abandonment or compromising the principle in question by the British Government. Surely, if this were the case, as according to Brigadier-General Winder's conception it certainly is not, it would have been an abandonment of it on the part of the American Government, if this restriction had not existed in the power, and would have been an extent of power which, it is confidently believed, His Excellency did not expect would be conferred on the occasion—nor indeed could it be supposed that a power to treat relative to the adjustment of this principle would have been conferred upon a person in the situation, and under the circumstances which Brigadier-General Winder was when he received the power.

Brigadier-General Winder further supposes that His Excellency had and can have, in the ordinary course of things, no power to settle and adjust this question unless by special delegation, and this, if known to the Government of the United States, would have drawn from them a correspondent delegation of power with a view to its adjustment.

But the Government of the United States were aware that His Excellency possessed as incidental to his military command, the power of making exchanges relative to the prisoners made from and by his command, which did not compromit the principle of the British Government on this point, and therefore had in view to delegate a corresponding power to Brigadier-General Winder, as it is considered they have entirely done.

The Government of the United States conceived that a relinquishment of the twenty-three original Hostages taken by them would be compromitting the principle on their part, and declined to give a power to this extent—they, on the contrary, do not ask a release of the twenty-three men sent to England, because that would be relinquishing it on the part of the British Government. The power to negotiate upon this question, it is presumed, has been delegated to the commissioners about to assemble at Gottenburg.

But General W. is at a loss to perceive, that because he does not possess this power a negotiation is to stop, which could originally only have contemplated, and been expected to contemplate, the exchange, as far as could be done without broaching that question. And the letter of the Secretary of State to His Excellency, of the 19th

March, and his contemporaneous instructions to Brigadier-General Winder, while they look to the largest possible exchange, yet reserve, and express to do so whole
and entire, the right on this system of retaliation, and
he most sincerely believes his propositions of yesterday's
date entirely attain this object to both parties.

Brigadier-General Winder, conscious it would be useless to submit any observation on the other parts of
Colonel Baynes' note, as he believes them completely
embraced in one of the propositions of his note of yesterday, entirely conformable to Colonel Baynes' wishes ;
and because, possessing no other powers or instructions
than those already communicated, he supposes it more
important, at the present moment, to obviate the objections to proceed in the negotiation, which he flatters himself the foregoing remarks will have a tendency to effect,
and which unless he can effect, would be time uselessly
spent, as no result could flow from it.

Brigadier-General Winder submits these remarks in a
spirit of unreserved candor and cordiality, and without
the loss of a moment ; —and flatters himself, that, viewed
by Colonel Baynes with the same spirit, they will be
found entitled to strong and conclusive weight.

(Signed)   Wm. Winder,
         Brig.-Gen. U. S. Army.
    No. 3.

      Montreal, April 11th, 1814.

Brigadier-General Winder has received Col. Baynes'
note of this morning and has read it with all the attention which the subject of it was calculated to awaken,
and however much he regrets that he is not able to accomplish all that he hoped and wished, yet he is gratified
in believing, that much may be accomplished in strict
conformity with the principles upon which His Excellency feels himself bound to act as detailed in Col. Baynes'
note of to-day, and also entirely within the powers and
instructions which Brigadier-General Winder has received and submitted from his Government. Colonel
Baynes' note states, '' that the confinement of the
twenty-three American officers, and an equal number
of non-commissioned officers, is considered as the first
stage of retaliation, on the part of the British Government, and will be persevered in so long as the twenty-
three soldiers, for which they are held as Hostages are

kept in confinement, and cannot be effected by any exchange that does not emancipate the twenty-three British soldiers.''

What Brigadier-General Winder proposes, therefore in entire conformity to this principle is, that the British officers put into confinement in retaliation for the confinement of the above forty-six American officers and non-commissioned officers shall be released and exchanged to such an extent as an equivalent value of American officers confined in retaliation for them, or who may be prisoners of war, other than the above forty-six, shall be released and exchanged.

Brigadier-General Winder, in his note of the 9th made his proposition as extensive as he was allowed, but considered at the same time, that if, in its whole extent, it was not acceptable to His Excellency he would hold himself ready to embrace any modification of them, which might be more acceptable, and within Brigadier-General Winder's power.

This proposition appearing to Brigadier-General Winder to be so entirely within the principles contained in Colonel Baynes' note he feels the most sanguine assurance of its acceptance, and, without incumbering it with anything else, he hastens to submit it without delay.

(Signed) Wm. Winder,
Brig-Gen. U.S. Army.

No. 4.

Headquarters, Montreal,
Adjutant-General's Office,
April 12th, 1814.

Colonel Baynes has to acknowledge Brigadier-General Winder's note of the 11th inst., and is commanded to acquaint him, that the Commander of the Forces consents to an exchange of Hostages, and all others, prisoners of war, in conformity to the scale of the cartel, under the previous stipulated conditions recited in his note, viz.—That the twenty-three British soldiers first confined as hostages, and the forty-six American officers and non-commissioned officers confined as Hostages, in retaliation for the same, remain untouched and be not included in the present proposed exchange.

It appearing that the American Government assert to

have placed seventy-seven British officers in confinement
as Hostages, and the right to retaliate in an equal number
being assumed by the Commander of the Forces, it would
be necessary to place thirty-one American officers in similar restraint, in order to hold seventy-seven to restore in
exchange, but to avoid the performance of so unpleasant
a task, it is proposed that it be taken for granted that
this further act of retaliation has been carried into effect,
and that the number of Hostages on both sides, being
equal in number, amounting to seventy-seven are declared
released as Hostages, and placed on the footing of ordinary prisoners of war, to be exchanged as such, in conformity to the cartel.

That this measure take place immediately in Quebec,
and with the least possible delay in the United States and
Halifax.

The exchange contemplated is to include every individual held as a prisoner of war connected with the
Army of British North America, commencing from the
first act of hostilities on either side, excepting only
twenty-three British soldiers, and the forty-six American officers and non-commissioned officers to be reserved
as Hostages, it being further stipulated that the last mentioned forty-six will be placed on the footing of ordinary
prisoners of war, and exchanged as such whenever the
twenty-three British soldiers are so released or delivered
over for exchange.

The details contained in Brigadier-General Winder's
note of the 9th inst. are accepted of, as forming the outline for mutual arrangement for carrying this exchange
into effect.

(Signed)   Edward Baynes,
                Adjutant-General, N.A.

No. 5.

Headquarters, Montreal,
    Adjutant-General's Office,
        April 12th, 1814.

Colonel Baynes has to acknowledge Brigadier-General
Winder's note of this day, and is commanded to acquaint
him that the Commander of the Forces has no objection
to the principle upon which his exchange is proposed by
the Secretary of State as a preliminary measure to his
entering upon the proposed negotiation, provided that

the basis upon which that negotiation is to be conducted is in its principle admissible, and holds out a fair and a reasonable prospect of producing the desired end.

His Excellency considered the proposal as stated in the Secretary of State's letter of 19th March as coming under that description, and the accompanying letter of instructions of the same date, comporting with the same, he did not hesitate to grant his consent to the proposed exchange of Brigadier-General Winder, as a proper preliminary measure—but a subsequent communication from the Secretary of the United States being received by Brigadier-General Winder, and represented by him to have been introduced into the first instructions, alterations in themselves inadmissible in principle, and that the same had been omitted by error in transcribing the first copy, and were therefore to be considered as forming the text and spirit of the proposition. The Commander of the Forces considered himself absolved from his assent to a document, which had, from the act of the proposing party, become a nullity; and thereby cancelling whatever might have emanated from it, and that he was at liberty to revert to the alternative suggested in the Secretary of State's first letter, and reject the proposal *in toto*.

Colonel Baynes is directed to inform Brigadier-General Winder that it is not His Excellency's intention to sanction any partial exchange, except for the express purpose stated in the Secretary of State's letter, with which he thinks it highly expedient and proper to comply, but he must require from that officer a most direct and unequivocal assurance that he is *authorized to treat and ratify, without further reservation on the part of his Government*, a negotiation on the principles stated in Colonel Baynes' note of the 11th and 12th, and in General Winder's note of the 11th instant—in which case his exchange will be declared full and complete.

Brigadier-General Winder will excuse this demand, which has become necessary from the doubts which he has himself created, as to the nature and extent of the restriction recently placed upon him by his Government.

(Signed)   Edward Baynes,

Adjutant-General N.A.

No. 6.
Montreal, April 13th, 1814.

Brigadier-General Winder very much regrets that he should have failed in communicating to Colonel Baynes in the last interview the extent of the powers communicated to him with requisite precision.

It was the intention of Brigadier-General Winder to have stated that his powers extended without restriction, to propose and agree to an exchange of all British prisoners of war taken from the command of Sir George Prevost, except the twenty-three men put into confinement in retaliation for the twenty-three men sent to England, to which extent he now assures Colonel Baynes his powers extend, embracing all the subjects contained in Colonel Baynes' notes of the 11th and 12th, and Brigadier-General Winder's of the 11th.

As it was not the intention of Brigadier-General Winder that His Excellency should have the least question as to the extent of his powers, he cannot but feel mortified, that an idea should have been entertained for a moment that he intended to render them in the least degree doubtful, and he trusts this avowal will remove all such impressions, and enable Colonel Baynes and himself, upon the adjustment of Brigadier-General Winder's exchange, to proceed without delay to the arrangement.

(Signed)   Wm. Winder,
Brigadier-General, U.S. Army.

General Order.

Adjutant-General's Office,
Headquarters, Montreal,
July 18th, 1814.

His Excellency the Commander of the Forces announces to the troops under his command, that having at the invitation of the American Government, deputed Colonel Baynes, Adjutant-General, and Lieutenant-Colonel Brenton, Provincial Aide-de-Camp, to meet on Thursday last at Champlain, Colonel Lear, late Consul General of the United States at Algiers—for the purpose of reconsidering the convention for the exchange of prisoners which had been entered into on the 15th of April last, between Colonel Baynes and Brigadier-General Winder ; and of removing whatever objections might be made to the due execution of it :—and the said meeting having taken place accordingly, all objections to the said convention were then and there completely removed ; and the same was, on the 16th instant, fully and definitely ratified by Colonel Lear, on the part of the United States ; (he having full power for that purpose) with a supplementary clause, by which the twenty-three British soldiers, and the forty-six American officers, the Hostages mentioned in the first article of the said convention, are declared to be included in that convention, and are to be released and exchanged, in the same manner as other prisoners of war, mentioned in the same articles, notwithstanding the exception to them therein contained ;—and His Excellency is pleased hereby to direct that this General Order be considered in explanation and confirmation of the said General Orders issued on the 16th and 2nd July, 1814.

Edward Baynes, Adjt. Gen. N.A.

The morning of our actual departure from Frankfort was, as will be believed, one of joy and exultation to us all ; and at an early hour most of the officers were already up, and with light hearts and cheerful countenances preparing for their journey.

Our horses were at length brought to the entrance of the hotel, before which nearly half the town of Frankfort had collected to witness our departure. Habited in our light and neatly-fringed Kentucky frocks, fastened by silver buckles attached to broad red morocco belts, we soon vaulted into the saddle ; and escorted by Lieutenant Mitchell of the rifle service, and Colonel Crocket, the Marshal of the state, a consequential gentleman, who had often vainly sought to subdue our refractory spirits into something like submission to his authority, we commenced our journey. The hand of kindness and the voice of gentlemanly consideration were extended to us by a few, among whom stood principally conspicuous Major Madison and the banker Mr. Sproule ; but on the countenances of the many might be traced very different feelings. Even while detesting our presence, they seemed to regret the approaching removal of their victims, and the insolence of their looks and observations bore sufficient testimony of their hostility.

Pursuing a route different from that by which we had reached Frankfort, we soon arrived at Newport,[1] a small town situated at the confluence of the Kanaway and Ohio rivers, and immediately opposite to Cincinnati, in the neighborhood of which latter place the prisoners from Chillicothe were awaiting the arrival of their officers. Large boats were procured for the passage of our horses, and having crossed the river the same evening, we were conducted to our old quarters, the principal hotel in Cincinnati.

On joining the men, we found, that independently of those whom the Americans had successfully employed every art to seduce from our service, two individuals were missing, in whose fate we had become previously interested. At the moment of departure from the harbour of Amherstburg, Captain Barclay had received two young Indian warriors, anxious to witness a naval combat, on board of the Detroit; and on engaging the American fleet, they were stationed in the tops with their rifles. This position, however, they found less secure than the trees of their native forests, and were soon assailed by showers of grape and canister which filled them with dismay. They instantly relinquished their rifles, and hastened to decamp. Too much frightened to adopt the safer and more usual mode of descent by the ladder of the rigging, they each grasped a loose rope pending from the yards, and in this manner glided with fearful rapidity to the deck, lacerating their hands in a cruel manner, and no doubt secretly regretting their spirit of adventure. Nor did they stop until they reached the bottom of the hold, where they were subsequently found by the Americans, lying within a large coil of rope, and in company with a pet bear, belonging to one of the crew, who had

[1] Newport is at the confluence of the Licking river and the Ohio. There is a Kanawha river, another branch of the Ohio, farther east. See map.

conveyed him there, as a place of perfect security from the enemy's shot. In our occasional visits to the encampment at Chillicothe, we always saw and conversed with them, and at the last which preceded our close imprisonment, we found them busily engaged in making bows and arrows—a work in which they were not interrupted by their guard, who probably saw nothing more in the occupation than amusement, or an agreeable employment of their time, but they told us in their own tongue, a little of which was understood by one or two of the party, that they were meditating their escape, and that the bows and arrows were to provide them with food in the woods. The intelligence now received was, that they had succeeded in effecting their design shortly after our departure, having managed to scale the picketing on a dark night, which they had selected for the purpose. What the final result of their enterprise was, we had no future opportunity of ascertaining ; but with the knowledge we possessed of the extreme facility with which the Indians find their way through the deepest and most extensive forests, we did not entertain a doubt of their having rejoined their tribe in safety.

The morning of our departure from Cincinnati was the last of Colonel Crocket's " guardianship " ; for we were handed over to an old friend, Mr. Steele, the Marshal of Ohio, a man as gentle, considerate, and unassuming, as the other was harsh, exacting, and overbearing. From this gentleman we received an account of the death of our old persecutor, Colonel Campbell.[1] This officer had been

[1] Lieut.-Col. John B. Campbell was in command of the 11th U.S. Infantry at the battle of Chippawa, July 5th, 1814, where he was severely wounded in the knee, from the effects of which he died. On May 14th, 1814, with a force of about 800 men, he landed at Long Point, Upper Canada, without opposition, burnt the village of Dover, Ryerson's Mills, Finch's Mills, killed the cattle and hogs of the settlers and burnt their dwellings. For this act he was brought before a Court of Inquiry at Buffalo composed of Brigadier-General Scott, Major Jessup and Major Wood. The verdict of the Court was, that Lieut.-Col. Campbell was justified in burning the flour mills and distilleries by the usage of war, but that he erred

desperately wounded on the Niagara frontier, whither he had been ordered with his regiment, soon after our departure from Chillicothe. The cap of his knee had been carried away by a cannon shot, and he died in extreme agony. If we had humanity enough not to rejoice at this intelligence, we certainly did not indulge in any very immoderate grief ; for the unfeeling conduct of that individual was still fresh in the recollection of many, and, above all, the insult of exposing us to public curiosity in the principal streets of a town in which he held the first military command—an insult we had every reason to believe originated with himself.

Our route from Cincinnati lay through the same dull region we had traversed the preceding autumn ; but with feelings far different from those we then experienced, did we now measure back our steps. The season too was changed, and instead of chill damps and penetrating rains, over the face of nature was spread the genial warmth of summer. It was the middle of July ; and though the ardent rays of a burning sun threw their oppressive lustre on our heads, while traversing the more open parts of the country, we much more frequently found shelter in thick and extensive woods where a solitary, winding and imperfect wagon-road alone marked the progress of civilization. Each moment of our journey brought us nearer to the more fortunate companions of our toils, and the final termination of our anxieties ; and with this heart-cheering perspective we reconciled ourselves to the privations incident to our more immediate position.

---

in burning the private dwellings, and that the active opposition of the inhabitants to the American interests was no justification.

Richardson is not the only writer who condemns the inhumanity of this officer. Alexander McMullen, a private in Col. Fenton's Regiment of Pennsylvania Volunteers, censures him for his acts on his descent on Dover.

For documents connected with the acts of this officer in Upper Canada, see " The Documentary History of the Campaign on the Niagara Frontier in 1814," by Lieut.-Col. E. Cruikshank.

Towards the close of August we again arrived at Sandusky, and during nearly the whole of the succeeding
month, were compelled to remain encamped on the small
marshy plain extending from the base of the hill on which
that fort is situated, to the edge of the river from which
it derives its name. Owing to the unjustifiable neglect
of those to whom that office was entrusted, not a boat was
in readiness for our transportation across the lake, and
we beheld this new and unlooked-for evil with dismay.
The finishing stroke was put to our calamities by the
introduction of intermittent fever into the camp, a malady
which necessarily arose from constant exposure to heavy
fogs and noxious exhalations from the stagnant waters
around us. Few of the officers escaped this cruel and
distressing scourge, and nearly one-half of the men were
attacked by it. With the view of having the former
more immediately at hand, the medical officers in the fort
caused them to be conducted to a small building contiguous to one of the gates, which had been previously used
as a stable, and admitted the air and rain on every side.
A handful of hay, covered with a blanket, composed our
couch ; and here, in a state of inexpressible misery, did
we languish beneath the effects of accumulating privation
and disease. Nourishing or refreshing aliment we were
utterly unable to obtain, and the absence of necessary
medicaments was severely felt. Either from ignorance
or indolence,—but we were given to presume the former,—
the medical officers, while they prescribed bleeding, would
not perform that office themselves, but entrusted it to a
drummer of the garrison, who certainly, to his credit be
it said, opened our veins with admirable dexterity. This
operation being performed on the arm of each patient,
half a pint of raw whisky was given us to drink. If this
potation was administered with an idea of burning the
disease out, the effect did not answer the intention, for
our stomachs were long inflamed in consequence of this
draught, and the fever raged with unceasing violence.

Heartily sick of our present abode, we begged to be removed to the tents we had lately occupied. This request was accorded ; but here we were visited by another severe inconvenience. The neighbourhood of Sandusky abounded in wolves, and our ears were nightly assailed with their dismal howlings. The noise generally commenced from one pack at no great distance from the fort, and was repeated by several others in succession, and from opposite directions, until the whole extent of surrounding woods appeared to be alive with them. There was something fearfully gloomy in this association of wild sounds, particularly when the night was far advanced, and the encampment hushed into silence and repose, yet, but for the danger actually apprehended, we should have been disposed to find amusement in their discordant yellings ; for these bold animals came frequently down from the adjacent hills, and by the pale light of the dying embers, we could distinctly see and hear them craunching the bones and fragments remaining from our meals. At our repeated solicitations however, fire-arms were accorded us ; and though we made no actual use of them, they inspired us with a feeling of greater confidence and security. Yet were we not even then entirely free from alarm, especially as our tents were detached at some distance from each other ; and more than one sleepless night did we pass with our fingers on the triggers of our muskets, and momentarily expecting to be attacked by these ravenous prowlers, against whose fury we invariably took the precaution to secure the entrance to our tents in every possible manner.

Our situation was now become truly pitiable, and some of the officers were compelled to part with their scanty wardrobe, in order to procure the common necessaries of life, from the few miserable settlers who had taken up their abode in the neighborhood of the fort, which they partially supplied with milk and vegetables. The former article was that most in requisition with the invalids, and, in addition to the wild fruits which we ate with avidity, contributed not a little to the increase of our malady. At length when nearly worn down by vain expectation and undermining fever, a solitary boat was seen slowly emerging from one of the angles formed by the windings of the narrow and unhealthy river, and in this we were embarked for Cleveland, a small harbour on the American shore, opposite to Long Point, in Canada, where we were to be finally delivered up. During this coasting voyage we were assailed by a tempest which upset our boat ; but as we had fortunately kept close to the land, the accident occurred in water not beyond our depth, and we easily succeeded in righting and dragging the vessel to the shore. Every article of clothing was, however, completely wet through, and no habitation being near, we were compelled to throw ourselves for the night on the damp beach, covered with blankets still dripping with recent wet, and suffering the extremes of cold and heat, as the various stages of our disease were developed. It required more than ordinary constitutions to resist these attacks, and one officer (Lieutenant Jones, of the 41st) subsequently perished. Our provisions had been utterly destroyed by the water, and our only dependence was on the scanty pittance obtained from the impoverished inhabitants along the coast. A few potatoes and a small quantity of rancid butter were all that could be procured by the American officer escorting us, and these we devoured with all the keenness and rapacity of famished wolves ; yet was our hunger never wholly appeased. At length the heights of Cleveland, where were at that time two solitary and miserable houses, appeared in sight, and we were now landed on the beach, where several of the officers imprudently ate large quantities of peaches which grew uninclosed and in abundance around. The accession of fever produced in consequence was great, and the night was passed in the ravings of a delirium little short of madness. On the following morning we were re-embarked in a small vessel lying in the harbour ; and leaving an officer behind to await the arrival, and superintend the transportation of the men who were advancing by land, we again set sail. Long Point, the place of our destination, was soon gained ; but with what altered feelings did we now behold that soil which, one short month before, would have been hailed with rapturous exultation ! Disease had worn away our persons, and our minds were deeply tinged with that morbid melancholy which is a characteristic feature in the complaint. Existence itself had nearly lost its value with its charms, and, in our then tone of feeling, liberty or captivity were situations of indifference. It had rained without intermission during the passage, and on the vessel being brought to anchor, we were summoned from the small filthy cabin, into which we had been thrown, to the boats waiting for our reception. In a few minutes we were landed, exhibiting to those by whom we were received on the beach the most distressing images of poverty, disease, exhaustion, and discontent. We arrived in Canada on the 4th of October, 1814, making just one year from the date of our captivity.

On my arrival in Canada I lost no time, dispirited and emaciated as I was from the effects of an ague which continued upon me for five consecutive months, without a single day of intermission, in parting from those with whom I had shared so many toils and vicissitudes, and hastening to join the King's Regiment (then stationed at Montreal and Laprairie), to which I had been gazetted some months previous to my capture at the Moravian-town. Nor is it uninteresting to add that my passage from Toronto to Kingston, was made in the St. Lawrence, Sir James Yeo's flag-ship, during the very last trip performed by that magnificent vessel, the vast dimensions of which will be understood, when it is known that she mounted not less than 112 guns, of various heavy calibre, and was manned by a crew, including all branches of the service, of one thousand souls. There were, also, if I do not greatly err, a seventy-four and two fifty gun ships, with numerous smaller craft, following in the wake of this Leviathan ; but war had now been so long carried on in the country as a matter of course, and on so extensive a scale of preparation, that these latter were scarcely regarded as anything extraordinary, even on the small and inland fresh water sea of Lake Ontario.

At length spring with her cheerful and invigorating attributes once more appeared, bringing with it a cessation of hostilities between Great Britain and the United States ; and intelligence having soon afterwards reached this country of Bonaparte's escape from Elba, and the consequent renewal of the war in Europe, we were hurriedly ordered for embarkation, to join the British Army in Flanders. The Headquarters of my regiment left Montreal for Quebec in the first steamer[1] (the John Molson), that ever navigated these waters, and we were speedily embarked in a transport waiting to receive us, and forming one of sixty sail, under the convoy of Sir George Collier in the Newcastle. Our route was to Ostend, but we were too late—as the battle of Waterloo, to have participated in which was worth the sacrifice of all our previous service, was fought before we were half way across the Atlantic.

Since that period, I had never revisited Canada, until the astounding and unexpected events of 1837 and 1838 again brought me to my native land, to aid if necessary in vindication of her wounded honor.

[1] The first Steamer on the St. Lawrence was called the Accommodation, not the John Molson. The name of the owner however, was Honorable John Molson.

THE END.

ADVERTISEMENT.

(To first edition)

Notwithstanding all the care we have personally bestowed upon the correction of the press, so many glaring typographical errors have crept into the present edition of this narrative that, were it not for the time necessary to prepare a second, we should unhesitatingly commit the impression to the flames rather than suffer it to go forth to the public.

This difficulty will be obviated should the work be stereotyped, in which case all to whom the publication is now gratuitously sent shall be furnished with new copies.

APPENDIX

I

Major Muir's Official Report of the Expedition to Fort Wayne.

II

Letter from Colonel John Askin, Strabane, to Captain Charles Askin, of the Militia, stationed at Chippawa.

III

Letter from John Richardson, to his uncle Captain Charles Askin at Queenston.

IV

Letter from Colonel Elijah Brush, Detroit, to Colonel John Askin, Strabane.

V

Notes on Illustrations.

I

Expedition to Fort Wayne.

Major Muir to Col. Procter.

Miami River, 2 miles above Fort Miami,

Sept. 30th, 1812.

Sir,—I beg leave to acquaint you that on the morning of the 27th instant, as I mentioned to you in my former letter of the 27th, it was intended to have attacked the enemy on his march, and everything was ready for that purpose; however in the morning it was thought necessary to send out a reconnoitring party to see if he was likely to move, and Captain Caldwell and Lieut. Askin, of the Militia, and a party of sixty Indians were sent out for that purpose. In the course of an hour, some shots were fired and our parties returned, leaving one Indian, whom they reported to be killed, and said that the enemy was on his march towards us. Still no further steps were taken by the Indians to prevent his progress. Soon after another Indian came in and reported that the enemy was within less than two miles of us, and that another Indian had been killed by them. I then requested Colonel Elliott to inform me what the Indians intended to do; he went to Round Head (the principal chief) and returned immediately saying, " I might choose any place in the plain which I thought best adapted to the use of the guns, and that Indians would flank them." I told him I should occupy the road skirting the wood ; where they would be ready to act in any situation as soon as this arrangement took place, and the troops were at their stations as a guard to the guns. Colonel Elliott rode up to me and said the Indians would not come that way, and requested I would retire through the woods and stop at the first place where I could take up a good position, and that they would flank us as they said before. We then commenced our retreat and at the distance of about four miles in our rear there was a small opening in the woods where they supposed the guns might be disposed of to advantage, but I soon convinced them to the contrary by showing them that the guns could not possibly throw a shot more than one hundred yards in any direction, and I told them the guns were brought for the purpose of battering Fort Wayne, but would not answer to fight in the woods, and that as soon as we arrived at Fort Defiance I would endeavor to send them off, and should then be at liberty to act according to circumstances. I then made every arrangement and had the artillery and stores embarked in boats under the direction of Lieut. Troughton, with orders to proceed to Amherstburg with as much expedition as possible. This service being arranged and sent off, I went to the Indian Camp where the Indians were at Council, and was soon given to understand that they were determined to meet the enemy at an advantageous spot in the morning. The next morning (the 28th) about an hour before daylight I received a message from Colonel Elliott saying that the Indians had been conjuring all night, and that the Mackinac and the Sagina Indians were going to leave the camp. This being the case, I made no doubt, but a retreat had been agreed upon, and intended by the whole, and gave directions for the cattle and baggage to proceed. In less than half an hour afterwards I received another message from Colonel Elliott saying that Indians were determined to fight and requested I would move on the troops. I immediately ordered them to march, and was at their camp in a few minutes. Colonel Elliott then came up to me and begged that I would hold the men for a few minutes as the Indians were not yet ready. I then observed them moving off, bag and baggage, in bands of six and seven at a time, in every direction. I mentioned what I had seen to Colonel Elliott, who told me they were going to hide their things and would return immediately. The chief of the Mackinac Indians then came up and took his leave, saying that the Indians were divided amongst themselves, and that he would take home his young men, adding that those who had horses might remain, as they could easily run away in case of defeat. He then marched off with the principal part of his band, which consisted of two hundred young men. I then observed to three or four of the interpreters that were standing by me, " I thought the camp began to be very thin." At that instant a young Huron said that by the time we got to the fighting ground we should not have half the number that were then present. This gave me a pretty clear idea of what I might expect. I was, however, determined to see, and we all marched off for the ground that it was intended we should fight on, which was the east bank of the north, or little Miami River, branching off from the other about three miles above Fort Defiance. Soon after our arrival at the place Colonel Elliott and I went to look at the ground, and on our return a prisoner was brought in by one of the Indians, who said that he had strayed from the army about four days before, and that he had not eaten anything, during that time. We then examined him respecting the army, and he informed us that it was commanded by General Harrison as far as Fort Wayne, when he was obliged to return to the Wabash in consequence of some of their towns having been burnt by the Indians, and that as soon as he had quieted them he was to return to the command of the army, and bring with him the force he took to the Wabash. That during his absence the army was commanded by General Winchester ; he further said that the army was three thousand strong, consisting of the following regiments, viz. : Wells' Regulars, Lewis', Allen's and Scott's Volunteers from Kentucky, Simmerole's cavalry, 250 strong, and 150 mounted riflemen, with one six-pounder and 70 waggons. That they were short of provisions, but that they expected another army of the same strength to meet them at Fort Defiance which was to bring provisions for both armies, and four pieces of cannon, and that both armies were to have met at Fort Defiance on the 26th inst : and that it was generally thought it was intended on their meeting they should proceed to Detroit. During this conversation I recollected what I had been told respecting the number of Indians I should have, and as nearly as I could judge there were not more than from 320 to 330 present. I mentioned this to Colonel Elliott, and told him I considered it would be madness with such a handful of men to think of opposing an army of such a force ; besides, it was running the risk of being completely locked in, without the smallest chance of success, or even escaping. He then told me that two of the Indian conjurers had dreamt that they should be successful that day, and that they were determined to fight. I then told him to acquaint the Indians, that I could not see the smallest prospect of success, but on the contrary, should I engage, the whole of the troops under my command, must inevitably fall. I was determined not to throw away the lives of so many men, and for no purpose. He then went to Round Head and informed him of my determination. Round Head then came to me with an interpreter and urged the necessity of trying their success in compliance with the dream of the conjurers, and that at all events we might drive back their advance guard. I agreed that that might be done, but what would be the advantage, when while we were engaged with these few men we run the risk of being cut off from our baggage and provisions, and at the same time allowed the enemy to get so near that to retreat with my troops would have been morally impossible. He repeated that as to being surrounded and cut off we could easily prevent that by retreating through the woods. I told him that might answer for his people very well, but would not for mine, and that if he would collect the warriors and young men of his nation I would wait for them at the camp we left in the morning, and we might then retreat in a body. To this he agreed, and we commenced our retreat accordingly. Lieutenant Troughton, who will deliver this letter, will give you every information respecting our retreat to this place, as we overtook him the first day, and he has been with us ever since. He will also account to you for some stores he was obliged to destroy in order to get down our guns. Some Indians who had been sent up the Glaize river on the 27th to examine into the truth of the report the prisoner we took made, respecting an army being on its way down by that river, returned without having seen anything of the army, but they discovered fresh footsteps and heard bugles sounding very distinctly, and from that they imagined the enemy were encamped not more than two miles from the Fort. Previous to this they had heard two cannon shots in the same direction but at some distance further off. Colonel Elliott this day assured me that he would send out parties with white men to reconnoitre and watch the movements of the army, from whom we should receive information according as anything material should occur. Before I conclude, permit me to assure you that every praise is due to the officers of my little army for their exertions in endeavoring to forward the expedition and for their zeal and cheerful compliance with all orders on every occasion. The men also behaved remarkably well, and I have no doubt that could they have been brought into action with any hopes of success, their conduct would have been equally good.

(Signed)   A. C. Muir, Major, and Captain 41st Regt.

Commanding.

Colonel Procter,
Commanding, Detroit.

II

Letter from Col. John Askin, Strabane, to Capt. Charles Askin of the militia stationed at Chippawa:

Strabane, Dec. 28, 1812.

My dear Charles,

Last night I heard that Capt. Hall said he was going to Queenston and that he would call for my letters. I expect him every moment, therefore will have what I can ready and write you the rest by the very next opportunity. Your long and very welcome letters of the 11th and 14th of last month reached me on the 24th inst. Prior to their arrival we had not a word of what had taken place in your quarter, nor has anyone written the intelligence but yourself, therefore not only us but all the gentlemen here are obliged to you for the circumstantial account you have given, and I am surprised (the duty being so hard) how you got time to write so much. I cannot anywise account why battles fought near Queenston the latter end of last month are not officially made known to Col. Procter here, but such is really the case, for he wrote me a line begging to know the part of your letters which related to public news. Indeed, the battle of Queenston was not fully known here for near a month afterwards. News in this quarter, we have none at present. The American force at the Glaize, if there is any there still, do not make their appearance. The militia for the present are let return home, Capt. Elliott's and Maisonville's companies excepted, who are stationed at the River aux Raisin. We are happy to learn that we have so fine a fellow for your inspector as Lt.-Col. Bisshopp. The cowardice of the Americans is really surprising; it would seem as if the

Hand of the Almighty interfered in our behalf. However we might wish for peace, if it should be on the conditions of giving back the posts we took, a war would be much preferable, for should it take place we will lose the Indians and the trade and in a very few years Canada with it; but that a peace can be made without the concurrence of the Indians I can't think possible. Surely England will not abandon a people to whom we are not only indebted for the preservation of our Posts but also for the taking of those we got. I beg you will try and send me the public papers and as many of them as you can, for they will be all new to us who have not got any, and you must cover them so as it cannot be known that they are newspapers, otherwise I will not get even one of them, and we are very anxious to hear what is going on at sea. Capt. Hall will give you any little news of this place, and I must defer writing on your private matters until another opportunity, except to say that Brush being disappointed in not being able to get the oxen over has returned them, which is a matter of no consequence, for so many cattle have been been bought by the Government this fall that there will be a scarcity of oxen in the spring, and 40s. per 100 I thought too low to sell them to Government at. We are all here in good health, and pray for your happiness here and hereafter.

Adieu, my dear Charles,
Your tender father,
John Askin.

III

Letter from John Richardson to his Uncle, Captain Charles Askin.

Amherstburg, 4th February, 1813.

My Dear Uncle,—

You have doubtless heard ere this of the engagement at the River Raisin on Friday, the 22nd inst. (ult.); however, you may probably not have heard the particulars of the business, which are simply these: On Monday, the 18th, we received information that the Americans, under the command of General Winchester, after an obstinate resistance, had driven from the River Raisin a detachment of Militia under Major Reynolds (also a party of Indians) which had been stationed there some time. That they had sustained great loss from the fire of our Indians, and from a 3-pounder, which was most ably served by Bombardier Kitson (since dead), of the R.A.

On Tuesday part of our men moved over the river to Brownstown, consisting of a Detachment of R. Artillery, with 3 3-pounders and 3 small howitzers, Capt. Tallon's Company (41st Regt.), a few Militia, and the sailors attached to the Guns. An alarm was given that the enemy were at hand. The Guns were unlimbered and everything prepared for action, when the alarm was found to be false.

On Wednesday the remainder of the army joined us at Brownstown, where (including Regulars, Militia, Artillery, Sailors and Indians) we mustered near 1,000 men. We lay, this night, at Brownstown. Next day the army commenced its march towards the River Raisin and encamped, this night, at Rocky River, which (you know) is about 12 miles beyond Brownstown and 6 on this side the River Raisin. About two hours before day we resumed our march. On Friday at daybreak we perceived the enemy's fires very distinctly—all silent in their camp. The army drew up and formed the line of battle in 2 adjoining fields, and moved down towards the enemy, the Guns advanced 20 or 30 paces in front and the Indians on our flanks. We had got tolerably near their Camp when we heard their Reveille drum beat (so completely lulled into security were they that they had not the most distant idea of an enemy being near), and soon after we heard a shot or two from the Centinels, who had by this time discovered us. Their Camp was immediately in motion. The Guns began to play away upon them at a fine rate, keeping up a constant fire. The Americans drew up and formed behind a thick picketing, from whence they kept up a most galling fire upon our men, who, from the darkness of the morning, supposed the pickets to be the Americans ; however, as it grew lighter, they discovered their mistake, and advanced within 70 or 80 paces of the pickets, but finding that scarce one of their shots took effect, as they almost all lodged in the fence. Being thus protected from the fire of our men they took a cool and deliberate aim at our Troops, who fell very fast, and the most of the men at the Guns being either killed or wounded, it was thought expedient to retire towards the enemy's left under cover of some houses. I was a witness of a most barbarous act of inhumanity on the part of the Americans, who fired upon our poor wounded, helpless soldiers, who were endeavouring to crawl away on their hands and feet from the scene of action, and were thus tumbled over like so many hogs. However, the deaths of those brave men were avenged by the slaughter of 300 of the flower of Winchester's army, which had been ordered to turn our flanks, but who, having divided into two parties, were met, driven back, pursued, tomakawked and scalped by our Indians, (very few escaping) to carry the news of their defeat. The General himself was taken prisoner by the Indians, with his son, aide, and several other officers. He immediately dispatched a messenger to Colonel Procter, desiring him to acquaint him with the circumstance of his being a prisoner, and to intimate that if the Colonel would send an officer to his Camp to summons the remainder of his army to surrender, he would send an order by him to his officer then commanding to surrender the Troops. Colonel Procter objected to sending one of his own officers, but permitted the General to send his aide (with a flag). The firing instantly ceased on both sides, and about 2 hours afterwards the enemy (460 in number) laid down their arms and surrendered themselves prisoners of war. A good many of our officers were wounded in the engagement, but none of them killed. The following is a list of them: R.A., Lt. Troughton (slightly); Seamen attached to the Guns, Capt. Rolette, Lt. Irvine, Midshipman Richardson (severely); 41st Regt., Capt. Tallon, Lieut. Clemow (severely); Militia, Inspecting F. Officer Lt.-Col. St George, Capt. Mills, Lt. McCormick, Paymaster Gordon (severely), Ensign Gouin (slightly), R. N. F. Regt, Ensign Kerr (dangerously); Indian Depart., Capt. Caldwell, Mr. Wilson (severely). This is as accurate an account as I can give you of the Engagement. I will now give you an account of my feelings on the occasion. When we first drew up in the field I was ready to fall down with fatigue from marching and carrying a heavy musquet. Even when the balls were flying about my ears as thick as hail I felt quite drowsy and sleepy, and, indeed, I was altogether in a very disagreeable dilemma. The night before at Rocky River, some one or other of the men took my firelock and left his own in the place. It being quite dark when we set out from that place, I could not distinguish one from another. Enquiry was vain, so I was obliged to take the other (without thinking that anything was the matter with it). When we came to the firing part of the business I could not get my gun off. It flashed in the pan, and I procured a wire and worked away at it with that. I tried it again, and again it flashed. I never was so vexed—to think that I was exposed to the torrent of fire from the enemy without having the power to return a single shot quite disconcerted the economy of my pericranium ; though if I had fired fifty rounds not one of them would have had any effect, except upon the pickets, which I was not at all ambitious of assailing like another Don Quixote. Our men had fired 4 or 5 rounds when I was called to assist my brother Robert, who was wounded, and who fell immediately, and which led me to suppose that he was mortally wounded. However, when he was carried to the doctors I found the poor fellow had escaped with a broken leg, which torments him very much, and it will be some time before he gets over it. I think it is highly probable we shall have a brush with the *valiant* Harrison, who is said to be at the Rapids of the Miami River, or near them. If so, I think we shall have tight work, as we have lost in killed and wounded in the action of the 22nd 180 men (exclusive of Indians).

Pray remember me to my cousins, and,

Believe me,

My Dear Uncle,

Yours affectionately,

JOHN RICHARDSON.

Mr. Chas. Askin,)
Queenston.   }

Medals granted in 1848 for Fort Detroit, Chateauguay and Chrystler's Farm.

The Fort Detroit was awarded to "CHIEF JOHN NAUDEE, WARRIOR, GUIDE AND SCOUT"; the Chateauguay to "JOSEPH BEAUCAIRE ROYAL ARTILLERY"; the Chrystler's Farm to "PRIVATE PETER BROUSE CANADA MILITIA"; the two bars to "CHIEF JACOB PHEASANT, WARRIOR, GUIDE;" the 3 bars to "PTE. JEAN BTE LECLAIRE CANADA MILITIA."

IV

Letter from Col. Elijah Brush, Detroit, to Col. John Askin, Strabane.

Detroit, 20th October, 1813.

Dear Sir,—I recvd. your note last evening relative to the application of Mrs. Richardson.   It is not in my power to go to Sandwich as you wish.   In the first place I have no horse, and I am unable to walk that distance and return ; besides I am every moment engaged in my domestic concerns which are all out of sorts, and likewise I am preparing for fishing.   It would be of no use even if I were to go, for as to Doct. Richardson, I settled it with Commodore Perry before he left here that the Doctor should return home the moment that Commodore Barclay could be left with safety—I will write Mrs. Richardson on the subject.   As my salt has not yet arrived and I am about to commence fishing, I beg you will not dispose of the barrel at your house ; I may want it, and think probably I shall before mine gets up.   You can examine the enclosed letter I propose sending to Mr. Pattinson, and if you approve of it please return it by Edmund.   If there are any additions or subtractions you wish to have made please signify them.

Yours truly,

E. Brush.

V

Notes on Illustrations.

purchased his Majority on June 26th, 1793, and on Oct. 27th, 1797, purchased the Lieutenant-Colonelcy. He served in Holland in 1799, and in the Baltic in 1801, and came to Canada in 1802. He was made Colonel in 1805, and, after a visit to England, succeeded to the command of the troops in Canada in September, 1806. On June 4th, 1811, he was appointed a Major-General on the staff in North America, and on Sept. 30th was appointed President and Administrator of the Government of Upper Canada, an office he held at the time of his melancholy death . . . . p. 64

12. GENERAL LEWIS CASS . . . . p. 80

13. QUEENSTON, 1812. This view is from the Canadian side of the river near Vrooman's Point, looking up the river. The village of Queenston is plainly seen, also the road winding up the heights to the Falls . . . . . p. 104

14. LIEUTENANT-COLONEL JOHN MACDONELL was born at Glengarry, Scotland, on the 19th of April, 1785, and came to Canada with his family in 1792. He was educated at Cornwall under Bishop Strachan, admitted a student at law on 6th April, 1803, and called to the Bar of Upper Canada in Easter term 1808. He was appointed Attorney-General of Upper Canada on the 28th of November, 1811, and in the spring of the next year was elected by the county of Glengarry a member of the Legislative Assembly of Upper Canada. When war was declared, he was selected as Provincial Aid-de-Camp by Major-General Brock, and accompanied that officer to Detroit, where he drew up the articles of capitulation, by which Hull's army, the town and fortress of Detroit, and the State of Michigan passed under control of the British and Canadian arms. He was mortally wounded on the morning of the 13th of October, 1812, while gallantly leading the regulars and militia up the Heights to avenge the death of his chief, and died the next day at the early age of 27. His remains repose beside that of Brock under the monument on Queenston Heights. They fought side by side in defence of Canada and in death they are not separated. Canada had no more noble or illustrious defender than Lieutenant-Colonel John Macdonell.

There is a brass tablet erected to his memory in Osgoode Hall, Toronto.

For the silhouette of Lieutenant-Colonel Macdonell, and the picture of the Gold Medal for Detroit, I am indebted to Mr. John Alexander Macdonell, K.C., of Alexandria, author of that valuable history, "Sketches of Glengarry in Canada," whose grandfather, Colonel Duncan Macdonell, was a brother of the Lieutenant-Colonel . . . . p. 108

15. MONUMENT TO BROCK. On the 14th of March, 1815, the Legislature granted by Act £1,000 "for the constructing of a monument to the memory of Major-General Sir Isaac Brock," and on Jan. 30th, 1826, a further sum of £600 was granted to complete it.

On the 13th of Oct., 1824, the remains of Major-General Brock and his gallant Aid-de-camp, Colonel John Macdonell, were taken from a bastion of Fort George, where they were first interred, and placed in a vault beneath the monument.

On Good Friday, April 17th, 1840, this monument was irreparably wrecked by a rebel of 1837, named Lett, who had managed to explode within it a quantity of gunpowder. A monster meeting was called for the next 30th of July at Queenston Heights, for the purpose of adopting measures for the erection of another monument. The meeting was a great success ; a building committee was formed, and arrangements were made for soliciting subscriptions from the people of Canada. In 1853 the new monument, the one shown in this volume, was begun. The corner-stone was laid on Oct. 13th, 1853, by Lieut.-Colonel Donald Macdonell, Deputy Adjutant-General of Militia, and brother of the gallant officer who had shared in the glory and met the fate of Major-General Brock, 41 years before. On this day the remains of the two brave men were deposited in two massive stone sarcophagi in the vault prepared for them in the new structure . . . . p. 112

16. SIR ROGER HALE SHEAFFE was born in Boston on July 15th, 1763. His father died when he was young, and Earl Percy, afterwards Duke of Northumberland, took an interest in him, gave him a military education and purchased for him an ensigncy in the 5th Fusileers. On March 22nd, 1798, he reached the rank of Lieut.-Col. of the 49th Regt. On June 4th, 1811, was promoted to the rank of Major-General. He won the battle of Queenston Heights by a flank attack, thus placing his men on

equal terms with the invaders. For this he was created a Baronet by patent dated Jan. 16th, 1813. He was Administrator of the Government of Upper Canada from Oct. 20th, 1812, to June 18th, 1813. After the close of the war he returned to Edinburgh, where he died on July 17th, 1851.

He left a manuscript description of the Battle of Queenston Heights that is similar to all well known accounts, in which he gives praise to the militia and the Indians, who really won the battle. . . . . p. 122

24. THE FORT AT AMHERSTBURG, 1901. This is the view of the ruins of the north embankment of the Fort and the ditch, looking westward. The remains of the northwest bastion may be plainly seen. The river and Bois Blanc Island are in the distance. The dark place at the end of the ditch is the ruins of a covered way or tunnel that led from the ditch to the water's edge. The ruined sally-port may be noticed as a slight depression in the embankment. To guard the covered way leading from the river, a battery was placed in the foreground of the picture.

A short history of Fort Amherstburg, written by Mr. C. C. James, M.A., Deputy Minister of Agriculture for Ontario, has been published in pamphlet form by John Auld, M.L.A., of the Amherstburg " Echo." . . p. 206

30. ADJUTANT-GENERAL EDWARD BAYNES, entered the army in 1783, and served at Gibraltar, in the West Indies, Cape of Good Hope and the East Indies. In 1811 he was Colonel of the Glengarry Fencibles, and served during the War of 1812 as Adjutant-General of the Forces in North America. He died at Sidmouth,

MAJOR-GENERAL HENRY PROCTER entered the army, as an ensign in 43rd Regt., April 5th, 1781, at the age of 16 ; Lieut. in Dec. following ; Captain 1793 ; Majority 1795 ; Lieut.-Col. of 41st Regt. Oct. 9th, 1800 ; Col. July 25th, 1810 ; Major-General June 4th, 1813. For his reverse at Moraviantown he was suspended from rank and pay for 6 months. In opposition to the general verdict of most historians of this war, I have come to the conclusion that Procter was used disgracefully. No account has been taken of the valuable services he performed. With less than 1000 whites and a very unreliable Indian following he destroyed three American armies, as large as his own. Reinforcements he asked for were not sent. His soldiers became stale and dispirited because of neglect from headquarters. The defeat at Moraviantown was the inevitable result of this neglect. He died at Bath, England, Oct. 31st, 1822, aged 59 years.

LIEUT.-GEN. HENRY ADOLPHUS PROCTOR, born 1784 : Cornet 2nd Life Guards, Jan. 14th, 1801 ; Capt. 82nd Regt. May 16th, 1805 ; Major April 30th, 1812 ; C.B. July 19th, 1838 ; Col. 97th Regt. Nov. 29th, 1852 ; Brig.-Gen. June 20th, 1854. He came to Canada with the 82nd Regt. in July, 1814, and served on the Niagara frontier. He died at his residence, Aberhafesp Hall, Montgomeryshire, Wales, May 13th, 1859, aged 74 years.

Errata.

P. 96, l. 7. For "Miama" read "Miami."

P. 236, last line but one of note. For "position" read "positions."

P. lxvi. For "Ponchartrain" read "Pontchartrain."

INDEX

Printed in the United States